Jacopo Sadoleto

1477-1547

Humanist and Reformer

JACOPO SADOLETO
Portrait by an Unknown Artist

Jacopo Sadoleto

1477-1547

Humanist and Reformer

By Richard M. Douglas

HARVARD UNIVERSITY PRESS
Cambridge, Massachusetts · 1959

*Publication of this book has been aided
by a grant from the Ford Foundation*

Library of Congress Catalog Card Number 58-12965
Printed in Great Britain

To Betty

pella sua paziènza

Preface

Studies of early Catholic Reform were once so heavily charged with anticipation that every zealous Bishop, like each new Theatine monk and every founding Jesuit, was said to belong to a single movement which led to the Council of Trent. What this perspective obscures is not only the great variety of reform projects locally preached and applied all over Europe, but also the range of disagreement among the reformers themselves. It likewise neglects the important difference between the activities of individuals, writing or working by themselves without recognition or support from Rome, and the corporate action of the whole Church, working later through the deliberative procedures of a council which was called on the Pope's initiative and conducted under his direction. If individual reformers prepared a way for the Council of Trent, they did so as much by their failures and feckless improvising as by their scattered achievements. If support for conciliar doctrine gained force among them during the early years of the religious schism, there were ancient fears still to be overcome in the hierarchy and the function of the council to be rediscovered in the Curia before it could materialize. The opening of the Council of Trent in 1545 became inevitable only after lesser remedies were found to be inadequate.

In the same way, the image of Sadoleto's career can be distorted by anticipating his later activity as a theorist and agent of reform too early. He went to Rome from Ferrara shortly before 1500 hungry for recognition as a man of letters, and it was poetry rather than piety which won him his first living in the Church. He died in Rome a Cardinal, still celebrated for the elegance of his Latin style and known only in late life as a public partisan of Catholic reform. Indeed it was not until the last fifteen of his seventy years that Sadoleto was closely associated with such reform-minded figures as Gasparo Contarini and Gianpietro Caraffa—just at the time when the first signs of cautious interest in a council began to appear in the Holy See.

Even then, Sadoleto preferred to confine his exertions as reformer to his own diocese and to his writing. It was not altogether by choice that he became one of the few prelates of Luther's generation who was directly engaged in nearly every major turn of papal policy from the St. Peter's indulgence of 1515 to the convocation of the Council in 1545, for Sadoleto came to abhor the "active life" as he experienced it in the Roman Curia. The vocation most congenial to him, and therefore the one most carefully rationalized in replies to those who tried to take him away from it, was that of the scholar in learned seclusion from the world, living in his Provençal diocese, engrossed in his books. He argued that this was the kind of duty (*officium*), the particular obligation (*munus*), for which God intended him. Moreover, here was the style of life—the *ratio vitae*—which Bishop Sadoleto was determined to maintain as long as he lived. In his case the word *munus* signified a permanent obligation in a particular place to a life of study and writing.

But his contemplative ideal was never wholly fulfilled. Instead of the simple *ratio vitae* which Sadoleto coveted for himself, he was called to perform a variety of roles which issued from another kind of obligation, quite unlike the self-imposed demands of a humanist scholar. The second set of obligations came from the outside, imposed by men in the Vatican who interpreted duty differently and called him from his books to projects of curial reform, papal diplomacy, and the affairs of the Council.

This book, which draws on some previously unknown or unused manuscript material, examines the career of a singularly independent figure of Catholic Reform through the various roles, both private and public, which he assumed during a lifetime parallel to Luther's. It deals primarily with Sadoleto's efforts to define his career as a scholar and a prelate, and with his responses to controversies in which all that he valued was threatened or under attack—the sanctity of peace, the religious unity of Europe, the authority of the Church, the cause of liberal studies, and the scholar's claims to learned leisure. Moving back and forth as he did from the active to the contemplative life, Sadoleto acquired the perspective of one who was both a critical observer of Catholic Reform, admonishing its partisans from a distance; and, just as often, a participant in the Pope's projects of reform, who later worked for a future council which he alternately favored and feared. In Rome he was associated with what is often described as the "Middle Group" of Catholic reformers, those who sought a reformation of the Church and clergy within the limits of tradition. But Sadoleto's connection with this element was often as tenuous as the existence of the group was brief. He took his identity from no group or faction, but rather, like his friend Erasmus, from the ways in which he stood alone.

The first of my obligations in point of time and degree is to Professor Myron Gilmore of Harvard University. A Fulbright grant for study in France made it possible for me to consult Professor Alfonse Dupront at the University of Montpellier before working in the archives of Avignon and Carpentras. I am also grateful for the various kindnesses of M. Charles Breton of the University Library at Montpellier, and for the hospitality of Dean Jean Cadier at the Faculté libre de Théologie Protestante. M. Georges de Löye, Conservateur of the Musée Calvet in Avignon, facilitated my work in that splendid library and later supplied additional material while I was working in Paris. In the Bibliothèque Inguimbertine at Carpentras, both M. Robert Caillet and M. Claude Sibertin-Blanc provided generous help with local history, bibliography, and manuscript material.

In Rome, Monsignor Hugh O'Flaherty of the Holy Office graciously aided my research in Vatican City, where I was privileged to consult the late Prefect of the Vatican Archives, Monsignor Angelo Mercati. I am indebted to Reverend Joseph Grisar, S.J., of the Gregorian University, and particularly to Dom Anselm Strittmatter, O.S.B., who was then at the Collegio Sant' Anselmo, for his considerable help on various occasions.

I am also indebted to Professor Lewis Spitz of the University of Missouri, Professor Felix Gilbert of Bryn Mawr College, Professor William F. Church of Brown University, Professor Peter Riesenberg of Swarthmore College, Professor A. L. Pellegrini of Vassar, and to Dr. E. H. Wilkins. Mlle. E. Droz, Professor P. O. Kristeller, and Reverend Walter J. Ong, S.J., read the manuscript and offered many useful suggestions, although the responsibility for errors of judgment or accuracy is, of course, my own.

Finally, I should like to thank the American Council of Learned Societies for a generous grant-in-aid toward the cost of publication.

RICHARD M. DOUGLAS

Amherst, Massachusetts.
April 1958

Contents

Illustrations

JACOPO SADOLETO. From *Jacobi Sadoleti S.R.E. Cardinalis Epistolae Leonis X. Clementis VII. Pauli III, nomine scriptae. V. A. Costanzi (Costantius), ed.* (Rome, 1759) [p. civ]. *Frontispiece*

Little is known about the original form of the portrait from which this engraving was made except that it was probably executed in relief as part of the monument to Sadoleto at S. Pietro in Vincoli in Rome. The monument itself has disappeared; Costanzi could merely state, in 1759, that it was "at one time" in the church. It may have been dismantled after Sadoleto's remains were taken for reburial in the cathedral of St. Siffrein at Carpentras in 1646. There are two oil portraits of Sadoleto at Carpentras, one in the Musée Inguimbertine, the other in the rectory.

SADOLETO'S STÈMMA. From Alphonse Chacon (Ciacconius), *Vitae et res gestae Pontificuum Romanorum et S.R.E. Cardinalium* (Rome, 1677), Vol. III, col. 610. *Title page*

As a prelate of the Church, Sadoleto was entitled to adopt heraldic arms, represented by the *stèmma*. His personal insignia appears on the shield (*scudo*), which is surmounted by the clerical hat. The two cords of six tassels (*fiocci*) traditionally signify the rank of Bishop.

DETAIL OF FRESCO BY GIORGIO VASARI. In the Palace of the Cancelleria, Rome. Photograph, courtesy of the Direzione generale dei Monumenti musei et gallerie pontifiche, Vatican City. *Page 208*

In 1546 Vasari was commissioned, at the suggestion of the celebrated historian Paolo Giovio, to decorate the great courtroom of the Palace of the Cancelleria with four frescoes honoring the Farnese family and the ponticate of Paul III. Giovio described the second fresco as that "ubi praemia dispensat Paulus." Here the Pope is shown conferring honors and titles on certain of those he nominated to the Sacred College. Giovio himself appears as the bareheaded figure behind Paul III and identified those beside him as

Reginald Pole, Sadoleto, and Pietro Bembo (whose hands rest on the back of the Pope's chair). (A. Ronchini, "Giorgio Vasari nella Corte di Cardinal Farnese." *Atti e memorie delle RR. deputazione di Storia patria per le provincie modenesi e parmensi*, II [1864], 126,n.1.) It seems likely, however, that Giovio was careless or mistaken in placing Sadoleto between Pole and Bembo. Vasari himself stated that Sadoleto is portrayed in the fresco, but the artist left nothing with which to establish the Cardinal's place in this panel. Nevertheless, the mystery has been plausibly solved by Dr. Ernst Steinmann. After examining every major likeness of the three capped figures in line with Giovio, Steinmann concluded that it is really Gasparo Contarini, rather than Sadoleto, who stands between Pole and Bembo. Sadoleto is the hatless and bearded old man at the left, wearing a red mantle, and seemingly reluctant to be led to a place among the three Cardinals behind the papal throne. (Ernst Steinmann, "Freskezyklen der Spätrenaissance in Rom. I. Die Sala Farnese in der Cancelleria," *Monatshefte für Kunstwissenschaft*, III [1910], 55–56, with plates.) Sadoleto's guide seems clearly to be moving him toward the "novi creati" at the right. Contarini's right hand, like Bembo's head, is turned toward Sadoleto in a gesture of welcome, but Vasari evidently meant to portray Sadoleto as one who accepted his nomination to the College of Cardinals with some kind of reluctance.

Jacopo Sadoleto

1477–1547

Humanist and Reformer

I

The Young Scholar

Few princes of the Italian Renaissance more closely resemble Machia-velli's profile of the model ruler than the Dukes of Este. Niccolò III, who fastened the claims of his usurping line on Modena and Ferrara in the fifteenth century, is the archetype of Machiavellian style. After early acts of violence and conquest to consolidate his power, Niccolò gave his people thirty years of peace and good order, and was loved and feared as the creator of lasting stability. It was to him, said a contemporary, that

Ferrara owed its transformation from a mire-bound and evil-smelling place into one of the cleanest, healthiest, most populous, and sightliest of cities. Niccolò paved the streets and laid sidewalks, replaced tile structures with stone houses, raised forts and towers and fortified the suburbs.[1]

Power passed quietly to three of Niccolò's sons, who followed the paternal example to emerge among the most secure and resplendent princes of Italy. Soldiers, diplomats, and patrons, the Estensi seemed also to perfect the techniques of that amoral and improvising statecraft which for Jacob Burckhardt was the special genius of their kind.

The Estense regime, however, was not the plastic creation of the Dukes alone. This orderly despotism originated just as much from the proven failures of communal democracy in the cities they mastered and ruled. In Ferrara and Modena, as elsewhere in the northern plains, tyranny was accepted as the condition of survival, the only alternative to internal chaos and the steady danger of interference by covetous neighbors. Spread out between the subhills of the Alps and the

Apennines, this fertile and river-webbed basin was then one of the most densely populated regions of Europe as well as "the most blood stained spot on earth." Like the Visconti in Milan at the western end of the plains, the Estensi rose to power as the despotic guardians of stability and independence, tightening their authority over subjects who could not live in peace without it and imposing an elegant tyranny over men who took *libertà* to mean freedom from domestic strife and security from foreign conquest.

The life span of Cardinal Sadoleto's father, Giovanni (c. 1440–1511), fell in the time when the Estensi came into the fullness of their power. The Sadoletti belonged to the middle ranks of the new bourgeoisie which increased with the commercial prosperity of Ferrara during the later fifteenth century and gradually worked its way into the civil bureaucracy as lawyers, military administrators, diplomats, jurists, and professors.[2] But neither this class of civil servants nor the wealthier merchants of the bourgeoisie ever secured real political autonomy for itself in Ferrara or Modena. The rise of the middle class was checked if not altogether blocked by the Dukes, jealous and absolute tyrants who would not tolerate the formation of a politically independent bourgeoisie. Families like the Sadoletti therefore found their fortunes hinged to those of the Dukes, as indeed did the artists and writers who were supported at their court.

By the end of the Quattrocento Ferrara was an important center of princely patronage.[3] If pageantry and diversion were closer to the tastes of the Estensi and their courtiers than a serious concern for learning and letters, the Studio at Ferrara (as the University in Ferrara was called) was high in the second rank of Italian universities and received as much ducal support as it did supervision. Furthermore, at least in the genre of epic poetry the court of Ferrara was unrivaled anywhere else in Europe by virtue of the *Orlando* cycle and the supremacy of the poets, Boiardo and Ariosto. The accent on public architecture, court spectacles, and chivalric literature, however, offers a sign of the Dukes' attitude toward patronage. Niccolò III carefully provided a classical education for his sons and brought Guarino to the Studio as their tutor. But he trained them to be statesmen and soldiers who looked upon the arts as a means of embellishing their authority and upon writers and painters as state functionaries working "under the wings of the Estense eagle," whose role it was to glorify the Dukes and their regime. In few courts of the Renaissance were humanists more rigorously required to defend the established order of society or to write more faithfully in praise of the state. Ferrara, in effect, was a barracks. The same discipline which made it the "most symmetrical and least picturesque city of Europe" fell with equal severity upon writers who depended on public subsidy. Poets and painters found themselves spied upon and ordered about as though they were mercenaries in the Estense army.

Thus, there is no mystery in the fact that the house of Este never attracted a durable and independent school of scholars or writers resembling those who once gravitated toward Florence. Creative spirits in Ferrara were usually transient and with rare exceptions moved on to the more buoyant freedom of Padua or Rome. The cultural climate of Ferrara and Modena seemed far more congenial to the soldier, bureaucrat, merchant, and jurist than to the independent man of letters. The sons of Giovanni Sadoleto who entered the professions and the civil service stayed on to work for the Estensi, while those who aspired to literary vocations moved to Rome and the papal Curia. All of them, however, profited in some way from Giovanni's high standing with the Dukes. In late life the Cardinal looked back on his family's indebtedness and service to the dynasty in a letter to Ippolito II: "I feel the greatest bond of affection and obedient respect to you," he wrote in 1539, "because nearly all my kinsmen, past and present, were born and educated under the sovereignty of your house, to which they have been wholeheartedly and consistently faithful, and by which they have been justly honored. . . ."[4]

Although Giovanni Sadoleto rose rapidly in the new bourgeoisie, his origins remain obscure.[5] We know of him first as a student of civil and canon law at the University of Ferrara, where he soon received praise from his masters and favor from Duke Borso. A jurisconsult in Modena at the time of his marriage to Francesca Machiavelli,[6] he taught at Pisa before returning in 1488 as professor of law in the University of Ferrara on the invitation of Duke Ercole I.[7] Giovanni's brother

Niccolò likewise made a career of the civil service, first as a municipal official in Modena and later as Ferrarese ambassador to the courts of Naples and France.

Aside from Cardinal Sadoleto, the most prominent of Giovanni's five sons was Alfonso, whose career in civil law, public office, and the University ran close to his father's. Until later life, at least, Alfonso was more prosperous than any of his brothers and certainly the most active in politics. Frequently elected to the Conservators of Modena, he was also appointed *podestà* in Cesena, Florence, and Bologna, as well as Counsellor of Justice in Florence, and Modenese envoy to the Roman Curia in 1526. Leo X made him a Knight of the Golden Spur and Count Palatine in 1518, possibly to honor the family of Bishop Sadoleto, but just as likely to conciliate the Modenese, who at the time were sullen and hostile subjects of the Church, impatiently awaiting their opportunity to bring back the Dukes.

Ercole, another of Giovanni's sons, seems to have been bitter and frustrated in the career at which Alfonso thrived. Although he also held public office in Modena and taught law at the University, he was a poet by temperament and desire, yet envious of Alfonso's success, and resentful of whatever help his brothers occasionally offered.[8] Lodovico, the youngest, had a strong interest in architecture and classical scholarship but never distinguished himself as a public servant. Jacopo's favorite brother, Giulio, followed him to Rome and briefly lived in the household of Cardinal Bibbiena before his early death in 1521.[9]

Alfonso alone, therefore, seemed to prosper in the service of the Dukes,[10] and yet until Jacopo settled in Provence as a Bishop in 1527, when a swarm of relatives began to surround him there, nearly all the Sadoletti remained in Ferrara or Modena. Educated in Estense schools and dependents of the Dukes, they pursued the law as a path to public office, their condition rising or falling with the status of the Estensi during the decades of foreign invasion. Jacopo was the only member of his family to find an independent career outside his fatherland and the first of the Sadoletti in two generations to escape the shadow of the Dukes.

This first or second son of Giovanni and Francesca was born on July

12, 1477, and probably spent his childhood in Modena and Pisa before
the family moved to Ferrara in 1488.[11] There Giovanni put him into
the hands of tutors before sending him to the University[12] at a time
when its principal ornament was Niccolò Leoniceno, a favorite of
Ercole I and a versatile scholar whose talents ranged from mathematics
and medicine to philosophy and classical letters. Jacopo attended
public lectures at the Studio. He was introduced to Latin and Greek
literature, and perhaps to philosophy as well, but his primary interest
was Latin letters.

At this time also Sadoleto first met the gifted Venetian humanist,
Pietro Bembo, who had accompanied his father on a diplomatic
mission from the Signory to Ferrara in January 1498. Both Sadoleto
and Bembo were still intended for the law and public life, although
already both were balking at parental expectations and were aspiring
instead to literary careers.[13] The friendship between them which lasted
for fifty years, despite widening differences of temperament, literary
taste, and sense of vocation, began with the common interests and
ambitions shared by the two young scholars at Ferrara.

What Jacopo took from his brief period of formal study was a
stimulated interest in classical literature and the formation of his Latin
style. It was ultimately this talent which gave him access to a career
in the Church, at a time when the educated Italian prelate so often
knew more Cicero than Augustine. Otherwise, the value of his study
at the University was thin. Not having had a disciplined foundation in
philosophy or theology, he was later forced to instruct himself in those
areas of systematic knowledge over which bitter and subtle controversy
broke out in the wake of the Protestant revolt. Along with other
Italian humanists who entered the hierarchy in Luther's generation,
Sadoleto later discovered the limitations of study confined to the
classics and the praise of antiquity. But in his early years Latinity opened
a high road to preferment.

Soon after his twenty-first year, sometime between 1498 and 1499,
Sadoleto left Ferrara and his family for Rome.[14] A place had been
found for him in the household of a distinguished patron, under whom
Jacopo was to continue his studies. The notable feature of the decision

which took Sadoleto to Rome is the fact that he seems to have considered it permanent. At no time in the years immediately ahead did
he even mention the possibility of returning to Ferrara or Modena.
Any explanation of this is conjectural. The most plausible one seems to
follow from Sadoleto's early vocation to letters and scholarship, and
therefore in his fear that by returning to Ferrara he would run the risk
of having to enter the government of the Dukes in one role or another.
In contrast to his brothers and cousins but like many others intended
for the law, Jacopo wanted to pursue the arts not as preliminary to
jurisprudence but as a proper vocation in itself. By making such a
decision he implicitly repudiated the kind of career in which his family
was engaged, the career which humanists patronizingly called the *vita
negotiosa*, "the busy life." In the earnest and active city-state society of
northern Italy, in Venice no less than in Ferrara, those who were
educated at public expense were usually expected to accept some kind
of civic office, and upon all who hoped to remain in official favor hung
the obligation of public service.

By leaving Ferrara, Sadoleto thus cut himself off from the practices
of his kinsmen and escaped an inevitable commitment to the *vita activa*
in the regime of the Estensi, whether as writer and scholar or magistrate
and professor. Ariosto, the poet who attached himself to the Dukes
soon after Sadoleto departed, became the brightest luminary of their
court, but even so his *Orlando* was written in the course of endless and
dangerous missions for Cardinal Ippolito d'Este. As military captain,
private secretary, diplomatic envoy, and political governor, he worked
actively in the Estense government for twenty-five years before entering a retirement which was won at last, he sighed, "by my own
earning."[15]

Ironically, however, Sadoleto's progress toward the privacy of the
contemplative life was even more difficult. In moving to Rome, as
he was painfully to discover, Jacopo merely exchanged one form of
dependency for another and abandoned the prospect of a career in the
state for one in the hierarchy of the Church. The decision to quit
Ferrara, to be sure, permanently reset the course of his life, but it
neither relieved him from the claims of patronage nor provided him

with what Philip Melanchthon, following Plato, once called the "sacred silences" of the well-placed scholar.

Jacopo's first patron in Rome was Cardinal Oliviero Caraffa, a wealthy Neapolitan, *papábile* in five conclaves, a savant, canonist, and theologian who was then Dean of the Sacred College. Sadoleto was to remain with Caraffa for twelve years, living in the austere but magnificent Orsini palace (over which the Cardinal had life use) on the Piazza Navona. Nothing survives to explain how a young and still unknown Modenese gained a place for himself in so prominent a household. Bembo by this time already had a literary reputation, but Sadoleto did not. Certainly Giovanni, who approved of his son's decision to study in Rome,[16] had neither name nor influence enough to secure such gilded hospitality for his son, but it is doubtful that Jacopo left for the eternal city without recommendation. Help may have come from the Estensi themselves through their diplomatic connections in Naples or through the intercession of Cardinal Ippolito I. In any event, Sadoleto was received into the household of a prince of the Church, deserting the ordered bourgeois ways of his family for the heaving turmoil of Borgian Rome.

But the atmosphere of Caraffa's palace on the Piazza Navona was starkly unlike that of Alexander VI in the Vatican.[17] Whether deliberately or by accident, Jacopo was placed with a puritan in a city of wickedness. There were a dozen other Cardinal patrons in Rome at this time, including Giulio de' Medici, Riario, Farnese, Soderini, and Sanseverino; but none of them was Caraffa's equal in erudition or moral stature. An early patron of printing, a sponsor of Bramante and Filippino Lippi, Caraffa was among the most learned and responsible Maecenases of the city and also one of the most pious, belonging to that small circle of incorruptibles in the Sacred College who represented the conscience and tradition of ecclesiastical reform.[18] As a member of a papal commission in 1497, for example, Caraffa candidly set forth the abuses of venality and corruption in the Curia with an argument for a general reformation of the Holy See and the College. Neither he nor his collaborators were declared enemies of the Borgia regime, but they reopened the case for reform in one of the darkest decades in the history of the Papacy.

Jacopo's studies unquestionably took a new turn under Caraffa's direction in that the secular classicism of Leoniceno's lectures was now supplemented by reading in the literature of Christian antiquity and in later Christian history. Moreover, Sadoleto was at least introduced to the works of the Greek and Latin Church Fathers[19] because Caraffa intended him for the priesthood. Yet it is difficult to estimate the depth of Caraffa's impact on Sadoleto's formation, and in trying to do so one must avoid the temptation of assuming that Jacopo's twelve years with the Cardinal were the start of his religious vocation. There is a good deal in Sadoleto's later life which suggests Caraffa's position on curial reform, for example, but it is unlikely that Jacopo absorbed these concerns at a time when his own were so intensely literary. It may be more accurate to say that the period with Caraffa tempered the transition from Ferrara to Rome, during which his education was enriched and extended under a learned and pious, but apparently not a stimulating mentor. Sadoleto evolved to the stature of Caraffa in the course of his own mature life through experience and disillusionment. When he left the Cardinal's household, his reputation was that of a classical scholar and Latinist; it was, in fact, to be Luther more than Caraffa who turned Sadoleto to a consideration of the issues of ecclesiastical reform and the perspectives of Christian humanism. Yet even as a Cardinal, Sadoleto never fully managed or tried, as Caraffa had, to subordinate the role of scholar-humanist to that of priest, or to regard the classics merely as an avocation.

We know somewhat more about the effects of the world beyond Caraffa's quiet *palazzo*. Jacopo's memory of Rome in these years went back to the literary colony, to the study of Greek under Fortiguerra, to meetings with humanist friends at Angelo Colocci's garden on the Quirinal, and to association with men like the younger Beroaldo, Castiglione, Paolo Giovio, Blosio Palladio, Andrea Navagero, Mario

Maffei, and Bembo.[20] He looked back wistfully on Rome as "that city so dear to me that I can love nothing more fondly," as the matrix of his education and all that he valued in learning and friendship.[21] Although Caraffa kept him occupied with study and secretarial duties, Sadoleto found time to identify himself with the swelling number of poets, artists, and scholars who formed the Roman Academy.[22] Then under the presidency of his friend Colocci, the Academy was a rather pretentious but open society of the learned, where Sadoleto and Bembo were readily received. The Academicians shaped Jacopo's literary development far more decisively than the masters at Ferrara had and did so more visibly than Caraffa, who tended to avoid the literary gardens and their votaries.

When Sadoleto went to Rome, he was an aspiring poet who took Vergil, Horace, and Lucan as his models. Of his early poetic works, however, only one—*De Cajo Curtio et Curtio Lacu*[23]—survives; the rest were destroyed at his own request.[24] He considered the poem worthy of dedication to Angelo Ubaldo, but added that poetry was now alien to his taste and style. The work itself is laboriously imitative, praising the deeds of a legendary patriot of Roman antiquity, but it probably found its way to the gardens of the Forum during the early years of Sadoleto's residence at Caraffa's. Far better known, however, is a poem of 1506 celebrating the Laocoön group which a peasant's plow had struck on the Esquiline.[25]

The statue provoked a sensation in Rome. Sent with Michelangelo to the vineyard where it was discovered, Giuliano da San Gallo promptly identified it from the account in Pliny as the work of three sculptors from Rhodes in the reign of Augustus. Julius arranged to have the statue installed in the Belvedere "with the ceremonies reserved for religious relics." Michelangelo took assurance for his own emerging style from the tension and pathos of Laocoön and his sons, while Sadoleto turned to a discarded medium to praise the discovery in verse. For him the unearthing of the sculpture symbolized a brilliant new age in the life of Rome. After centuries of darkness, while the work lay buried in Titus' palace, Romans were now entering "a second life" and "a new day," able once more to understand the grandeur of the Augustan era.[26] It was of such things, moreover, that fame was won in the gardens of the Academy. Here were lines, wrote Francesco Arsilli, in which "the breathing marble of Laocoön glows." And soon after writing the poem Sadoleto received the first fruits of preferment at S. Lorenzo in Damaso.[27] The benefice was conferred on him by Cardinal Caraffa, who was responsible in turn for raising the notorious fragment of "Pasquino" from the earth to a pedestal of honor in the Piazza Navona.

According to the younger Beroaldo, the Bolognese poet and Vatican librarian, Jacopo was also occasionally drawn to the Roman demi-monde in these years. Beroaldo named him among several rivals for the favor of Lucrezia Cugnatis, the most dazzling courtesan in Rome, who called herself "Imperia." The daughter of a prostitute in the Borgo, Imperia before her death at twenty-six had no peer among the thousands of *cortigiane* in Rome and received the attentions of Cardinal Piccolomini, the banker Chigi, Raphael, Aretino, and Beroaldo himself. If the poet only intended an ironic jest at the expense of Sadoleto, whom Bembo later described as "the most innocent of all," it was one deliberately repeated in at least three places in his works.[28] There is no reason to assume that Beroaldo invented these claims, but Imperia like Vergilian verse did not belong to Sadoleto's mature life. An habitual gravity, which Beroaldo also noticed, becomes steadily more evident in his writing and, with rare lapses, in his manner. Except for an elegiac poem to the Fregosi of Genoa written in 1541, he entirely deserted the model and medium of Vergil for the prose style of Cicero, just as he abandoned the society of Imperia for that of Vittoria Colonna.

The earliest prose treatise[29] which can be positively attributed to Sadoleto was one of four on the theme of Christian truce and a crusade against the Turks.[30] These exhortations, although largely innocent of current political reality, display a deep and enduring concern for the peace and unity of Christian Europe. Despite his affection for Modena Sadoleto instinctively thought of political geography in terms of European Christendom. At a time when the infidel became the diplomatic ally of Venice and France, he rhetorically but feelingly invoked the idealism of St. Bernard. His first appeal, *De bello suscipiendo contra Turcos*, was addressed to Louis XII, who was rivalled only by Julius II in troubling the peace of Italy.[31] It is at once a warning about the dangers of princely discord and a plea for the restoration of a Christian commonweal under the King of France. Here Sadoleto abandoned the humanist view of the Middle Ages as an interlude of barbarian night before the advent of "new time" (as in his *Laocoön*), and praised the grandeur of the French crusading tradition from Charles Martel to Louis IX. The treatise acknowledges the continuity of secular history in Christian time, if only in the form of war on the infidels.

Even in the isolated society of letters in Rome Sadoleto could not ignore the chaos in Italy which followed the French invasions. The oration to Louis XII foretold a fixed and firm neutrality in Sadoleto's political reflexes which he held for the rest of his life, however contrary it might be to patrons or superiors. No humanist of his generation stayed more distant from political partisanship or grew more anxious over the dangers of European war. The tone of the *Contra Turcos* is very close to that of the *Querela pacis*. Erasmus, if indeed he wrote the Complaint of Peace, found the author of Christian discord in Julius II and the truest sanctuary of Christ in France, but he shared Sadoleto's disgust that Christian princes should be at peace with the Turks while at war with one another. Sadoleto's first prose treatise, moreover, was an oblique criticism of the Estensi, for the principal Italian ally of Louis XII was Duke Alfonso of Ferrara. The Estensi were soon to pay dearly for their support of the French when the Pope went to war against Ferrara and Modena in his campaign to pacify northern Italy with the sword. In 1510 Modena fell to the Duke of Urbino, whose victory opened a period of occupation which lasted for seventeen years under the heavy rule of imperial and papal governors.

While the northern war reached its climax, Cardinal Caraffa died in January of 1511 at the age of eighty-one.[32] Jacopo was still weighing the choice of a new patron in March but seemed preoccupied with other matters. Every hour, he wrote, brought a new calamity, including violent death to one of Caraffa's stranded dependents and serious

injury to another. He went on to discuss his financial predicament in a
letter to Giovanni, who had already sent ten ducats together with a
letter of consolation on the Cardinal's death. Jacopo admitted his own
need but felt that Giovanni's was still more acute. Even without a
patron he now felt that his own resources were potentially greater
than his father's. And then at the end of the letter, almost as an
afterthought, he added: "I expect in the next ten days to become a
priest."[33]

Giovanni died the following November, three months after Imperia
and ten months after Caraffa. Jacopo may have taken comfort in
remembering that he had recently thanked the old man for things
that could never be repaid. Now, with the passing of his father and his
first patron, Sadoleto stood in a new relation to his kinsmen and *patria*.
By this time more Roman than Modenese, Jacopo no longer turned for
help to the Estensi or his family. The roles were reversed. He soon
began to represent the interests of compatriots in Rome while taking
care of indigent relatives whose fortunes declined with the adversities
of the Dukes.

Nevertheless, the humanist by necessity remained a dependent.
While the Sadoletti endured the oppressive regime of the first imperial
governor in Modena, Jacopo selected a new patron in Rome, now
being able to make a choice among several. During the last, convulsive,
eighteen months of Julius' reign he belonged to the household of
Federigo Fregoso, a prelate several years his junior, who had been
briefly a member of Caraffa's *famiglia* in the Parione. An accomplished
philologist whose major interest was oriental languages and a Maecenas
whose generosity exceeded Caraffa's, Fregoso had more tolerance than
the Cardinal for the Roman Academy and extended his hospitality
more widely. Here Sadoleto was associated with Raphael and with
Bembo, who had returned to Rome from Urbino in 1511.[34] But the
new household dispersed almost as quickly as it gathered, for at the
death of Julius II and the election of Giovanni de' Medici early in 1513,
Fregoso hastily departed for Genoa.

This time the loss of a patron was soon made up, for one month
later both Sadoleto and Bembo were summoned to the Vatican and

the court of Leo X. Once again the paths of Leoniceno's young auditors intersected. Each had abandoned his native city, drawn to Rome by the promise of patronage and the quest of literary recognition. Having chosen to avoid the courts of secular princes, Bembo and Sadoleto began their ecclesiastical careers in the service of the first Medici Pope.

II

Papal Secretary:
The Court of Leo X

Before leaving the Conclave in which he was elected on March 11, 1513, Leo X appointed both Bembo and Sadoleto to the Apostolic Secretariat with the rank of Domestic Prelate and the title of Domestic Secretary.[1] This nomination was the new Pope's first gesture of deference to the Roman Academy and likewise his acknowledgement of a tradition by which papal secretaries were chosen on the basis of their literary talent rather than for their experience in curial affairs. Thus the new appointees stood in the line of Poggio, Flavio Biondo, Leonardo Bruni, and Aeneas Sylvius, selected to draft the official Latin documents through which the Pope communicated with heads of state and members of the hierarchy.[2]

Until recently the Domestic Secretary had exercised considerable authority in the Curia, for under the reorganization of the Secretariat by Innocent VIII in 1487 this principal secretary virtually monopolized the secret diplomatic correspondence of the Holy See. To Leo X, however, the practice of his predecessors seemed cumbersome and ill-suited to the needs of efficient diplomacy. He soon deprived the Domestic Secretary of supervision over the work of the nuncios, for example, and placed this responsibility in the hands of a new official, a Cardinal Vice-Chancellor, who became the prototype of the modern papal Secretary of State. As a result of this reorganization Sadoleto and Bembo had no independent jurisdiction of their own but served rather as ornamental *breviatores* who drafted public documents in the Pope's name, specializing in administrative correspondence while their lesser colleagues in the Camera treated questions of doctrine and ordinary discipline.[3]

The bulls and briefs drafted by the two Domestic Secretaries were sealed *sub bullo* or with the fisherman's ring, and occasionally countersigned by the Vice-Chancellor. This office was held first by Cardinal Bernardo Dovizi da Bibbiena,[4] Leo's former preceptor, private secretary, and conclavist, who now directed the permanent papal nunciatures established by the Medici Pope. Bibbiena was also the rather solitary leader of the pro-Spanish faction of the early Leonine Curia, convinced that only a close tie with Spain could deliver Italy from further harassment by the French. Opposing him, although no less devoted to the *libertà d'Italia*, were Cardinal Giulio de' Medici and the Pope's brother Giuliano, while Leo himself remained ostensibly neutral.[5]

Bembo's early alignment with the francophiles is perfectly clear, and during the first year of the new pontificate it was his support which Bibbiena tried hardest to detach from Giulio de' Medici. But Sadoleto's sympathies are dim and difficult to specify. He seems to have remained on good terms both with Bibbiena and Cardinal de' Medici, taking no active part in papal diplomacy or curial politics, either through indifference or lack of conviction. Although frequently the author of documents in support of Leo's official or public policy of reconciliation, he made no visible and certainly no important commitments of his own. Nor was he expected to. As Domestic Secretary he found himself a servant of the Pope, a guided hand rather than a collaborating head in curial administration and never occupied with court intrigue in the manner of men like Giberti, Aleander, or Pietro Ardinghelli.

He showed the same lack of interest in the perennial issue of ecclesiastical reform. When Egidio da Viterbo addressed the Lateran Council on the urgency of reformation in 1513, Sadoleto praised the orator for his rare gifts of eloquence but disregarded the body of the speech, with its bold defense of the council as an instrument of reform.[6] Sadoleto's

2+

own conversion to the role of a Catholic reformer was still many years away. As Domestic Secretary he had a close and continuing view of papal government but no decisive part in it. He attended consistories and ceremonies of state as well as private deliberations of the Curia, at which he read or spoke, as he wrote, in the name of Leo X.[7] But during his early years in the Secretariat he remained the professional Latinist and Ciceronian, a humanist in the service of a Pope who himself looked unsympathetically on the advocates of reform and skeptically on the partisans of ecclesiastical councils.[8]

Until he was fifty Sadoleto knew Rome and the Curia only, as it were, at first hand. He was not able to acquire perspective on the Vatican or on the issues of reform until he was able to see them from his remote diocese in Provence. Nor did he find reason, in the service of Leo X, to undertake the study of patristic doctrine or the labors of biblical exegesis. Therefore it is a mistake to include Sadoleto at this time with Cajetan and Prierias among the small group of theologians in the Leonine Curia.[9] He had gone to Rome as a poet and steadfastly saw himself as a man of letters; Leo X placed him in the Secretariat not as a priest but rather as a skillful Latinist to adorn the public language of a prodigal patron.

In order to avoid the hardened formulae of diplomatic usage, the Medici Pope specified that Italian be employed in secret correspondence with his nuncios and legates. Latin was reserved for the documents the Holy See issued in its formal relations with secular powers and the hierarchy, on occasions when Leo X chose to speak as the common head of Christendom. As Domestic Secretary, for example, Sadoleto expressed the Pope's satisfaction with the general truce of 1513 between France and Spain. He drafted papal exhortations to peace in Italy and the Empire, warning the princes in the Pope's name against the dangers of Turkish expansion. He composed briefs to heads of state as required by protocol, gravely thanking Emmanuel I of Portugal for the gift of a white Indian elephant to the papal menagerie or congratulating Francis I at the time of his coronation.[10]

Whether or not Sadoleto supported Leo's fateful policy on indulgences—a question which probably can never be settled,[11] his name was conspicuously attached to a number of important documents regulating this traffic. It was through him that Leo granted the right to preach an indulgence for two years to the cathedral chapter at Trier in 1515, and later the explosive concession of the St. Peter's Indulgence to Albert of Halberstadt.[12] Sadoleto pursued certain details of administering these indulgences in briefs to the papal commissioner Arcimboldi, Tetzel's superior.[13] And three weeks after Luther posted his theses at Wittenberg, Sadoleto was again in touch with the Archbishop of Mainz, this time in connection with the efforts of another papal agent to obtain Latin manuscripts for Leo X, to be bought with funds collected for the reconstruction of St. Peter's.[14]

There were also particular papal briefs to be written to private individuals, or on behalf of servants and dependents of the Holy See. Through Sadoleto the Pope commended Erasmus to Henry VIII in 1515 and granted exemption for the sage of Rotterdam from the disabilities of illegitimate birth and disregard of the canon law. Leo X likewise had Sadoleto petition Francis I to release Jacopo de Saulis from detention in Lyons and through him extended papal privileges to protect the publications of other Leonine humanists. Correspondence with curial officials, members of the Medici family, or the Florentine government fell also to the Domestic Secretaries. In fact so extensive was the scope of Latin briefs in the first half of Leo's pontificate that other members of the Secretariat accused Sadoleto and Bembo of monopolizing its work.[15] The Pope accepted their complaint but managed to turn it to his own advantage by requiring lesser scribes to buy the privileges of drafting *brevi particolari* for 25,000 ducats. By the same agreement the Domestic Secretaries were confined in principle to writing the more public documents, the *brevi di stato*, although the rising volume of administrative correspondence in the coming four years could easily have brought about such a redivision of labor anyway.

To occupy so prominent a place in the Curia was high tribute to a son of Giovanni Sadoleto. Jacopo was not simply another client in the throng of dependent Italian humanists who surrounded Leo X, but one singled out for particular recognition; and while embellishing the

Pope's Latin, Sadoleto's name followed his briefs to courts and chancelleries all over Europe.

The other side of Sadoleto's life in Leonine Rome was occupied with the literary world of the city, which reached its spectacular zenith in the reign of the first Medici Pope. Leo X proved himself worthy both of the subtle Cosimo in diplomacy and of his father, Lorenzo the Magnificent, as a patron of letters and the arts. It was not in Florence but in Rome that Medicean patronage waxed most extravagant and —superficially at least—most indulgent.[16] Leo X looked upon the promotion of learning as both a prerogative and an obligation.[17] Not only the droves of suddenly stranded writers and poets, but likewise the frantic creditors who invaded the Vatican palace after the death of Leo X bore witness to the fact that the recent splendor of Roman life had come about through the boundless generosity of Giovanni de' Medici.

No longer a newcomer to literary circles in Rome by the time he entered the Secretariat, Sadoleto ranked as one of the more prominent figures of the lettered community and was himself the head of a group of humanists who met at his vineyard on the Quirinal Hill. Situated on the Monte Cavallo in a region then inside the walls but sparsely inhabited, this villa developed into one of the celebrated "suburban gardens" of the city. Sadoleto bought the property in May 1518.[18] Rich in antique ruins and favored by the summer breeze, it lay in the same area of the Quirinal where Pomponio Leto and Platina had built their villas. For Sadoleto it provided asylum from the strenuous life of the court together with an appropriate place in which to receive his literary friends, a retreat from pestilence and heat no less than from the Vatican.

The elite of the literary colony formed what Sadoleto called "that blessed society of friendship" which captured his interest and fired his enthusiasm for the classics so persistently then and during the years of retirement from the city.[19] For both Bembo and his colleague it was the Roman Academy which made Rome attractive, and the Curia which ultimately made it intolerable. In his well-known letter to

Colocci, who was also an apostolic secretary, Sadoleto recalled the names and distinctions of luminaries in this circle. Among them were "careful and acute Casanova, fluent and sonorous Capella, eloquent Vida, whose verse came so close to antique splendor; chaste and prudent Beroaldo, and the gifted company of Piero, Grana, and Blosio, whom our generation calls distinguished in song and speech."[20] There were Ciceronians like Girolamo Negri, Venantio, and Francesco Bini; Latinists like Camillo Porcio, as well as Paolo Giovio, Lazaro Bonamico, Mario Maffei, and Marcantonio Flaminio. Raphael, the most honored artist in Leonine Rome and the papal court, was a particular friend of Bembo and Sadoleto, whom the painter consulted, according to von Pastor, when he composed the "School of Athens."[21] Castiglione, likewise a member of this group, sent the manuscript of his *Cortegiano* to Sadoleto in September 1518 at the suggestion of Count Canossa, because of certain reservations about having it published.[22]

But the literary achievement of both the Domestic Secretaries was negligible while they were in the Camera of Leo X. The pontificate of Leo X was generally a fallow period, undistinguished, as Gnoli reminds us, by a single outstanding literary work. Sadoleto's epistolary style was formed and constantly exercised during these years, certainly to the advantage of his fame as a Ciceronian.[23] Yet his own work was neglected to the extent that it is impossible to attribute a single major treatise to him between the years 1513–1521.[24] Compared to later periods spent in Provence, this was the most barren of his career.

We may conclude that he failed to write simply because he lacked time. It is also likely that his leisure was too often given over to talk, to the banquets and sociability of the gardens, or taken up by the incessant diversions of the papal court itself. The Pope rarely had the company of poets on his hunting and fishing expeditions to Magliano or Lake Bolsena, but they were always present in numbers at table and during the many lavish *divertissements* at court. Leo's household was animated by buffoons and jesters, the foremost of whom was the Dominican Mariano Fetti,[25] a professional clown who first gained notice in the household of Julius II. And Sadoleto, despite his reported gravity, was willing to take his turn with Mariano and the jesters, winning some reputation as a court wit.[26]

The literary friends of Leo X, moreover, participated in a series of crises, both real and imaginary. Sadoleto and Bembo were among the first to defend Christophe Longueil or Longolius, a Flemish humanist whose appearance in Rome in 1517 promptly divided the city into battling factions.[27] Although lionized by the Domestic Secretaries and their friends, Longueil was unable to live down an oration he once delivered at Poitiers, in which he belittled the cultural achievement of Rome while citing the greater literary glory of France. Roman patriots violently denounced the foreign poet as a "barbarian" and at the urging of a young firebrand, Celso Mellini, summoned him before a "popular tribunal" on the charge of "treason" in April 1519. Longueil fled north in terror, stopping to visit Erasmus at Louvain before going to England, while Budé praised him to Sadoleto from Paris.[28]

Even after the controversy burned itself out following Mellini's death, Longueil remained a peevish problem for Sadoleto, to whom the temperamental Fleming turned as his only real friend in Italy.[29] In defending him with earnest tenacity and conviction, Sadoleto and his friends eventually overcame the literary and political chauvinism of Mellini. However, Sadoleto and Bembo alike were unable to see, as Erasmus did so easily, how trifling and artificial the issues were, or how absurd Longueil had been in his apologetic appeals to the "Conscript Fathers" and the "votes of the tribes." The Domestic Secretaries were close enough to such bombast to identify themselves with the poet and uphold his cause as their own.

It is not too much to say that Longueil's "trial" was taken more seriously by many in the Curia than Luther's,[30] whose case was virtually suspended during the year 1519, not because of Longueil, of course, but rather through neglect and indifference. Yet the impact of Luther's early doctrines was widening. As the hour of Longueil's confrontation with the Capitoline tribunal drew near and his enemies accused him of looting libraries in Rome for Erasmus and Budé, Erasmus himself was taking careful and serious notice of Luther. Accusing critics already charged him with accepting and even of originating Luther's radical position. While Sadoleto and Bembo were defending Longueil and the universal cause of good letters, Alberto Pio attacked Erasmus and other northern humanists for inflaming the young against worthy theologians and for mocking the dignity of the priesthood.[31]

Most of the papal court and the Pope himself held out against Erasmus' critics, albeit with a more cautious enthusiasm than they had given Longueil. The exception was Girolamo Aleander, a member of Cardinal de' Medici's party and later papal nuncio to Germany, who became the most passionate of all Erasmus' enemies at this time.[32] Confronted by Luther's defiance in burning the bull *Exsurge Domine* and the books of the Canon Law, and by what he considered to be his clandestine part in Luther's apostasy, Aleander thundered against Erasmus in a letter to Rome in November 1520. The Nuncio was further outraged to find that some one in the Curia was informing Erasmus of these reports and charges.[33] Although it is impossible to identify the source, we do know that Erasmus' partisans in Rome were few but included Sadoleto and Bembo,[34] both of whom stoutly opposed his ecclesiastical enemies. Aleander also complained to the Vice-Chancellor about the Pope's toleration of this crypto-Lutheran, angered by a brief which Sadoleto wrote to Erasmus to acknowledge recent assurances of good will toward the Holy See.[35]

One need not postulate an "Erasmian party" in the Church to suggest that the free spirit of Rotterdam had already created a division among the humanists and within the hierarchy. Leo X, to be sure, was eager to enlist Erasmus' support against Luther. Equally significant, however, was the alienation of Aleander, an accomplished scholar and classicist, from Catholic humanists like Sadoleto and Bembo.

The two Domestic Secretaries were generously rewarded by the first Medici Pope. By the time Bembo left Rome for Padua in 1521 he had accumulated twenty-seven benefices, held with extensive dispensations for their use through a series of briefs which his colleague Sadoleto drafted on the Pope's instructions.[36] Sadoleto fared as well. In October 1513 Leo X conferred a number of exemptions upon him at Jacopo's instigation: he was enabled to receive four simple benefices and four *beneficia curata*, two canonries and two ecclesiastical pensions, release from the obligation of residence where traditionally required, and the right to assign or give away 1,000 ducats of beneficed income.[37]

It is less probable, however, that he directly sought for himself the Provençal diocese of Carpentras, which the Pope conferred on him on April 17, 1517, two days after its Bishop died in Rome.[38] Then at Loretto as a pilgrim, Sadoleto declined to accept the charge. A good deal has been made of this refusal, which may have been sincerely intended, but the *nolo episcopari* was also a convention by which a nominee was expected to declare his unworthiness. Moreover, Jacopo was promptly invested with the diocese, released from the obligation of residence and permitted to appoint a vicar-general in his place. The yearly revenue of this modest see, located in the papal state of Venaissin, northeast of Avignon, was around 1,600 ducats and therefore somewhat more than Bembo received from his principal living at S. Giovanni in Bologna.

Each of the Domestic Secretaries came into his major benefice in the same year, neither any more innocent of self-seeking than he was free of need. Bembo looked on preferment as the recognition of literary merit, and Sadoleto seems to have regarded his minor livings in the same light. But once a Bishop, Sadoleto consistently took his new office as a *cura*, the source of responsibility as well as privilege. While an absentee Jacopo kept in close touch with the diocese through serious and active procurators, carefully promoting the welfare of both the see and the town through his connections in the Vatican.[39] In these matters he may well have acted more from a sense of duty than out of love for a place still unfamiliar and unseen. The recent publication of fresh evidence about the Oratory of Divine Love in Rome makes it no longer possible to claim Sadoleto as a member of the society at this time.[40] Therefore, Jacopo's solicitude for a small and distant see in Provence is the first trace we have of his interests as a churchman—

a kind of concern which never stirred in the breast of his friend Bembo.[41] Although they continued to share the broad vocation of humanist, they now began to move toward the choice of working careers along different lines.

From the standpoint of the two Secretaries the Pope acquited himself well in the Longueil affair and in the initial disputes over the orthodoxy of Erasmus. Despite the gathering crisis in matters of doctrine, discipline, and diplomacy, Leo X also continued to be the most eager and unsparing patron in Italy. Yet both Bembo and Sadoleto began to grow restive and disillusioned in the Curia, increasingly ill at ease in the turmoil of the court and unable to lead a productive literary life while attached to it. During the latter half of Leo's reign they began to recognize the dilemmas of the dependent humanist. A month after he was made Bishop, Sadoleto confessed to Tiepolo that he wanted "nothing more earnestly than to devote myself to those studies without which life is not worth living," and from which he had been cut off by the constant and heavy demands of four years in the Secretariat.[42] He resented the sacrifice of studious leisure to the regimen of his office and coveted the precious quiet, the *otium* of the humanist—not only time and tranquility, but freedom and autonomy as well. On the other hand, he seemed not yet ready to break away and confessed he would yield to the Pope's desire that he remain in the Secretariat.

In the meantime the assignments which Sadoleto received during the last years of Leo's life reflect a new gravity in the problems confronting the Curia. The Pope failed to take seriously the reform sentiment so widespread in Christian Europe and so explicit in the Lateran Council, but he did share the general anxiety about the advance of the Sultan's forces in the Middle East. After the Turkish conquest of Aleppo, Damascus, and Jerusalem, the conciliar fathers approved the collection of a tithe for three years to support a crusade and pressed for a universal truce among the Christian princes at the close of the Council in March 1517. The Pope had already ordered a commission of the Sacred College to study the problem and work out detailed plans for joint action by the princes.

Ignoring the cynicism which answered these proposals in Germany

2*

and the casual indifference with which Venice signed a treaty with the Sultan in the fall of 1517, Leo X stood fast in his determination to fight the Turks. On March 3, 1518, he created four Cardinal-Legates to preach the crusade and published a bull calling for a five-year truce among the secular powers. A series of penitential processions began in Rome on March 12, and two days later the Pope himself walked barefooted from St. Peter's to Santa Maria sopra Minerva for the concluding ceremony.[43] There, after Mass, Bishop Sadoleto preached the crusade in a Latin sermon, warning that a holy war was now the sole means of saving Christendom from enslavement.[44] He argued that God had permitted the infidel to flourish because of the wickedness of Christians and even to reach the edge of triumph before providing the instrument of their defeat by a holy alliance of all Christian peoples. Confusing reality with his own wishes, the orator rejoiced in the support which the princes now, at last, were willing to give the crusade.

Much of the sermon was lost on the audience, according to Paris de Grassi, because of the weakness of the speaker's voice. But the Venetian ambassador heard enough to demand that Sadoleto's references to the historical opposition of Venice to the Turks be deleted from the discourse before it was printed.[45] The Signory meanwhile kept the Sultan minutely informed of military preparations for the crusade, which in turn met vigorous resistance in Germany and equivocation in France, while Erasmus skeptically asked how much better the Pope would govern the Orient than the Turks if the crusade should succeed.[46]

Late in March 1518 Sadoleto completed a set of instructions for Cardinal Farnese, the new Legate to Germany, with particular attention to the necessity of assuring the Germans that the special tithe requested by the Pope would be spent on the crusade alone.[47] When at the last minute Farnese was replaced by Cajetan, he drew up letters accrediting the second mission to the German princes.[48] And Cajetan left Rome on May 5, soon to find himself before a hostile Diet at Augsburg in midsummer.

By now Sadoleto was involved in a far more serious order of curial business than he had previously handled. The instructions to Cajetan contained no reference to Luther, but while the Diet was in session the Legate received two briefs, both by Sadoleto, which dealt with Luther alone. The first, dated August 23, was written to enforce Luther's citation before the Auditor of the Camera as ordered by Ghinucci and Prierias in July.[49] In view of the Emperor's cooperation with the Legate, Cajetan was instructed to take Luther into custody and to demand imperial assistance if necessary. On the same day the Pope had Jacopo write a brief to the Saxon Elector, requesting his help in handing Luther over to the Legation. But when Frederick balked at having the Wittenberg professor sent to Rome, another brief was sent to Cajetan on September 11, condemning Luther as a notorious heretic but granting consent to have his case examined at Augsburg.[50]

The Pope's interest in German affairs was further quickened by the death of Emperor Maximilian I in January 1519. Cajetan was promptly told to oppose the candidacy of Charles I of Spain and to support one of the German Electors instead. Sadoleto worked on dispatches bearing on the imperial succession during the spring of 1519,[51] his duties extended partly by the Pope's new attention to Germany and likewise by Bembo's reduced activity in the Secretariat, which began with his prolonged illness in the summer of 1518. From Gregorio Cortese, then at Lérins in a Benedictine monastery, Sadoleto learned that he was expected momentarily to take up his episcopal duties in Provence.[52] While the ailing Bembo took his ease in the Vatican gardens, Sadoleto replied that although he wanted nothing more than to go to Carpentras and resume his studies, he saw no honorable way at present to leave the Secretariat.[53] Desire again yielded to duty, for the Curia was currently engrossed in delicate arbitration with the princes; with four Legations afield the business of the Camera was exceptionally heavy.

Bembo, however, was far less responsive to the obligations of his office. In late April 1519 he left Rome for Venice on the plea of bad health, perfunctorily fulfilling a papal mission at Mantua en route. Ill and burdened with debts, he went north, as he put it, to seek the healing effects of Venetian air and stayed for over a year. Once back in Rome he detected that Sadoleto, like himself, had grown restive in the Vatican but predicted that the Pope could probably persuade his colleague to stay on.[54] While Jacopo won momentary relief from his duties, he did nothing to break away from them, irritated though he was by the rigors of the active life and aware that he had already floundered in it too long.[55] He told Longueil of his craving for quiet and even wrote of going to Carpentras; what mattered most, however, was "to bring forth something from myself" and to plunge into serious study and writing.

At no time in his earlier career had Sadoleto stated his intentions so positively or defended the literary vocation so emphatically against the *vita activa*. On the other hand, the letter to Longueil is merely the praise of something still out of reach.[56] He had resolved, he said, to devote his energy as much as possible to scholarly pursuits. But even the promise has a ring of futility, for he went on to complain of the confusion in the city and of the strain he found in trying to work in a place "so likely to deceive and disturb the mind." Rome, or at least the Vatican, had become an abomination.

In the early summer of 1521 Bembo decided to leave the Curia for good, again on the pretext of poor health but actually for more complex reasons.[57] One was his affection for Fausta Morosina, whom he had taken from Rome to Venice in 1519, and his desire to live with her again.[58] There was also his disappointed hope for a red hat as the means of financial independence. But just as compelling was his disenchantment with the Curia and the Pope's style of patronage, which in Bembo's eyes was fatuous, chaotic, and uncritical.[59] He longed for Padua, for its climate and calm, and above all for freedom to write. Therefore what passed again for a leave of absence was tacitly understood to be his resignation from the Secretariat.

Even before Bembo departed, Sadoleto found himself drawn deeper into the Pope's efforts to achieve diplomatic security while trying at the same time to gain control over the fresh floods of defiance in Germany. Bibbiena died in November 1520 disgraced and repudiated, though himself a late convert to francophilia just at the time when papal diplomacy was shifting toward the Emperor. Cardinal de' Medici's primacy was now complete. The Vatican also looked to

Charles V for help against the Lutherans. On January 18, 1521, the Pope had Sadoleto compose an urgent brief to the young Hapsburg prince, imploring him to publish the recent bull of excommunication against Luther and to execute the ban on his followers throughout Germany. In a sweeping statement of two hundred words the Domestic Secretary recalled the duty of the Holy See to "purge the Lord's vineyard of reptiles" and the duty of the Emperor to labor for the faith in enforcing papal discipline.[60] Still lacking Charles' support, however, Leo was forced to solicit help wherever he could find it. In the following weeks Sadoleto was asked to send off similar pleas to Joachim of Brandenburg and Duke George of Saxony, along with new instructions for the nuncios on the suppression of Lutheran heresy.[61]

Leo spent the early months of 1521 in a last effort to deal concurrently with Francis and Charles V, hoping to play off one against the other to his own advantage. But in the midst of his double-dealing were dark fears of the French in Milan and of the heresies in Germany, so that at length he turned to Charles V as an ally of necessity against France and the German heretics, trusting that a strong tie to the Emperor would assure the welfare of the Holy See and the independence of the peninsula from French domination. The text of a treaty between Charles and the Pope was ready early in May and presented to the Spanish ambassador on the twenty-eighth.[62] If we accept a note appended to it in 1549, the document itself was prepared by Sadoleto though revised and closely glossed by Giberti.[63]

At a single stroke Leo X undertook a bold policy based on Bibbiena's original position and designed to satisfy his own aspirations as Pope, Medici, Catholic, and Italian. It ended papal neutrality with an offensive pact against France, binding the Emperor to evict the Most Christian King from Milan and to protect the Holy See against enemies of the faith. The short-run results of the alliance were highly successful, albeit at the cost of compounding the Pope's financial ruin. But the ultimate effect was to replace one foreign oppressor with another, expelling the French from the Upper Country to expose the region and later Rome itself to the Spanish. As Pope Clement VII, Giulio de' Medici was to reap the whirlwind which swept the imperialists across the Tiber in 1527, though for the moment he had the satisfaction of driving the French out of Milan in November 1521.

On learning of these victories in Lombardy, the Pope is said to have exclaimed, "This pleases me more than my tiara." A week later he was dead, succumbing to fever on the night of December first. Late at night on the third Sadoleto met the Cardinals in the *camera para-mentorum* to discuss arrangements for the Pope's funeral.[64]

Panic surged through the city; with hundreds of other curialists and dependents of every condition, the Domestic Secretary found himself abruptly deprived of a patron. Sadoleto's release from the *vita negotiosa* had come about unexpectedly, but while many of the Leonine humanists and other dependents left Rome, Sadoleto retired from the Vatican to his Quirinal vineyard, and waited.

III

Papal Secretary:
The Court of Clement VII

Leo X was succeeded by the son of a Flemish boatwright, who took
the name of Adrian VI. The crowd in St. Peter's square which first
heard this news on January 9, 1522, denounced the election as an outrage. To a Roman diarist the pious obscurity chosen by the Conclave
was an "homo barbaro, de natione vilissimo de Fiandre,"[1] who was
then living "in outlandish Spain." The widespread confusion which
settled over Rome and the Curia after Leo's death was aggravated
by rumors that the new Pope did not intend to go to Italy. Cardinals,
curialists, artists, and writers were still moving out of Rome in great
numbers, and so many of Leo's former dependents had gone to Spain
to seek favor or employment from the new Pontiff that the Sacred
College forbade such journeys entirely, fearing that a modern Avignon
might arise there. The closing of many Roman banks made credit
virtually impossible, while angry creditors milled around the papal
palace with unpaid claims on the Holy See.

As one of Leo X's huge household Sadoleto remained in Rome through
these weeks of confusion until late in March 1522, when he went to
Modena.[2] Whether this was merely a long deferred visit to his mother
or connected with the death of his brother Giulio at the end of the year
we do not know. It is certain, however, that the sojourn was cut short
after two weeks by word that the Pope was preparing to go to Italy.
Lancellotti gives an explanation for Sadoleto's brusque departure from
Modena on April 10:

On this day the most Reverend Monsignor Sadoleto, Bishop of Carpentras, left Modena for Rome, having received word that His Holiness, the newly elected Pope, is soon to arrive there, and because he was secretary of the late Pope Leo, he would like to assume the same office with the new Pope; M. Jacopo arrived from Rome two weeks ago.[3]

Four days later Girolamo Negri reported that Adrian, "having been informed by Bishop Cosentino of the integrity and erudition of this man, wants [him] for the same office."[4]

Back in Rome, Sadoleto went to his vineyard again. The rumor that the Pope was en route to Italy turned out to be false, though widely accepted, and the Bishop soon returned to his books. There is nothing to show that he corresponded with Adrian while the Pope was in Spain but a good deal to suggest that Monsignor Sadoleto expected and indeed hoped for nomination to the new Apostolic Secretariat. The fact that he hurried back to Rome so suddenly and remained there for another year strengthens the assumption that Sadoleto was an expectant office-seeker. On the other hand, he knew well that his future depended on the Pope's attitude toward him and that his standing with Adrian was entirely conjectural.[5]

In May 1522 Adrian prepared at last to leave Saragossa. After numerous delays the papal fleet put to sea on August 5 and reached Ostia on the twenty-eighth. He went to Rome the following morning, receiving the tiara in a pompless ceremony on August 31. The new pontificate, which to Italians had been a ghostly and unfamiliar shadow play until now, soon appeared in its full austerity. Nothing could have been more brusquely different from the elegant style of Leo X. Luigi Gradenigo described Adrian as a solitary, a man of few words and without a confidant in the Sacred College. Many of the limited circle around him were politically inexperienced and inept; "stupid and stolid louts," was the picture Negri gave of the Dutch Datary Enkevoirt and Dirk van Heeze, the pontifical secretary.[6]

Nevertheless, the Pope's counsellors also included such worthy and able men as Gian Pietro Caraffa, Cardinal Campeggio, Cajetan, and Cardinal Schinner. The advance of Lutheranism, following the Diet of Worms, and the obvious failure of Leo's political countermeasures had alarmed these men and made their admonitions about reform more pressing. The new Pope, who himself had belonged to the reform party in Germany and to Cardinal Ximenes' group in Spain, could hardly have identified himself with a group more seriously concerned about the status of papal authority or the condition of the Church.[7]

But Sadoleto's friend Negri, describing Adrian's severity and reforming zeal, added his doubts that the Pope's good intentions would come to anything because "Nature abhors sudden mutations" and because corruption was too deep to be quickly dislodged.[8] Bembo expressed the view of most sophisticated Italians when he found Adrian's regime worse than the chaotic interregnum which preceded it. Theologians and reformers overwhelmed the poets, parasites, buffoons, and *bon vivants* whose flight was completed by the Pope's arrival. With the Academy in exile, it soon appeared that of all the Leonine literati only the ungrateful Paolo Giovio found favor with Adrian VI. The Vatican became a cloister.

Erasmus, moreover, was the single humanist whose services and presence in the Curia were directly solicited by the Pope; Adrian's purpose was to strengthen the authority of the Vatican by asking Erasmus to write against the new heresies from Rome. In the first of several invitations, dated December 1, 1522, Adrian offered him neither honor nor wealth but a reminder of duty, and urged him to come to Italy at the end of the winter. A second invitation was sent in January 1523.[9] But Erasmus declined, alleging poor health and poverty of talent, although by conviction he felt that mere verbal attacks on Luther without reform in the Church would accomplish nothing.

Adrian had hesitated for months before writing to Erasmus, and it may be that he likewise postponed a decision about Sadoleto. The Pope had apparently considered him before leaving Spain; in January 1523 it was rumored again that Adrian intended to bring Sadoleto back to the Curia, but nothing came of it.[10] Sadoleto remained in isolation on the Quirinal, at last engrossed in his writing and entirely out of touch with the Vatican. Now, for the first time in his adult years, he gave himself entirely to his writing.

By the spring of 1523 he no longer anticipated recognition from across the Tiber, an attitude for which Negri offers a trivial but not irrelevant explanation:

[Sadoleto] is well, . . . secluded from the public and indifferent to preferment, especially in view of the fact that the Pope, while reading a certain elegant work in Latin the other day happened to remark, "This is the work of a poet," as though he were ridiculing eloquence. And again, when he was shown the Laocoön in the Belvedere as a wonderful and excellent thing, he said, "Those are the idols of the ancients."[11]

Sadoleto's final decision to leave Rome for Carpentras and his diocese was made sometime in March 1523. It has been suggested that certain enemies had accused him of tolerance toward Lutheranism and that he was therefore ordered into virtual exile.[12] Another supposition is that his youthful past and possibly his association with Imperia provided weapons for his critics, but Cantù, who offers this hypothesis, is probably in error when he adds that Sadoleto had also been charged with falsifying a papal brief while in the service of Leo X.[13] Such an accusation did develop, to be sure, but not until after Sadoleto had been at Carpentras for several months.

Negri's version attributes the decision to Sadoleto's own choice. He reported that

Sadoleto has been entreating the Pope for six months [for permission] to go to his diocese and will leave soon after the [Easter] holiday. . . . All Rome is incredulous that His Holiness has given him leave to go, but I do not wonder, for the Pope does not know him. . . . Rome in truth is no longer Rome. Rid of one plague, we are now stricken by a greater.[14]

Negri went on to foretell the ruin of the Church under Adrian and said that the majority of good and honorable men in the city envied Sadoleto his chance to leave, without explaining why it was that a Bishop needed papal consent to assume residence in his see. On the eve of his friend's departure, Negri's tone was even gloomier:

Sadoleto is leaving, to the great sorrow of this entire court. And I believe that if in these days we followed the ancient custom of rending our garments for grief, he would find no less than 20,000 men who would do so, just as Cicero did. To every decent man it appears that the goodness and virtue of Rome depart with his lordship: and indeed it is so.[15]

Therefore, if Sadoleto left under a cloud of suspicion, or at the Pope's command, we cannot know it from Negri. He failed to explain, however, why Sadoleto waited for ten months after Leo X died to ask leave to go to Provence. This belated request appears to have been submitted within four to eight weeks after Adrian's arrival in Rome, that is, in October 1522. Either Sadoleto received an evasive reply from the Pope which later became negative, or he simply surmised that there would be no place for him in the new regime once he had time to observe it, with the result that he left as soon as good weather returned the following spring.

We know little about his state of mind in leaving Italy, though Negri says he intended to stay in Carpentras for about a year, depending on conditions in Rome and Italy in general.[16] Such a statement makes his departure seem voluntary, implying that he still intended to pursue his career in Rome, whether as a curialist or not. By the time he left, his literary plans at least were settled. They included a treatise on ecclesiastical government, a work on Cicero's *De gloria*, a commemorative essay on the death of Giulio Sadoleto, commentaries on several Psalms and parts of the Gospels, and completion of a treatise "on the dissensions in Philosophy."[17] Obviously less monolithic than Bembo's projects of the same period, these intentions place Sadoleto well apart from the more strictly secular interests of the Academicians. There is now an unmistakably theological tone in these projects, but at the same time the Bishop en route to Carpentras still thought of himself primarily as a classical scholar.

The journey was to include a stop at Modena before proceeding by way of Milan to Avignon. A pair of mules carried his bed and clothing, the rest of his belongings being sent by sea. Northern Italy was afflicted by war and plague, while plundering and unpaid troops menaced the traveller on every side. After thirty-four days, toward the middle of May, Sadoleto first saw Carpentras in the luminous beauty of the Provençal springtime. Welcomed at the gates by his

people, the Bishop was gratified to learn that the plague, which
threatened to overwhelm the town before he appeared, completely
vanished at his arrival. So great, he explained to Cardinal Egidio, was
God's beneficence to him.[18]

Carpentras pleased Sadoleto immensely and seemed to provide him
with much of the same kind of asylum that Petrarch had found after
leaving papal Avignon for Vaucluse.[19] Although Jacopo missed his
friends in Rome, there were books to take their place and the towns-
men, even if unlettered, were hospitable. To Egidio, who congratulated Sadoleto for his decision to "seek a haven of quiet and tranquility
from the tempests . . ." of Rome, Sadoleto replied that nothing could
be more placid than his new life and nothing more welcome than the
relief it provided from his labors in the Curia.

The diocese of Carpentras was hardly considered a prize by ambitious
place-seekers.[20] It was a rural see of modest resources and heavy duties,
since it served as the capital of a small papal state and the seat of
temporal government in the Comtat Venaissin. Fifteen miles northeast of Avignon, the town itself seems incidental to the blue masses of
Mt. Ventoux nearby and the scorched colors of the hills and plains
below. Less punished than Avignon by the mistral in its haste from the
Alps to the mouth of the Rhône, this region also suffered abrupt
climatic changes—intense dry heat and late frosts, as well as drought
and floods. For the peasant *contadini* of Sadoleto's diocese, life was a
constant battle against nature and men.

On the other hand, Provence offered special compensations to the
Italian humanist. Gregorio Cortese complained of the cultural bar-
barism of the Riviera, but for Sadoleto's generation the interior held
a rich fascination derived from the literary traditions of Provence, so
that Bembo, Colocci, Antonio Tebaldeo, Pole, and his friend Beccadelli felt a particular fondness for the adopted land of Petrarch and
looked upon it as another *patria*.[21]

Sadoleto's first visit to Carpentras fell during an era of calm preliminary to one of acute and widespread distress the following year.
In 1524 the plague, a bad harvest, and the depradations of French
troops provoked anguished complaints to Rome from the syndics and

consuls of the Comtat, but Sadoleto was gone before these troubles began. Consequently, the impression he received of his role as Bishop was deceptively soothing and gave few signs of what his pastoral problems would be; at the moment Carpentras seemed fully to satisfy his desire for isolation and quiet.

Nothing remains to disclose his reactions to the end of the viciously maligned and tragic pontificate of Adrian VI, or to the election of Giulio de' Medici as his successor. Adrian died in September 1523, his end precipitated by the severity of the Roman summer. Relief at his passing was unrestrained, and in circles which Negri frequented the election of Giulio de' Medici after another long and stormy interregnum was greeted with wild enthusiasm.[22] To humanists and Leonine curialists the election of Cardinal de' Medici signified a new day, ending the dark severities of the foreigner, Adrian. Moreover, the Leonine exiles reflected the sentiment of the populace itself, which joyfully welcomed the choice of the Conclave on November 18 and fastened the same expectations on Clement VII which had been placed on his cousin a decade earlier.

On the day of Clement's election word spread that the new Pope intended to name Giberti as his Datary and Sadoleto, together with the poet Blosio Palladio, as his Secretaries.[23] On November 29 or 30 a courier was sent to Carpentras with a papal brief containing Clement's invitation, almost a year to the day after Adrian VI, for entirely different reasons, first asked Erasmus to go to Rome. Negri had expressed the fear, however, that Sadoleto's love of Carpentras might lead him to refuse the post, and a letter from the Bishop confirmed this anxiety. Sadoleto had recently learned of the charge that he had falsified a papal brief as Domestic Secretary to Leo X, the report apparently having been circulated late in the reign of Adrian VI. Sadoleto dismissed the accusation as a vile calumny, adding that "others will now see, as a result of my experience, what great folly it is to serve princes in this office."[24] But Negri comforted himself with the thought that his friend, who at that time had not learned of Giulio de' Medici's election, could not graciously refuse the appointment he was about to receive. Negri also knew that the new Pope, rejecting the names of other candidates, had specifically designated the Bishop of Carpentras as one of his principal secretaries.

And Sadoleto evidently accepted the nomination with dispatch. Despite a sojourn with Cortese at Lérins, he was in Rome by the end of January 1524, his first letter in the name of Clement VII being written to Reginald Pole on the thirty-first.[25] Bembo was aware of his return by the middle of February and himself returned to Rome later in the year, hoping again to find preferment.[26]

Sadoleto had stayed in Carpentras for less than a year, suddenly willing to give up the solitude that was to mean so much. No doubt he complied with Clement's invitation partly out of obedience, but he was reluctant to leave Rome in the first place and considered his absence temporary, as we know from Negri. To hold, as some have,[27] that the Bishop only returned to Rome on condition that he be allowed to go back again to his diocese three years later is to accept the highly questionable argument which Sadoleto used in retrospect in order to justify his precipitous departure in 1527, just before the Sack of Rome.

Sadoleto's arrival in Rome at the start of 1524 coincided with the carnival atmosphere which filled the opening weeks of the Medici restoration. The return of the plague chastened this mood somewhat, but it was generally assumed that the character of the Leonine era would prevail again. Castiglione, back in Rome briefly as Mantuan envoy, found the city congenial again and his friends once more installed in the Curia. Although the papal household displayed an unexpected parsimony, it was larger than that of Adrian VI and offered the usual good will of the Medici to men of letters, if not their habitual generosity. Humanists such as Coloccio, Blosio Palladio, and Giovanni Battista Sanga were restored to the Secretariat, and the Borgo Vecchio, where Sadoleto now took lodging, regained some of its lost animation as the favored district of provincials and foreigners in Rome.

In many ways, however, Clement VII brought far more bitter disappointment to his partisans than did Leo X. The eleven years of Clement's pontificate formed a period of passage, full of desperate improvising and disaster, into the era of Catholic Reform. Disillusionment with the second Medici Pope resulted both from his inability to deal with the monstrous dilemmas he faced and equally from his character defects. Contemporaries were quick to see that the Pope's greatest weakness was irresolution, a fateful inertia in the presence of decision.

Hailed at the start of his reign by Mario Maffei as one who would soon restore Christendom to its pristine virtue and purity,[28] Clement VII began his pontificate with earnest plans for the reform of the Curia and the clergy. No less than his predecessor he received a series of admonitions and abundant counsel on the suppression of heresy and the introduction of ecclesiastical reform. The early months of his reign provided encouragement for Catholic reformers when the Pope showed interest in the correction of curial abuses, and when he made Caraffa the Vicar-general of Rome in the spring of 1524. Examination of the Lutheran heresy was continued in the Curia and through Campeggio's Legation in Germany, from which the Cardinal wrote Sadoleto expressing his private satisfaction with the Pope's "holy and sincere intention to correct and reform the condition of the Curia," while congratulating Sadoleto for his own exertions in behalf of reformation in Rome.[29]

But these early signs of promise, as the Bishop explained twelve years later to Duke George of Saxony, soon melted away. Clement VII, he conceded, was

a good man by nature, devoted to things righteous and honorable, if only he might have been true to himself and firm in his own counsel. Under this Pope I hoped that a means would be found for healing dissension. I worked vigorously and pressed him continuously in this matter. Steps were taken for summoning bishops from all over the world in order that by their efforts and advice the condition of the priesthood, which had so ominously declined, might be restored to its ancient status. The foundation was laid for serving and honoring the concerns of religion more piously, and for rescuing the clergy from its baseness and depravity. The effort at length began to prosper, when the worthy, moderate, and devout Pope, though indeed too feeble in keeping his counsels, was forced to descend into war and the enmities of the princes, and to suspend his pious intentions by the scheming of certain men who exerted excessive influence on him.[30]

This appraisal of Clement's failure, to be sure, was made after the Pope's death. However, it also contains the same views which Sadoleto expressed to his friends, albeit with less candor, in 1527 and 1528. During his three years in the court of Clement VII he was not a conspicuous partisan of reform, but it was also at this time that he first became sensitive to the condition of the Curia and the urgency of reform.

The Pope similarly disappointed those who continued to demand a general council. His own opposition, stronger than that of Leo X, was strengthened by the doubts or open resistance of many experienced observers of the Lutheran movement, including Cajetan, Campeggio, Aleander, Eck, and Cochlaeus, who were also aware of the political difficulties it would create. The Pope's position had support in the Sacred College and among the curialists, who looked upon conciliar reformers with suspicion and fear. Others, like Archbishop Fisher, warned that the time for reconciliation with the heretics had passed and that to summon a council now would amount to a concession toward those who had no will or intention to abandon their errors.[31]

For his own part the Pope equivocated and obstructed the conciliarists, magnifying the difficulties they raised without examining the merit of their arguments. He took the traditional course of the Medici by turning from reform and the council to political alliances and diplomacy, under the illusion that the Lutheran movement could be successfully treated as a political problem. His viewpoint was based on a half-truth, but because of his diplomatic inconstancy it became quite impossible to exploit whatever limited chances of success this policy contained.

As an Italian and a Medici, the Pope was no less preoccupied with Italy, counting its freedom from foreign intervention as indispensable as the pacification of Germany. After a year of honest effort to maintain the neutrality of the Holy See and to secure peace between Francis I and the Emperor, Clement began his pathetic efforts to use the force of papal diplomacy to assure the political autonomy of the peninsula, or at least of the Medicis' sphere of interest. What he sought was a delicate equilibrium between France and the Empire, to be adjusted by the application of his own diplomatic weight.[32] But the variables were so numerous and unstable, the views of his political advisers so conflicting and his own temperament so irresolute, that papal diplomacy failed even more visibly than the attempted reforms of 1524.

Once again Sadoleto had no active part in the formulation of papal policy. Compared to the discordant theories of involvement pressed on the Pope by Giberti and the imperialist Nicholas von Schönberg, his was a doctrine of strict neutrality and political detachment. Sadoleto was an Italian to the marrow of his bones, but in politics he thought in terms neither of Modena nor indeed of Italy, but rather of Christian Europe. The role of the Holy See in politics, as he expressed it in instructions to one of the nuncios, should not be that of a self-interested party but that of a father toward his son.[33]

Sadoleto's duties under Clement VII provided constant exposure both to the Hapsburg-Valois rivalry in Italy and the domestic turmoil in Germany, as well as to the Turkish advance in eastern Europe. The troubled and pessimistic reports of the nuncios impressed on him the urgency of a neutral policy in the Vatican and the need for a general pacification of Germany, menaced by heresy and princely disobedience no less than by the Sultan. From one of Lorenzo Campeggio's letters it appears that Sadoleto had begged him to warn the Pope about the importance of political neutrality, but while Campeggio agreed with the wisdom of such doctrine he declined to express himself to that effect in writing.[34]

Under Clement VII Sadoleto was again one of two Domestic Secretaries, serving together with the rather inactive Benedetto Accolti, a Florentine humanist and prelate who had been an *abbreviatore* for Leo X.[35] But Jacopo's duties had become significantly more important, for he was now charged with both the Pope's public correspondence and with the secret correspondence between the Vatican and the nuncios.[36] To the obligation of writing elegant Latin was added responsibility for a critical area of curial intelligence. Dispensing with Leo's reorganization of the Secretariat, Clement VII did not appoint a Cardinal to supervise the work of his *segretario intimo* and preside over the administration of foreign policy, even though Clement himself had once had this role. In effect, he restored the office of Domestic Secretary to what it had been after the reforms of Innocent VIII and thus allowed it to recover jurisdiction over the nuncios, who now addressed their dispatches, in many cases, directly to Sadoleto. Although giving Sadoleto a free hand with the missions to Germany and eastern Europe, Clement personally dealt with those involving Italian affairs and therefore with envoys to the Emperor or Francis I. But during the three years which he spent as Clement's principal secretary, Sadoleto, with varying degrees of authority, handled the great bulk of the Pope's correspondence.[37]

Clement's neutrality came to an early end in December 1524 when he concluded a secret agreement with Venice and France against the Emperor. The commitment was made largely on his own initiative, despite the influence of Alberto Pio and Giberti, as an attempt to contain the French in Milan and to preserve the independence of Parma and Piacenza. The immediate result was to enrage Charles V, who roared at the Pope's treachery and threatened retribution, implying even that it might mean imperial favor toward the Lutherans.

The Pope's purpose was not to defy the Emperor so much as to guarantee the *status quo* in Italy, but the new shift to France produced a holocaust in the peninsula which rumbled all over Europe. Unaware of the gravity of his decision, Clement wrote to the Emperor through Sadoleto on the day the treaty was published, addressing him in affectionate and benevolent language as he explained that the agreement with Francis I was a "counsel of peace," designed to secure "our tranquility" and the welfare of Christendom without prejudice to the Emperor or thought of private advantage.[38] Sadoleto also wrote the Doge to emphasize the Pope's concern for peace as a means of creating unity against the Turks, and announced the treaty to Henry

VIII as a device to end the war and protect the Holy See.[39] The Secretary persisted in the task of justifying the Pope's action for weeks to come. He explained to the German Electors that the intent of the treaty was merely to guarantee each party from harm in a pact which was by no means hostile to Germany.[40]

He also drafted instructions for papal envoys in northern Italy, where the Pope vainly continued his efforts to secure an accord between Francis I, the imperial viceroy, and Charles de Bourbon. Clement's wishes were communicated to Cardinal Salviati, the Legate to Modena and Reggio, who was in touch with Spanish forces in the North, while his brother Lorenzo reported on the French. Cardinal Salviati summarized the terms and counterclaims of each side in a letter to Sadoleto in January 1525, urging the necessity of speed in seeking an accord that would secure peace in the northern plains.[41] But the fate of Lombardy was sealed as though the Pope's peace missions did not exist. In the course of a few hours the French hold on Pavia was broken and the King himself taken prisoner on February 24, 1525.

Through Sadoleto's briefs we can follow the melancholy progress of Clement's diplomacy in the two years between the Battle of Pavia and the early months of 1527. The Pope's public correspondence, formal and restrained, discloses his beneficent intentions but shows little of his own desperate predicament. Without troops and all but ignored by his French allies, he turned to appeasement of the Emperor, despite the pleas from Venice and other Italian states to organize the defenses of Lombardy. Sadoleto was the hand but not the heart behind those briefs to Charles V which acquiesced in the defeat of the French while taking comfort in the hope that the Emperor would now turn to the labors of peace and pacification. Writing to Charles in May, Sadoleto reminded him of the two great dangers with which Christendom was besieged, as though to say that with Francis I in captivity, the Emperor acquired sole responsibility for protecting Europe from the Turks and the Lutherans.[42] While it is true that both the foreign and domestic menace increased in 1525, the papal brief was at best a feeble instrument of persuasion. The Emperor, called a "second

David" whom God had sought out to deliver his kingdom, remained
no less preoccupied with his private interests than the Pope.

And the private interests of the Pope were treated by his Domestic
Secretary in quite another manner. The contrast between Sadoleto's
rhetorical *brevi di stato* and his terse instructions to the agents of Medicean politics appears vividly in two concurrent tasks he performed in
June 1525. The first was a conventional brief to Charles V, expressing
the Pope's satisfaction with a recent treaty, described not as a new
union but as an old friendship revived.[43] The second was a secret
dispatch to Francesco Guicciardini,[44] the Pope's principal military
adviser who was then Governor or *Presidente* in the Romagna, where
he was to work out a system of defense against the imperial forces in
Lombardy. It was delivered by Niccolò Machiavelli, whose plan for a
national militia in the papal states had temporarily won Clement's
attention and interest.[45] While Guicciardini and Machiavelli were
studying the military potential of the Romagna, Sadoleto addressed
the Pope's affectionate greeting to Charles de Bourbon, the imperial
commander and ally of the Emperor, now ominously and restlessly
at large in northern Italy.[46] Indeed it was just such firebrands as
Bourbon whom Guicciardini was desperately trying to immobilize.
Papal diplomacy, as in the era of Leo X, was steered by several com-
passes.

Another category of secret correspondence under Sadoleto's direction dealt with German affairs, for Clement VII freely delegated his
authority here in order to concentrate his energies on Italy. Although
bitterly aware of the disorders in Germany and of the Turkish threat
to Hungary and Austria, he insisted on regarding both the *malum
domesticum* and the *malum externum*—heresy and the Turks—as similar
issues, that is, as political problems. Disturbed by the more immediate
question of peace in Italy and security for the states of the Church, the
Pope wanted to stabilize his position in the peninsula before trying to
suppress the Lutheran princes or fight the Sultan. As a result of this
emphasis, his missions to Germany were treated with relative neglect.

Correspondence sent to Rome from the Cardinal-Legate Lorenzo
Campeggio and the Nuncios Rorario and Andrea da Burgo were

addressed almost entirely to Sadoleto,[47] following the practice which existed before the Secretariat was reorganized by Leo X. While much of this intelligence was seriously inaccurate or misleading, these reports contained an enormous amount of factual matter and close observation, which gave Sadoleto direct knowledge of the Lutheran movement. Certainly the most meticulous and useful dispatches were Campeggio's. His letters to Sadoleto, sent from all parts of Germany, Bohemia, Hungary, Poland, and Austria, contained careful and detailed evaluations both of princely and popular sentiment in these regions. The Legate was particularly disturbed by the deterioration of political stability in Germany and by the apparent weakness of the Catholic princes. He insisted, however, that neither doctrinal nor political discussion would be profitable so long as the Emperor was absent. The destruction of heresy depended not only on the active efforts and presence of Charles V, but equally upon general peace in Europe. As it was, he warned, the rumored alliance between Clement VII and the French late in 1524 simply made the Lutherans more arrogant by encouraging them to believe that Charles would now have to give them his support.[48]

The jurist Campeggio almost wholly ignored the theology of the Lutheran revolt. Sadoleto shared neither his political interpretation of heresy nor the appeal to a policy of force in Germany, but he emphatically endorsed the Legate's argument that reform in the Church and peace in Europe were indispensable to any lasting religious settlement. Under Leo X Sadoleto had acquired a Roman and myopic vision of the outer world, but in the following decade his perspective was gradually changed by what he saw of papal diplomacy and by what he read in Campeggio's dispatches about the disorder in Germany and eastern Europe.

The Pope, however, still looked at Europe through the lenses of the Italian and the Medici, if not of the Roman, and persisted in giving his attention almost exclusively to peninsular politics. By October 1525 imperial troops had seized the Duchy of Milan and thus destroyed the equilibrium already upset by the collapse of the French in Pavia. Against the insistent demands of Giberti and his circle, Clement continued in his efforts to appease the Emperor, while Castiglione and Cardinal Salviati assured him of Charles' peaceful intentions. Sadoleto also produced papal briefs in support of Clement's naïve hopes that Charles intended now to turn to the arts of peace and that he might even restore Milan to Francesco Sforza.

Toward the end of 1525 the Pope began to see that his confidence in Charles was misplaced and that the Emperor's docile manner might be the mask of deception. On December 19, while informing both the Doge and Henry VIII of the Pope's watchful attitude, Sadoleto went on to say that the Holy See would go to war if the oppression of Milan was not lifted.[49] During the spring of 1526 the drift from appeasement was quickened by the release of Francis from captivity in Spain and by the heavy price of freedom imposed on him by the Treaty of Madrid. Support for France arose not from sympathy with its King but out of fear that the Emperor might soon dominate the continent as he did the Italian peninsula. Milan, as it turned out, was not only the "bilancia di tutta Italia," as Guicciardini put it, but the fulcrum of Europe as well.

At last, therefore, the Pope agreed to join the coalition against Charles V. The League of Cognac, conceived as a holy alliance, was formed on May 22, 1526, to include Francis I, Clement VII, the Doge, and Francesco Sforza. Giberti's policies reached their full triumph with the whole Italian peninsula nominally solidified against the Emperor. The voices of protest were few. Castiglione months earlier had admonished the Pope that such an alliance would bring ruin to the Holy See, and in Rome Sadoleto likewise tried to dissuade the Pope from war with Charles V.[50] The Domestic Secretary reportedly argued that the real enemy of Christendom was not the Emperor but the Sultan, who at that time was preparing his final assault on Hungary.

Nevertheless, Sadoleto's pen remained at the Pope's disposal, working for measures which Jacopo both feared and disliked. During the summer of 1526 preparations were being made for a war of deliverance. On June 6 Sadoleto informed Guicciardini of his appointment as papal lieutenant in the States of the Church and general of the papal army, later adding full diplomatic authority to these powers in dealing with Francis I and his ministers.[51] It was Sadoleto who composed the notorious brief of June 23 to Charles V, notifying him of the Pope's adherence to the League of Cognac and enumerating the Emperor's offences against the Holy See.[52] So severe was this rebuke that Clement later tried to soften it in a following letter, but he merely shifted the burden of explanation to the dispirited Castiglione.[53]

How the Pope justified himself to Charles V matters little, for the war had already begun and Sadoleto was soon caught up in the dismal details of its prosecution. He sent a brief to the Swiss concerning the use of mercenaries in the papal army; he dispatched instructions to Andrea Doria, the Pope's naval commander, and received complaints from Guicciardini about the conduct of Francesco Sforza along with his own proposals for the attack on Genoa.[54] Through Sadoleto the Pope remonstrated with Francis I for failing to fulfill his obligations to the papal offensive in Lombardy and bitterly complained of this default to Henry VIII.

Then, as though to fill the cup of affliction, Clement learned that the Sultan had annihilated the Hungarian army at Mohacs. Only days later another disaster suddenly broke on Rome and the Curia when the Colonna on September 20 stormed through the Porta S. Giovanni as auxiliaries of the Emperor and quickly moved across the city to the Vatican with 4,000 plundering troops. No sooner had the Pope taken refuge in S. Angelo than the papal palace, the sacristy of St. Peter's, and a number of curial dwellings were ransacked, including the apartment and stable of Bishop Sadoleto, who had followed the Pope to safety.[55] The season of calamity, foretold by Castiglione and evidently feared by Sadoleto, had now begun. Penurious, bewildered, and almost ignored by Francis I, the Pope now felt the boundless vengeance of his enemies. Sadoleto recounted Clement's desperate predicament in a brief to King John III of Portugal a month later. Candor overtook the Secretary in describing the chaos of counsel among the Pope's advisers when he confessed that "we found ourselves in conflicting opinion and thoroughly confused about what we should do." They could only agree to send nuncios to all the kings and princes, informing them of the plight of Hungary and the urgency of peace, as well as of the Colonnas' humiliating assault on Rome.[56] It was as though Clement, through his Secretary, sought to exchange the role of a beleaguered Medici prince for that of the paternal Vicar of Christ.

The Secretary himself, however, was little more than a puzzled and increasingly distraught observer of this rising disorder. He lived and worked among those who took decisions and made what passed for policy, but he was not one of them. It would be misleading, therefore, to dwell further on his public career in the reign of Clement VII without pausing to examine the manner in which Sadoleto ordered his private life as a prelate and writer attached to the papal court. A certain discontinuity between public duty and private interests runs through and even distinguishes his career in the Church; and while a fusion of the active with the contemplative life was often necessary, it was seldom harmonious. What occupied his mind among friends on the Quirinal had little to do with the claims which fell on him from the Vatican. These hills seemed to polarize his life in Rome. The Tiber, separating them, was a chasm which Sadoleto never easily bridged.

D espite the turmoil in the Curia and the heavy demands of his office, Sadoleto found time for his studies and retained contact with his diocese. Although more deeply engrossed in curial business than ever before, he managed to combine an active occupation with his literary interests. While living in the Trastevere in order to be closer to the Pope, he could still retreat to his vineyard, and Negri tells of summer days when Sadoleto received members of the Academy at his villa.[57] He kept in touch with Bembo and the Paduan humanists, and through Bembo began to correspond with Reginald Pole, who was then studying at Padua.[58]

By this time Sadoleto was also well acquainted with Erasmus,[59] now embattled both with the Lutherans and with a small but intent band of critics in the Church. The Pope himself, however, held steadfastly to his faith in the Rotterdamian, believing like Adrian VI that he was indispensable as an ally against Wittenberg. Through Sadoleto, Clement VII expressed his own good will and sent a modest gift to Erasmus in the spring of 1524. In November the Domestic Secretary wrote of having received a new book from Erasmus, the recent *De libero arbitrio*, not yet read for want of time.[60] During the late months of 1524, Sadoleto responded to pleas from Boniface Amerbach to intervene with the Pope in behalf of Botzheim, who had been accused of sympathy with Luther and summoned to Rome.[61] Sadoleto did enough to earn the thanks of Erasmus, who expressed his gratification with the outcome of the case and assured Sadoleto again of Botzheim's innocence, adding that mere association with Lutherans in itself was no proof of guilt at a time when contacts with heretics were so difficult to escape.[62]

In the summer of 1525, frustrated by bad weather in his plan to go to Rome, Erasmus wrote to congratulate Sadoleto for his commentary on the Fiftieth Psalm. Generally critical and sometimes contemptuous of Roman Academicians, Erasmus said he took new hope from the fact that such a work could come out of Rome.[63] He praised Sadoleto for simplicity and clarity of style no less than for his success in drawing out the significance of the text.[64] This was Sadoleto's first exegetical work, presumably started at Carpentras and completed in Rome, where it was published with a papal privilege of ten years in 1525.[65] The content of this work on the Psalm, *Miserere mei, Deus*, need not be treated at length here. This is David's prayer, following the seduction of Bethsheba, for the forgiveness of his sin and the purification of his iniquitous nature. Sadoleto likened David's plight to that of mankind, alienated from God and seeking divine mercy, having come to know penitence through despair. The interpretation which Sadoleto put on these verses and their implication for the relationship of man to God is one which repeatedly emphasizes David's dependence on grace. But even so it failed to satisfy Luther. The Wittenberg professor, whose eye fell on an incredible variety of religious literature, found the commentary untheological throughout, insensitive to the nature of grace, and neglectful of the role of Christ in the redemption of man.

In the dedicatory letter to Giberti, Sadoleto explained his view of textual criticism as practiced in the commentary. In place of using a single mode of analysis he defended a fusion of the literal, moral, mystic, and allegorical interpretations, in order that the meaning of the text might be more fully disclosed.[66] Sadoleto followed Colet and Erasmus in his use of a radically different exegetical method which dispensed with the apparatus of the scholastics in order to emphasize "the text instead of the history of the text." He also showed a new awareness of current theological issues by selecting the Fiftieth Psalm as his first exercise in biblical commentary. While Campeggio enlarged his knowledge of the politics of the Reformation, Erasmus and Giberti alerted Sadoleto to some of the more recent techniques of textual criticism. Behind the Bishop's new concerns, however, was the provocation of Luther.

Sadoleto likewise found time to promote the welfare of his diocese. The citizens of the Comtat, like those of Modena, were burdened with a military occupation during part of Sadoleto's first year in Rome as Secretary to Clement VII, and each community needed an advocate in the Curia. After the Modenese complained to the Holy See about the ruinous conduct of papal troops under the Marquis of Mantua and Giovanni de' Medici, they sent Alfonso Sadoleto to Rome to represent their grievances to the Pope.[67] In Alfonso's brother the consuls and citizens of Carpentras also found a spokesman in Rome.

Soon after their Bishop returned to Italy, the *contadini* were beset by pestilence and bad harvests, and by the presence of French troops quartered in the Comtat. Equally oppressive was the privileged status of the Jewish moneylenders in Provence, whose rights, sanctioned by the Roman Camera and its dependent courts in the County, entitled them to have Christian debtors imprisoned. The interior of Provence, and particularly Avignon and Carpentras, had been a haven for persecuted Jews since the Middle Ages.[68] The Papacy made a practice of protecting them as soon as it learned to profit through the sale of special privileges to them. Local tribunals, accountable only to Rome, upheld interest rates up to twenty-five per cent for Jewish money-lenders. The bankers in turn often acquired parts of the harvest through advance purchase of the crop or by outright possession in default of payment. Foodstuffs thus acquired were usually sold at inflated prices in a region where drought and frost were common.

Clement VII oscillated between severity and reckless indulgence toward the Jewish community, but in August 1524 he issued a bull which closely restricted its prerogatives as creditors and usurers.[69] The bull, however, was not enforced, and a year later a Jewish delegation recovered their former privileges from the Cardinal Camerario by paying a new tax. Tension between the bankers and peasants in the county grew more serious, and so the problem lay until Sadoleto returned to Carpentras. Meanwhile, the Pope's confirmation of privileges sold to the Jews by the Camera did not prevent the Bishop from arguing the case of the debtors, or from writing what Negri called a "most elegant oration against the Jews,"[70] setting forth the grievances of the debtors and the disastrous effects of cameral privilege. The treatise was never published, but from Negri's summary it appears to have judged the Holy See for the sale of privileges as severely as it condemned the Jews for exploiting their protected status. The remarkable feature of the work is Sadoleto's willingness to identify himself with his diocese even though attached to the papal household.

Attention to the affairs of his see took other forms as well. Sadoleto reorganized the cathedral chapter at Carpentras by obtaining a bull which stipulated that all revenues and prebends attached to St. Siffrein be divided into equal shares among the canons. Other questions of clerical discipline were treated in diocesan synods held each spring under the Bishop's vicar at Carpentras. In the fall of 1525 he began to besiege the judicial *conseil* of Toulouse with entreaties to settle a controversy between the diocese and one Domino de Muris.[71] The Bishop accused de Muris of blocking action on a case which had been tied up in the court at Apt for thirty years before being transferred to Toulouse. Sadoleto was also party to the dispute in that he demanded restitution of the two villages which De Muris had seized and plundered in the Venaissin. The Bishop obviously had no taste for such matters but doggedly kept up his protests with a demand for immediate settlement.

Sadoleto's commentary on the Fiftieth Psalm and his pastoral polemic against the Jews point to new interests in one who earlier had aspired to fame as an imitator of Vergil. So, too, does his attention to the welfare of Carpentras. His emerging concern with biblical studies represents an effort beyond the range of his classical poetry and Ciceronian eloquence, and the mastery of style which he developed under Leoniceno. Similarly, his labors as priest and prelate lay outside the world of the Roman Academy and belonged more to that of Oliviero Caraffa.[72] The rhetorical tradition and the cult of secular Latinity which flourished in the literary gardens of Leonine Rome left clear traces on everything he wrote in later life. Yet the intellectual categories within which the Leonine humanists thought and wrote proved to be no longer adequate, by themselves, for Sadoleto as he approached his middle years. His earliest major work after the death of Leo X was the first part of a dialogue, *De laudibus philosophiae*, intended to be a defense of secular wisdom and the contemplative ideal. But his venture into exegesis took him beyond the pale of the Academicians. Poets like Beroaldo and patrons like Chigi had no more interest in biblical commentaries than Imperia or Fra Mariano had in diocesan synods or crop failures in Provence.

On the other hand, the literary promise of Sadoleto's youth was still not fulfilled if he is compared to his friend Bembo, the first of the Medicean exiles and by now the literary dictator of his generation. Living in Padua and by 1526 the father of three illegitimate children, Bembo had become the object of "enthusiastic admiration and all but idolatrous worship."[73] His thought and energy were now wholly engaged in his writing, and the scope of his work was closely defined. Sadoleto, however, had not yet managed to leave the Curia and seemed still unable to stabilize or unify his literary plans. What opportunity he had for study and writing was divided between widely dissimilar tasks, so that he had no real identity among Italian humanists except as a Latin stylist.

Nevertheless, one dilemma was soon to be resolved, if only by accident. Sadoleto spent the first forty years of his life in the shadow of princes and patrons—the Estensi Dukes, Cardinal Caraffa, Fregoso, and the Medici Popes. Restricted by the demands of patronage, he had never known, though he often craved, the enjoyment of sustained and meaningful personal freedom. Bembo achieved it by deserting the court of Leo X in 1521. Sadoleto was to achieve it abruptly when he abandoned the service of Clement VII in 1527, only days before the Sack of Rome.

If the Pope's commitment to the League against Charles V accomplished nothing else, it simplified the problems of papal diplomacy. Policies of neutrality, equilibrium, and appeasement gave way to war after Clement joined the coalition against the Emperor in May 1526, so that curial business, thereafter, was chiefly concerned with military matters. Sadoleto's official duties declined proportionately. With the fighting concentrated in Italy, most of the negotiations with the imperialists were conducted directly between representatives of both sides in Rome.[74]

To the humiliation which the Vatican suffered from the Colonna raid was now added the progress of the imperial forces in northern Italy, where Georg von Frundsberg led his wild *landsknechte* across the Po in November. Impetus to their advance was given by the avarice of the troops and the ambition of Frundsberg's collaborator, Charles de Bourbon. The Duke, having failed in his invasion of Provence in 1523, and disappointed in his efforts to seize the French crown with the support of Charles V, now turned to the invasion of Italy as the road to personal power and rank among the sovereigns of Europe. And at the start of 1527 there seemed to be nothing which would stop him. Bourbon and Frundsberg joined their armies near Piacenza in February and started down the Via Emilia toward Modena and Bologna at the end of the month, helped in their progress by Alfonso d' Este. Hungry and unpaid, these troops became an increasing threat to their leaders, whose control over them began to depend upon frantic promises of booty and pillage in Rome.

The Pope's despair soared in the face of this peril. Almost bankrupt and virtually deserted by Francis I, he tried to buy off the imperialists in March, when negotiations for an armistice were started. Before the abortive agreement was ratified, Sadoleto explained the Pope's decision to the Doge in one of the last briefs he wrote for Clement VII.[75] The letter simply informed the Doge that there was no alternative to such a truce; the Papal States as well as Tuscany might otherwise fall, and the Holy See was plainly unable to resist the enemy alone. But Bourbon refused the treaty. The Duke, after the death of Frundsberg, ran south at the heels of his own army.

Cardinals Farnese, Orsini, and Cesarini begged the Romans in April for money to organize the defense of the city. Others, like Giberti and the Pope, held vainly to the belief that money could still halt Bourbon's rapid advance. Negri wanted to share this hope but suspected it, doubtful that the imperialists could be held to their word. If not frightened, he was eager to go to Padua or Venice to escape the Curia. "This Court," he told Micheli, "has now become a chicken yard. Every day makes us more aware of the iniquity of the times and of a desperate situation."[76]

Sadoleto, on the other hand, evidently warned Negri of impending attack on the city and urged him to leave before it struck.[77] But the Bishop's foresight, which he attributed to Providence, was not especially remarkable in view of the growing exodus from the city. Sadoleto left Rome in haste on either the sixteenth or seventeenth of April.[78] From the many self-justifying letters he sent back to Italy from Carpentras, we know more about this journey than any other he made. He departed with the Pope's consent, obtained through Giberti; Sadoleto acknowledged the Datary's "kindness" and "mediation" in enabling him to go, and described Giberti as "the giver of my tranquility."[79] Sadoleto later explained to Francesco Bini that the Pope had given him leave for three or four months.[80]

From Rome he went to Civitavecchia, accompanied by two kinsmen, Camillo and Paolo Sadoleto.[81] There they embarked for Nice. During the passage both crew and passengers fell victim to the plague, so that when the ship arrived at Nice, authorities ashore would not allow the cargo to be discharged. Consequently the part of Sadoleto's library which had survived the Colonna raid, including many Greek and Latin manuscripts laboriously collected, remained aboard and was never seen again. The refugees stayed at Nice for two days before they resumed their travels with borrowed pack animals on April 27.[82] It was precisely at this time that Bourbon broke camp on the Arno to begin the final stage of his march on Rome. The rabid *landsknechte* were south of Viterbo when the Bishop and his nephews arrived in Carpentras on Friday, May 3.

On Monday, under cover of a thick fog, the slaughter and wreckage began in Rome. Churches, monasteries, palaces, and private dwellings alike were ravaged for a week with a fury that exceeded the power of witnesses to describe. Seeming more intent on destruction than booty, the invaders tore open the tombs of St. Peter's and stabled their horses in the Vatican Palace and the Sistine Chapel. The Borgo, including Sadoleto's house, was sacked again, and thousands of every age and condition fell victim to the frenzied invaders. Sanuto estimated that in two *rioni* adjacent to the Vatican 2,000 bodies were thrown into the Tiber and nearly 10,000 others were buried.[83]

Few of Sadoleto's friends or curial associates escaped without physical suffering, deprivation, or captivity. The quarters of nearly all the curialists were plundered and most of the Cardinals forced to pay enormous ransoms for their safety. Giberti, Salviati, and Schönberg fled to S. Angelo,[84] where the Pope again sought refuge before he was placed in the custody of imperial troops. Sadoleto's colleague Accolti lost his entire library, as did Giraldi, Coloccio, and Egidio da Viterbo. Plague, famine, and malaria spread through the ruins, and the papal household was not fully restored for sixteen months.

Meanwhile, in May again, the people of Carpentras welcomed their Bishop.

IV

Fugitive

The two decades of Medici rule, from 1513–1534, were years in which a soaring confidence later burst into disorder and bewilderment. Erasmus, once the prophet of a golden age, now confessed his despair. Guicciardini interrogated the recent past without presuming to understand it, convinced that the golden age had ended at the death of Lorenzo the Magnificent, twenty years before a Medici wore the tiara. And toward the end of the Medicean Papacy Sadoleto, like Erasmus, began to feel that the worst was yet to come.[1]

Although the Sack of Rome was by no means universally deplored outside of Italy, it was often taken for proof that the times were evil and hopelessly out of joint. The Venetian diarist Alberini summed up three common responses among his countrymen in accounting for the calamities of 1527:

Opinions respecting the course of human events are varied and diverse. Some believe that they occur according to the favor of a false goddess, called *Fortuna* or Fate by the ignorant; some, from the disposition in which we ourselves make and ordain events; others (in my view more accurately) contend that everything necessarily depends on the will of God, who orders and disposes to whatever end it pleases him.[2]

Men of Sadoleto's convictions tended frequently to regard the Sack of Rome as God's vengeful judgment on a wicked generation and a depraved city. But just as often they invoked the course of fate or human agency and the malevolence of men.

From the quiet of his diocese Sadoleto expatiated for more than three years on the Sack of Rome and tried to interpret it in the light of his own hasty departure from the Curia. Many had fled from the city in the wake of the invasion, but he alone among the Pope's nearest associates had left when Bourbon's horde appeared.[3] Thus his many letters from Carpentras after the event are a continuing apology for the course he had taken.

Negri informed Sadoleto that his flight was severely judged in the Curia and that his critics even included men like Giberti.[4] Giberti, however, was an author of papal policy and bore responsibility in which Sadoleto had no personal part. Before the Pope returned to Rome from Viterbo, Giberti retreated to his own diocese in February 1528, disillusioned, and eager to resume his priestly duties at Verona in a setting of studious quiet. He was also alarmed by the Pope's recent drift from Francis I toward the Emperor and hoped to dissociate himself from what he considered a new and dangerous kind of diplomacy.

Throughout his letters of self-justification Sadoleto argued that certain papal advisers had deceived the Pope and that they had abused his good nature or exploited his weaknesses.[5] He wrote as one whose own warnings had been ignored, assuming the viewpoint of a distressed observer who looked back on conditions which he had deplored but could not control. Negri probably repeated Sadoleto when he said, "since you found that your counsels were not approved by those in authority, you departed shortly before all was sunk in catastrophe . . ."[6] The Pope's guilty advisers, the general corruption of the age, and the evil state of the Curia provoked the wrath of God, who first "punished the innocent in order to recompense them with a greater good" to follow.[7]

At other times, however, Sadoleto entirely dispensed with the argument from divine judgment. In fact what makes these letters interesting is the erratic and often contradictory nature of his explanations. Occasionally, for example, he invokes a cruel *fortuna* to explain the events which had carried him north; it was fate rather than God's hand which deprived him of his library[8] and plunged him into a "new and unfamiliar" life. Sometimes he follows Erasmus in attributing

3*

the destruction of Rome exclusively to human actions. When he replied to Erasmus' letter castigating the invaders themselves for the ruin of Rome, Sadoleto remarked that although there were many moral defects in the city, "virtue nevertheless ruled the greater part." Therefore, explanation of the disaster was to be sought in the viciousness of the *landsknechte* and their leaders.[9] But this was to say, in effect, that God would punish those whom the Bishop elsewhere described as the chosen agents of divine anger.

His efforts to exempt the Pope from responsibility were likewise inconsistent. He wrote to Clement VII of the obstacles which others had placed in the way of papal reform, so that vice and impiety prospered until Providence finally interceded.[10] Failure to reform the Church and the court led to catastrophe through the fault of "perfidious men." The disaster, however, could also be made the "gateway to sound morals and holy laws," provided that men worked to restore the honor of the priesthood and the grandeur of pontifical dignity. Human and divine agency were thus said to be joined together. While writing to Negri only a few days later, he charged the Pope's counsellors with refusal to reform and purify the *sacerdotium*, whereupon the Bishop abruptly reversed himself to criticize Clement for obstructing the will of God. Because the Pope drew back from those drastic measures which circumstances required, he had aggravated the disease instead of curing it.[11] A year after his departure from Rome Sadoleto wrote to the Pope on the urgency of a sweeping reformation in the Church. Expressing himself "perhaps too boldly," he reiterated his belief that both the faith and the Church had to be restored to a pristine dignity under the leadership and initiative of the Holy See.[12] The success of any pontifical reformation would depend upon the selection of pious and cultivated priests as well as scrupulous care in the collation of benefices. Counsel of this kind may also be read as a statement of the Pope's past errors, with an accent on human responsibility for the present condition of the Church.

Discussion of reform and a general council was renewed everywhere after the events of 1527, and few doubted the argument that effective remedies required papal support and initiative. But in

Sadoleto's often conflicting observations on the state of the Church and the clergy there appears no acceptance of his own participation in the conditions he deplored, no troubled sense of his share in corporate accountability. He repeatedly gives the impression of looking at the Church from the outside, as if the Church were really the Roman Curia seen from Carpentras. A willingness to tell Francesco Bini, then papal secretary, that in going to Carpentras he was not deserting the Pope so much as placing himself "near another and greater Holiness, to whom I consider myself even more obligated,"[13] does less to set him apart from his priestly contemporaries, however, than to illustrate the candid individualism so widespread in the pre-Tridentine hierarchy.

Fully aware of seeming to abandon the Pope at a critical time, he acknowledged to Giberti on reaching Provence that he had done so in order also to achieve the personal goal of a more serene life in the service of God.[14] He wrote of having come at last into a haven of calm after being adrift in heavy seas. He spoke of having repudiated a career in Rome for "those letters and the study of those noblest arts, through which we have the means to know ourselves and come closer to God." Although often expressing his devotion to Clement VII and his willingness to rejoin the Pope in an emergency,[15] Sadoleto also made clear his intention to retire permanently from the Curia and to stay in his diocese.[16] Suggestions from Salviati and Accolti that he return to the city were rejected out of hand.[17] God had delivered him from tempests which he was determined never to see again. The very nature of curial service was distasteful to him. Rome embodied all he cherished as the heart and soul of Latinum: it was "this beloved city," "the noblest and most glorious of all." Yet he left no doubt that he would spend the rest of his life at Carpentras, where he could be his own master, at liberty to serve God and the cause of good letters as he saw fit. To Bembo, who naturally approved the decision and reminded Sadoleto that he now had to recover much lost time,[18] the Bishop explained that he had not been born for bondage, and bondage was the word (*servitus*) he now used to describe the life of a curialist.[19]

This was a view which he expressed with notable candor to the

Parisian humanist Germain Brice, with whom Sadoleto felt a certain kinship in passing up a public career for the contemplative life. He had forsaken the agitation of Rome both to regain tranquility and to achieve a "free and self-determined manner of living," as well as to follow the muses. "Long harassed by countless cares and anxieties, which I bore and endured in conformity with another's will, I betook myself, disheartened and weary, to a place of quiet."[20] And when Cardinal Contarini later implored him to go back to Rome as a member of a new commission on reform, Sadoleto answered that he preferred to remain where he was. Happiness, he said, lies "in serenity and freedom of the mind, in doing those things which proceed from our own free choice."[21]

Having spent so much of his life "in things alien to me," Sadoleto also asked whether he had not given enough to the service of princes, friends, and the Church.[22] Here is the suggestion that the man of letters earns his way, as a matter of right and merit, to honorable leisure. He knew well enough that the timing of his departure from the Curia had aroused sharp criticism in Rome, despite the approval of humanist friends. But Sadoleto, who spoke vaguely in 1528 of an understanding with Clement VII respecting the duration of his service in the Secretariat, subsequently claimed that it was fixed at three years before he ever returned to Rome in 1524.[23] Yet it is significant that he never alluded to a specific arrangement of this kind while Clement lived and never, therefore, in his early letters of self-vindication. He invoked— or more likely contrived—this argument in 1545 as a means of strengthening his refusal to answer another papal summons, contending that Clement VII had accepted his departure in 1527 as the end of his obligation to the Curia.

As a place of refuge in the midst of disorder, Carpentras represented what Sadoleto had tried to find in his Quirinal vineyard, the quiet that he sought after his reputation was secure. If it was true that Italy remained the common fatherland of all men, he found that the individual's truest *patria* lies wherever he is most content, in whatever place he can accomplish most.[24] At Carpentras, in his garden and among his books, Sadoleto discovered the freedom and autonomy which had been wanting in Rome.[25] While he rejected common cause with the priestly estate, he welcomed it with such men as Erasmus, believing that the literate and well-educated, through their study and writing, could contribute to the restoration of stability and right religion.[26]

Therefore all of us who are instructed in the liberal arts and consecrated to them must not grow weary or faint-hearted in alleviating, each in his own way, this great calamity and disaster, or in perfecting the works of peace and piety, though we do less in public and the society of men. . . .[27]

Let us both, my Erasmus, to the utmost of our capacity, succor the Christian faith in its infirmity, oppressed at this time not only by the reign of evil and a host of wicked men, but by every manner of foreign and domestic adversaries, as well as by the instruments of war and impiety—a faith close to collapse, unless God . . . sustains and upholds it.[28]

Sadoleto interpreted the role of the Christian humanists as members of a priesthood of the pen, joined by a common obligation to defend an imperiled faith, but set apart from the active world. At the same time, Sadoleto found it necessary for the rest of his life to defend the contemplative ideal as a positive and constructive good against those who called it an evasion of public duty. He praised it as the nobler alternative for men like himself, dismissing the *vita negotiosa* as the simple pursuit of power and wealth. Whereas he may have been pleased with the invitation to Rome in 1523, Sadoleto contested every future summons he received during the final twenty years of his life. Quite unexpectedly he had become a rarity among Italian ecclesiastics in establishing himself as a voluntary and a happy expatriate.

But as an expatriate Sadoleto had no desire to make his isolation absolute. He kept in touch with humanist circles in Rome, Padua, and Venice, and managed to be informed on the affairs of the Curia and the progress of heresy. In 1530, for example, we find him inquiring about Luther and the projected Council from Cajetan and Fregoso, adding his intention to be present if it should take place.[29] Cardinal Accolti sent him current intelligence drawn from reports of legates and nuncios, while Sadoleto in turn corresponded with such other members of the Sacred College as Tournon, Gonzaga, Trivulzio, and Du Prat, as well as with Bini and Blosio in the Secretariat.[30]

Nevertheless, Sadoleto looked at the world beyond as through a veil. Physical remoteness and intentional disengagement further clouded his vision of matters with which he had once been directly occupied. A certain hopelessness about the present afflicted him throughout the last two decades of his life; a measured pessimism caused him to keep the veil intact, as though the errors of the recent past were too great to be soon corrected, and those of the moment too disheartening to be closely examined.

The fascination of Rome had swiftly dimmed, making Carpentras suddenly meaningful as a refuge from the rigors and dangers of curial service. When he reached the diocese in May 1527 the question of place, at least, was settled; and in some ways the choice of place was the most crucial of a humanist's career. Moreover, a sense of vocation was at last emerging. Sadoleto appeared, at fifty, to have found himself. The *landsknechte* had forced a decision.

In letters to outsiders the Bishop usually wrote as though he were now wholly isolated from the world, occupied only with his studies and writing.[31] He had never been happier than he was in Provence and hoped that the Comtat Venaissin, where men seemed tranquil by nature anyway, might soon become the most peaceful place in Christendom.[32]

However, Sadoleto often failed to mention his own efforts to achieve this halcyon ideal or his labors to secure the welfare and independence of his people. It is difficult to know in what degree he was involved in pastoral matters, but he once described his new life to Negri as being so filled with them that he was able to spend only leisure moments in the pleasures of study.[33] The completion of his commentary on the Ninety-third Psalm, the first treatise to issue from retirement, had to be delayed because he was too much engrossed in the litigation at

Toulouse and the controversy with de Muris to have time to write.[34] While by temperament Sadoleto preferred his books and a life of learned solitude, he was nevertheless a jealous and willing prelate, alert as much to the obligations as to the prerogatives of his office.

Although he produced nothing quite comparable to Contarini's *De officio episcopi libri duo* (1516),[35] his own views, given at the opening of his work on the Ninety-third Psalm,[36] were strikingly close to those of the great Venetian. Both insisted that the fabric of the faith is no stronger than priestly virtue makes it,[37] that the faithful inevitably imitate the vice or virtue of the clergy. They agreed that the *sacerdotium* had universally fallen into dishonor and impiety[38] and attributed popular contempt for it to the universal plague of avarice. Sadoleto felt that the majority of the priesthood was so lost in cupidity that lay respect had all but vanished.

As one who placed himself in a minority in the Church, Sadoleto went on to suggest that the clergy of the Comtat, if not of the French nation too, was now obliged to strive even more intently to bring honor to their calling, avoiding every suspicion of the greed and self-seeking which prevailed in Rome.[39] "Though thou, Israel, play the harlot," he admonished, "let Judah not offend."[40] Tolerance for nepotism and pluralism in Judah, however, appear to have been rather liberal.

In one respect his interest in the diocese was necessitated, for Sadoleto as well as a growing clientele of kinsmen drew their living from it. Immediately after reaching Carpentras he surveyed the monastic dependencies and general resources of the diocese.[41] This inventory contains over fifty entries, including forty-five priories of the Order of St. Ruf, over which the Bishop enjoyed rights of provision and from which he received income.[42] In fact, through such jurisdiction, as perpetual commendator of the Abbey of Santa Maria de Grezo,[43] Sadoleto obtained a major source of his maintenance, most of which was paid to the manse in kind.[44] The nature of these dependencies was such, therefore, as to require close and minute attention.

Yet there is little in Sadoleto's correspondence to suggest that he found it difficult to regulate the strictly internal affairs of the diocese.[45]

Small and compact, it included no jurisdiction capable of competing against his own. Procurators had maintained effective discipline over the parochial clergy in his absence while the Bishop supervised the cathedral chapter from Rome. In April 1528 he introduced new statutes for the government of the canons of St. Ruf before an assembly of its membership, enforcing a more literal observance of their rule and limiting their personal freedom somewhat,[46] but such measures were evidently accepted without resistance.

Far more complex than the internal government of the diocese itself was the relation of his authority to other jurisdictions in the papal state of which the see of Carpentras formed a part.[47] The status of its Bishop was complicated by the fact that the Papacy exercised temporal as well as ecclesiastical authority in Avignon and the Venaissin. In addition to the Archbishop of Avignon, the interests of the Holy See were represented by a host of lesser officials.[48] The extent of their prerogatives in the Comtat constantly distressed Sadoleto and threatened what he hoped would be the splendid isolation of his retirement, not to mention the traditional liberties of his people. Moreover, the presence of these officials forced him to extend his role beyond the limits of the diocese proper.

By virtue of his episcopal office at Carpentras Sadoleto contended that he was the "primo membro et prima persona" of the Comtat Venaissin and thus responsible for the defense of its rights.[49] But his claims oversimplified a vexed and ambiguous question. The temporal government of the county belonged in theory to a rector, traditionally appointed by the Pope alone and invested with authority over all aspects of secular rule except taxation. In principle the rector's was also the court of last instance before appeal to Rome, a privilege on which the *contadini* vigorously insisted. But under the Legation of Cardinal Clermont (1513–1541) the office was filled by Gisard de Corneillon, a severe religious from Agde, who also assumed the duties of Vice-Legate and promptly antagonized both the laity of the Comtat and the Bishop of Carpentras.

The *contadini*'s complaints to Rome about the violation of their rights and the oppressive rule of the rector won full support from

Sadoleto, who accused Rome of misgovernment and unwarranted interference by sending special commissioners into the area to defend the interests of the Holy See. As the controversy grew hotter, he finally became reconciled to Cardinal Clermont but intensified his attacks on the papal commissioners.[50] Sadoleto argued that the inspectors were not only violating the autonomy of the Legation, but seriously alienating papal subjects from their respect for Rome.[51] The commissioners fired back with their own charges; they found Sadoleto excessively ambitious and eager to usurp authority which did not belong to him, seeking power for himself by flattering the Legate.[52] The dispute lasted for three years before the Bishop eventually won his point against the commissioners; his efforts to protect the rights of the rector, however, came to little.

His success was as mixed in dealing again with the Jewish bankers of Carpentras. Hard times befell the county once more between 1530 and 1532, when drought and the time of the plague made famous by Rabelais were followed by crop failures and a famine so grave that the Legate found himself obliged to provide food for 2,000 families over a period of several months.[53] In the wake of this crisis grievances flared up again against cameral privileges granted to the Jews when the estates of the county drew up a long cahier of complaints in 1532.[54] The deputies bitterly protested that the special privileges of the Jews were upheld by ecclesiastical courts and the local camera to the point that infraction was punishable by excommunication and fines, while the Jewish creditors were able to obtain judicial sanctions for imprisonment and confiscation both of landed property and chattels.[55]

At Marseilles in 1533 Sadoleto prevailed upon Clement VII again to withdraw the concessions given eight years earlier.[56] The Pope restored the limits he had previously placed on the commercial and judicial prerogatives of the Jewish bankers in 1524. Creditors were forbidden to speculate in foodstuff or to seize landed property in default of payment, while the extent of usurious contracts was more narrowly limited. These measures failed to end the conflict, however, for the Jews continued to find influential support both in the local

Camera and in Rome. Sadoleto stubbornly fought against the sale of dispensations to the Jews but obtained no more than temporary relief for his people in Provence.[57]

By this time Sadoleto had earned a reputation as a zealous and militant prelate,[58] quite willing to enter the *vita activa* at least so far as it concerned the material and spiritual welfare of his diocese. Although his private leisure turned out to be less than he expected and others imagined,[59] and although suffering chronic nostalgia for lettered friends in Italy,[60] he abhorred the thought of leaving the diocese either for Rome or the service of a secular prince like Francis I. At Carpentras he enjoyed a kind of independence which he had never known before, and it is significant that Sadoleto was rarely more spirited or aggressive than he was when episcopal prerogatives or the rights of his people seemed threatened in Rome or locally by curial deputies.

The Bishop also believed that the Church was on trial before its own, that the loyalty of Catholics was being strained by the abuse of ecclesiastical power as well as by the immorality of priests. Such was his opinion with respect to the conduct of the rector and the commissioners, and toward the protected status of the Jews. Deeply distressed by the alienation of Christians as the result of ecclesiastical misgovernment, he urged the Pope to put an end to the charges of heresy, for example, which his subordinates were making against certain merchants in Avignon.[61] His change of heart toward Cardinal Clermont was influenced by what Sadoleto looked upon as measures of constructive reform which the Legate started in the improvement of judicial procedures in the county. During the dispute with the commissioners Sadoleto congratulated Giovanni Niccolai, then Vice-Legate and Bishop of Apt, for the public instruction in the Epistles of St. Paul which had been started at Avignon under an Italian Dominican.[62] He also had warm praise for the Legate in writing to Clement VII about the Cardinal's acts of public charity and his reform of provincial monasteries. Through such labors as these, he said, the Papacy could recover honor and dignity in the province. Sadoleto often felt that the predicament of the universal Church was beyond remedy, but he was quick to praise and support concrete action at the local level.

An absentee Bishop himself for nearly a decade, he now showed no embarrassment at insisting upon the necessity of episcopal residence. Anything else, he reminded Salviati when the Cardinal tried to urge him back to Rome, was desertion.[63] In writing to Mario Maffei, who had left his see at Cavaillon in 1530, he put aside his wonted gentleness to reproach a friend for grave negligence and warned that the diocese was on the edge of rebellion against Maffei's vicars.[64]

A more immediate concern was Jacopo's search for a schoolmaster for the college at Carpentras. Sadoleto was astonished by the ignorance and illiteracy of his people[65] and asked friends in Padua, Rome, and Paris to find him an able teacher. He had moral support for the project from the Prior of S. M. de Grezo, who was eager to establish a classical curriculum throughout the order of St. Ruf. Negri, to whom the Bishop wrote first, replied that qualified masters in Padua were unwilling to leave Italy and unimpressed by the salary offered at Carpentras.[66] Brice was no more successful in Paris. Sadoleto patiently continued the search for two years before a candidate unexpectedly turned up in the fall of 1535.[67] This was Florentius Volusenus (Volusene), a Scot who had gone to Paris in 1528 after studying at Aberdeen.[68] Passing through Avignon en route to Italy, he heard of Sadoleto's interest in finding a teacher and went to Carpentras, reports the Bishop, to meet its celebrated Latinist and to apply for appointment to the new academy.[69] Volusene was promptly hired, his salary being contributed by the municipality and the Bishop himself, while Sadoleto turned to Cardinal Lorraine, a former patron of the Scot, for additional funds.

Other visitors also found their way to Carpentras in these years. Reginald Pole stopped briefly en route from Avignon to Padua in 1532 after leaving England in January.[70] He departed with letters for Bembo and Lazaro Bonamico, together with a draft of Sadoleto's *De liberis recte instituendis,* one of the more durable fruits of Jacopo's literary progress at Carpentras. Alfonso, the Bishop's brother, spent several months with him in 1533, and Negri talked of making a visit the next year.[71] Learned friends in the region were few. At Avignon, in addition to the celebrated Alciati, there was J. F. Ripa, who taught civil law there and whom Sadoleto tried vainly to retain in 1534 against the orders of the Duke of Milan that he return to Italy. Those at Carpentras formed an anomalous company but were sufficient at least to help Sadoleto test Volusene's "wit and intelligence" at table in the episcopal palace, and included the Bishop's physician, whose professional visits must certainly have been as numerous as his social calls, for in spite of his apparently robust frame Sadoleto was never in good health at Carpentras.

For this reason, and because he was sedentary if not somewhat indolent as well, the Bishop remained close to the diocese. Commissions and journeys on personal or episcopal business were usually assigned to his cousin Paolo, or to various other procurators; Sadoleto had no taste for travel and seldom went as far as Avignon.[72] His only avocation was viniculture and gardening. The rural retreat at the priory of San Felice, which he described in the Roman manner as his "hortos suburbanos," was embellished by planting which he supervised with pleasure and interest. Maffei felt obliged to explain to Clement VII why the Provençal fruit and particularly the apples which Sadoleto sent from Carpentras were superior to the pears of Cavaillon; Jacopo's trees had an advantage in soil and climate, said Maffei, as well as that of careful attention.[73] And among the favorite wines of Paul III was one which Sadoleto supplied from the region.[74]

In addition to his concern for literary and diocesan matters Sadoleto gave tireless attention to the welfare of his family. Above all he was determined to advance the fortunes of Paolo Sadoleto, who had accompanied him in the flight from Rome. This was the cousin who was made the author's interlocutor in the treatise on education, the one whom he regarded in the place of a son, and the companion whom Sadoleto made his suffragan and heir.

P aolo Sadoleto's father, also named Jacopo, was a cousin of the Bishop and like so many of the Sadoletti a lawyer and minor official in the regime of the Estensi.[75] Properly speaking, therefore, Paolo was not, as the Bishop occasionally put it, "my brother's son,"[76] but "fratris Patruelis filius,"[77] the grandson of Giovanni Sadoleto's diplomatist brother, Niccolò. Little is known of Paolo's father except what we can learn from brief allusions to the offices he held at Modena, most of them minor posts in the bureaucracy.[78]

It is clear, however, that Paolo early preferred the humanities to law. After studying under Lilio Giraldi at Ferrara, he went to Rome and entered the household of his curial kinsman, then in the court of Clement VII.[79] But virtually nothing else illumines Paolo's early life until, after reaching Carpentras, he emerged as Jacopo's very active assistant and procurator.

A year after they arrived, for example, Paolo was packed off to Lyons with instructions to see Sebastian Gryphius—for Jacopo was then looking for a publisher[80]—and to visit Federigo Fregoso, again a political exile and currently Abbot at St. Benignus in Dijon. Fregoso sent what must have been a sizable part of his library to Sadoleto at this time, having learned of the Bishop's losses at Nice a year earlier.[81] In late May 1529 Paolo set out for Modena, soon after his father's death, the first of several occasions on which he attended to the financial affairs of the younger Sadoletti and of others who depended on the Bishop's assistance.[82]

More relevant to his "uncle's" episcopal concerns, however, was a journey to the court of France which Paolo made in 1532. Jacopo carefully prepared the way with letters to Guillaume du Bellay and Cardinal Lorraine, instructing Paolo to follow their counsel closely.[83] Although the stated purpose of this visit was merely to pay the Bishop's compliments to Francis I, Jacopo may well have had the security of his diocese in mind. The Comtat was periodically overrun by French troops, for one thing, and the Most Christian King was not fully reconciled to papal provision in the archdiocese of Avignon, contesting the investiture of the Bishop of Apt by nominating a candidate of his own in 1533. To be on cordial terms with the French crown was therefore indispensable, and the Sadoletti succeeded to the extent that Jacopo was later invited to join the royal court.[84]

At the time of Paolo's mission to Paris, his cousin was again in bad health, suffering from a disorder which Jacopo considered too "unworthy" to name but which he put to the effect of certain local wines. Whatever the ailment, it was enough to keep him away from his books between November and March of 1531–32 but not so acute that it diverted him from nepotistic designs for Paolo's future. During these months, with varying degrees of help from friends in Rome, the Bishop began to negotiate for papal recognition of Paolo as his coadjutor, with the right of succession, in the diocese of Carpentras.

Sadoleto moved discreetly, knowing that the request was certain to arouse criticism. Oliviero Caraffa had denounced such nominations in his memorial on reform to the Borgia Pope, and Clement VII was himself known to dislike them.[85] Sadoleto therefore tried first to build up support from others before approaching the Pope. In addition to Giovanni da Pescia, one of the few papal commissioners in the county whom Sadoleto could tolerate, he entrusted the case to Antonio Cornazano, previously associated with the diocese and now in Rome, and especially to his friend Cardinal Benedetto Accolti.[86] Then, in June 1532, Sadoleto challenged Clement's opposition to concessions of inheritance by pointing out that Leo X had granted a *decreta coniutoria cum successione* in behalf of Antonio Verantio and that as Domestic Secretary he had prepared the decree. Why then should Carpentras be denied the same thing?[87]

The answer arrived in a month. Accolti reported that the Pope was evasive, agreeing to issue the decree only on condition that Sadoleto's friends find some means of avoiding a precedent by which the Vatican might be expected to grant like favors to others. Such terms, of course, were impossible. So Accolti, accompanied by Trivulzio and del Monte, saw the Pope again.[88] This time Clement yielded, at least for the moment, and Paolo's nomination appeared to be secure.

Sadoleto wrote extravagant thanks in October[89] but the authenticating document, the *scheda consistorialis*, was still unsigned.[90]

In view of Clement's procrastination Sadoleto decided a year later to confront him in person, making one of his rare journeys from Carpentras in order to be at Marseilles when His Holiness arrived for the wedding of Caterina de' Medici to the Duke of Orléans in October 1533.[91] Intruding on a formal occasion of state and at a moment of critical diplomatic negotiation, Sadoleto managed nevertheless to obtain the diploma of appointment for his nephew without fee—*sine pretio ullo*.[92] He said nothing of this to Bembo in describing the trip but expressed pleasure at the Pope's cordiality to him,[93] reassured by the apparent good will of the Pontiff toward one who had abandoned him in 1527.

Certainly the new status which the Bishop procured for Paolo was the most notable of Sadoleto's achievements as a nepotist, but it was by no means the only one. A relative who also enjoyed special favor was Paolo Sacrati, whom Jacopo provided with several benefices, including a canonry at Ferrara in 1531, while another of the Sacrati received provision at Carpentras.[94] Gian Francesco Sadoleto, the coadjutor's brother, was in the line of the Bishop's kinsmen who held Jacopo's benefice at S. Lorenzo in Damaso before moving to Carpentras; and Camillo Sadoleto settled permanently in the Comtat after accompanying the Bishop from Rome in 1527. The priories of S. Maria de Grezo supplied livings for additional nephews and one Paolo Emilio Sadoleto became Abbot in the monastery at Carpentras. In later years other nephews, cousins, and a sister, Francesca, left Modena and Ferrara permanently for Provence to live under the benevolent if fretful auspices of Bishop Jacopo.

So widely deployed were the Sadoletti and so needful of assistance that the Bishop periodically had to call on friends in Italy to promote their interests or intercede for them. Accolti worked not only in Paolo's behalf but likewise for Jacopo's morose and thankless brother Ercole[95]; and Salviati evidently helped Paolo Sacrati find further preferment in Ferrara. Jacopo turned again to the Estensi after they returned to power in 1527, though now in the interest of his family and not of himself. During one of his missions to Italy, for example, Paolo received instructions tendered in the spirit of a Polonius or Lord Chesterfield for dealing with the Duke at a time when young Paolo was still trying to pay his father's creditors in Modena.[96] He was also urged to seek a pension from the new Pope, Paul III, in order to settle the estate and help the Bishop's brother Alfonso.[97]

If retirement from the Curia ended the strain of living in Rome, it failed to free Sadoleto from the constant financial cares which haunted him for the rest of his life, decisively affecting his conduct as well as his career in the Church. No doubt it would have been a simple matter to live on his own had he been unwilling to share it with his kinsmen, but such was never the case. The fortunes of the Sadoletti deteriorated seriously during the years of imperial and papal government at Modena, and even though they must have profited from the restoration of the Estensi in 1527, the family had increased considerably in the meantime. So, too, had Jacopo's sense of obligation. And as a result he resolutely tried to enlarge his resources, if only to assist his nephews while alluding constantly to his own great penury.[98]

Because of the simplicity of his life and his protests of indifference to wealth and honors,[99] Sadoleto liked to say that he had nothing in common with the avaricious prelates in which the Church abounded. This feeling of singularity, shot through every aspect of his life, grew especially noticeable during his later years. It became a spring of that self-assurance he revealed as a critic and reformer of the Curia and clergy in the reign of Paul III[100] and may also account for the fact that he never felt obliged to justify the nepotism in which he was so deeply engrossed. Equally notable is the easy conscience with which Jacopo laid claim, as a matter of right,[101] to special privileges and exemptions, or sought additional dispensations in Rome. He willingly defended his retirement to Carpentras, like the favor he sought for Paolo, as rewards for service to the Holy See and the Medici Popes. He looked at preferment for a prelate, like patronage for a writer, as a form of legitimate compensation.

Few Italian Bishops, however, would have accepted the isolation and meager revenues of Carpentras as a permanent prospect, yet

Sadoleto seemed content to spend the rest of his life in a Provençal garden. Aside from periodic favors for his dependents, he asked no more than to be left alone to enjoy the rights and duties of episcopal office and the uses of leisure. No longer a curialist, he saw himself as priest and scholar, free to interpret his religious vocation as he saw fit.

V

Exegete, Pedagogue, and Theologian

Once in Provence, Sadoleto repeated Poggio's definition of "dignified leisure" as the enjoyment of writing and study in a place of rural quiet, and found as Cicero had that he was never "less idle than in studious leisure."[1] The Bishop now regarded Rome as the worst rather than the best of all possible locations for the scholar. Carpentras, not the Curia or the Quirinal, was to provide "otium cum dignitate": the possession of time and calm which Sadoleto, like Erasmus and Bembo before him, had learned to value so highly. And during the first nine years of "retirement" his literary output exceeded that of the previous thirty.

Between 1527 and 1536 the erstwhile poet and Latin secretary produced three new works of exegesis and three long treatises. In 1530 he completed a dialogue on education, perhaps the most durable thing he ever wrote, followed in turn by the second part of his defense of philosophy and then by an ambitious interpretation of Paul's Epistle to the Romans. Other works were revised or projected. As the Bishop described this new writing to distant friends and circulated manuscripts among them for comment, however, it was obvious that he still wrote for a double public. Sadoleto recognized the impossibility of pleasing men like Bembo and Reginald Pole at the same time and appeared willing to address himself in turn to each without making a full commitment to the preferences of either. This attitude seemed to trouble the critics more than the author. Moved by the humanist's stout confidence in the power of the pen and the utility of right knowledge, Jacopo saw his role at Carpentras as the defense of good letters and Christian orthodoxy alike. To his mind each cause was worthy of the Christian scholar, especially at a time when liberal studies and the faith were in serious peril. He was no less convinced that such dedication on his part was enough, by itself, to justify his withdrawal from the Roman Curia.

The first work to issue from retirement was a treatise on the Ninety-third Psalm, dedicated to Federigo Fregoso as a friend and former patron who had urged Sadoleto to apply himself to sacred studies.[2] Erasmus, having earlier praised the Bishop's commentary on the Fiftieth Psalm as "the first product of your great piety," complimented him on the second with equal enthusiasm.[3] The new work was at once an exegetical exercise and a tract for the times, treating the sunken condition of the priesthood together with the failures of the Pope and his advisers, as well as the superiority of the contemplative life.[4]

Sadoleto knew in advance that Bembo would have little respect for writing of this kind and easily anticipated his friend's objections. The *Asolani* were in revision at the time, and while Jacopo complimented Bembo for his gifts with the vernacular, he likewise reproached him for neglecting Latin and for wasting his talent on unworthy studies.[5] At least during the first years of withdrawal to Provence Sadoleto found more in common with Erasmus than with his old colleague. Soon after Sadoleto reached Carpentras Erasmus left the troubled atmosphere of Basle for Freiburg, seeking his own "harbor" there in 1529.[6] Although the melancholy of his last years often stands in bleak contrast to Sadoleto's contentment in Provence, they were still bound by a sense of like purpose and mutual esteem. Despite greater distance they corresponded frequently on subjects ranging from Luther to literature and the condition of the Church, each in his way a self-appointed censor and critic, observing at a distance a world from which he felt himself alienated.

On most issues Sadoleto and Erasmus were in general accord until a year or two before the northerner died. Erasmus trusted and respected Sadoleto, who was probably the closest of his Italian friends.[7] For his part the Bishop counted Erasmus among the few before whom there was no need to justify himself or explain his role, although he was habitually cautious in acknowledging this friendship to others and discreet to the point of timidity in appraising Erasmus' religious position.[8] Together they regarded the religious crisis less in terms of simple rebellion at Wittenberg than as a sign of collapsing unity in Christian Europe, aggravated by corruption in the Church and the failure of leadership among princes and prelates alike. They shared a fear that the public mood was hostile to free discussion and liberal studies—to all that each represented. Each in his way despaired of seeing an early end of the schism, fearing that opportunities for reconciliation had been squandered through needless blundering in the Curia during the early years of Luther's disobedience.

Their friendship, however, was not without strain, and on at least one point the censors found fault in one another. Sadoleto repeatedly took Erasmus to task for intemperate attacks on his Catholic critics. The Bishop saw no value in becoming embroiled in controversies of this kind and had little patience with his friend's irascibility, insisting that Erasmus was exhausting himself on petty disputes when quiet and constructive defense of the faith was needed so desperately.[9] Erasmus confessed to volatility but answered that "your people" in the hierarchy were either too quick to suspect his orthodoxy and loyalty, or too slow in gratitude for his services to the faith.[10] He reminded Sadoleto that those who deplored his quarrels with Catholics were often ignorant of his strictures against the Lutherans, just as they were of the abuse he suffered from men like Aleander and John Eck. Tunstall no less than Sadoleto needed to know more before finding fault with him.

Erasmus' belligerence, of course, gained him nothing, but at the same time Sadoleto at Carpentras displayed his own distance from the heat of the religious conflict. He refused to see that the Church itself was seriously divided on the question of reunion and reform, or that issues necessarily involved personalities as well as principles. Believing that men like Erasmus and himself should address themselves only to God's work and to one another, he practiced the Erasmian injunction to aloofness from faction far more literally than Erasmus did, certain that peace and unity could be promoted by those who labored with the pen rather than "among men in mundane affairs." The duty of the humanist in providing relief from the common disaster was perfectly clear.[11] Erasmus, if less sanguine, had not deserted this conviction, fatigued and harassed though he was.

In the meantime he sent his recent commentary on the Eighty-fifth Psalm (83) to Carpentras and later forwarded the edition of St. Basil which Froben published in 1528.[12] Soon after Erasmus completed his own pedagogical treatises of 1528–29,[13] Sadoleto began a dialogue on liberal education which was the first literary work of consequence to come out of retirement and the most frequently published of all his works.[14] Like the *De laudibus philosophiae* which appeared three years later, this was probably a treatise long intended but often postponed for lack of time. And even before finishing it he spoke of a desire to give up the classics entirely for sacred letters.[15]

A defense of the liberal arts by an active teacher (Sadoleto was carefully directing Paolo's reading at this time), the dialogue also came out of the Bishop's anxiety over the future of sound learning. It is primarily a discourse on curriculum rather than a manual for the teacher and shows no evidence of borrowing from Erasmus' recent works. Both he and Erasmus defended the Petrarchan emphasis on tutored virtue, conceiving of education as a precondition of the moral life, but Erasmus was far more explicit in his accent on religious instruction. Sadoleto's curriculum assigned these studies to parents rather than the master.[16] But he followed Erasmus and Vergerio in citing Plutarch as the safest guide to sensible theory among the ancients and invoked Plato above all as the ablest philosopher of antiquity. Let it be Plato, however, and not those medieval interpreters whose crude style always corrupts philosophy and good writing.[17]

Having set forth the separate functions of each learned discipline in long and digressive detail, Sadoleto goes on to say that the sum of all such studies—from grammar to music—is their fusion in philosophy.[18]

The end of the liberal arts is properly the cultivation of wisdom, derived from the modes of *scientia*, and wisdom (*sapientia*) in turn is the perception of essences and of immutable things. Philosophy marks the stage of intellectual formation farthest removed from the bonds of sense and primitive nature, the point at which knowledge generates virtue and harmonizes desire with reason.[19] So far the doctrine has a faint Augustinian ring. But when he claims that the conquest of philosophy marks the perfection of the individual and his likeness to God, without important reference to faith and none to grace or revealed truth, Sadoleto's *sapientia* is allowed to rest on natural capacity alone.

In other words the mind by itself can move toward beatitude and the "divine original." Wisdom is not piety so much as a high form of virtue which follows right knowledge. Common among the ancients, it is rare in the present age, though certainly the possession of Bembo, Erasmus, and Aleander, just as it was of Plato and Cicero.[20] Sound study fulfills human potentiality for good and leads to the likeness of God. Philosophy must be guided by faith in God, but through a curriculum in which the formal knowledge of God is lacking.

Small wonder then that Bembo's lavish compliments were dimmed by Pole's complaints. The young Englishman by now had virtually abandoned the classics for theology, confessing to Sadoleto in the fall of 1532 that he had scarcely read a Latin author in four years.[21] Whereas Bembo's criticism was confined to style and usage,[22] Pole fixed his attention on the content of the dialogue and on Sadoleto's willingness to rest his case on a purely secular concept of wisdom. The course of studies set forth here is worthy of Plato and Cicero, he said, but it strands the Christian among the ancients in "an alien and infidel port."[23] What of the true end of the voyage? Pole reminded Sadoleto that the true goal of all learning is knowledge of revelation; any curriculum which omits theology thus omits its proper substance.

Sadoleto replied equivocably, saying once that philosophy by definition includes theology,[24] but later that the program he outlined was meant to instruct a youth no further than his twenty-fifth year, while the study of theology belongs to later life. He promised, moreover, to discuss the harmony between human and divine wisdom in his *Hortensius*, the projected second part of the *De laudibus philosophiae*, which would be "notable for its praise of theology." But Pole was not satisfied and refused to drop the issue as Sadoleto assumed he would.[25] So the Bishop later argued, and somewhat irritably, that philosophy is the foundation of all theology and that without the liberal arts Augustine, for example, could never have been a respectable theologian.[26] The effect of these replies was only to restate the value of the classics without accounting for the omission of scriptural theology from his treatise.

Once the willing and enthusiastic disciple of the Paduan humanists, Pole, by 1533, found old friends like Bonamico tiresome and pedantic, corrupted by Pomponazzi and the rhetoricians.[27] Far more congenial to him were the theologians and reformers whom he had recently come to know in Venice, where the circle of Gasparo Contarini, Cortese, and Alvise Priuli now received the respect he once gave the Paduan literati.[28] Sadoleto, in Pole's opinion, was suspended between these two groups, still an incomplete partisan of sacred studies and Catholic reform.

P ole delivered a copy of the *De liberis* to Padua in the summer of 1532, after visiting Sadoleto in Carpentras. With the completion of this treatise the Paduans began to ask what their distant friend ought to undertake next. Bembo recorded one such conversation in a letter to Sadoleto that autumn:

When Pole and I fell into a long discussion about you and the work you now have in hand—the *Hortensius* and the interpretation of St. Paul's Epistle, he raised the question about the kind of writing to which you now should give your maximum effort and answered in favor of St. Paul. I emphatically disagree. I feel it is far wiser to complete your dialogue as soon as possible. For although the first part of the work aroused great expectation, you left it for many years unrewarded and unsatisfied; now, with considerable leisure at your disposal, you must admit that you are little better off than if you had never started it, or than if no one expected anything from you.[29]

Bembo found support for his argument from Bonamico[30] just as Pole did for the contrary view from Giberti.[31] But Sadoleto escaped what for others might have been a dilemma by dividing his efforts between his *Hortensius*, which was to conclude the *De laudibus philosophiae*, and an exposition of St. Paul's Epistle to the Romans. He began the *Hortensius* early in 1531, interrupting himself to start work on his new biblical commentary in October,[32] only to resume the treatise on philosophy the following year.[33]

If it was to Bembo's encouragement that he owed completion of the *De laudibus philosophiae*, the plan of the work was entirely Sadoleto's. *Phaedrus*, the opening half of the treatise, was written in Rome after the death of Leo X and finished in 1523 during Sadoleto's brief sojourn at Carpentras. Subtitled "The Accusation of Philosophy," this section presents an indictment of *sapientia* and the contemplative ideal in order to prepare the ground for the humanist's refutation in the second part. Sadoleto's antagonist is Tommaso Inghirami, known as Fedra, whom de Nolhac once called "the archetype of the Roman prelate in the Renaissance."[34] Diplomat, poet, and papal archivist, he becomes at Sadoleto's hands the cynical mocker of speculative thought and a champion of the *vita negotiosa*, a straw philistine whom Sadoleto intended to destroy in the *Hortensius*.[35]

Fedra treats Sadoleto as a misguided friend who has chosen to "fix the temple of his life in Philosophy," despite the counsel and hopes of active men, to pursue a vain ideal of wisdom in a life of indolence.[36] To Fedra the philosopher is a social parasite who confuses words with things while confounding himself with questions which cannot be answered. He contributes nothing to the common welfare and manages only to lose himself in meaningless disputation,[37] unaware that final things are inscrutable or that truth is always relative to historical time and social utility. The good and useful life is the life of deeds and civic virtue, not that of declamation; the soldier and the statesman are the noblest types of all, for they fix their careers in society, not in pedantic and barren solitude. And in a startling passage near the end of the treatise Fedra contrasts Sadoleto's contemplative ideal with two models of *prudentia* which the Bishop had refused to follow, according to his accuser, in his own life. One was Oliviero Caraffa, in Fedra's opinion a man skilled in the ways of mundane success, both able and willing to guide Sadoleto to worldly honors and influence. The other is Giovanni Sadoleto, represented here as a father who sent Jacopo from Ferrara to Rome to gain knowledge of the world and standing in the papal Curia for the advancement of himself and the prosperity of his family.[38] It is a puzzling passage, ostensibly included to discredit Fedra rather than Giovanni Sadoleto or the Cardinal, but one cannot help wondering if it offers clues of Jacopo's estimate of his early preceptors.

The second part of the dialogue was Sadoleto's attempt to recon-struct the lost *Hortensius* of Cicero and to deliver philosophy from the degrading effects of medieval commentaries.[39] Wisdom and eloquence were to be rejoined and philosophy freshly adorned—at Fedra's expense. The Bishop saw the *Hortensius* as his part in restoring the whole corpus of Greek philosophy, a labor in progress everywhere in Christendom, he confessed, though originating in Italy. The case for philosophy lies in its power to lead men beyond transient good and mundane honor, and outside of Fedra's *prudentia* to the sublime knowledge of God and eternal things. But the treatise is clearly not the work of a philosophic mind and is awkwardly built on a series of rhetorical affirmations, unsupported by coherent argument. It is a literary defense of humanist opinion about the nature and character of knowledge, a significant statement of humanist piety but trifling as a work of philosophy.[40]

Hortensius belongs instead to humanist literature on the dignity of man, interpreted as a being uniquely endowed with reason and capable of acquiring the likeness of God. By virtue of his freedom, man is able to ascend through degrees of good to the divine, or of despising the good and corrupting his being. But because the rational faculty is impotent without cultivation, it must be nourished by philosophy, vaguely interpreted here as *ars artium* or *scientia scientiarum*, the highest order of knowledge, which "addresses itself to the category of things

4+

divine and eternal . . ."[41] He explained *sapientia* in turn to Fregoso while writing the *Hortensius* as the application of formal knowledge to the quest of God, wisdom being that which intellect acquires from study of the liberal arts once they coalesce in philosophy.[42] Whoever acquires wisdom is thereby emancipated from sensual appetite and error, being finally brought to the knowledge of good and the image of God. Philosophy perfects the nature of man by instructing him in absolute good: wisdom recognizes the existence of God as creator, just as the philosopher perceives that salvation lies in the Christian faith.[43]

These brief allusions to Christian doctrine, however, appear only at the close of the dialogue and have little relevance to the body of the treatise. The progress of the philosopher is toward union with God, not of reconciliation to him, so that the dialogue is fashioned in the context of only the most dimly christianized Platonism in which intellect rather than grace achieves and completes the perfection of man. Here then is a secularized doctrine of wisdom in which revealed truth has no place and theology no function. The promise given Pole that the *Hortensius* would be a praise of theology went unredeemed.

Consequently the *De laudibus philosophiae* justifies the same kind of complaint that Pole had raised against the treatise on education. Protests against Sadoleto's theory of knowledge and his doctrine of human nature came only from friends and private individuals so long as he wrote as a humanist; but once he offered his concept of human freedom in the name of Christian orthodoxy, the Sorbonne and the Vatican were obliged to remonstrate.

Sadoleto readily admitted that his book of Commentaries on St. Paul's Epistle to the Romans proved to be an exceptionally difficult enterprise.[44] Like so many Italian humanists of his generation he had no theological training and only began to study patristic theology in retirement, toward the age of fifty. What he knew was therefore self-taught and rapidly acquired.[45] If to these limitations are added an inveterate contempt for the scholastics and a clear preference for the Greek fathers, Chrysostom in particular, it is obvious that he was ill prepared for the heavy seas of doctrinal controversy which were then running.[46]

His objective in the Commentaries, as he explained it to Erasmus, was to chart a new course between Augustine and Pelagius on the issues of merit and grace:

> I have dared, as you will see for yourself, to turn from the course long since used and followed by others, and to set forth on another which seemed to avoid the perils of the questions and to lead more boldly and splendidly to the truth.[47]

His "altera via," as he called it, would show that Pelagius' was the error of pride, in which so much is attributed to man that the action of grace is all but eliminated,[48] whereas Augustine left nothing to man but the necessity to sin in the presence of an arbitrary God.[49] The problem was thus to reexamine the first Epistle of St. Paul—the text itself and not the commentators—in order to clarify the extent to which there is "something in us" for salvation.[50] In doing so, and in spite of Fregoso's admonitions, Sadoleto claimed to have had the help of God in bringing new light to the text and in finding things previously unknown about it.[51] He was equally certain that his Latin translation of the Greek text had restored the grammatical purity of the Epistle and brought its meaning into clearer focus.

Sadoleto took the view that right knowledge of Scripture is cumulative. Each age, by further study, uncovers a fuller depth of understanding. Augustine's limited command of Greek reduced his capacity to interpret St. Paul, with the result that critical passages of the Epistles had been long misread. The Lutherans, moreover, were now exploiting such obscurity to advance their deceptions, taking refuge in the dark places of theology which the commentators had previously failed to illuminate, while using popular ignorance of Greek to lead men into fraudulent doctrine.[52]

So the purpose of the Commentaries was the reconstruction of Romans by applying the more recent methods of textual criticism. It was Sadoleto's self-assurance as a linguist which led him to speak of finding new doctrinal certainties in the course of making a new Latin translation. Consequently the treatise was more polemical by inference than in substance, and not until the third book, which is largely a defense of Catholic ceremony, did Sadoleto become visibly apologetic. However, the Commentaries fall short of developing a systematic analysis of Pauline theology, just as they do of pursuing the close linguistic scrutiny which the author promised. The form of the dialogue is virtually abandoned at many points, and what begins as a work of exegesis in the first of the three books ends with a hurried miscellany in the third, which closes with an exhortation to a crusade against the Turks. Thus Emil Gothein was able to say that "a less dogmatic commentary on a scriptural text was not written in the sixteenth century."[53]

On the other hand, Sadoleto did attempt in the treatise to grapple with the prime dogmatic issue of the Reformation era. The Commentaries were his effort to interpret the relationship between the omnipotence of God and the dignity of man by demonstrating an essential harmony between the action of grace and the freedom of the will. As he put it to Fregoso,

I am restoring to our will the assent of the soul and the disposition by which we offer ourselves in willing obedience to God, so that he may shape and guide us as he chooses; yet every worthy action, every laudable fruit of good work, and whatever merit there be, I attribute without reservation to divine grace.[54]

His declared purpose was to reaffirm the capacity for free assent in man's response to God without seeming to limit the function of grace. Sadoleto quarried his argument directly from his own study of the text, to the extent of neglecting patristic and scholastic tradition as well as the recent literature of Pauline commentary. What emerges from his reading of St. Paul is an ambitious and ranging account of justification which accents the continuity from the human order to the divine. To the extent that Sadoleto's position can be reduced to a formula, it is to argue that man is justified through a process which he begins and God completes.

The argument develops in reverse, as it were, from man's ultimate reconciliation to God or from the indwelling of God's justice in man, rather than from the fall of man toward a progressive restoration of the divine image in him.[55] For Sadoleto the process of redemption develops out of a basic capacity for good, a natural capacity for faith and the knowledge of God. Man is perfected and salvation is completed by grace, without which there is no access to God. But even though we lack merit sufficient to achieve salvation, there is "something in us" that we bring to the start of our regeneration.[56] To the mercy of God man himself is able to contribute the beginnings of faith and a right inclination of the will, which God perfects.[57]

The beginnings of salvation proceed out of the desire to be saved and the movement of the will to seek God. In spite of sin we retain the power to seek liberation from it as well as the freedom to accept or obstruct the action of grace, although Sadoleto never worked his way into the clear on this point. At times, for example, he appears to say that the action of man and God in the beginnings of salvation is simultaneous:

The true beginnings of proper inclination and desire proceed from God in such a way that they also issue from our will; when of our own accord we turn ourselves to the greatest and sovereign good, we find in it a powerful force to which we are drawn, and yet (*tamen*) the freedom of our soul is not constrained.[58]

The power of willing is certainly to a degree in us, and just as we cooperate with the action of God in us, so too have we some capacity for striving and exerting ourselves, as though in raising our hands to God we are first lifted up by him and then made just.[59]

Elsewhere he asserts that those who believe in God are capable of offering something antecedently on which grace may descend in the form of right disposition to God:

There is nothing of ours which is worthy, nothing bearing any power or principle of merit, yet (*tamen*) it is necessary that something proceed from us on which the grace and justice of God may rest; this is not the effect of meritorious work, but of a proper disposition toward God, which comes to us through faith alone in Christ.[60]

Man is said to be devoid of merit, yet capable of seeking God before receiving grace; he is helpless without grace, but able nonetheless to take part in escaping from helplessness.

Sadoleto tried to solve the dogmatic issue by using what, in effect, is little more than a grammatical device. In the foregoing passages he concedes the primacy of God in the work of salvation, only to restrict and limit God's role with an assertion of man's freedom. The grammatical device in each case is an adversative clause, the word "however" (*tamen*) introducing statements which not only declare that man cooperates with grace, but also that he inclines his soul to receive God in the first place.

The whole order [of divine justice] is so wrought . . . that we bring to God a faith which is nourished by his gift and strengthened in us, yet (*tamen*) there remains some part of our will in it. Faith calls forth the justice of God, . . . not only forgiving those who come to him, but also endowing them with the same justice and the same form of righteousness which are his.[61]

There are many testimonies of Scripture attributing everything to God, and these are not to be gainsaid. I acknowledge that it is improper either to contest the witness of Scripture or to deny the propriety of attributing every good to him; however, (*tamen*) I likewise believe, without committing this error, that there also remains a place and function for our will. . . . Our election is from God, . . . and our disposition to Christ, our knowledge of the kingdom of heaven and our hope of attaining beatitude are the gifts of God, and these are the first and greatest, yet (*tamen*) they are conferred on us with the consent of our wills.[62]

The force of the qualifying *tamen* here again is to set off man's part from God's and to reserve to human will the *bona voluntas* which, according to Sadoleto, is the beginning of salvation. Justification is God's work, and not man's, yet man begins what God completes.

To support this ambiguous distinction Sadoleto appealed to another: to the difference between God's part as efficient cause, and as final cause.[63] As efficient cause God is said to work in man, without any sort of human cooperation, to perfect whatever we possess of faith, hope, love, and will. As efficient cause God strengthens those already existing faculties by which men are saved, and through which the elect, for example, are called to glory. But insofar as God works also in man as final cause, his grace is present in such a way that the will is free, just as free to obstruct or refuse grace as to cooperate with it. In this way God is not the compelling and disposing "effector," but rather the object of our will and inclination, the thing sought or rejected by our own choice. Giulio Sadoleto, the principal interlocutor, summarized his brother's position in this way:

I see that this distinction of yours preserves the glory of God in such a way that it does not deprive us of the freedom of our will, and I also see, as Paul has shown, that . . . God is not only the inducement and incitement of our will, as its end, but likewise its moving and impelling master. . . .[64]

Giulio's insight, however, is difficult to share.

The *tamen* shows Sadoleto's "new course" to be a twisting path which veered far closer to Pelagius than to Augustine. If Giulio's part in the dialogue was that of a reformed Pelagian whom Jacopo had rescued from error, Jacopo identified himself as one following those Fathers "who leave something to us in such a way that they still (*tamen*) attribute all our merit and virtue to the glory of God."[65] The distinguishing feature of this position is its defense of an inherent justice which the believer activates by exercising his freedom. What menaces the orthodoxy of the Commentaries was the author's willingness to find a movement of the will in the beginnings of salvation which seems at the least to coincide with the action of grace, rather than to follow from grace.[66] For Sadoleto the corrupting effects of sin are not enough to prevent the soul from undertaking its own regeneration. Yet to claim that man himself brings forth the beginnings of justification is quite different from the doctrine that he participates in it by virtue of prevenient grace. The Church for a thousand years had rejected the argument that such *initia* proceed from man without the foregoing action of grace. Augustine's attention to this point[67] was confirmed in the Council of Orange (529) and reiterated by St. Thomas.[68] Luther acknowledged it[69] no less than did Erasmus in the *De libero arbitrio* a decade before Sadoleto wrote. In defending the freedom of the will against Luther, Erasmus conceded that the first impulse is that of grace as principal cause, while the will of man is secondary though free and collaborative.[70]

The particular kind of emphasis which Sadoleto placed on human freedom in the Commentaries may be explained, like that of Erasmus, as a reply to Luther. But these accents had still deeper resonance in the Bishop's thought. His understanding of St. Paul grew out of a philosophy of man which was frequently more classical than Catholic and more Greek than Christian. In the *De liberis* and again in his *De laudibus philosophiae*—which had nothing to do with the doctrinal controversy—runs the same assertion that man, through his own exertion, can raise himself from base nature to goodness and the likeness of God. Like other Catholic humanists Sadoleto turned in the Commentaries to those parts of Christian tradition that deal not with human sinfulness but with the potentialities of frail nature, which through free will and the grace of a beneficent God may be sanctified and restored to godliness.[71] In the treatise on the Ninety-third Psalm Sadoleto declares that man is "not bound but free," unique in dignity above all other forms of being: last in sequence of creation, he stands outside the bonds of necessity, endowed with mastery of his will and with freedom over all things. Applied to the quest of the good, such freedom brings him to equality with the angels.[72]

In writing the Commentaries Sadoleto felt confident that he had corrected the Vulgate and clarified the meaning of the text without in any way limiting the omnipotence of God. But others were less certain. Those who examined the treatise in the light of Catholic tradition found his rejection of Augustine too great and his qualification of Pelagius too small.[73] The "altera via" therefore stood in need of early mending.

Although Fregoso was one of Sadoleto's most faithful friends and therefore among the first to see the Commentaries, he was also the first to warn the Bishop against claiming too much for his interpretation of St. Paul.[74] Erasmus was also an early if somewhat more guarded critic. He received the opening dialogue during the spring of 1533 along with a request that he sound out Froben about publishing the treatise.[75] Erasmus' comments have not survived, but from the silence which followed from Carpentras he assumed that they were not well received.[76] Sadoleto did not write to him again until after the work was finished eighteen months later. Only then did he acknowledge Erasmus' "corrections" and said merely that they had been applied to a revision of the first book.[77] Erasmus thought well of its literary qualities but feared that brilliance of style had sometimes dulled the edge of piety.[78] He confided his more serious reservations to Damian à Goes after the Commentaries fell under official censure: "I foresaw this," he recalled, "I cautioned him . . . as far as it is correct to admonish a person of his rank. He put great effort into this work. [And now] I hear it is disapproved by the Sorbonne."[79]

The stages by which the censure materialized are not always clear and cannot be fully reconstructed. We know, however, that Sadoleto sent the Commentaries to Paris in the spring of 1534,[80] asking Brice to deliver the manuscript to "fair-minded judges" at the Sorbonne with the further stipulation that they be men learned in the classics.[81] While awaiting the Faculty's opinion, he wrote to Brice again in June in a mood that is both querulous and defensive.[82] He mentioned having read "all the interpreters" of St. Paul and emphasized the great value of a more precise Latin translation, calling attention again to his efforts to draw out a more definitive meaning from the text. "What wrong," he demanded, "have I done in this?" The work should be welcome because it exposes the heretics in their deliberate corruption of the Greek version.[83] But something was amiss.

In the meantime the Faculty of the Sorbonne deputized two of its members to examine the treatise and sent the Bishop a preliminary report, together with a request for clarification of several of its passages.[84] The examination of books at the Sorbonne was customarily assigned to small commissions in whose hands an author's fate was decided without further consultation in the Faculty as a whole. By this time, moreover, an earlier and rather well-diffused respect for the liberal arts may have declined among the younger theologians[85]; Sadoleto evidently knew this and saw that a good deal depended on the

4*

kind of men selected to examine his work. One of the two deputies who read the Commentaries was Mathieu Ory, prior of the Dominican convent in Paris, a protégé of Cardinal Tournon, and later the grand inquisitor of France. In him, at least, Sadoleto's hope for readers sympathetic to classical studies may well have been disappointed, not to mention his hope that Brice could influence the choice of his judges in Paris.

The ultimate disapproval of the Sorbonne doctors appears to have followed publication of the treatise at Lyons early in 1535,[86] for by the spring of that year Sadoleto had still not received word of their final opinion.[87] But by the time he was struck by the Sorbonne's disapproval, he had suffered a humiliating shock of rebuke from the Vatican. During the summer of 1535 the Commentaries were put under a ban by the Master of the Sacred Palace, Tommaso Badia.[88] In doing so the Dominican Badia, himself a Modenese, invoked the power of preventive censorship established twenty years earlier in the Lateran Council.[89] He forbade publication of the Commentaries and told Sadoleto to have them immediately withdrawn from sale,[90] citing his failure to examine the work of the later scholastics and his neglect of prevenient grace in treating the nature of justification.[91] The weight of these objections thus fell on the limited scope of the author's theological formation as well as on his sympathy for a semi-Pelagian doctrine of merit.

The Bishop met this criticism in a burst of outrage and unbelief. It was one thing, he said, to be privately reprimanded, but the "prohibition of the book, made so expressly and so uncivilly, has grieved me to death . . ."[92] Never, Sadoleto continued, had he suffered greater indignity. Now that the report of Badia's action had spread to Avignon and Lyons, he was almost ashamed to show his face[93]; and to make matters worse, it looked as though the censure were supported by the whole Curia rather than by an individual, for Sadoleto tenaciously attributed the ban to Badia personally and not to his office.

Bini, the Domestic Secretary, then informed the Bishop that he had further antagonized Badia by his replies to the censure, but Sadoleto was unrepentent. He simply answered that the Maestro's objections were poorly reasoned and went on to defend his own right to dispute them.[94] He also made obvious his displeasure in being rebuked by a Thomist for ignoring the later scholastics and for the implication that he might not be qualified to discuss theology in the first place:

I do not deny that there is ignorance in me but say only that if those who go to Paris to study theology receive doctor's degrees in six years, I who have studied it continuously at Carpentras for eight cannot be so ill endowed as not to derive some profit from it, and even if I have not studied Durandus, Capreolus, and Occam, I have studied the Bible, St. Paul, Augustine, Ambrose, Chrysostom, and those most worthy doctors who constitute the tower of true knowledge.[95]

But what mattered most was to have the prohibition withdrawn. In early September Sadoleto dispatched Paolo to Italy, charged with a number of commissions,[96] the most important of them being to pay homage to the new Pope, Paul III, and to deliver to him a "bella Apologia," as Negri put it, for the Commentaries.[97] Once Paolo left, Sadoleto relaxed somewhat, diverted for the moment by purely parochial concerns—the uncommonly heavy *vendange*, the care of his gardens at San Felice, the arrival of Volusene, and again by the Jewish bankers. He also returned to his *Hortensius* and started another work long postponed which he called *De gloria*.

Nevertheless, he had not given up his determination to chasten Badia or to have the ban lifted. In Rome, on the Bishop's instructions, Paolo presented himself to Cardinal Contarini, nominated to the Sacred College in May and consecrated in October,[98] with the purpose of enlisting his support against Badia. Paolo reported favorably on his efforts in the Curia in a letter written November 3, which reached his cousin at Avignon together with a letter from Contarini. Sadoleto was delighted.[99] Paolo's reception in Rome seemed to dispel any fear of a general hostility toward the Bishop in the Curia and indicated that Badia was now willing to accept the clarifications of disputed passages in the treatise which Sadoleto had sent him. Contarini's letter pleased him even more, not only for its content but because the Cardinal had written on his own initiative and done it so gently. In him Sadoleto felt he had found at least a friendly critic, if not an advocate, in one from whom even censure would be far more palatable than from Badia.

Although Contarini's letter of early November is missing, Sadoleto's of the twenty-sixth reveals the substance of the Cardinal's objections to the Commentaries and provides a singularly candid defense of the work.[100] Here, for example, he conceded the error of neglecting prevenient grace but added that such a distinction, although used by Augustine against Pelagius,[101] was seldom observed by Chrysostom, Basil, or Ambrose. The argument from *gratia praeveniens* he interpreted as a polemical refinement rather than an article of fundamental Catholic dogma. He agreed, however, that he might have more fully emphasized the effects of original sin as well as "the restitution of our will by the Holy Spirit."[102] Yet, in discussing his claim that the believer participates in the beginnings of salvation, he cited the warrant of Greek patristic doctrine again and argued that it is neither Pelagian nor contrary to Catholic belief to attribute something to human will, even though all merit is from God.[103]

Contarini calmly turned aside Sadoleto's efforts to align him against the Maestro. The Cardinal's skill as a mediator comes out vividly in a letter to Sadoleto written toward the end of December 1535.[104] "Why," he asked, "did you send me your interpretations of those places which the Master of Sacred Palace, a good and a conscientious man, had annotated, and why did you seek my opinion on them?" He dismissed the ban as unimportant now that the "Magister has read your explanations and found them satisfactory, and is so pleased that you intend to change those passages in the Lyons text which will clarify its meaning to your readers."[105] Contarini added his personal hope, however, that the Bishop would be careful not to leave such openings to his critics again and limited his private views to a single point. Commenting on Sadoleto's discussion of *caritas* and the effects of baptism, the Venetian observed that the treatise does not use the language of the "later theologians" when they speak of prevenient grace, "although you say some things which convey the same sense."

So Contarini refused to take sides, being eager to pacify Sadoleto while supporting the Maestro's case for revising the treatise. He agreed to help restrain Sadoleto's publisher in Venice, by official pressure if necessary, from issuing an uncorrected edition of the Commentaries before Gryphius published the second emended edition at Lyons.[106] And at least for the moment Contarini's offices were successful. While Sadoleto felt that he still bore "the stigmata of dishonor," he finally stopped his attacks on Badia and agreed to amplify certain parts of the original text.[107] Nothing, however, was deleted from the first edition. Badia permitted the Bishop merely to enlarge the objectionable passages without reconstructing his general position. The most important of these changes, which appears only in the second and in none of the later editions, is a two-page insertion in which Sadoleto elaborated the interpretation of merit and the beginnings of salvation in his discussion of Romans 8:29–31.[108] Later in the same book he introduced a brief reference to the action of prevenient grace and the disabling effects of sin in the section on Romans 9:7–26.[109] But these concessions scarcely affected the principal argument of the treatise.

Contarini's mediation and the assurance of friendly feeling toward him in the Vatican eventually soothed the Bishop, whose capacity for anger was the single defect of character that Fiordibello cited in his life of Sadoleto. Far from being treated as though he were one of the "rebels against the Church," as he once put it to Blosio, he emerged from the dispute with his reputation quite intact, and even before the Commentaries were reissued he was invited to return to the Curia by Paul III. Nor did acceptance of Contarini's arbitration mean that he altered his understanding of human freedom and the action of the will. Writing to the Cardinal in 1536, for example, Sadoleto again took occasion to challenge Augustine, arguing that "if I do not agree with [his doctrine], I do not therefore dissent from the Catholic Church," which in censuring only three *capita* of Pelagius leaves the body of his works open to discussion.[110] Contarini by then was far more interested in persuading Sadoleto to go to Rome and let the question rest with only passing mention of his own profound assent to Augustine's doctrine of justification.[111]

So the victory was Sadoleto's, at least for the present. The few changes which he supplied to the text of the second edition were trivial, and nothing was done when he omitted them entirely from two new editions which appeared at Venice in 1536 and Lyons a year later.[112] At the time Sadoleto wrote the Commentaries, encouragement and tolerance of the amateur theologian were still generous indeed. He was convinced, we must recall, that his private study of patristic doctrine at Carpentras qualified him to embark on a fresh examination of Pauline theology. Moreover, his previous works, most of which anticipated his theological position in the Commentaries, had been given wide approval from men like Fregoso and Erasmus, who encouraged Sadoleto's earlier efforts as exegete. Pole in particular had endorsed his plan to interpret the Epistle to the Romans, as did Cardinal Tournon[113]; Clement VII once requested him to comment on two disputed passages in the Gospel of St. John,[114] and Cardinal du Bellay, as we know, suggested that he continue his exposition of Paul even while the Commentaries were being criticized. The treatise on Romans proceeded out of confidence taken from the assurance of pious and learned friends, many of whom suspected the professional theologian and encouraged doctrinal speculation among well-meaning but ill-qualified amateurs.[115]

Yet while Sadoleto successfully overcame the objections of the Curia and the Sorbonne, he failed to win lasting recognition as a theologian, largely because he never acquired the perspective of theology. Technical competence and mastery of doctrinal tradition were wanting in him, to be sure; but so, too, was the theologian's sense of distance between God and man. Sadoleto hardly recognized any discontinuity between nature and grace and endowed human nature with a capacity to take on the likeness of God virtually—it would seem—by powers of will and intellect alone. In such diverse works as the treatise on the Ninety-third Psalm, the *De liberis*, *Hortensius*, and the Commentaries there appears the same tendency to merge man's order with God's, the same assumption that natural wisdom on the one hand and *bona voluntas* on the other can provide human nature with the initial means of assuming identity with the divine.

His failure as a humanist theologian may also be measured by the distance which separated his understanding of doctrinal tradition from the principles which later triumphed in the Council of Trent. Sadoleto intentionally rejected the scholastic doctors old and modern, and in his emphasis on scriptural theology illuminated by philological analysis he gave only slight attention to the Fathers. But Trent soon exposed the audacity of Sadoleto's methods by defending the scholastic tradition against Lutheran and Catholic innovators alike, while setting Christian Aristotelianism against modernists of every kind.[116] The new exegesis developed by men like Valla, Colet, Erasmus, Giberti, and Sadoleto found partisans in the Council, to be sure,[117] but their position collapsed under the new weight which the fathers restored to the old authority of scholastic tradition.

It is true, however, that in formulating their decree on justification the conciliar fathers had to pass through many shoals of recent error on the part of their coreligionists.[118] Seripando warned the theologians when considering certain aspects of disputed doctrine to take care lest they condemn such Catholic apologists as Egidio da Viterbo and Contarini, or the zealously anti-Protestant Albertus Pighius, whose doctrine of grace so much resembled Sadoleto's.[119] Seripando himself was identified with Contarini's support of a twofold justice. But the formula which the Commission on Justification finally developed in January 1547 belonged to the Dominicans. The Council itself was to become a triumph of militant monasticism, drawing its inspiration not from Padua or the Christian humanists, but from medieval Paris and the monastic schools.[120]

On the other hand, while the theologians at Trent found it necessary to reject the contributions of Contarini and his friends to the clarification of Catholic dogma, the conciliar fathers also owed a certain debt to these men in their capacity as ecclesiastical reformers. Conspicuous among them was the Bishop of Carpentras, summoned to Rome in his sixtieth year not as Latinist or papal secretary, and certainly not as a theologian, but as a prelate called to the Vatican for a project of reform in the Church.

VI

Curial Reformer
and Cardinal

When Paolo arrived in Rome in November 1535 to muster support for the Bishop's Commentaries, the Vatican was humming with talk of a general Council. A year before he succeeded Clement VII, Cardinal Alessandro Farnese had openly committed himself in principle to reform and the Council, and soon after the Commentaries appeared at Lyons, nuncios were afield to promote the Council in Germany, France, and Spain.

As estimates of popular and princely response began to accumulate in Rome, the Venetian ambassador drafted a long report to the Signory on these developments and particularly on what he took to be the private views of the Farnese Pontiff.

Whoever considers and searches the Pope's heart can discover that although he talks in public of his desire for the Council and [denies] that he fears it, he will gladly flee from it and will never strive to bring it about. And this is the universal opinion of the cardinals who are closest to him, who admit that his words are empty and false, and that although he has said he wants it, . . . all will come to naught, nor does His Holiness, by any means whatever, want it to take place. . . . It may therefore be concluded that the Pope, far from desiring the Council, will soon abandon it, although, as you see, he says otherwise.[1]

The ambassador went on to explain why a Council would present dangers to the Holy See. For one thing, reform of the clergy might easily embarrass the Curia and the Pope himself. Doctrine could not be discussed without taking grave risks, and although Paul III was well aware of abuses in the papal court, he knew also that a Council might drastically reduce his financial resources while threatening his authority over investiture and the temporal wealth of the hierarchy as well.

Soriano's analysis, however timely, was incomplete and somewhat myopic. In the first place, he assumed that control of the issue rested with the Pope alone. Paul III, to be sure, had already recovered a good deal of the prestige and authority which his Medici predecessor squandered for ten years, but in doing so the new Pope invoked the support of new men and old principles which had a force of their own; moreover, he had committed himself to a course from which it was steadily more difficult to deviate. And like the Medici Popes, he had further to reckon with the enormous will and mounting political power of Charles V.

Determined now to turn all his energy to ending the religious and political chaos in Germany, the Emperor confronted the Pope in Easter week of 1536 with his own unyielding demands that a general Council be called immediately. Under pressure to implement his earlier declarations, Paul III in consistory on April 8 announced the convocation of a Council, while Charles continued to thunder provocatively against Francis I. Knowing that French hostility to any such convocation still disquieted the Vatican, Charles left deputies behind to press his demands on the Curia when the imperial suite started north on April 18. And after a month of debate the conciliar bull was published on June 4, declaring that the Council was to assemble at Mantua in May 1537.[2] By ironic coincidence this month would mark the tenth anniversary of the Sack of Rome. The Emperor's part was as decisive in the one instance as in the other.

To the Bishop of Carpentras these negotiations were little more than a distant rumble and a series of rumors dimly heard. In 1535 his horizon still ended at the gray-blue hills of Provence: Rome was only a cruel memory, something fled, and at best the source of dispensations confirming his own deliverance from it.[3] When talk of a Council had reached him five years earlier, he turned skeptically to Fregoso to ask if it was to be taken seriously or dismissed as a sham. The latter seemed more likely, and while insisting that he would attend any Council which showed prospects of success, the wiser choice then seemed to stay where he was.[4]

Sadoleto's reaction to new reports of a Council under Paul III was more sanguine, if only because the Pope was opposing a general Council to the "free national synod" that the Lutherans demanded.[5] Beyond this, however, he declined to comment. When he heard that Paolo had committed him to write a treatise for the Pope, Jacopo answered with irritation that although he could not refuse, neither would he write anything which touched on the conciliar issue, nor would he declare himself publicly on a topic so controversial.[6] The Bishop liked what he heard and knew about the Farnese Pope, but his suspicion of the Curia and distaste for further involvement in the Vatican were as intense as ever.

Yet even before the status of the Commentaries was settled, there was new discussion of recalling him to the Pope's service. It came first from Giovanni Battista Grassi, papal chamberlain and Bishop of Viterbo, who at the end of 1535 tried to persuade him to go to Rome, apparently as tutor to the Pope's grandson, young Cardinal Alessandro Farnese.[7] More significant and pressing, however, was Contarini's desire to bring Sadoleto back to the Curia, although whether his purpose was originally the same as Bishop Grassi's we cannot know. At the end of his letter to Sadoleto of December 29, 1535, most of which dealt with revision of the Commentaries, Contarini wrote that he was "most eager to enjoy [Sadoleto's] company";[8] and in replying the Bishop acknowledged reports that Contarini had discussed with Paolo the prospect of his return to Rome and the subject of new "honor and distinction" for him.[9] Sadoleto dismissed these efforts, whatever they were, by saying that "nothing could be more inimical" to his private interests, which lay deep in "tranquility, . . . peace of mind," and self-determination. Contarini's proposals were abhorrent because they would require the abandonment of personal freedom for a return to the *vita negotiosa* by one who had experienced "each condition and way of life," and who was now resolutely attached to quiet and liberty. He added, as though to anticipate the Cardinal, that his life at Carpentras was one which also served the Church, and concluded with a plea that he not be forced back into "turbulence and wild confusion."

There followed a long and rhetorical admonition to Contarini against nourishing false hope for the deliverance of the Church:

O most learned and excellent Contarini, may your hopes never deceive you! By your singular goodness and virtue you are lead to trust that what should be done has indeed already been done. Do you not believe, if there were hope of accomplishing substantial good, that I would offer and dedicate myself, not to honors . . . but as the chief Apostle said, to death and the cross . . . ? Believe me, the vice and the base passions of our generation are closed to probity and wisdom. In the Pope we have an extraordinary leader, intent upon worthy ends. But he is no stronger than the depravity of the times. The body of Christendom is sick, afflicted with that kind of disease which defies the present remedy [the Council]; more devious measures are required to bring it back to health, just as the disease came on bit by bit over a long course of time. To restore health and dignity to the Christian Commonwealth will require great patience, a variety of cures, and secret counsels.[10]

If a Council is held after such recovery begins, Sadoleto said he would attend, as he admitted he should, but he made equally clear his conviction that present hopes for an effective Council were badly misplaced. In the meantime, therefore, he begged the Cardinal to respect his wish to stay at Carpentras.

On the same day in March 1536 Sadoleto notified the Pope that "nothing could be more disagreeable than to be torn away from this place in which . . . I am situated by firm and perpetual resolve. . . ." In repeating his pledge to attend a future Council, he went on to say that aside from attending it he saw no way in which he could be useful to the Curia. In case of some unforeseen urgency which required him to leave Provence for Rome, he stipulated in the strongest possible terms that there be no change in his present status and that he be permitted to return to his church, his studies, and his tranquility, "which I place far above all wealth and honors," after such service ended.[11]

Because he was occupied with the negotiations for the Council

which took place during the imperial visit to Rome in April, Contarini was unable to reply to Sadoleto's letter until after the Emperor
left on the eighteenth. While he helplessly accepted Sadoleto's refusal,
the Cardinal later advised him not to speak as he had written about the
condition of the Church, because such skepticism by itself was
dangerous if carelessly spoken.[12] Paul III answered Sadoleto on May 8,
confirming what Contarini had already written and accepting the
conditions which Sadoleto placed on any future absence from his see.[13]
But in closing, perhaps with the purpose of preparing the Bishop for
another summons, the Pope added that Sadoleto would "learn of
these matters in more detail from Contarini." Despite Contarini's
failure to bring the Bishop to Rome at this time, it is particularly
significant that his efforts to do so began in December 1535, four
months before the Council of Mantua was accepted in principle and
seven months before the Pope's second reform commission was
nominated in July 1536. Contarini's invitation to Sadoleto, first conveyed to Paolo, was issued to him not as one among several others,
but to him alone.[14] For this reason it is the more unfortunate that the
intent of the invitation cannot be precisely known, although it obviously bore on Contarini's role as reformer and advocate of the Council.
Jacopo's several allusions to new honors and titles further suggest that
some importance was to be attached to his duties.

Once the Council of Mantua was decided upon, however, Sadoleto
promptly stated his plans to attend it, although by force of habit he
spoke of the personal hardship that any such journey would entail for
him.[15] Then in his sixtieth year, chronically ill and always indigent,
he showed a striking consistency in interpreting his obligations as
priest and prelate. He held fast to the conviction that he had earned his
status at Carpentras as a matter of right and reward for curial service,
boldly turning aside a series of invitations, and even summonses, to
rejoin the papal court. Service of this kind, he seemed to argue, did not
bear upon priestly duty. But attendance at a Council was quite another
matter. This, he confessed to Contarini, involved one's "pious and
bounden duty to God, the Church and the Holy See."[16] The irony
was, however, that Sadoleto spent half the last decade of his life in

Rome, attached to the Curia, occupied with reform and diplomacy preliminary to a Council which neither he nor his coadjutor ever attended so long as Jacopo lived.

Once Paul III had committed himself to the Council and acquiesced in fixing a date for it, he created new expectations on the Holy See and thereby increased the necessity of reform under its auspices. The Curia fell under a new burden of proof in the spring of 1536 and equally under the obligation to reform itself, not only in order to demonstrate the Pope's integrity, but also to deprive his enemies and critics of the opportunity to demand measures of their own devising. Reform of the Curia and clergy, of the Church "in capite et in membris," was, with sudden emphasis, said to be indispensable, and the continued existence of abuses an obstacle to the convocation of the Council.

To the extent that the Farnese Pope planned to meet the urgency of reform, his means lay in the gradual formation of a reform party in the Sacred College. Never insensitive to the realities of family interest, secular politics, or curial conservatism, Paul III like his predecessors of recent decades used his power of nomination to reward the strong and the influential. Yet he successfully built up in the College a nucleus of earnest reformers, without vested interest in the Curia, through whom he tried to achieve the preliminary work of Catholic reformation. Indeed the selection of these men may have been one of his most constructive accomplishments. The most conspicuous of them, of course, was Cardinal Contarini, taken without notice from the notoriously anti-curial Signory of Venice and installed with honor at the Pope's side. The secret of Contarini's nomination, like that of others who followed him, may be sought no less in his innocence of Rome and of sacerdotal professionalism than in his reputation for piety and erudition. He was the symbol, if not the inspiration, of those

Pauline reformers who by accident or design had remained free from
curial venality, bureaucracy, and conservative bias.

On May 29, 1536, five days before the Council of Mantua was
promulgated, the Pope addressed the consistory about reform both of
the offices and the conduct of his curial subordinates.[17] A bull of June 2
assigned to the Council the task of undertaking the moral reform of
Christendom. In the consistory of June 21 he announced his plan to
summon a body of "optimi viri" to prepare the way for the Council.
Contarini notified Pole of his appointment on July 12, the day of
Erasmus' death, and instructions for assembling the commission were
secretly issued in the Farnese palace on July 21.[18] Although there is
little doubt that Contarini worked closely with the Pope in organizing
this reform commission, it was probably instigated under the Pope's
direction.[19] Contarini was certainly an active collaborator; it was he,
for example, who proposed that Gregorio Cortese be named to the
group,[20] but he described it to Pole as "a gathering of learned men
which the Pontiff has arranged."

The briefs of invitation were drawn up on the nineteenth and
twenty-third of July and sent to Gianpietro Caraffa, Cortese, Giberti,
Sadoleto, Fregoso, and Pole, all of whom were instructed to gather in
Rome at the end of the summer, to "assist us in preparing and disposing all manner of things" related to the Council.[21] Bartolomeo
Guidiccioni was excused on the plea of age, and the names of Tommaso Badia and Aleander added, according to Pastor, at Contarini's
suggestion.[22] All were Italian except Pole,[23] at that time in Venice and
still engrossed in his studies, having broken off all ties with Henry VIII
in May. Pole was a worthy addition in his own right, but his acceptance also marked a certain triumph for the Pope against the schismatic
king of England. All of those originally summoned were outside of
Rome, and none with the exception of Badia could be called a
curialist, although of course both Giberti and Sadoleto had earlier
belonged to the Curia of the Medici.[24]

The deputies who were already in Italy started to Rome in September, Pole travelling with Giberti and Caraffa, and Cortese with
Fregoso. Considerably more was involved for Sadoleto. During the

summer his diocese was overrun with French and Swiss troops while Montmorency directed the sack of Provence in the face of an imperial invasion. Sadoleto left Carpentras toward the middle of September, still anxious for the safety of his people and shortly before the prospect of war in the Venaissin had fully receded. Once again in bad health, he was eager to complete the long trip south before the autumn storms began. From Piacenza, where already he wrote of his longing for Carpentras, he moved on in haste to Modena, beset en route by a band of Spanish soldiers. And after spending ten days in his *patria*, he left on October 23 for Bologna and Rome, carried on a litter for at least part of the journey and accompanied by Lodovico Beccadelli and Maria Molza, as well as by the faithful Paolo.[25]

He was in Rome by November 1, returning after nearly a decade to a city which still showed scars of the *landsknechtes'* fury. Maffei had warned him to expect to find "a new city, a new Senate, and new curialists," almost empty of familiar faces.[26] In November he began to talk of his departure the following spring, when he intended to leave either for Mantua and the Council, or for France and "the pleasant haven of my studies, my leisure, and tranquility."[27] In writing to other friends about his presence in Rome, Sadoleto explained that he had come there against his will and out of a sense of duty, "forced" to give up his chosen way of life. But Jacopo was not the only member of the Commission who went to Rome reluctantly; Giberti and Caraffa were equally distressed by the prospects of public service.[28]

Meetings of the Commission of Nine were probably in progress before the end of the month and lasted until sometime in February 1537.[29] The formal opening of the Commission's deliberations followed an oration by the Bishop of Carpentras, who was easily the best Latinist of the group.[30] Absent from Rome at the time, Paul III missed Sadoleto's speech, a jeremiad in which praise of the present Pope was lost in denunciation of his predecessors and in stinging attacks on the unreformed clergy. Instinctively cautious though often indiscreet, Sadoleto spoke here with the passion of a Hebrew prophet, warning at the start that "if remedies for existing calamities are not soon found, we shall be faced no longer with mere admonition and correction, but with the final annihilation of us all."[31] Yet even on the edge of this destruction, he continued, our princes persist in waging war, deepening a chaos which Popes in their turn have chosen to enlarge rather than limit.

The leading theme of his address was to charge the Holy See with responsibility for the condition of the Church and with the loss of authority all over Europe. In the language of Christian idealism habitual to humanist and reformer alike, he looked back to the historical Papacy to find in it a pristine good now debased into evil:

Great was the dignity, majesty, and dominion of the Roman Pontiff in the era when, having been elected to this sacred station of highest honor, he was held not by profane lusts but dedicated and consecrated to God alone. At that time the Roman Pontiff was likewise the common father of all races and nations. He sought nothing for his own that was alien to the salvation of those commended by God to his care. He pursued no private advantage, no personal power, no gains from oppression and injury to others, but comforted and sustained all who seemed stricken with poverty or injustice.[32]

But from early innocence and virtue followed a lapse into avarice, self-interest, luxury, and intemperance, into the abuse of power and contempt for ancient law. As men abandoned their confidence in the *sacerdos* they lost faith in God, believing that providence no longer operated in the affairs of men. Behold, then, the hatred in which the clergy is held today, he said.[33]

Think of the Lutherans' demand that we be exterminated, and count the defections from the faith which have taken place beyond the Alps. We are reaping the putrid harvest of our sins. Let us admit, therefore, how far we have come from the religion of our forebears, how much we are despised in almost every nation. You—Sadoleto abruptly changed pronouns at this juncture—have now lost the obedience of eastern Europe. You have plunged Germany into faction and discord by the abuse of indulgences and the most ruthless exploitation, making it possible for wicked men to inflame the oppressed. You are even losing Italy; and what need be added, he asked, about

England, Hungary devastated by the Turks, and Rhodes, already lost?[34]

The only hope now lies in Paul III, alone among the Popes of this generation to abstain from conflicts between the major princes. The new Pontiff is a peace-maker who has summoned a Council at a time when nothing else can answer the needs of the *Respublica Christiana*, after centuries in which no general Council was honestly attempted. Our task, the orator said, before going on to praise each member of the Commission, is to bring back all neglected measures for the welfare of Christendom and to restore the morality of the priesthood. Given this company of men, our work should soon be achieved, so that "you may restore your ancient dignity and influence, the pristine authority of the Holy See, and the priesthood to grace with God and honor among men." The orator himself, however, often sounded more like a spectator than a participant in the labors ahead.

On the other hand, Sadoleto's remarks went well beyond the demands of mere rhetoric. There is a quality of bitter reproach here that is almost vengeful in its implicit judgments of the Medici Popes, if not of the entire papal succession of his own era. The Bishop's accusations, unlike his public exhortation to the crusade twenty years earlier, lay deep in his own experience and in his disillusionment with Leo X and Clement VII.[35] So, too, did the oration express the familiar and more general idea of "restitutio" or "restoratio" in the belief that contemporary Christianity at every level lay far below the normative purity of the early Church.

In spite of its asperities the oration won the approval of Paul III. Writing from Volterra on December 3, Mario Maffei informed Sadoleto that the stars seemed to confirm a popular rumor that he was soon to be honored by the Pope, Jupiter especially portending recognition and new dignities.[36] On the same day, Sunday, Blosio was instructed to invite the Bishop of Carpentras to the Pope's Mass *in capella*.[37] But the supreme honor, the red hat, was conferred on him three weeks later in what has been rather unconvincingly called the "Erasmian promotion."[38]

The nomination of December 22 was only in a limited way a sequel to that of May 21, 1535, which brought Contarini to the Sacred College. Included among the nine Cardinals in the elevation of 1536 were three authentic reformers in Gianpietro Caraffa, Sadoleto, and Pole (Aleander being reserved *in petto* at this time); but so, too, were there three manifestly unworthy recipients in Lodovico Borgia, Giovanni Maria del Monte, and Niccolò Gaetani, a young nephew of the Pope. Among the others one, Charles Hémard de Denonville, the French ambassador to Rome, was nominated as a concession to Francis I; another, the Datary Cristoforo Jacobazzi, was a professional curialist, while da Carpi and Filonardi were promoted in recognition of their services to papal diplomacy.

The three members of the new Commission were certainly nominated to augment the strength of reform sentiment in the College, and very likely at the suggestion of Contarini. But the Pope was sensitive to other considerations. For one thing, he wanted to reduce the power of the Medici element but could not afford to alienate the old conservatives either. Jacobazzi was therefore chosen to represent their interests in the promotion of 1536 just as Ghinucci and Simonetta were in 1535, while Borgia and del Monte were evidently named on the general demand of the College rather than by the Pope's preference. So at the most this election signified only a modest gain for the reformers, since it also increased the forces of obstruction and reaction as well.[39]

The nomination of Reginald Pole, settled upon in November if not sooner, was intended to defy his king and encourage his coreligionists in England. Nonetheless, Pole himself found it a frightening prospect, which he accepted largely on Contarini's persuasion.[40] Sadoleto also had reservations. He looked at his nomination from the perspective of Carpentras and San Felice, to see himself "recalled anew from port into the tempest. . . ."[41] He had learned to count the cost of preferment, knowing now that honors always carried obligation with them. This, perhaps, had been the most painful lesson of his career. He also looked at his nomination in the perspective of a lifetime: his first letter as a Cardinal was to Duke Ercole II, to whom Sadoleto pledged his loyalty, as though again aware that it was to the Estensi that the

Sadoletti owed their advantages.[42] He felt obliged to add, as he did for the information of humanist friends, that the election had come as a complete surprise to him.

In Modena it was quickly made the cause of celebration, as the Duke's subjects rejoiced in the honor which Jacopo Sadoleto had brought them. Lancellotti attributed the promotion to Sadoleto's literary reputation[43]; for the diarist he was still the man of letters who had won a place among the literati of Rome. On Wednesday and Thursday of Christmas week, the Modenese gathered in their *piazza* to honor a native son with "processions, masses, music, and bonfires," and all the citizens, according to Lancellotti, now believed that Sadoleto was eminently *papábile*.[44]

But in letters answering the congratulation of his friends, most of them humanists—Bembo, Bonamico, Negri, Maffei, Giraldi, Guillaume du Bellay, Alciati, Girolamo Vida, Brice, Nausea, and others—Sadoleto showed few signs of pleasure or ambition in his new office and was visibly troubled by what it involved. Like Pole, he had talked of refusing the nomination,[45] fearing at the same time that the Pope would find his grounds inadequate. Friends were quick to remind him that his misgivings were no better than private motives, prompted by his affection for Carpentras. This talk of refusal is not to be taken seriously, but Sadoleto was plainly distressed to admit that he was now obliged to remain in the Curia indefinitely. For him the Sacred College meant "the most binding servitude" and the loss of a private life.[46]

In this retiring classicist, however, there was also the churchman, whom Lancellotti had failed to recognize. Sadoleto was genuinely impressed by his colleagues in the reform Commission and by the Pope's support of their purpose.[47] He readily identified himself with Contarini and Pole during these weeks, sitting near them in consistory and living, as they did, in the Vatican Palace.[48] Occasionally he crossed the river to his Quirinal vineyard, where once again a coterie of literary friends gathered. The humanist is otherwise difficult to find in Sadoleto at this time, however, and even in corresponding with men like Bonamico and Bembo there is scarcely a trace of the pristine

Academician. For the time being he was preoccupied with the work of the Commission as the hour of the Council at Mantua drew near.

Members of the reform Commission, it must be remembered, worked on their recommendations to the Pope fully expecting that the Council would take place, as scheduled, in May. At the end of February Sadoleto replied to an inquiry about its prospects from Friedrich Nausea, then in Vienna at the court of King Ferdinand, to say that the Pope was already preparing for his journey to Mantua despite the dangers on every side.[49] Writing privately to a German Catholic and an outsider, Sadoleto now appeared to question the wisdom of holding a Council at this time, feeling that more was to be feared from it than hoped for, and that political conditions for its success were still highly unfavorable. By conditioning, if not by temperament, he was in many ways a pessimist who tended to consider darkly the motives of men in authority and to measure possibility with great caution. His own experience had taught him the value of observing the conduct of princes, frequently the condition of survival to an Italian of this era, so that as the time of the Council approached he became increasingly dubious of its prospects. If his oration to the reform deputies in November had the ring of the Christian idealist, his letter to Nausea was that of the skeptic who observed that conditions of travel were everywhere so bad that the Council would be seriously delayed even if held.[50] For his own part, Sadoleto confessed to Nausea that he "could find no safe remedy" for the corrupt and divided condition of the Church.[51]

By now the Commission had already completed its report, which was signed by Pole and Giberti before they started north on February 18. As Pole departed for England on a mission which was to leave him stranded at Liège, his colleagues prepared to submit their memorial in consistory before leaving for Mantua. Their deliberations were kept secret, and because no trace of the proceedings has survived, it is vain to speculate on the authorship of the memorial. We know only that the celebrated *Consilium de emendanda ecclesia* was presented to the Pope and the College, together with parts of a dissenting version by Cardinal Sadoleto, on March 9, 1537.[52]

The record of what took place at this consistory in the Camera di Papagallo depends almost entirely on an interpretation written by the ubiquitous Aleander, still embittered by his exclusion from the promotion of the previous December.[53] He explained that the report which Contarini read on March 9 had been discussed and approved by the deputies as a body, and that they in turn had already rejected a separate statement drawn up by Cardinal Sadoleto. Nevertheless, Sadoleto demanded that his own views be presented to the Pope and managed to gain enough backing to have at least parts of his private version read after Contarini presented the majority report.[54] Once again, however, Sadoleto's memorial was turned down; yet when on Aleander's suggestion the Pope agreed that those present should receive a copy of the principal memorial for private study, Sadoleto once more demanded recognition and arranged to have his remarks circulated in the same way.[55] Aleander unfortunately reveals nothing about the content or character of the dissenting version, saying only that parts of it were read by Cardinal Cesarini, and that while it was "elegantly written," it pleased no one, "for many reasons" which he failed to set forth.[56]

The problem is less one of accounting for Aleander's refusal to discuss this minority report than of explaining the unanimity with which it was repudiated. Was it more rigorous or more mild than the one which Contarini read for the rest of the deputies? Friedensburg, a Protestant historian, suggests that although Sadoleto accepted the majority position as far as it went, he was not content to rest with a mere rehearsal of abuses and therefore proposed original and positive recommendations of his own for their removal.[57] Certainly no member of the Commission interpreted the religious and moral crisis in more desperate terms than he, and few Catholic reformers seemed more skeptical of the traditional measures of reform. Consequently, it may be that Sadoleto abandoned the "search for precedents"[58] and proposed entirely new measures instead of advocating the reapplication of existing law. From the tone of Aleander's comments it seems quite possible that Sadoleto's position was thought to be too radical. The fact remains, however, that his private memorial has not survived and that the degree and direction of its deviation from the *Consilium* are still a mystery; we know simply of his stubborn isolation from the group and of its failure to incorporate his personal recommendations in the majority statement.

With the defection of Bartolomeo Guidiccioni, the second reform Commission lost its one potential opponent of searching criticism. Its nine members, uniformly agreed at least on the urgency of correcting abuses in the Church, therefore enjoyed a clear advantage over the previous Commission of August 1535, which was dominated by the private interests and caution of Ghinucci, Simonetta, and Jacobazzi. The *Consilium* of 1537–38, as finally published,[59] contains few innovating remedies measured to the present condition of Curia and clergy; but at the same time its critical sections, forming the bulk of the memorial, are notable for their candor and severity.

The document is largely a catalogue of abuses prevailing at all levels, from the Holy See to the parish, the cloister, and the school. It treats the gravest in some detail, combining description with suggestions for their removal, and placing greatest emphasis on the reckless collation of benefices and the neglect of canonical practices in the life of the clergy. The deputies denounced the condition of the monasteries and even proposed the gradual suppression of conventual orders. They cited the low level of religious instruction in the universities and dealt with the neglect of censorship. In one brief passage they also recommended that Erasmus' *Colloquies* be suppressed on the ground that such writing aroused impiety in the young—a prohibition which Luther answered with a bellow of outrage and Melanchthon with ironic contempt.[60] But Protestants like Sturm, as we shall see later, readily conceded respect for the main burden of the *Consilium* as a review of ecclesiastical abuses. The memorialists examined the misuse of episcopal authority and corrupt practice in diocesan administration. They attacked corruption in the administration of papal pensions, reservations, provisions, and expectations, specifically condemning the appointment of coadjutors with the right of succession. The Cardinals were cited for avarice and neglect of responsibility, and the Curia for tolerating the moral license which still flourished in Rome.

In locating the source of these evils the deputies were faithful to the analysis which Sadoleto elaborated in his opening oration and concentrated their attention on the exercise of papal authority. More specifically, the *Consilium* emphasized a doctrine advanced by the papal legists with respect to the plenitude of power in claiming that the Pope is master (*dominus*) of all benefices, and when by right the master sells what is his, it necessarily follows that the Pope cannot fall into simony. Therefore, the will of the Pope, whatever it be, is the rule by which his conduct and action are directed. Thus it follows that he may do whatever pleases him.[61]

Out of such sophistry and false principles—"as from a Trojan horse," says the memorial—springs the mass of corrupt practices which are carrying the Church toward destruction.

After praising Paul III for summoning a Council to meet three months later, the deputies countered the teaching of the legists with a precept from Aristotle's *Politics*. It was that in the Church, as in any state, "this rule be observed above all, that the laws be observed to the maximum," without exception or dispensation, there being no graver error in ecclesiastical government than neglect of the law.[62] By inference, therefore, the Church possess the means of its own regeneration; by enforcing the canon law, it can restore itself to a condition of "pristine sublimity." The Church has precedent and law enough to reform itself; what it needs is men to apply them.

Those who claim to find the principle and practice of despotism in the government of the Renaissance Church should reconsider the reign of Paul III and the debate over the issues of reform, reunion, and the Council which took place in the generation before Trent. The fortunes of the Pope's second Commission and its memorial offer a revealing instance not of papal absolutism but rather of its opposite. The deputies under Contarini's presidency, representing a minority viewpoint in the Curia and the College, had been assigned by the Pope to the study of reform at all levels of the hierarchy. Made with something less than genuine unanimity, their recommendations were pointedly critical of the center of power and the operation of the pontifical bureaucracy; the report likewise made assumptions which were immediately attacked both in the Curia and the Cardinalate, so that the deputies were eventually forced to take up defensive positions. In the process appears the familiar spectacle of awkward parliamentarism in the form of bitter factional strife and struggles for power, bad manners and invective, the clash of personalities, and the impasse of contrary principles. Reform in the pontificate of Paul III quickly displayed a collision of rival interests between which the Pope, for a time, attempted to be an arbiter.[63]

What confronts us here is not the factionalism which produced plots against the lives of Leo X or Paul III, and not the use of the College as a chamber of dynastic intrigue or the cockpit of political rivalries, but rather the use of the consistory as an ecclesiastical forum. The College under Paul III emerged, albeit with its Italianate preponderance, as a body whose members variously interpreted the meaning of the schism and debated the methods by which it might be ended. There is nothing startling in the fact that the Cardinals disagreed, but what is so often neglected is the intensity as well as the effects of their discord. Church historians sometimes overlook the controversies and overunify the processes through which the Curia reached its decisions in the years before Trent, so that we frequently lose sight of the dissenting reports, the gratuitous polemics, the voting divisions, the speeches, and the literature of advocacy and opposition so abundant in the decades between the appearance of Luther and the early sessions of the Council. One of the most vivid instances of this condition may be found in the reception which the reform memorial met in the College.

Among the first to challenge the *Consilium* was Nicolaus Schönberg, a moderate of varied experience in the Church, who in the consistory of March 9 raised the question of how such a candid statement on abuses might affect opinion in Germany.[64] In the Cardinal's own view it would probably do great harm and certainly achieve no real good. He questioned the timing of the memorial, holding that the condition of the Church did not justify the radical changes which the deputies proposed and warned that if reform were attempted now, the Lutherans would quickly claim credit for bringing it about. Gianpietro Caraffa, a dedicated partisan of reform though not of reconciliation with the heretics, answered for the deputies that any delay would be disastrous, and dismissed the argument from expediency with the precept that an evil should not be committed to achieve a good.[65] But the question of whether the *Consilium* was to be published was adjourned without decision because of differences of opinion in the College. Meanwhile, the Pope forbade public discussion of the report until its form and content were settled; but despite his precautions the *Consilium* soon found its way to Germany.[66]

A far more virulent and aroused attack on the memorial came from the pen of Bartolomeo Guidiccioni in a treatise addressed to the Pope.[67] Here the memorial was described as a monstrous presumption which, if applied and accepted, would lead to the ruin of the Church. To Guidiccioni the *Consilium* was the work of radical and insolent men who wanted to wreck the authority of the Holy See. He answered their complaint against the legists with the very argument the deputies had attacked. Guidiccioni declared that the Pope enjoys free and absolute authority over all ecclesiastical benefices, and that he is privileged to "found, change, transfer, or suppress" them at will. And one by one he ridiculed or denounced each section of the memorial which he was originally asked to help compose.[68]

Seeking both to answer these critics and to elaborate the philosophy of the *Consilium*, Contarini wrote two treatises of his own, also in the form of letters to Paul III, on the subject of papal authority.[69] Together with Sadoleto and Pole, he accepted the doctrine of the plenitude of power; his interest lay in defining and interpreting its original and legitimate form. In Contarini's view the doctrine rested on two principles. First, the authority of the Pope is divinely instituted and therefore to be exercised under divine law. Second, the Pope is *dispensator* and *servus*, not *dominus*, as some hold, so that he is by no means free to exercise his power arbitrarily. When the legists try to stretch his authority, they only debase it into the most corrupt kind of

5+

license for exploitation and abuse, thereby exposing the Holy See to the mockery of the Lutherans in their books about a "Babylonian Captivity." Contarini here reveals an assumption commonly made and defended by most of his associates in the Catholic reform movement, when he warned that the Protestant revolt had been provoked in the first place by the spread of abuses and the corrupt condition of the clergy. Sadoleto conceded as much in his Exhortation to the Princes and People of Germany by the admission that "the corrupt morals of the clergy and the vices of Rome supplied you with the pretext for overturning everything. . . ."[70]

Throughout Sadoleto's opening oration to the deputies in 1536, as well as the *Consilium de emendanda ecclesia* and Contarini's glosses on it, runs the common theme that the religious crisis was the whirlwind of corruption and that the Curia of the recent past, if not the present, its direct cause. Each of these three commentaries argued that reform was both an end in itself—the restoration of the Holy See to its proper authority and lost integrity—and the means of ending the schism. They held that to reform the Curia and the clergy is to disarm the leaders of heresy in Germany and to reassure the legitimate critics of the Church.[71] This was to insist, in other words, on the importance of reform for the eventual attempt at reconciliation, and in part to justify Catholic reformation as the instrument of reunion.

This point of view, so readily visible in most of the deputies of the second reform Commission, became the cause of their progressive isolation from prevailing opinion in the Curia, the College, and the leadership of the German hierarchy. Between the Lutheran radicals and the conservative majority in the Cardinalate, the circle of Contarini and his associates—Sadoleto, Pole, Giberti, Fregoso, Morone, Badia—constituted an ephemeral center.[72] But the duration of its influence was brief; strong and hopeful at the time of Sadoleto's nomination to the College in 1536, it was divided, disspirited, and reduced to helplessness by 1542. Of the nine deputies on Paul III's second Commission, more than half—Sadoleto, Giberti, Pole, Badia, Fregoso, and Contarini—were at one time censured for heterodox belief or for objectionable conduct in relations with the heretics.

Together they formed a splinter group in the College, numerically too weak to affect its corporate decisions and morally ineffectual without the positive and declared support of the Pope himself. By accepting Aleander's proposal that the memorial on reform be reviewed by the entire College, thus allowing the original *Consilium* to be tabled, Paul III tacitly agreed that the Commission had surpassed the tolerances of the majority. He seems to have taken the memorial as a referendum on the issue of reform *in capite* which disclosed the weakness and isolation of Contarini's support. Paul III did not desert the Cardinal, but neither did he favor his leadership in a moment of critical significance to the progress of Catholic reform. The old Farnese Pope knew the art of waiting and the value of compromise better than he knew his own principles, and what followed was the search for accommodation between discordant elements of the College.

Something of the same variety of opinion prevailed with respect to the Council. One month after the *Consilium* was presented, Sadoleto's friend Blosio, the Domestic Secretary, read in consistory a letter from Federigo Gonzaga concerning the question of military security for the Pope and prelates who were to meet at Mantua in May.[73] Duke Federigo, fearing a French attack from the Alpine passes as well as possible violence among the conciliar deputies and their retainers, decided to withdraw his offer of hospitality to the Council when the Pope refused to provide a garrison in Mantua. The Council was subsequently prorogued on April 20 until November 1, 1537, and the site left unspecified.[74]

In a letter to Cardinal Salviati, Sadoleto explained that the Pope and the College, after twice debating the question, decided that the presence of troops at Mantua would intimidate the Lutherans and jeopardize the outcome of the Council.[75] He and Schönberg, however, strongly protested against further delay in its opening, although they agreed that the location had to be changed.[76] Distressed by bickering over matters of place, time, and procedure, Sadoleto now warned that postponement would seriously injure the Pope's cause and might also cost the alienation of German Catholics still loyal to Rome.[77] Just as significant is the still uneven course of Sadoleto's attitude toward the Council. From outright rejection of it in 1535, he had passed to doubtful support and then to anxiety in the letter to Nausea of February 1537, only to argue in April that it could not be further delayed without real danger. Sadoleto, and perhaps Paul III, was afraid to have the Council held, and at the same time afraid not to have it.

From the start of his reign until the end of 1541 Paul III tried to deal with the problem of reform through the use of a series of *ad hoc* commissions. In doing so the Pope appeared to trust that the hierarchy was willing to reform itself, that the Cardinals, for example, would not only assent to the urgency of reform in principle, but would also participate in the process of limiting their own privileges.[78] But this technique of hopeful improvisation accomplished very little; it soon became clear that self-reform could never be constructively implemented, and that even among the reformers it was impossible to find general agreement and a common body of remedies.[79]

In 1518, while still loyal to the Holy See, Luther looked upon the problem of reform in a way that suggests both the skepticism with which Sadoleto answered Contarini in the spring of 1536, and the flaw of Paul III's initial policy:

The Church needs a reformation, but this is the province not of one man, the Pope, or of the Cardinals, as each of the most recent Councils demonstrate; but rather of the whole world, or indeed of God alone. And he alone, the creator of time, knows the hour of such a reformation.[80]

Yet Sadoleto also participated in the failure of the Pope and the Cardinals to reform the Church without a Council. On the other hand, as we have seen, he frequently dissented from the conciliar policy of Paul III as well as from Contarini's philosophy of reform, often a solitary in his own somewhat unsettled opinions. It may be for this reason that Sadoleto was not assigned to any of the small committees which grew out of the second reform Commission. Censured as a theologian and recently repudiated as a theorist of reform, he struck out finally on his own to deal with the issue of reunion and reconciliation.

VII

Conciliator

It was the repeated opinion of Erasmus that curial policy toward Luther and his followers was wrong from the start. If these heretics, he argued, had been handled like the Hussites, the present crisis might never have started, or at least would have been brought under control. By magnifying Luther's importance instead of ignoring him, by selecting intransigents to represent the Curia in Germany, and by failing to commit the issue to temperate and prudent heads, the Church had permitted a minor incident to become a major catastrophe.[1] As he once wrote to Sadoleto, "if this matter had been turned over to men like yourself, conditions would be less aggravated everywhere."

The tribute, however, was not entirely deserved. Sadoleto himself showed far less consistency on this haunting question than his friend imagined. In late life, to be sure, he agreed that the initial spread of heresy arose from needless severity and blundering in the Curia, but in saying so the Bishop forgot that he himself had been the author and instrument of the Pope's strong measures against Luther in 1520–21. As Domestic Secretary, for example, he composed the brief of January 18, 1521, which enjoined Charles V to publish and execute the ban against the heretics and to help the Pope "rid the Lord's vineyard of reptiles."[2] This was the brief which was intended to justify the strong turn of papal policy after publication of *Exsurge Domine* and the later *Decet Romanum Pontificem* of January 3, 1521. Erasmus, however, openly deplored Leo's new methods at the very time they appeared and found *Exsurge Domine* a document of unwarranted harshness; to him it was a "bulla terribilis" which could do nothing but fan the flames.[3]

In retrospect, however, Sadoleto adopted a rather similar if more generalized point of view. Both of the Medici Popes, he later admitted, had been guilty of ineptitude, Leo X by the use of uncompromising measures when moderation would have been effective, and Clement VII by his failure to convoke a Council or to initiate a reformation of the clergy.[4] The failure of Leo X, in other words, was one of too much severity in dealing with Luther, while Clement's was a failure of too little in reforming the Church. What we find here may be less a case of poor memory than a genuine change of heart; or more likely, the growth of a concern for reconciliation in Germany and reform in the Church about which Sadoleto seldom had troubled himself while attached to the Leonine Curia.

Yet if Sadoleto moved toward agreement with Erasmus on the original errors of the Papacy in dealing with the schism, he enjoyed less certainty about the course of future policy. He shared none of Erasmus' willingness, for example, to compromise on questions of doctrine, although with Erasmus he appealed beyond the scholastics to scriptural and patristic authority. His status was naturally more difficult and complex than that of Erasmus, who exercised great authority without the encumbrance of priestly office or accountability. Sadoleto's attitudes toward reconciliation and reunion, however, decidedly place him with the Catholic moderates of the hierarchy, far closer to Erasmus than to such advocates of force and repression as Lorenzo Campeggio, Caraffa, Cochlaeus, Eck, Johann Fabri, and Nausea.

Consistency in approaching the practical issues of reconciliation and the Council was rare among Sadoleto's contemporaries in the College except in the ranks of the conservatives. The crisis was too inscrutable, uncertainties too many and too sudden, and contact with trans-Alpine Europe too imperfect to enable any but the most doctrinaire to take assurance in their own judgment. During the last decade of his life Sadoleto vacillated within the limits of a position far less clearly defined than Erasmus', retreating to more secure ground under the rebuke and reprimand of his colleagues, and sometimes, though infrequently, adapting his opinions to those of a less conciliatory superior.[5] His late years offer a study in the reactions of a humanist in the hierarchy who was unwilling to yield on doctrine or the authority of the Church, while passionately committed to its reformation and the recovery of Christian unity. His was the anomalous predicament of the Catholic conciliator, eschewing force for persuasion and the sword for the pen, only to be rebuked by his coreligionists and ridiculed by those whom he sought to convert.

Sadoleto put his hope for reunion in a general policy of restraint and accessibility to negotiation on both sides, applying the spirit and the methods which the Medici Popes feared or rejected. More distinctly his own, however, was his faith in the utility of *rapprochement* and discussion between humanist moderates and intellectuals of each side. Sadoleto seemed to know with full certainty who such men were among the heretics. It never occurred to him that Luther himself was one of these, for the Cardinal looked upon Luther as a coarse and inflexible radical, a rabble-rouser and vile outlaw.[6] Oecolampadius, he admitted, was learned but still a militant rebel whose death he could not lament.[7] Calvin he took to be an arrogant man, driven by ambition and pride. It was not in these, but rather in men like Melanchthon, Sturm, and Bucer that he placed his hopes for contact between Rome and the Protestant world, persuaded that communication among the learned could never be destroyed in spite of doctrinal differences among them.

In June 1537, Sadoleto addressed himself on two successive days to Philip Melanchthon and Duke George of Saxony, hopeful in both cases of gaining the confidence of men with whom he had had no direct contact whatever. The seeming irony of his turning simultaneously to prominent leaders of hostile parties is more apparent than real.[8] Sadoleto evidently looked upon Duke George, of all the German princes, as one whose views were most consonant with his own; here, he felt, was not only a serious champion of the faith, but likewise a magnanimous man, the advocate of a Christian reformation and reunion of the churches.[9]

Sadoleto's first letter to the Duke, written from Rome on June 18, 1537, is largely a review of his own career and an apologia which interprets his service to the Medici Popes, his distress in their failure as reformers, and his recent return to the Curia. Sadoleto wrote as a Cardinal to an influential Catholic layman, pledging unsolicited support to one who may have concluded that he was seeking new patronage abroad.[10] But Sadoleto's real interest, to judge by subsequent letters, was to inform himself through the Duke of the religious condition of Germany, if not to test his own views on reunion and reconciliation against those of a Catholic prince in close contact with the Lutherans.

On June 17 Sadoleto wrote his celebrated letter to Melanchthon, greeting hin affectionately as "mi Philippe," "mi doctissime Melanchthon."[11] Here again Sadoleto introduced himself, writing quite as cordially as he did to Duke George, but now as one humanist to another in the "super-confessional community" of the learned.[12] Sadoleto's name and reputation had long been known in German Protestant circles, however, so that he was no stranger to Wittenberg. Commenting on the letter to Melanchthon, Luther described the author as one "who was a papal secretary for fifteen years, certainly an able and cultivated man . . . but cunning and artful withal, in the Italian manner. . . ." Luther also repeated his observation that Sadoleto had no understanding of theology and surmised that in writing to Melanchthon he was only preparing the way to bribe Philip back to Rome, perhaps at papal instigation, with the offer of a red hat.[13] Such a rumor, though chronic in Wittenberg, seems hardly to explain Sadoleto's intentions, although his motives are not entirely self-evident.

The letter is brief and respectful. It was written, he said, out of admiration for Melanchthon's works, which he had read with great pleasure, and from a natural desire to have the friendship of so learned a man. Sadoleto explained that efforts to write sooner had been cut off by a papal summons to Rome, referring almost with embarrassment to his renewed identity with the Curia and wistfully to his life as a Bishop:

It is difficult to explain how I was taken away from my erstwhile life of calm and contentment and brought into one so tumultuous and heavy with strife, or how many cares and concerns have afflicted me. . . . I once abandoned this kind of existence, by my own resolve, to seek the other; . . . I cannot rejoice in having what I did not want, and naturally regret having lost what I loved. But because God's will toward us is to be obeyed, we shall strive, through whatever aid and strength he gives us, to conduct ourselves honorably and righteously [i.e., as a Cardinal]. It is the purpose of my letter, *mi Philippe*, to say that I can no longer contain my desire . . . to express assurances of my cordial disposition toward you and the hope of yours for me: if in my affection for you I yield to my high opinion of your virtues, then you will be obliged, by your own generous nature, to receive me in the same manner. You will not deny me my longing for your friendship. For I am not one to despise a man whose opinion dissents from my own. Such is the conduct of a man proud in his own conceits, rather than gentle and kind, as I am by nature. I admire talent and virtue, and value the study of letters.[14]

Writing in his most studied and elegant style, Sadoleto followed this with further declarations of praise and esteem, setting no conditions on his invitation to friendship or to the suggestion that they enter into correspondence, "so that we who are separated by space may be joined in good will."

The letter made a considerable impression on Melanchthon, who sent copies to Camerarius and Veit Dietrich with generous comment on its Latinity; but he was reluctant to say more or to have the letter circulated.[15] News of the letter spread rapidly, however, first in Wittenberg and then all over Germany. Taken unawares by one whom he had previously noticed only as an antagonist, Melanchthon acted guardedly: "I have not yet answered Sadoleto," he told Camerarius, "but will soon write a reply which I shall send to you. I shall speak about personal friendship, as he did, and say nothing about public controversies."[16] But several weeks later, at the end of October, he was still undecided and so too were his friends.[17] In February of 1538 he spoke again of answering the Cardinal, although resenting the implication that Sadoleto might have expected by a single gesture to lead him and indeed all Germans meekly back to Rome—as though, he later added, by one compelling song from a curial

Orpheus.[18] By March he knew that Sadoleto was offended at the silence from Wittenberg; but having seen the *Consilium de emendanda ecclesia*, Melanchthon was shocked by the prohibition of Erasmus' *Colloquies* in a document signed by Sadoleto and Aleander.[19] From this he concluded that Sadoleto's humanism, like his religious tolerance, was fraudulent. Melanchthon never replied, and the spurious letter of Michael Braccetto, written to Sadoleto in Philip's name, came to nothing.[20]

With the exception of Osiander's passing curiosity, Melanchthon's friends showed no signs of suspicion to find that he had been approached so ingratiatingly by a Roman Cardinal. Sadoleto, on the other hand, enjoyed no such impunity, and while Melanchthon was pondering a response which he never made Sadoleto was greeted by a blast of Catholic protest from Germany. His principal critics, all men with long experience in the German Church, included Johann Dobneck, or Cochlaeus, court preacher to Duke George of Saxony; Johann Eck, the Ingolstadt professor whose effort against Luther Sadoleto had once praised as a papal secretary[21]; Friedrich Nausea, who once tried and failed to convert Melanchthon, and was now court preacher to King Ferdinand and Coadjutor in the diocese of Vienna; and Johann Fabri, Bishop of Vienna.[22] Together they formed the hard core of Catholic conservatism in Germany and represented the uncompromising position which Erasmus so often deplored. That Sadoleto should deliberately seek Melanchthon's friendship, and that such a letter should have been written in Rome, left them shocked and angry.

Evidently the first to react, Cochlaeus wrote Aleander from Meissen on October 7, 1538, to remind him that the Church had no greater or more dangerous enemy anywhere than Philip Melanchthon.[23] By placing his undeniable literary talents in the service of heresy, Cochlaeus warned, he has not only alienated large numbers of German youth from the Church but has strengthened the defiance of Henry VIII and inflamed the Scandinavians with hatred of Rome. Sadoleto's preposterous letter, by then circulating widely in Germany, has done more for Luther's cause than ten of Luther's own books. Cochlaeus urged Aleander to remonstrate with Sadoleto secretly and civilly, but

with the suggestion that he "hold the Church dearer to himself than
its most frightful enemy." Fabri was no less outspoken when he wrote
directly to Sadoleto in January 1538.[24] By then, he reported, the letter
was common property even outside Germany, to the astonishment of
Catholics and the glee of Lutherans, who now claimed to have won
a convert in the Sacred College itself! Acknowledging the severity of
his language, Fabri went on to say that Catholics scarcely expect such
blandishments from the Roman *cathedra*, whatever the magnitude of
Melanchthon's learning and Latinity. And like Cochlaeus, Bishop
Fabri found little in the Cardinal's attitude to show that he recognized
the heretic within the humanist.

   The exchange of views which Sadoleto provoked reveals something
of the breakdown in effective communication between the German
Episcopate and the Curia which the nuncios manifestly failed to
repair. Eck, Nausea, and Fabri regarded Sadoleto's conduct as the sign
of unbelievable naïveté and ignorance on his part and possibly even of
curial approval for such advances. The incident also exposed the wide
disagreement over Catholic policy in Germany which both Sadoleto
and his critics recognized. While the issue of Sadoleto's letter to
Melanchthon was still being discussed (as it was for several years),
Cochlaeus warned Giovanni Morone, the young nuncio to Germany,
that "neither the King of England nor the Lutheran princes will be
brought back to the true faith by persuasion or flattery, but only if
coerced by terror and the fear of force . . ."[25]

   Sadoleto was quick to recognize the implications of his position and
its remoteness from that of his German critics. Although his first
letters to Morone and Nausea are missing, those which belong to a
second exchange disclose a complete refusal of self-criticism and
remorse. His letter to Nausea on November 23, 1537, is a forthright
defense of his judgment in writing to a man "whose talent I admire,
whose learning I appreciate, and whose beliefs, obviously, I do not
share."[26] What offense is there, he demanded, in trying to approach
this man with the purpose of bringing him back to the Church, or of
observing simple courtesy in doing so? How can one's orthodoxy be
called into doubt by such a letter or the College dishonored? When he

wrote to Fabri in February,[27] Sadoleto made it clear that the tone of
the letter to Melanchthon was intentionally cordial because he wanted
to secure the confidence of a man worth saving. He bluntly added that
those who proceed "more contentiously and spitefully" have little
enough to show for their efforts, and reiterated his belief that the present
bitterness and sedition would never exist if clemency and restraint
had been followed from the start.

On the other hand, the uncompromising certainty of his German
critics had raised real doubts for Sadoleto, who concealed them before
Nausea and Fabri while admitting to Duke George that

I am uncertain as to how I should act toward [the Lutherans], whether rigorously
and sharply, or courteously and affably. It seems to me that the first method
could have had no worse results for those who have applied it. When I attempted the other and wrote to certain of them humanely and civilly, I know
how badly my effort was received by many of your people in Germany, who
attacked me either for having written to heretics, or for doing so in that
manner. If mine was a lapse in judgment, it was certainly not one of zeal or
piety. . . . Therefore, most excellent Duke, I beseech your distinguished
opinion, to which I will always give the greatest authority, as to whether I acted
wisely or not. You who have instructed me in standards of judgment and the
rules of general conduct in matters of this kind, will continue to be my guide.[28]

As early as October 1537 Morone had given Sadoleto his private
approval of the letter to Wittenberg, showing, as Sadoleto put it,
that "you have thoroughly understood the purpose and intent of my
writing . . ."[29] Morone at the same time informed the Cardinal of
the furor which his letter had touched off, and complied with a request
from Paolo Sadoleto that the Cardinal be notified of later developments.[30] Morone admitted that although discerning Catholics quickly
forgot about the letter to Melanchthon, those whose religion was
mainly a matter of hating and abusing the Lutherans still discussed it
because they were unable to understand it in the first place. He
advised Sadoleto not to try to justify himself to such persons; and in
giving his own views on Catholic policy toward the heretics used the
same language which we have already noticed in Erasmus and Sadoleto:

. . . it is far better to treat these modern heretics with clemency than to try to antagonize them with insults! and if from the start such a manner had been observed, the reunion of the Church might now be a simple matter.[31]

The nuncio was certain that wilful provocation of the Lutherans by various Catholic zealots had produced nothing but deeper hatred and bitterness.

Morone found himself drawn into another but more doubtful effort at conciliation, which also involved Sadoleto. In October 1537 the Dean of Passau, Rupert Mosheim (or Mosham), wrote to Paul III of his private plan for ecclesiastical reunion and expressed the desire to present it to the Pope in person.[32] At the same time he wrote Sadoleto, taking his sympathies for granted, and asked for the Cardinal's active support. Having met Mosheim in Prague and being aware of his design for reform, Morone informed Ambrosio Ricalcati, the papal secretary, that the Dean's thoughts were incomprehensible and his theology suspect.[33] Without knowing anything about Mosheim, however, Sadoleto replied to him on November 22, sending the letter by way of Morone together with another for Nausea.[34] Sadoleto's remarks to the Dean have not come down to us, but in the opinion of Johann Eck, who evidently read the letter, they were even more outrageous than those made to Melanchthon. Eck took this as another needless blunder which further damaged the prestige of the Holy See and showed Sadoleto again "too ready to write to these fools."[35]

At least to men like Eck and Fabri, Sadoleto's charity for Melanchthon and Mosheim was nothing less than scandalous. To us, on the simple appearance of these letters, he may also seem a victim of ignorance or innocence, of quixotic self-deception or blindness to the real issues of the schism. But the perspective of Fabri from Vienna or for that matter of Melanchthon in Wittenberg is only partial; and while the outcome of the schism vindicated Fabri and Luther rather than Sadoleto and Morone, it is with their immediate point of view that we are concerned here.

Furthermore, in relating Sadoleto and his critics to the issues of their generation we meet some bizarre contradictions among sincere and intelligent men who shared a common concern for the welfare of the faith. One measure of judgment is Erasmus himself. It was he whom

Sadoleto had repeatedly urged to avoid fruitless conflicts with Catholic extremists, and he whom Sadoleto once found too cordial toward Wittenberg.[36] It was Erasmus, in turn, who first but vainly tried to warn Sadoleto against the dangers of controversialist theology after reading the Bishop's Commentaries on Romans. Sadoleto, evidently too harsh for his colleagues in his advice on reforming the clergy, nonetheless put his hand to the prohibition of Erasmus' *Colloquies*, a form of disloyalty which Melanchthon regarded with angry contempt. Yet Friedrich Nausea, who turned so virulently on Sadoleto for his praise of Melanchthon, was also the author of a treatise in 1536 which describes Erasmus as "the most illustrious ornament of the Church," the "splendor of the earth and the wonder of the ages."[37] In the year before his death Erasmus used almost the same language to describe Sadoleto.[38] This was a time, moreover, when the mild Contarini was a leading patron of the early Jesuits, while the austere and militant Caraffa remained their hostile opponent. In December 1536, while Contarini and his colleagues worked at the *Consilium* for Paul III, nine partisans of Ignatius Loyola entered the basilica at Basle, "in the manner of pilgrim scholars," to pay homage at the sepulchre of Erasmus.[39] And Etienne Dolet, once the author of a tract denouncing Erasmus and the Protestant reformers, later dedicated a Latin treatise redolent with Lutheran doctrine to Cardinal Sadoleto,[40] whose own theology had been attacked for its semi-Pelagian excesses in the refutation of Luther. The defects of communication in Catholic circles were a matter not simply of distance but likewise of confusion in defining the issues, and it was such confusion which in no small way made the Council necessary. The images of Melanchthon and his conduct as Luther's spokesman reveal as many anomalies on the other side.

B̲efore he had been back in Rome a year, Sadoleto fell seriously ill again, plagued by recurrent fevers which left him almost incapacitated during the winter months of 1537–38. His affliction was probably a form of malaria, although whether it was the severe tropical form which took the life of Alexander VI among its first victims is impossible to know. Sadoleto periodically complained of fevers for nearly a year at this time but only later used the word "terzana,"[41] presumably to refer to the "tertian fever," a milder kind of malaria usually found in temperate regions. Robust in stature, bearded in the manner of Julius II, with the verticals of his beard and long, narrow nose imparting a somewhat mephistophelean aspect to his features, Sadoleto gave the appearance of considerable if rather awkward strength; but throughout his life he fell prey to illness, pulmonary and intestinal, as well as to cycles of chills and fever which increased with old age.

In January 1538 he was appointed to another commission,[42] this one instructed to work through the snarled questions of conciliar organization and procedure before the twice-prorogued Council opened on May 1 at Vicenza. While Sadoleto languished in his Vatican apartment, his eight colleagues struggled to adapt conciliar doctrine to the current crisis but found themselves too much divided in purpose and perspective to accomplish the task assigned to them. Now that debate in the College had turned from internal reform to the issues of reunion and the Council, the margin of agreement between Caraffa and Contarini steadily narrowed, foreboding the imminent collapse of the consistorial center.

For the moment, however, the urgency of preparing for the Council diminished before the Pope's renewed efforts to end the war between Francis I and Charles V. Believing that the Council was futile so long as hostilities continued, Paul III set out in March for a meeting with the princes at Nice in hopes of negotiating a lasting settlement between them. He therefore decided to postpone the Council indefinitely on April 25. Sadoleto was still too weak to take his place in the huge papal suite when it left Rome on March 23 but managed to overtake it several weeks later at Parma.[43] The price of this exertion was an acute relapse, so that the journey to Savona was especially difficult. Nevertheless he was able to remain with the papal court and was taken aboard one of the imperial triremes which carried the Curia to Nice late in May.

The congress at Nice was staged in the most lavish style of sixteenth-century diplomacy with the three principals attended by over two thousand retainers. During the two weeks of negotiation, however, the princes refused to meet one another face to face although each received the ambassadors of the other and consulted in person with the Pope in a Franciscan monastery east of the city. While the two hostile courts remained in elegant isolation, the Pope was obliged to operate through "flying legates" to the King and his rival. Sadoleto took part in public discussions with the ambassadors and in private conversations with each ruler, but served in no formal diplomatic capacity.[44] After Marguerite de Navarre arrived on June 8, together with Queen Eléonore, Sadoleto and Contarini met the King's sister at a banquet which the Pope arranged in her honor. There she and the Cardinals are said to have discussed theology together in what was probably one of the few congenial moments of the congress.[45] The political talks ended in a feeble compromise; the ten-year truce signed on June 18 only signalled the difficulty of peace and further darkened the prospects of the Council.

By the time Paul III returned to Rome Sadoleto was again at Carpentras, granted leave for a brief sojourn to recover his health. Looking back on the congress, the Cardinal was unwilling to commit himself on the present outlook for the Council and judged its chances thus to Pflug and Cochlaeus:

Whether or not it will take place I cannot say. Nevertheless, I continue to hope that it will remain a concern of the Pope: he [now] speaks confidently about it. Nor have I the means of knowing at this time what the Council can accomplish. In the first place, it depends not only on the Pope but equally upon the princes, and they appear to me to be concerned with other things, especially with a war against the Turks. Moreover, neither do I really know, nor if I knew would I dare say, what the outcome of a Council would be. I do believe that a great deal might be accomplished for the benefit of the Church if the Pope by himself undertakes to correct the moral condition of the Church, as indeed he promises he will.[46]

For his part Sadoleto was now moving toward an opinion which Paul III was not yet willing to accept. The Cardinal seemed to feel that if reform, and even perhaps the Council, were to take place at all, it would have to be done on the Pope's initiative, irrespective of the will of the princes.[47]

Sadoleto's anxiety over these issues was tempered by his joy in returning to Carpentras, where he arrived late in June 1538 to the tearful delight of his people.[48] With the Council prorogued there was little to occupy the College until autumn. Contarini also took advantage of this respite by spending the rest of the summer in his diocese at Belluno, on the edge of the Dolomites, temporarily assured that he was not needed in Rome.[49]

Although Jacopo's fevers persisted, a sense of well-being came back as he reached the Comtat, the result, he assumed, of "this climate and place, indeed of this freedom."[50] It seemed better not even to think about leaving at the end of the summer, but September promptly brought Cardinal Farnese's reminder that he was expected in the City immediately. Sadoleto had already resolved to wait until spring and admitted as much to his friends before requesting formal permission to stay on from the Vice-Chancellor and the Pope on October 15.[51] Aware that the work of the reform commissions was to resume and that he had been given only temporary leave from the Curia, Sadoleto at considerable length attempted to excuse himself from a prior commitment to the Pope. He conceded that it was no longer the state of his health which prevented compliance, but rather the condition of his finances. It was the high cost of living in Rome and the low level of his income which made it more advisable, he argued, to serve the Church in Carpentras; and at least for the present he refused to accept the Pope's previous offer of additional funds in the form of an annual cameral stipend.[52] Here Sadoleto emphatically drew a line between annual and monthly grants *ex aerario* on the one hand, and the kind of income that is intrinsically sacerdotal, publicly entrusted to priests for the performance of a priestly charge, on the other. He added that even if he should now go back to Rome, his presence would contribute nothing to the wisdom of those already there.

The complaint of poverty was hereafter to be more chronic and insistent than that of bad health in Sadoleto's relations with the Holy

See.[53] The fear of added financial obligation and the feeling that he could not afford to live as a prince of the Church had troubled Sadoleto from the moment of his nomination in 1536.[54] Seldom free from debt,[55] encumbered by provision for his nephews and recurrently by the needs of older kinsmen in Ferrara, he took the position that it was financially impossible to settle and stay in Rome. What sufficed to maintain him in his domestic and pastoral obligations at Carpentras was not enough, he claimed, even to support a household in Rome except on borrowed money.

This kind of problem was not uncommon. Contarini eventually found the costs of keeping up a Roman household to be prohibitive and therefore sent his household to Padua in 1542. But it is as difficult to test the reality of Sadoleto's embarrassment as it is to determine the extent of his resources. The diocese itself was worth 1,600 or 1,700 ducats and the pension at Verona around 600, but he had already assigned the latter to certain nephews.[56] If we include the revenue from smaller benefices and that which he received as a Cardinal, we may estimate his gross income for these years at something close to 4,200 ducats.[57] In view of the steady rise of prices in Italy, which Sadoleto was quick to notice,[58] this figure relative to the average income of Italian colleagues in the College was probably rather modest. Certain Cardinals in the conclave of 1524, for example, enjoyed ecclesiastical revenue as high as 50,000 ducats a year, although Lorenzo Campeggio's was only 3,000 and Cajetan's 2,000. However, Loyola had required only twenty-five ducats per year while studying in Paris.[59] Sadoleto's resources never stabilized and show signs of fluctuation and growth from the moment he entered the Sacred College. Was the monthly stipend of 200 ducats cut off, for example, when he left the Curia in the summer of 1538? Perhaps for a time it was; in a letter to Pole in 1540 Jacopo referred to his having unexpectedly received through Contarini's intervention "a share in those monies which are customarily distributed [only?] among those present" in Rome.[60] But what then was the monthly *subsidium* for which Sadoleto thanked the Pope three months earlier?[61] In 1542 he acknowledged receipt of vouchers for 500 scudi from the Datary "for my support for a month," asking that in the future such funds be deposited for him at Lyons to avoid delays while abroad on a papal mission.[62]

Sadoleto had no private funds with which to supplement his ecclesiastical income, having given up his share in Giovanni's estate to his brothers[63]; and was persuaded that he could give only the appearance of a poor priest, or at least of a modest prelate from a rural see, but certainly not of a Cardinal.[64] Now more than ever he became the sensitive *borghése*, fearing the "ridicule of the College" since he was required in Rome to associate with well-born colleagues from old and wealthy Italian dynasties whose means and manner of living lay far beyond his own.

Sadoleto's discomfort in the College may throw some light on the social status, real or imaginary, of other bourgeois humanists and prelates of his generation. Whereas the artist and writer encountered few obstacles in the path of recognition or minor preferment in the Church, major stations in the Italian hierarchy were generally reserved for the nobility. The Italian Episcopate, for example, was all but monopolized by aristocrats.[65] Once the dependent of patrons like Oliviero Caraffa and Fregoso, Sadoleto became the nominal peer of such men in his progress through the hierarchy, which was made possible by his reputation as a humanist. But with respect to wealth and social status his position in the College was anomalous, a condition to which he was highly sensitive. The feeling of his own singularity, acute in 1527 but more poignant as a Cardinal, may thus be the reaction not just of the humanist, but no less of the bourgeois Bishop and prince of the Church, ill at ease amid the wealth and mannered elegance of his colleagues in the College.

Yet the lack of money was not the only kind of malaise he experienced in Rome, for Sadoleto was never wholly at peace with himself while away from his books. If disqualified from serving the faith by means of wealth and status, he could still do so by his writing.[66] This self-picture was one which Sadoleto tirelessly elaborated; as he once told Guillaume du Bellay, he was a "simple man," too unsophisticated and unpolished to think of accepting a place in the court of Francis I. Beneath the appearance of modesty, however, was the desire to avoid the active life at virtually any cost. So, in November 1538, Sadoleto was again deep in his studies and thriving *in otio* not knowing whether his excuses for delaying his return to Rome were acceptable to the Curia or not.

Negri, that compulsive bearer of ill report, soon wrote that friends and enemies alike were unimpressed by the Cardinal's reasons for remaining at Carpentras.[67] The plea of poverty was rejected, he wrote, because others in the College stayed on to serve His Holiness even under a similar handicap; moreover, it was generally agreed that the times were such that stately living was unbecoming anyway. Others claimed that "you received your promotion with unseemly indifference, placing less value upon it than on your own convenience and comfort ..." More neutral observers stated that Sadoleto was elevated to the College not so that he would abandon the Curia but to stay in Rome to assist the Pope, who had honored him so generously.

Through continuing absence Sadoleto was neglecting a particular assignment which Paul III had given him before leaving Rome.[68] He had been instructed to direct a broad and thorough reform of an Italian monastic order, the Girolamiti (Hieronymites) or Eremites of St. Jerome of the congregation of Pietro di Pisa.[69] Originally introduced to Italy from Spain in the fourteenth century, this congregation now consisted of forty houses under two provincials and had fallen into scandalous indiscipline. Before departing for Nice Sadoleto had made an investigation of the order through two procurators, whose findings he called incredible. So he ordered a general chapter to convene at Ferrara in the spring of 1539, but decided in August of the previous year to ask Caraffa to assume responsibility for holding two preliminary chapters—probably one for each province—as soon as possible.[70] In other words Caraffa was to act for Sadoleto, but the Cardinal refused on the grounds that he was then too busy with other matters.[71]

As his departure for Rome was postponed from one season to the next, Sadoleto later tried to enlist the help of Benedetto Accolti and Contarini, to whom he wrote twice on this subject during the summer of 1539, and later of Tommaso Campeggio.[72] Tentative reform of the order was begun in 1540 by its general, Bernardo di Verona, and Campeggio evidently took further measures in 1541, causing Sadoleto to assume that little remained to be done.[73] But the general chapter had not yet taken place. Pole refused to involve himself in it and advised Campeggio not to do anything further until Sadoleto returned to Italy that spring.[74] The general chapter was not held until 1549, two years after Sadoleto's death; and whatever his initial interest may have been, there is nothing to show that he ever actively shared in its preparation.

In the meanwhile a summer's leave stretched out into an absence of four years. If the Hieronymites were abandoned to their own devices, the diocese of Carpentras unquestionably profited from the presence of Sadoleto, once again a resident Bishop and only the very titular Cardinal S. Calisto. So far as possible he again assumed the role and style of life so painfully abandoned in 1536, dedicating himself to the Comtat and its relations with Avignon and Rome, scrutinizing the conduct of the Legation and boasting that he had checked the spread of heresy which broke out during his sojourn in Italy.[75] But even stronger than his attachment to the welfare of the diocese was his interest in letters and his desire to write.

The character of his writing during these years and for the rest of his life indicates, however, a distinct change from the themes which had occupied the first period of retirement. If he sought then to complete the work of earlier inspiration, largely literary and philosophic, before turning to theology, in this second interval of retirement he became more often the ecclesiastic, drawing subject matter out of his recent experience in Rome and from his own somewhat shifting views on reconciliation with the Protestants. If he appeared to some to have forsaken the burdens of his new office, he still accepted the accountability of a humanist prince of the Church who was identified with the labors of Catholic Reform and the Council. What continuity there was between his service on the second reform Commission and his life at Carpentras lay, therefore, in his writing—in his letter to Johann Sturm of July 1538, his Exhortation to the Princes and People of

Germany (spring and summer of 1538), and his open letter to the Genevans (early 1539).

The letter to Sturm developed directly from the illicit publication of the Reform Commission's *Consilium de emendanda ecclesia*, which was widely circulated in Germany during the latter months of 1537.[76] Luther first saw it in vernacular translation early in 1538 and soon acquired a printed copy of the Latin original.[77] Later in the year it was twice published in Rome, without the Vatican's prior knowledge, and again in Milan and Cesena. In fact, so carefully had the document been guarded in Catholic circles that when Cochlaeus saw it in March 1538 he demanded to know whether it was authentic or merely a forgery by the heretics.

The memorial reached Sturm and his friends at Strasbourg just as it had reached Cochlaeus in Meissen, exactly a year after it was presented in consistory. Then Rector of the *Hohe Schule* in Strasbourg, Sturm belonged to the moderate wing of Protestantism which had not yet despaired of ultimate reconciliation with Rome. He also shared a measure of Sadoleto's confidence in communication between sincere and learned men of both sides, while like his theological mentor, the apostate Dominican Martin Bucer, he held high hope in Paul III as a partisan of reunion. But the effect of the *Consilium* on Sturm was to disappoint these expectations, and it was in order to express his disillusion that Sturm—no doubt on Bucer's urging—replied to the authors of the memorial. His letter, dated April 3, 1538, appeared as a preface to the *Consilium* itself, which was published by the Protestant press at Strasbourg.[78]

Generally temperate and never malicious, Sturm's letter is the effort of an irenic Protestant to appraise the work of Contarini's Commission and the progress of Catholic reform. He congratulated the deputies for their attack on extremist theories of papal power and for their willingness to demand that the Pope's authority be bound by the ancient laws of the Church. To hold, as the *Consilium* does, that "the Pope must honor the same laws which he wishes the Church to obey," is to make a concession which removes "a very great part of the controversy between us." But the body of the letter was concerned with the defects of the memorial, and in Sturm's view the most serious of these was its failure to examine the disputed issues of Christian doctrine. Why, he asked, was there no discussion of religious ceremonies and the sacraments, and not a word about indulgences? Why no attention to popular ignorance of the Gospel or to the problems of theological instruction?

Sturm goes on to prescribe various reform measures of his own, including the convocation of a prosynod consisting of representatives from both parties to deliberate on the issues of reform in advance of the Council.[79] He distinguished the Cardinal-deputies from those whose only purpose was to exterminate the Lutherans, for in Contarini and his colleagues Sturm found both the will and the authority to rebuild the dignity of the Church; but he also warned them of the obstacles in their path, as though to remind the deputies that theirs was a small voice.

Although his references to Contarini and Fregoso were entirely sympathetic, Sturm tended to deal with Sadoleto more severely, largely on the basis of what Sadoleto had written in his Commentaries on St. Paul.[80] Sturm found him willing not only to undertake the defense of Clement VII as a worthy Pope and righteous Christian, but also to judge the doctrine and works of Luther without knowing them at first hand.

Sturm's edition of the *Consilium* drew widespread interest and attention in northern Europe. Such was its sale in Saxony that Cochlaeus was unable to find a copy by mid-July, and in the meantime it had received particular notice in Paris. His letter to the Cardinals became widely known to the Catholic hierarchy, in which reaction ran from hostility to indifference.[81] The indefatigable Cochlaeus lost little time in answering Sturm,[82] who likewise felt the wrath of Johann Eck. But while theirs was the broader interest of German Catholic polemicists, Sadoleto's was the private concern of an injured party.

The Strasbourg Rector's remarks to the Cardinals must certainly have been on his mind before leaving Italy for Nice and Provence, because the reply to Sturm was among the first letters he wrote from

Carpentras after the congress ended.[83] The letter, dated July 15, 1538, may well have been meant to make up for the ill-fated overture to Melanchthon from Rome a year earlier. In any case, he was far more alert to the judgment of others and on this occasion he cautiously circulated his reply both in Germany and Italy before sending it to Strasbourg. Indeed nine months elapsed before Sadoleto's letter was known in Wittenberg and a year before it reached Sturm in the author's own hand.[84]

Although Sadoleto's manner in this letter is less ingratiating than it was in writing to Melanchthon, his position remained the same, so that he also approached Sturm as a learned man worthy of respect. Sadoleto either would not or could not restrain his conviction that letters and learning bind men together with ties which are unbroken by doctrinal differences. Notwithstanding Cochlaeus and his friends, he still believed that Latinity is the "mediator of good will." The same longing for common agreement is present here and the same profession of friendship for men like Bucer and Melanchthon. On the other hand, there are patronizing intervals in this letter which cannot be found in the letter to Wittenberg. Sturm was charged with the misuse of his talents, with the practice of calumny and a want of *humanitas* which, Sadoleto added, is expected only in men like Luther. But after taxing Sturm for an "atrocity" of usage in his letter to the Cardinals,[85] Sadoleto went on to say that his judgments on the heretics in the Commentaries were intended for Luther alone, and not for the like of Sturm, still unknown to him when the dialogue was written. If Sadoleto further intended here to refute the charge that he had attacked Lutheran doctrine without having read Luther's works, he did so very obliquely indeed, finding himself embarrassed by a question to which it was impossible to give an answer acceptable to Catholic and Protestant readers alike. Quickly and somewhat evasively he moved on to say that Sturm for his part had condemned Clement VII without knowledge of the man, and concluded by comparing his own epistolary *humanitas* with Sturm's reckless accusations. And yet in the last line Sadoleto reaffirmed his personal affection for Sturm, Melanchthon, and Bucer. This brief letter of Sadoleto's, however, wholly neglected to meet Sturm on the ground he had taken in his letter to the Cardinals, which criticized them severely for their silence on the doctrinal issue of the schism. Jacopo solved the problem of rebuttal largely by ignoring it.

Even though Sadoleto was careful this time not to approach Sturm as an equal, having conceded that he might have addressed Melanchthon "more humbly" than befits a Cardinal,[86] he reminded Cochlaeus again that Christian decency requires one to plead gently (*leniter*) with such persons and to avoid recrimination. But such lessons were lost on both Protestant and Catholic rigorists in Germany. Luther interpreted Sadoleto's letter to Sturm not as the song of Orpheus but as the "baseness of the devil," who seeks to alienate righteous men from the Gospel. "That Sadoleto," he warned, "really wants Philip, not Sturm." Luther added that if Melanchthon acquiesced, he could go to Rome—with wife and children—to be made a Cardinal,[87] while Cochlaeus, who also heard rumors that the Holy See was renewing its efforts to tempt Melanchthon to Italy, repeated his admonitions to the Curia. Once again he urged Contarini to recognize the danger of hoping to reason with men like Sturm, Melanchthon, and Bucer, and of Sadoleto's folly in trying to do so. Eck for different reasons found nothing to distinguish the letter to Sturm from those to Mosheim and Melanchthon, and the professor again conveyed his anxious irritation to Bishop Fabri and Contarini.[88] For the present, however, Rome took no visible steps to silence or chasten Sadoleto, although Eck and Cochlaeus were ultimately vindicated, for Sadoleto's letter to Sturm was placed on the *Index* of 1559.[89]

Sadoleto's gestures toward Melanchthon and Sturm generated far wider interest than his one general treatise on the Lutheran schism. Completed in the early summer of 1538,[90] the *Ad principes populosque Germaniae exhortatio gravissima* was never published in Sadoleto's lifetime, although it circulated briefly among friends and critics in Germany and Italy. That this open letter to the Germans was perhaps the least noticed and the most abortive of his works seems largely to be explained by its indifferent reception at the court of Duke George of Saxony. It merits attention, however, as an important disclosure of

Sadoleto's more public interpretation of the schism in Germany and the nature of Protestantism.

The Exhortation in many ways resembles the letter to the Genevans which Sadoleto composed the following spring. Each is a highly-charged polemic with respect, at least, to the leadership and doctrine of the Lutheran and Calvinist heresies. Each is a plea for the restoration of Christian unity and therefore becomes an argument for reconciliation, albeit on narrowing terms, being directed only toward the moderates on the assumption that the more radical leaders of the movement were quite beyond reach. In both treatises Sadoleto openly acknowledged the doctrinal issue, critically relating the theology of Luther and Calvin to the dogmatic tradition of the Church as one who had taken upon himself the exposure of Protestant error. In both instances, moreover, he wrote as a Cardinal, without having previously discussed his purpose or point of view with his colleagues.

The letter to the Germans attempts to make a global interpretation of the Lutheran movement in that Sadoleto tried here to find a relationship between leaders and followers, to deal with the role of abuses in the rise of heresy, and to unmask the corruption of doctrine by Lutheran theologians. The instigators of the movement, he noticed, had set themselves up to be the bearers of a new and purer knowledge of the Gospel, but what, he asked, is their authority? If they repudiate tradition—the word of God and the works of the Apostles, the interpretation of the Fathers and the Councils—then they insist upon serving as judges in their own cause. He charged that Lutheran doctrine appeals only to ignorance and simplicity, or to hatred; to rustics and generally not to men of learning. The innovators are men choked with ambition and vanity, driven on by their own destructive fury. Yet in trying to separate Luther from his more learned and less aggressive followers, Sadoleto restated his desire for discussion and the exchange of views with men presumably like Melanchthon, for example, who were said to share his own distaste for violence and disorder.[91]

At this point Sadoleto concedes that a wave of abuses was allowed to spread through the Catholic clergy, the Curia and especially the German Church after an earlier holiness had run its course.[92] He praised the decision of the Germans at the Diet of Speyer to submit their *gravamina* to the Holy See and promised fuller redress of such grievances in the general Council promoted by Paul III.[93] He described himself as one who had opposed the sale of indulgences under Leo X and who would not defend them now. But memory is a blind servant. As Domestic Secretary Sadoleto himself had drawn up for Leo X the bull of March 31, 1515, which enabled Albert of Brandenburg to collect the notorious indulgence at Mainz and Magdeburg, while several years later he persuaded the Pope to authorize the sale of a plenary indulgence to expedite the building of the new cathedral at Carpentras.[94]

It was perfectly true, he admitted, that the condition of the Roman Curia had long given cause for criticism, the origin of such corruption being the same avarice which makes reform a slow and difficult process, the same avarice which besets men and institutions everywhere. But the present Pope, he said, has already initiated the work of reform through the recent Commission of Nine, while the conduct of the heretics is only negative and destructive. Abuses therefore are "our fault," but disorder and sedition in Germany are "yours."[95] It is one thing to protest against corruption in the Church, but why seek to overthrow all Christendom? It is one thing to remonstrate against specific misuse of papal authority, but quite another to deny that "he who serves at the altar must live by the altar," or to deny authority to the Pope over the Christian world. Sadoleto was willing to say that abuses had supplied a pretext for rebellion to the heretics, repeating what he had told the deputies on reform in his oration of November 1536, and to echo what Contarini had written to the Pope in elaborating the purpose of the *Consilium*. The fact that a third of the Exhortation was given to a discussion of abuses indicates once more the extent to which he was willing to involve the Papacy and the *Sacerdotium* in responsibility for the schism.[96]

But he gave just as much attention to what he considered the deliberate distortion of doctrine by the heretics, or more precisely by their early leaders, whom he accused of inventing new dogma as a means of creating disorder.[97] If the Catholic side could be charged with the abuse of authority, so, too, could the heretics be held responsible for the corruption of dogma. The false doctrine of justification *sola fide*, in Sadoleto's view, was artfully contrived to inspire rebellion, to liberate men from spiritual and moral responsibility, and to release their most violent passions. While the Gospel enjoins peace and unity, the Lutherans have stirred up strife and dissension; they have created a swarm of warring sects and armed the common people against their leaders, plundering the Churches more wantonly than the Turks—and all this by the arbitrary warrant of justification by faith.

Sadoleto then attempted his own refutation of the central themes of Lutheran theology.[98] It was here for the first time, rather than in the Commentaries on Romans, that he undertook a fully polemical argument, for by contrast the earlier work belongs to the category of exegesis and apologetics. In the Exhortation he wanted to demonstrate the fallacy of justification *sola fide* by the use of contravening texts in order to show that Luther had refused to consider the whole Gospel. The method was loosely dialectical in that Sadoleto began with Luther's basic passages from St. Paul in support of justification by faith,[99] turning thereupon to texts which provide what he called the "testimony of good works,"[100] and finally to the "principle of synthesis" (*ratio concordiae*) by which seeming contradiction is reduced to harmony. Sadoleto's conclusions are first brought to rest on Corinthians 13:13, which he cited in order to challenge Luther for debasing charity to the order of works. His intent here was to demonstrate the nature of justice and the conjunction of faith, charity, and works with hope. The *ratio concordiae* is again illustrated from Ephesians 2:8–10, which he rendered in a literal translation from the Greek rather than after the Vulgate.[101] Once again he invoked the argument from *bona voluntas*, by which he meant an initial movement of the will toward God or the voluntary disposition of the soul toward grace. Sadoleto explained the text from Ephesians to mean that

in one aspiring to God through Christ is seen a certain manifest faculty and disposition of the will toward right conduct. The nature of justice in us is made perfect when it accomplishes and exerts itself in pious deeds and contains the practice of righteousness (*justitiae*), joined with the will to act righteously.[102]

By his mercy and goodness God perfects the imperfect beginnings of faith, right will, and good works in us: having himself disposed us to righteousness, he demands good works as well as faith in order that his commandments may be obeyed. Such then is the nature of justice that we are disposed at once to faith and works, to love and obedience.

In this treatise Sadoleto carefully set off the "original authors of these dissensions" and false doctrines from "certain more moderate men among you," who, for example, concede a place to good works even though they deny the effective value of works to salvation. However severely he dealt with Luther and his teaching, he returned to the plea for religious unity and peace, to the Pope's labors for reform, and the imminent Council at Vicenza. However inadequately he grasped the substance of Lutheran theology, Sadoleto wrote the Exhortation as a serious, if frequently stern conciliator, standing in judgment both of corruption in Rome and of wilful rebellion in Wittenberg. And throughout the treatise runs the acknowledgement of legitimate grievances in Germany together with the assurance that they would be resolved through discussion in the Council. Implicitly, however, the area of legitimate grievances did not extend to doctrine, but included only the institutional practices of the Church. Therefore his position followed the *Consilium* and lay open to the same kind of Protestant criticism which Sturm developed in his letter to the Cardinals.

Not knowing whether such a work was timely, he wrote Duke George of Saxony in September 1539 to ask whether it should be published, or whether it was too inflammatory to accomplish anything. "I profoundly desire not to antagonize any one or to spread dissension," he said. "I wish only to exhort men to peace, hoping to write what the Lutherans will accept without resentment and Catholics with complete equanimity."[103] A sanguine and unrealistic posture indeed, but one to which Sadoleto was genuinely committed. Later in the winter he twice asked Cochlaeus for his opinion of the treatise, indirectly admitting that the realities of the schism were too remote and complex for the outsider to fathom. Should the Exhortation be printed, or put away? What is there, he asked, that a single individual can contribute to the reduction of tension in Germany?[104] If Cochlaeus and the Duke replied, however, their letters have not come to light. From the fact that Sadoleto revised the treatise again in 1540 without subsequently publishing it, we may conclude that he was not encouraged to make anything of it.

With the appearance of the Commentaries on Romans he no longer enjoyed that assured and extravagant praise which once greeted his writing so consistently. The themes of these later works confronted him with a new public which was necessarily more critical and more deeply in the world. The common ties of erudition and sound Latinity which bound him to Padua and Bembo turned out to be of little moment when extended to Wittenberg and Strasbourg, or Vienna and Meissen. The attempt to win Melanchthon's confidence by praising his literary achievement turned out to be as fruitless as reforming Sturm's religion by correcting his Latin and his manners.

After returning to Rome in 1536 Sadoleto was forced back into contact with the present in all its frightful and bewildering immediacy. Carpentras still provided relative calm and autonomy, but certainly not the same isolation which he had found there a decade earlier. The difference lay both in the character of the new pontificate and the effect of Sadoleto's promotion, which bound him inescapably to Rome. What gives special character and significance to Sadoleto's later career was the recurrent disagreement between him and the Holy See, between him and his colleagues, over precisely what constituted proper behavior as a Cardinal.

VIII

Controversialist

By prolonging his absence from one year to the next, Sadoleto was obliged once again to justify himself to the Roman Curia. In doing so the tone he took was sometimes that of the Epicurean in his garden. It is both prudent and profitable, he argued, to seek what enables one to live well and happily. When one sees that public evils grow worse every day, why then should he not surround himself with private good, the center of which is the liberal arts and the study of theology?[1] He reminded his curial friends that while fulfilling the duties of a good shepherd at Carpentras, he also applied his studies and writing to the profit of the Church. Although he readily acknowledged his desire to remain in the Venaissin for personal reasons, he was also convinced that his presence there was indispensable to the welfare of his diocese.

It is ironic that Pietro Bembo, once with Sadoleto a fugitive from the Curia, should at this time have abandoned his own studies and leisure in Padua and Venice for Rome and a place in the Sacred College. Having been named Cardinal in March 1539,[2] he spent the next two years in the City, caught up in consistorial politics and actively committed to the ill-starred labors of Cardinal Contarini. Bembo's exertions to behave like a prince of the Church were often a curious and sometimes a pathetic spectacle. Yet for so strict a prelate as Aleander his nomination was a glory to the faith and a credit to the Pope, certain to meet with wide approval everywhere in Germany. An astonishing opinion from a rigorist like Aleander and thoroughly fanciful.[3]

Of more interest to Sadoleto was the sojourn of Reginald Pole at Carpentras for six months during the spring of 1539. He first appeared at the end of January en route to Spain as Legate to Charles V, only to break off the mission when the Emperor concluded an alliance with England. Stalked and harassed at every turn by the agents of Henry VIII, and profoundly depressed by the fate of his kinsmen in England, Pole returned to Avignon and then to Carpentras in March, seeking his own *portus* there and later in a Franciscan monastery nearby. Pole was delighted by the Comtat—by the solitude of the cloister, the kindness of the monks, and the hospitality of Sadoleto.[4] This interlude was his first respite after three years of abortive missions and persecution. In August he wrote to Contarini to say that although the effect of his rest at Carpentras had been salutary, he was by no means ready to return to the Curia, fearing that the "seeds of consolation would be suffocated" if he were to be so soon in Rome again.[5] Pole therefore begged Contarini to have him released from a summons which Farnese sent in July. Contarini seems to have anticipated the request and wrote on August 8 of the Pope's consent to stay longer.

Except for occasional visits with Sadoleto at S. Felice, Pole remained in seclusion at the monastery. The Bishop was evidently willing to interpret his friend's desire for isolation as therapy for grief and fatigue. Pole's secretary, Lodovico Beccadelli, reacted differently to the quiet of Provence. As a Petrarch scholar he occupied himself during these months with a study of the poet's life and soon entertained platonic fantasies about a local peasant girl, whom he chose to look upon as a latter-day Laura.[6] But the time for such adventures was brief. At the end of the summer Pole voluntarily informed Contarini that he was now ready to return to Italy if needed and offered to be in Rome by Christmas. He would have to take the usual precautions in travelling and asked that the Holy See make special arrangements for his security in Rome. Nevertheless, Pole now put himself completely at the Pope's disposal.[7]

Such was not the case with his colleague at Carpentras, although the question of returning to Italy had been on Sadoleto's conscience since the start of the year. Even before Pole turned around from his mission

to Spain, Jacopo told Pighius of plans to leave Carpentras in a few
months, possibly to redeem earlier promises to Caraffa and Farnese
that he would reach Italy by April.[8] In March, however, Sadoleto
wrote Del Monte to say that his departure would be put off until
autumn, and when the summer ended he decided to postpone it
indefinitely.[9] Reengaged "in an active life in the service of a contemplative ideal," Pole later supported his friend's wish to stay on,
explaining to the Pope that Sadoleto was urgently needed in his diocese
and in the Comtat.[10] For his own part the absentee continued to claim
that he was financially unable to live in Rome and that the welfare of
his people depended on his presence. While among them he said he
could serve the Church far more significantly by writing in its behalf
than by living penuriously in Rome as a useless and possibly an idle
member of the Curia.[11] He made clear his determination to stay at
Carpentras until there were more compelling reasons for returning to
Rome.

Meanwhile, Sadoleto continued to write. Each of the four periods of
his residence at Carpentras measurably increased his literary output,[12]
and if one were to subtract from his total achievement the works
produced while he was in Provence, only the early *De Bello suscipiendo
contra Turcos* and the incomplete first draft of his *Exhortatio* to the
Germans would remain. Most of the things he began after leaving the
Pope at Nice were concerned with the issues of reunion, reform, or
the exposition of doctrine. In one sequence he produced his letters to
Melanchthon and Sturm, together with the *Ad principes populosque
Germaniae exhortatio*. In another, he wrote an open Letter to the
Council and People of Geneva and then undertook the more ambitious
De christiana ecclesia. The letter to the Swiss is the work of a Catholic
polemicist, whereas the treatise on the Church is the complaint of a
Catholic reformer.

6+

The *Epistola ad senatum populemque Genevensem*[13] springs rather suddenly into view during the early months of 1539, unanticipated so far as we know by any marked interest in early Calvinist doctrine or by any known contact with Swiss Catholics corresponding to Duke George of Saxony or Cochlaeus. Nor is it possible to say when it was that Sadoleto became aware of Calvin or Farel and the revolutionary movement in Geneva. Sadoleto's friend Cortese had no knowledge of Calvin or the *Institutes* until the summer of 1540, even though the Abbot had taken pains to examine Luther's early writing.[14]

In the spring of 1539, however, Farel reported that the recent Catholic counter-offensive on Protestant Geneva was the work of Sadoleto and Cardinal Tournon.[15] It is entirely possible that Sadoleto wrote his appeal to the Swiss at the request of Tournon and Pierre de la Baume, the exiled Bishop of Geneva; but there is nothing to show that he attended a colloquy at Lyons in December 1538, where the strategy of Catholic restoration in Geneva was discussed by de la Baume, Tournon, and others.[16]

Sadoleto's Latin letter to the Swiss closely followed the Lyons conference in time, however. It was dated March 18, 1539, and delivered to the Small Council in Geneva two weeks later.[17] Less forceful than his Exhortation to the Germans, this appeal for the unity of the faith was also addressed to the rank and file of the movement and not to its leaders. Calvin is portrayed here as a plotting anarchist whose motive for rebellion was his own failure to win ecclesiastical preferment and recognition.[18] Although the tone of Sadoleto's remarks to the Swiss is paternally cordial, he made no such concessions to them as he did to the Germans about abuses in the Church, possibly because he had been generous enough on this subject already. The accent here fell on the unity of Christian tradition and on the sanctity of the historical Church rather than on the returning probity of the contemporary Church. The treatise is therefore a defense of authority against disobedience and of dogmatic tradition against innovation. As the ark of salvation, the Church provides the means of distinguishing truth from error. It is the perpetual authority of fifteen hundred years rather than the arrogant invention of the past twenty-five. Strifeless, infallible, and informed by the Holy Spirit, the Church of tradition is likewise the only proper guardian of Christian peace and concord.

Sadoleto also turned again to the inadequacies of Protestant doctrine on justification.[19] To preach justification *fide sola* is to say that the believer is excluded from responsibility for his moral conduct and from participation in his own salvation. Faith is a mere beginning to which the believer must add a pious disposition and the will to obey. Salvation follows the movement of the will toward God as well as the performance of good works. Faith properly understood embraces all the Christian virtues, so that no interpretation of faith is complete if it omits the love of God. Just as nothing of our own can be sanctified without grace, neither can a man be saved without *caritas*.

Weeks before John Calvin was invited to answer Sadoleto in the name of the Genevans, Contarini reviewed his colleague's doctrinal position in the letter from an Augustinian perspective. Like the Commentaries on Romans, Sadoleto's letter to the Genevans opened up differences between Contarini and himself, this time on the nature and action of *caritas* although more generally again on the question of merit.[20] The particular point at issue was Sadoleto's claim that charity is not an effect of righteousness but the very substance of it: charity or love *is* justice, being the "form" or animating principle of *justitia*.[21] Contarini treated this assumption as an error and a great simplification; he reminded Sadoleto that since the issue was not dogmatically settled and thus only a matter of scholastic opinion, it could not be stated so categorically in view of disagreement among Catholic theologians.[22] It would be well, therefore, to avoid offering the heretics an opportunity to embarrass the Church on so ambiguous a point. Whereas Sadoleto insisted on the identity or concurrence of *caritas* and *justitia*, holding that it is *caritas* which achieves justification, Contarini answered that love follows faith and is actually the result of justification. He claimed to follow St. Thomas and derived Sadoleto's viewpoint, ironically, from the same Scotus and Durandus whom Badia had accused Jacopo of neglecting in the exposition of Romans. Contarini emphasized a *caritas infusa*, while Sadoleto wrote of *caritas* as the believer's work, something which precedes justification and gives substance to faith. But the principal difference between them grew out of Sadoleto's emphasis on the necessity of human cooperation in achieving salvation, and Contarini's almost exclusive attention to faith in the redemptive agency of Christ. Such dissonance placed Contarini closer to Calvin than to Sadoleto in a way which became even more evident two years later.

For the moment, however, Sadoleto preferred to call off the debate entirely. He found no more pleasure in disagreement with Contarini than he had on earlier occasions with Pole, Fregoso, or Erasmus. So in a letter to Contarini of May 22 he abruptly proposed that the issue be dropped—on the ground that the weather was now too hot for further argument. There was a time for everything, and summer was customarily a season of rest and inactivity for the Bishop, who withdrew as much as possible to San Felice and suspended serious work altogether until fall. The period of indolence was generous, usually lasting, as he explained to Contarini, from May to October,[23] when the sun burns deep into the limestone hills of Provence and sears the luster of its springtime colors. This was the season when learned leisure gave way to idleness, when *otium* became *otiositas*. In July he began to draw back from his plans to leave for Italy in September, seeing "nothing to attract me there and much that keeps me here." In a letter to Farnese several weeks later he confessed his fondness for the Venaissin but went on to say that his presence was required to keep down the heretics and was valued by French officials as far away as Toulouse and Grenoble.[24] He was troubled only by the commitment to reform the monks of S. Onofrio.

Sadoleto's adversaries meanwhile were busy at his expense, and the center of their activity was Strasbourg. Having at last received the Bishop's letter of the previous July and indignant that so many others should have seen it first, Sturm finished his reply to Sadoleto on July 18, 1539.[25] He took notice at the start of Sadoleto's condescension and harshness, of his insults to the Protestants, and then asked what hope for reconciliation there was if it could not be placed in "you, Contarini, and Salerno" (Fregoso)? Men even of your moderation, he concluded, are ignorant of everything the heretics are striving for.

Why, he asked, have you not restored ancient discipline over the clergy? Why does corruption still infect the hierarchy in all degrees and in every nation? Why are the traditional canons of the Church still unenforced? Our people simply dissent from yours, but they do not desert the Church. Rome leaves everything unchanged and uncorrected; while accusing us of heresy and error, the Curia will not even bother to refute our arguments.

On July 24, a few days after Sturm's letter was completed, it was suggested in Berne that Calvin be invited to answer Sadoleto's letter to the Genevans, the Bernese Council having failed to find a local respondent after a search of four months.[26] The *Epistola ad senatum populemque Genevensem* was delivered to Calvin at Strasbourg in mid-August by the Protestant theologian Simon Sulzer. After some hesitation Calvin yielded to the urging of his friends and wrote his long and closely-argued reply in six days.[27] It was published at the end of the month, and rushed through the press in time to be exhibited at the September book fairs at Geneva, Frankfort, and Lyons.

This response to Sadoleto, written with passion and great intellectual vigor at the height of Calvin's youthful powers, went far beyond Sturm's irenic moderation.[28] Sadoleto's treatise, not addressed to Calvin but implicating him on every page, shows signs of fatigue and was clearly less substantial than that of his thirty-year-old antagonist. The Cardinal's letter was loosely reasoned and habitually rhetorical, whereas Calvin's was taut and aggressive. Calvin's manner was correct and in its way respectful; he recognized Sadoleto as one who has "fulfilled his duty so well to good letters and the liberal arts," but he also deplored the Cardinal's abusive language, his ignorance about Geneva, his doctrinal ambiguities, and his careless charges about Farel and himself.[29]

Against Sadoleto's constant emphasis on the unity of Catholic tradition and the sovereignty of the Church, which the Cardinal defined as the spirit of Christ, Calvin opposed the sovereignty and authority of the Word of God, disputing Sadoleto's definition as vague and uncertain. The Church is meaningless, he continued, unless it be founded on the Word of God: Christ said that it is to be governed

by the Holy Spirit; but to give mortals proper guidance, he added
that they are the Lord's who keep his Word. Calvin wrote in the
conviction that his was an essentially conservative ideal, intended only
to rebuild what had fallen. No one, with the possible exception of
Melanchthon, had stated the argument more boldly or emphatically.
In Calvin's view the unique model of the true Church was the Church
of the Apostles, from which he claimed the historical Church had been
led away by the Popes. In this way the Word of God had been ignored
and the liberty of the Christian destroyed.

Calvin's reply made a great deal also of the doctrinal issues, which
Sturm accused the reform Cardinals of neglecting altogether, and set
forth a summary defense of his doctrine of salvation.[30] But the argument that justification is the free gift of grace, "nullo operum merito,"
moves into sudden contrast with what Calvin described as Sadoleto's
astonishing interpretation of *fides* and the claim that *caritas* is the
"principal and most effective cause of salvation. Who, Sadoleto,
would ever have expected such a statement from you? Those who have
one spark of divine light realize that salvation resides in nothing else
than God's adoption of them."[31] He taxed the Cardinal again with
theological ignorance for his interpretation of authority and even with
that contempt of theology "so common among those who have not
experienced anguish of conscience." This was perhaps the sharpest
thrust of all, for it was aimed at the poverty of Sadoleto's insights into
the psychology of religious experience. Calvin sounded like Sturm,
however, when he protested that the Church now tolerated the abuse
or neglect of its ancient canons, that its discipline had vanished, and
that the clergy was now contemptuous of duty and law while
Christendom lay submerged under the illegitimate power and pre-
tensions of the Papacy.

Sadoleto's letter to the Genevans was the last of five attempts, all
made in the twenty months between July 1538 and March 1539, to
break through the frontiers of disputed doctrine. Aside perhaps from
the letter to Melanchthon—certainly the most sincere and ingenuous
in this series—each by its nature was an exercise in futility. However
hopeful his expectations may have been, these efforts to communicate

with the Protestant world by way of Melanchthon, Sturm, the German Protestants, and the Genevans, if not also through Mosheim, led immediately to recrimination and bitter feeling between one side and the other. The self-righteous and uncompromising tone of all parties to this correspondence is readily obvious. Sadoleto and Sturm patronizingly exchanged accusations of truculence and distortion, the same charges recurring in Sadoleto's letter to the Genevans and in Calvin's reply. Calvin, moreover, attacked the Cardinal for being so impious as to speculate on the defense of a Protestant (obviously meant to be Calvin himself) before God in the Last Judgment, but went on to do the same thing in his own behalf, exploiting the device in twice the space Sadoleto had taken.[32]

The ultimate effect of Sadoleto's letters was merely to bring embarrassment and further censure upon himself at home, and to solidify Protestant leadership abroad, while widening in a small way the gulf between Italy and the North. The replies of Sturm and Calvin to Sadoleto, for instance, brought praise from Luther in a letter to Martin Bucer during the fall of 1539:

Health to you, and pray give reverent respects to Masters Sturm and Calvin, whose little books I have read with unusual pleasure. I should hope for Sadoleto that he believe God is the creator of men even outside Italy. But this opinion does not penetrate Italian hearts, since they alone above all others put aside perception for pride.[33]

Melanchthon observed that Calvin's answer to Carpentras earned new esteem for him at Wittenberg; more than that, it seemed to help draw Calvin and Luther out of the mutual skepticism with which they once regarded one another. Luther was later seen rereading Calvin's answer to Sadoleto, complimenting it again as a thing with "head and feet" as he rode to visit the ailing Melanchthon in 1542. But on these replies from Strasbourg, not a word at Carpentras. In Germany, however, Cochlaeus and his friends kept up their protests to the Vatican about the damaging effects of Sadoleto's practices as a misguided agent of reunion.[34]

The simplest and most discerning counsel on the whole question of Catholic apologetics and communication with the Protestants came from Contarini in a letter to Cochlaeus. "I have long been convinced," he said, "that we will be more effective with our adversaries if they are not antagonized by what we write; and at the present time nothing can be submitted to them—however pious or irreprehensible —which does not antagonize them bitterly."[35] It was his way of suggesting that Catholics be temperate, or better yet, altogether silent.

These letters to the heretics illuminate only one side of Sadoleto's reflections on the condition of Christendom during the pontificate of Paul III. Another and equally significant kind of opinion is to be found in his address to the Cardinals of the reform commission in 1536 and in personal letters bearing on issues of ecclesiastical government and policy.[36] Sadoleto implored the Germans and the Genevans to return to the faith which he had defended in his Commentaries on St. Paul, and also to the Church of which he was, within the hierarchy, so harsh a critic. Before completing his letter to the Genevans he was already at work on a long new treatise written in the spirit of his oration of 1536, arguing for a thorough reformation of the clergy. Just as in earlier years he used to write for a double clientele—one represented by Bembo and the other by Pole, so now he addressed himself as a Catholic apologist to Protestant critics of the Church, and simultaneously as a Catholic critic to his associates in the Roman hierarchy. One audience lay beyond the Alps, the other in Italy.

The new treatise, variously known as *De christiana ecclesia*,[37] *De exstructione catholicae ecclesiae*, and *De aedificatione ecclesiae*, was started either late in 1538 or early the next year.[38] After completing the first of four projected parts, Sadoleto had the manuscript circulated in Italy during the summer of 1539. At the end of the year he finished the second part, evidently a treatise on the sacraments, but until the end of January 1541, he permitted only the opening section to reach his friends.

The model for this work may possibly have been the well-known *Enchiridion* (1536) of Archbishop Hermann von Wied of Cologne, whose rather extreme views on councils and ecclesiastical reform were familiar to Sadoleto and his circle. Sadoleto praised the work and intent of the Archbishop but also detected something of the heterodoxy which later carried its author over to the Lutherans and the *Enchiridion* to the *Index*.[39] More immediately influential was Pighius' *De ecclesticae hyerarchiae principatu*; in fact so similar was this work to his plans for the *De christiana ecclesia* that Sadoleto once talked about abandoning his own treatise altogether.[40]

The first book of the *De christiana ecclesia* is a glorification of the early Church and at times suggests a theme of Calvin's response to Sadoleto. But Sadoleto finds the principal evil of the modern Church not in its departure from the Word of God but from the early traditions of a moral and responsible clergy. In his view the corruption of the clergy is the source of all the present upheaval in Christendom and the proper focus of any significant reformation.[41] Whereas he defines the Church for the Genevan heretics as the Spirit of Christ, he defines it for a Catholic public as the estate of the Bishops under the authority of the Pope.[42]

To Sadoleto the substance of the Church is the clergy, and if the Church is the collective means of salvation, the priest is the particular instrument in a world inimical to God. It is through the *sacerdotium* that we are sanctified; the priest is mediator and interpreter of God's law, the vessel of divinity who conveys the promise and the means of salvation.[43] Whatever the Church may be at any point in history necessarily depends, therefore, on the condition of the priesthood. The contemporary Church, "as a result of the sinking of its foundations, will list over toward collapse and ruin unless it be rebuilt on new bases . . . after the model of its ancient form." The genius of the early Church was its vigilance over the clergy. "Our wise and saintly ancestors," Sadoleto admonished, knew the value of a disciplined and well-educated priesthood, and respected the distinctions between priestly orders. Unless the clergy is soon brought back to this condition by the strict enforcement of traditional law, the destruction of

6*

the Church is inevitable. Here Sadoleto shared the conviction so common to most humanist critics of the Church that reform is a matter of restoration and the return from present corruption to past purity.[44] His appeal to a pre-existing good is as clear in his ecclesiology as in his classicism, and the canons of right government in the Church as obvious to him as the models of literary perfection.

Although he carefully charted the circulation of his manuscript through the hands of a dozen readers in Italy, Sadoleto found himself once again under violent attack. Pole discovered that the treatise had reached a hostile public in Rome and that Sadoleto was being bludgeoned by his own statements, taken out of context, from an incomplete draft.[45] Contarini again went to the Bishop's defense, although he, too, had found fault with parts of the work. Granting that it needed considerable revision, Sadoleto still hoped to publish the *De christiana ecclesia*, but publication was evidently prohibited; Paolo's efforts to bring the treatise to grace twenty years after his cousin died were also blocked in Rome.[46] So the *De ecclesia*, like the letter to the Germans, was kept from the printer by the objection of Catholic critics. If we recall the tempest over his Commentaries on Paul, his minority report as a member of the reform Commission in 1537, and his several letters to the Protestant community, we may also find another degree of isolation from the hierarchy and even from the Church which Sadoleto tried with such frequently dubious success to defend. He was suspended, as Schultess-Rechberg observed, between a strong desire to work for its good, and the fear in doing so of suffering its reproof.[47]

As a critic of society and the Church, what he most deplored was not the want of good laws so much as the absence of moral men; he seemed to say that it was the present race of princes and prelates which had to be restored to a higher place.

Although strict and solemn laws are not lacking, custodians of them are and long have been; so that an opportunity or rather a great inducement to live immorally has been presented not only to the vicious, but equally to those whom right discipline might possibly have made good.[48]

As a moralist Sadoleto's anger fell no less on the princes than on the clergy, for in secular government he found the same contempt of ancient law which he attacked in the priesthood. While the Turks advanced unopposed across Hungary in 1541, he warned that there was no good to be expected from Christian rulers and no evil not to be feared from them. In his *De regno Hungariae*[49] he wrote of a "faithless generation," living in "wretched and calamitous times," afflicted by God's wrath for its depravity and discord, its avarice, irreligion, and heresy. The Turks are the creatures of divine outrage and their success the result of division among Christian princes. Common men are the victims of their indifference to the common good, and their internecine wars threaten ruin to the entire Christian commonwealth. Given the wickedness of such rulers, moreover, Christians are helpless to provide for the public safety and can do no more than look to their own.

Sadoleto long regarded the Comtat Venaissin as an enclave of innocence in the midst of an immoral society, a minuscule utopia which would become the most moral and peaceful place he knew:

If there remains anywhere a trace of quiet and calm, it is certainly here, where men are given to a serene and tranquil life by nature rather than by laws.[50]

How striking that one who found so much to denounce in the secular and ecclesiastical orders alike should have discovered an earthly paradise in his own diocese. His affection for Italy never diminished, yet Italy too, he warned, stands on the brink of ruin, having fallen prey to plundering princes who know only how to pursue their selfish ends, to grind down their people with taxes and live in rioting. The source of all Italy's troubles is the oppression practiced by princes who regard their subjects as slaves.[51] The remedy for Italy, like the remedy for all Christendom, is the restoration of that "ancient virtue and proud discipline" which once flourished in its governments, and the recovery of the "ancient dignity and honor of our forebears."

For Sadoleto, as a matter of habit and conviction, the measure of church and state, like the measure of good letters, was the test of antiquity; such was the rationale of humanist and reformer alike. We must remember, however, that the test of antiquity and the myth of a golden age were often no more than a means of protesting against current evils. And as a frequent critic of the Church, Sadoleto repeatedly surpassed the limits of its tolerance, isolated as he was from the College and alienated from the Curia. On one occasion, however, Sadoleto found himself on the conventional side of an issue, while Contarini and Badia—his critics of 1535—were on the other.

In 1540, while Jacopo worked over the first book of his *De christiana ecclesia*, Paul III renewed his efforts to secure reform and reorganization in the papal bureaucracy. At the insistence of Charles V and the Archduke Ferdinand the Council was suspended again in May 1539, while the Emperor pursued phantom hopes of settling the religious controversy by discussion with the Lutherans. The imperial policy of *détente* in Germany required a passive role of the Vatican, at least in terms of the Council, so that the Pope had no other present alternative than to resume the more limited projects of curial reform. Once again he discussed plans in consistory for a "reformation of the clergy and the Curia," while the nuncios urged the necessity of reform abroad. The Pope recalled Giberti to Rome and tried again to bring back Sadoleto as well, but the Bishop of Carpentras, although now receiving a stipend usually reserved only for Cardinals resident in Rome, refused to leave his diocese.[52]

At the end of August Paul III appointed four new commissions of three Cardinals each to study the reform of all the major curial agencies.[53] This was intended to be a fresh start, for the Pontiff had terminated all previous reform activity in April in order to cut off the controversies which had arisen over Contarini's program for reorganizing the Dataria. The new investigative group of twelve, including four members of the great Commission of 1536–37 (Contarini, Pole, Caraffa, and Aleander) continued its labors until the latter part of 1542. At the end of the first year, on the basis of a new decree against episcopal absenteeism, Cortese felt that "un gran principio alla reformazione" had now taken place.[54] Sadoleto was less certain; he wrote Cervini that he wished the Cardinals success in their present work but observed that the promising start of a general reformation, presumably that of 1536, was "later, I know not how, rather deflected from its course."[55] While the four commissions of 1540–42 undoubtedly accomplished a great deal more than those of the previous two years, the obstacles to self-reform by the College were as much intact in 1543 as they had been in 1537. And early in 1543 Morone informed Granvelle, the imperial Chancellor, that the Pope had now deferred all questions of reform to the Council in view of the difficulties which seemed to block his own efforts.

Parallel to the ineffectual work of the four papal commissions ran the Emperor's attempt to supplant both a general Council and a national synod with colloquies between the representatives of each party in Germany. Catholic opinion tended to be skeptical of the plan and often anxious about its consequences; such observers as Cochlaeus, Aleander, and Morone doubted that there was any real basis for discussion and saw no advantage to the Church in further talks. Morone felt that Rome had already allowed the Emperor to go too far in controlling the form and character of the coming colloquy at Worms. But a certain momentum had been built up in the movement for negotiation which the Holy See was as yet unable to arrest; for the time being, imperial policy prevailed over the Pope's.

The conference at Worms, which began in November 1540, was regarded as a preliminary to wider talks in the Diet at Regensburg which was to open in July 1541. The Church was already represented in Germany by Cardinal Tommaso Campeggio and Badia, as well as by the Nuncio Morone, Johann Eck, Cochlaeus, and the theologian Johann Gropper. But while the Colloquy of Worms was in progress, demands were made for a more authoritative papal delegation. Bernardino Santio, Bishop of Aquila, wrote the Vice-Chancellor on December 15 that unless the Pope sent an influential deputy who was also acceptable to the Emperor, neither the Colloquy nor the Diet would be of any value to the Church; and he suggested that the Vatican consider sending such a man as Farnese himself, Cervini,

Ghinucci, Caraffa, Contarini, or Sadoleto.[56] The Legate Campeggio later discussed the same question with Granvelle, who in turn felt that Lutheran theologians might find Italian Catholics more tolerable than German; his candidates, in order, were Sadoleto, Pole, or Fregoso.[57] The choice of the papal agents then in Germany fell on Contarini, whose appointment as *legatus a latere* was confirmed in consistory on January 10, 1541.

Accompanied by his diocesan vicar Girolamo Negri, who was to be the Cardinal's confidential secretary on the mission, Contarini reached Regensburg in March, hopeful that genuine progress toward religious unity could be made in the Diet and encouraged by the agreement reached at Worms over a formula on the interpretation of original sin. His instructions from the Pope, however, should have tempered the Cardinal's optimism, for he was required first to determine whether the Protestant delegation was willing to accept the principle of papal supremacy as divinely instituted, and whether it would accept the sacramental tradition unaltered.[58] Furthermore, the Legate was not given the generous proxy which Granvelle had so strongly advocated, the Pope's mandate reading that no authority could be given with "full power to reach agreements" because of the magnitude of the issues.[59]

Our present concern is not the entire drama at Regensburg[60] but only with Contarini's response to Article V of the "Book of Regensburg." On April 23, two days after the Emperor designated the colloquists for each side, he gave the Legate a book of twenty-three articles which had been worked out in secret conversations between Gropper and Bucer as the formulae of doctrinal accord. Contarini suggested a score of corrections to them, while Eck—taken out of his habitual role of controversialist and virtually forced into the talks— found the entire document unacceptable as the basis for discussion. Contarini's interest went rapidly to the fifth article, the statement of justification, which after extensive revision was ready on May 2.[61] The next day the Legate enthusiastically reported that he had reconciled the theologians of both sides to the article on "justification, faith, and works,"[62] without mentioning the disfavor which the formula had aroused in Gropper, Eck, and Melanchthon. Nevertheless, the most significant commitment was that of Contarini himself to this classic statement of "double justification."

Contarini wrote a personal defense and elaboration of the article on May 25 in a short treatise *De justificatione*, which he sent to Cardinal Gonzaga.[63] The Legate was highly pleased with the formula and hoped that it might dispel the general assumption of the past twenty years that Catholic doctrine was, in substance, semi-Pelagian. He explained to Gonzaga that the hope of salvation must be founded in the justice or righteousness of Christ alone, and not on the sanctity inherent in us. Inherent justice is imperfect and by itself inadequate, unless fulfilled and perfected by the imputed justice of Christ; these then are the two elements of salvation, but because of sin we cannot be justified unless an alien, divine righteousness is imputed to us. So in Contarini's view the justice inherent in the Christian believer recedes before the justice of God: it is grace above all, if not alone, which accomplishes salvation. Although the Cardinal did not argue dogmatically in his treatise, his exposition was thorough and easily simplified. Paolo Sadoleto, for example, summarized the doctrine to the effect that "we are to look not to the justice which inheres in us, but must depend on the justice of Christ."[64]

Contarini's support of the doctrine was met in Rome by hostility and suspicion. No one in the College vigorously or publicly defended him. Bernardino Ochino quoted Farnese as saying that of the fifty Cardinals about to meet in the consistory of May 27, "at least thirty will not know exactly what this justification is, while most of the remaining twenty will dispute and oppose it, and whoever tries to defend it will be considered heretical."[65] To some, Article V was strange and unfamiliar, to others simply a dangerous concession. Having left Rome for Capranica to find greater security from English agents, Pole sent Luigi Priuli back to the City to canvass opinion in the Curia, and learned from his secretary that the College showed no enthusiasm for Contarini's doctrinal concessions.[66] And on May 29 Cardinal Farnese informed Contarini that although the formula might be consonant with Catholic teaching, it would have to be made far more explicit and precise before the Holy See could approve it.[67]

Without any support in consistory, Contarini's only sympathetic contact in the Vatican was the immensely untheological Cardinal Bembo, who tried hard to spare his compatriot from knowing how great the opposition was.[68] Contarini's most enthusiastic partisan in Italy at the time was Reginald Pole, but because of his absence from the College he was unable to contribute much to the Legate's cause. However, Pole unreservedly praised the Regensburg formula on justification, which he described as "a precious jewel," always in the hidden treasure of the Church but only now disclosed to every one.[69] In the same letter he confessed that some had maliciously accused him of leaving Rome in order to avoid the embarrassment of defending Contarini in consistory, adding that he would certainly have returned to Rome in the Legate's behalf if discussion of Article V had continued any longer.

Reaction from Sadoleto at Carpentras was quite different: first, a protest and an admonition, then a somewhat pained apology. From Vergerio in Regensburg and from someone in Rome,[70] Sadoleto received copies of Article V together with Contarini's expository letter to Gonzaga of May 25—unaware of Contarini's connection with either.[71] He was profoundly troubled by the Lutheran quality of double justice and saw it merely as another sanction for moral license, his most recurrent objection to doctrine of this kind. To conclude that men are saved not by inherent justice but antecedently through the justice of Christ would be more calamitous for the Church than yielding to the Protestants on clerical marriage. Furthermore, Sadoleto seemed eager to have his views known at Regensburg. He not only conveyed them in a letter to Vergerio, but suggested that Beccadelli pass on to Contarini the brief statement on double justification which the Bishop had drafted at Carpentras. Sadoleto also attacked the doctrine in a letter to Ambrogio Catarino (Polito), whose work *De perfecta justificatione* he liked and whose theological judgment he trusted.[72] "I have never been able to convince myself," he said, "that faith alone, by itself and without works, ought to be held sufficient for gaining the kingdom of God."[73] Far more congenial than the Regensburg doctrine was Catarino's argument from the formula "fides cum operibus conjuncta." But he also begged Polito to reply immediately with respect to his own estimate of the Regensburg Book, for Sadoleto no longer trusted himself on matters of dogmatic definition.[74]

His own answer to Article V was the little treatise *De justitia nobis inhaerente, et de justitia Christi imputata*,[75] written without knowledge that he was thus taking issue with doctrine that Contarini supported. Is it a Catholic opinion, he asked, to say that "we depend not on the justice inherent in us . . . but rather on the justice of Christ which is imputed to us through the merit of Christ"? It seems far closer to the Lutheran position on faith. Moreover, it is ambiguous. Either the righteousness inherent in us accomplishes something for our salvation, or it does not. Scripture demonstrates that we are saved according to our merit and good works, our free will acting concurrently with the operation of the Holy Spirit in us. Once again Sadoleto emphasized man's capacity to cooperate with grace in the process of justification:

We must indeed depend to some extent upon the justice inherent in us and upon our own good works for acquiring the promise of God, in that we acknowledge that the justice in us comes from God, our free will cooperating and consenting, even though we are to place the greater hope and trust in the justice of Christ and his merit before God. . . .[76]

Such is the Catholic position, Sadoleto argued, which the Regensburg doctrine distorts because it so fully depreciates works and the value of human exertion for spiritual good, as well as the continuity between man and God through union in the merit of Christ.

Not until after Contarini left Regensburg for Italy did Sadoleto learn whom he had censured in attacking Article V of the Book.[77] Nor did he discover until August of 1541 the part Contarini had taken at the Diet in pressing the case for double justification on the Vatican. Mortified to find that he had contradicted a close and loyal friend so bluntly, he explained his regret to Campeggio and repeated it to Beccadelli[78]—the greater, no doubt, for the memory of Contarini's gentleness when their roles were reversed. Yet the fact remains that our semi-Pelagian now stood closer to orthodoxy than the profoundly

Augustinian Legate to Regensburg, who was under a barrage of loose charges in Rome. Paul III had reprimanded him before the Diet ended and further limited his powers as procurator. Caraffa virtually accused him and Badia of joining with the Emperor in a capitulation to the Lutherans in crucial areas of dogma,[79] and when he returned to Italy Contarini found that there were even those who regarded him as a heretic. In reality, of course, he looked back at the Diet as a dismal failure and on toleration of the Lutherans as a dangerous illusion; he recommended to Charles V that the Book be suppressed and took away from the colloquies only his personal attachment to the principle of a twofold justice.

Regensburg disclosed not only the range and variety of Catholic opinion on questions of doctrine, but also the futility of the Emperor's trust in negotiation as well as the urgency of a universal Council. The theological discussions of April and May cast doubts on the orthodoxy of Contarini and Badia, and likewise on the Emperor, Granvelle, Gropper, Pflug, and Pighius, although in all cases suspicion was carelessly grounded. Morone, nonetheless, wrote to Paul III in the wake of the Diet to stress the need for "a settled form of doctrine which can be read, taught, and preached everywhere." Yet Morone in turn offered as a model the Cologne *Enchiridion*, indirectly the source of many ideas drawn into the Book of Regensburg and later condemned.[80] Regensburg provided other lessons. Even before the Recess Negri admitted that Contarini and the rest of the Catholic party lost hope that anything would come of the discussions: it is too late, he conceded, and passions are too deeply aroused.[81] For his part, Melanchthon now looked upon reunion as an illusion,[82] the differences exposed at the Diet being too great for any group of colloquists to reconcile.

Before the theological discussions ended on May 22, the Curia decided to revoke its assent to a policy of temporizing and renewed formal negotiations over a general Council. The origins of Trent, says Jedin, lay in the talks which took place between Morone and Granvelle at Regensburg late in May.[83] And on June 15 Contarini was told to inform the Emperor that the suspension of the Council was to be withdrawn immediately; the Holy See now reclaimed its authority and instructed Charles V to make no further efforts to hold a national synod in Germany. With the recess of the Diet on July 29, 1541, all pending questions of dogma were referred again, as Erasmus had always implored, to the general Council.

By this time both Sadoleto and Contarini had participated in different aspects of a common failure, Sadoleto through his appeals to the Protestants and Contarini through his direction of the curial reform movement and of the Catholic representatives at Regensburg. The fate of Sadoleto's *De christiana ecclesia* was, in effect, the same as that of the Legate's *De justificatione*. Soon after the Diet ended, not only the issues of doctrine, but questions of reform and reunion were removed from the province of improvised individual effort and deferred to the Council. The collapse of the colloquies at Regensburg revealed the impossibility of finding common ground between Rome and Wittenberg. Symbolically, the failure of the talks stood for the failure of Contarini and the few who supported him. His appointment as Legate probably represents a concession not so much to an individual as to a policy or principle, of which Contarini stood for the theory and the Emperor the political application. In any event, each admitted its failure. The Cardinal returned to Rome falsely accused and often ill-treated, although by no means disgraced in the eyes of the Pope. In January of 1542, Paul III made him Cardinal-Legate to Bologna, "the most important and at the same time the most honorable Legation in all the States of the Church." But it now seemed as though the tide of reconciliation had rushed out, to strand him, almost alone and deserted, at the end of the Diet.

Leadership in the Sacred College was passing swiftly from Contarini and the conciliators to Caraffa and the intransigents. Contarini and Caraffa appear to have collaborated harmoniously on the early program of reform under Paul III, but they fell out over the issue of reunion and the objectives of Catholic policy in Germany.[84] By the end of 1541 it was clear that the only consensus within Contarini's Commission of 1536 rested precariously on the issue of internal reform. Such was the lesson of the summer. Contarini discovered, for example, that Sadoleto had rejected the doctrine of double justification just as energetically as Caraffa had. On the other hand, Sadoleto could take little comfort in his own labors of conciliation, for they turned out to be no less futile than Contarini's and just as severely criticized.

Thus the coherence of the so-called "Erasmian party" turns out to be a fiction. Whatever identity and prestige its members enjoyed as a group in 1536 had vanished by the end of 1541. Whatever solidarity they originally had had as reformers they eventually lost as theologians. Dispersion further reduced their influence through the absence of Pole, Cortese, Giberti, and Sadoleto from Rome; and within two years after the recess of the Diet of Regensburg, Fregoso, Aleander, Contarini, and Giberti were dead. The initiative returned to the Pope, whose emphasis now fell on the Council.

IX

Arbiter and Legate

On the second of January, 1542, Sadoleto received a letter from Farnese recalling him to Rome "a causa del Concilio" along with every other Cardinal then absent from the City.[1] The summons meant, in effect, that Jacopo would have to leave for Italy within the next two weeks if he were to take his place in the College, as the Vice-Chancellor stipulated, before the start of Lent on February 26. Drawn at once toward obedience and protest, Sadoleto promptly reminded Farnese of the hardships that such a journey involved for one of his age and infirmity, but he also knew that there was no honorable ground for refusal.[2] Moreover, this time he was "not merely invited but rather forced" to comply, although it was the middle of March before he managed to leave Carpentras. And after the usual respite in Modena the Bishop started south through the spring rains, arriving in Rome at the end of April.

So rapid was progress toward the Council now that the Pope had already fixed its site at Trent on the basis of Morone's recent negotiations in Germany. The contents of the bull of convocation, however, were still being discussed in consistory, where further talks took place on May 5 and 11. Once the details were worked out, the tardy Bishop of Carpentras was pressed into the familiar role of drafting the document itself, which convoked the Council for November 1.[3] There is a familiar ring to this language. In many respects the bull *Initio nostri hujus Pontificatus* reads like a series of extracts from the Bishop's own declarations on the state of Christendom. Verbally, at least, Sadoleto and Paul III were in full accord.

Once again Sadoleto was back in the Curia in a season heavy with crisis and important decisions. His absences from Rome during the years 1517–1547 occurred in periods of relative inactivity under both Clement VII and Paul III. Jacopo's separation from the Curia at Nice in 1538, for instance, took place at the beginning of an uneasy truce and likewise at the start of the Pope's acquiescence in the Emperor's new projects for a religious settlement in Germany, following an interlude in which the Holy See had worked intensely for reform and the Council. Sadoleto's prolonged leave in Provence extended over the full interval of the conciliar suspension and ended with the start of reactivated papal leadership in the promotion of the Council. The magnitude of papal enterprise might almost be plotted by the location at a given moment of the Cardinal S. Calisto.

His return to Rome in 1542 coincided with another mounting problem as close to his own concern as to the growth of new policy in the Curia; this was the steady rise of heresy among Italian intellectuals in various cities of the peninsula, fanning out from Venice to a dozen other cities in the northern plains. By now one of the most acutely infected was Sadoleto's own *patria*. Lutheranism in Modena grew rapidly during the decade of the 'thirties and flourished particularly in the small but influential body of literati and professional men who formed the Modenese "Accadèmia."[4] This society, which first appeared around 1530, was presided over by the humanist physician Giovanni Grillenzoni and drew to itself an impressive group of men whose interests were broad and restless. Among other things its forty-some members were said to be occupying themselves with dubious theological discussion and bold criticism of the Church. Modena by 1540 was both an important humanist center—which it was not during Sadoleto's youth—and an outpost of religious heterodoxy. In a report dated April 2, 1540, the Inquisitor Morbino found that "the greater part of the citizens and noble and learned men" of the city were sympathetic to false doctrine. Morone, the absentee Bishop of Modena, was told in the course of his mission to Germany that there were more heretics in this diocese than in the entire city of Prague.

The Holy See took notice of these conditions as early as 1536, when Paul III ordered a vigorous campaign against corrupt doctrine in Modena. Five years later he instructed Gregorio Cortese to investigate the progress of heresy in the city but shifted responsibility to Morone after the Legate returned from Germany in the spring of 1542. Astonished by what he found in the diocese and eager to take control of it, Morone at the same time was unable to cut his way through the thicket of new doctrine which surrounded him, for in no sense was he a theologian. In fact, "with the best intentions he allowed the work on the *Benefit of Christ* to be published in his diocese and circulated, little knowing that it contained the starting point of the very errors which he was now called upon to assail."[5] The Vatican, meanwhile, grew impatient for action.

But when the Pope was questioned about the incidence of heresy in Modena at the consistory of June 11, Sadoleto interrupted to ask that the matter not be opened to general discussion by the College and advised His Holiness to disregard loose rumors accusing the Modenese Academy. However, Jacopo promptly turned to his compatriots for reassurance.[6] He described his action at the consistory in a letter written the following day to Lodovico Castelvetro, an Academician and Conservator of Modena, to whom Sadoleto expressed his own doubts that learned men could support doctrine unworthy of true Christians. Referring to members of the Academy as his "dearest friends and brothers," he admonished them nevertheless to give up whatever novelties of belief they might support and to rid themselves of tainted members.

A few days later the Pope urged Morone to intensify his official efforts to expose and punish the heretics of his diocese. Morone had already persuaded Contarini, then in Bologna, to draw up a confession of faith similar in form to the Academicians' own creed. Intended to be a test and declaration of orthodoxy, the catechism was a series of questions which included a list of Lutheran errors. Morone's hopes for the confession were quickly disappointed; instead of subscribing to it the Academicians arrogantly defied their confused and mild Bishop, while the Pope created a commission of six (to include Morone and

Sadoleto) "on conditions in Lucca and Modena."[7] Morone's personal efforts, guided in part by Contarini, had come to nothing. What then of Sadoleto's?

Several prominent members of the Academy replied to their Cardinal compatriot during the first week of July and uniformly declared themselves innocent of the charges against them.[8] Thanking Sadoleto for his "faithful and friendly protection," Castelvetro wrote on July 2 to assert his own complete orthodoxy and to deny any affinity for "new and unseemly beliefs."[9] Grillenzoni described the Academy as a group associated originally for the study of Greek without any concern for religious literature whatever. The rumor about heresy in its membership was merely the work of gossips and local Dominicans. The doctor pleaded total ignorance of the Bible and sacred letters, adding that he had been denounced because he dared criticize "the idlers, evil-doers, hypocrites, and ignoramuses of this city," in which Fra Bernardino [Ochino] was abused "for having spoken too much about Christ." Alessandro Milano wrote to say that his interest also lay only in "profane studies" and to express his distress at the charge of heresy, while Francesco Greco, whom Grillenzoni identified as the first victim of the Dominicans' charges, wrote his eloquent disavowal on the seventh. The burden of all these letters was to deny, in effect, that the Academicians had any interest in religion at all.

Sadoleto was now more convinced than ever that his countrymen were falsely accused.[10] On July 14 he read Castelvetro's reply in consistory and called it proof of the man's "innocence and integrity." Just a day earlier, however, Contarini wrote to Morone from Bologna, accusing the savants, on the basis of Morone's reports, of "spiritual arrogance and pride, mother of all evil, joined with great ignorance" in matters of doctrine.[11] Although he conceded the existence of heresy in Modena, the unfortunate Morone fell under the suspicion of Roman zealots for his temporizing and clemency, which nonetheless he continued to justify in principle.

A month later Sadoleto stopped at Modena on his way north as papal Legate to Francis I. A conference was held on August 30 at the house of the Cardinal's brother Alfonso,[12] where Jacopo, together with Morone and Cortese, met with representatives of the city to discuss the matter of subscription to Contarini's forty-one articles by those who had previously refused.[13] At the end of a long colloquy, dominated by Cardinal Sadoleto, three of the Conservatori agreed to sign the formulary. Both at the conference and in the preface which he added to the *Confessio fidei* Sadoleto appealed as much to the local patriotism of the Modenese as to their piety.[14] At least for the present Contarini's profession of faith became the catalyst of accord, for it won adherence from forty-four prominent citizens, including Grillenzoni and Castelvetro. Time would prove, however, that the settlement was meaningless.

En route to Modena Sadoleto found himself involved in another controversy when he stopped briefly at Siena.[15] During an interview with Francesco Bandini, the Archbishop, he evidently went to the defense of Aonio Paleario (Antonio della Paglia), then professor of classics at Siena and a member of the Paduan circle who was about to be tried for heresy before an inquisitorial court. Precisely what the Cardinal did in Paleario's behalf is difficult to establish, but circumstantial evidence indicates that he managed to have the charges revoked and the trial cancelled.[16] In any case, this was neither the first nor the last occasion on which Paleario received help from Sadoleto, who habitually thought of della Paglia as an accomplished humanist, not as a religious innovator.[17] Paleario won high praise from the Bishop for his hexameter *De immortalitate animorum* (1536). Sadoleto merely criticized certain formal aspects of the poem and later commended it to Gryphius as a work of rare merit and firm orthodoxy.[18] Sadoleto's patronage continued even after Paleario's interests became more doctrinal than poetic, and in 1547 both Sadoleto and Bembo helped to place him as professor of eloquence at Lucca, although they were now disturbed by his theological radicalism.

Sadoleto's support of Paleario and the Modenese Academicians was part of a series of his contacts with persons of doubtful orthodoxy. One was with the Florentine Pietro Carnesecchi, a dependent of the Medici who served in the Apostolic Secretariat under Clement VII before entering Pole's circle at Viterbo and the doctrinal penumbra cast by women like Giulia Gonzaga, Renée de France, and Vittoria Colonna.[19] However, Sadoleto took a more particular interest in Marcantonio Flaminio, also a humanist of the Leonine period, who later drifted toward Valdés and Vermigli before being drawn back to orthodoxy by Cardinal Pole.[20] And although Sadoleto never lived among the free spirits of Viterbo, an agent of the Holy Office reported that "Cardinal Sadoleto often used to visit the Marchesa di Pescara," likewise a friendship which began while he was in the court of Leo X.[21]

In none of these associations, however, was Sadoleto implicated in the manner of Pole, Giberti, Morone, and even Contarini during their later years.[22] For one thing, absence from Italy kept the Bishop's connections more occasional and epistolary than they might otherwise have been. He was never so repeatedly the patron of the "Italian reformers" as was Giberti of Carnesecchi, Pole of Flaminio or Contarini of Vermigli. Furthermore, the basis of Sadoleto's interest in Paleario, Flaminio, and Castelvetro was a common respect for Latin letters; those for whom he actively interceded he looked upon as humanists like himself, chastening rather than encouraging or ignoring their flights from orthodoxy. Yet Sadoleto was by no means immune to the affinity of his friends for the searching inner piety of those in the Viterbo community. He tended to look upon Catholic reform as an institutional problem, although he was still receptive to the highly personalized and undogmatic devotion of one like Vittoria Colonna.[23] It was in the Viterbo group, rather than in the reform commissions, that the Oratory of Divine Love reached its fulfillment, notwithstanding the mutual interests which drew one group to the other.

A different element of the early Oratorians, represented by Gianpietro Caraffa and his adherents, looked with scorn on the tolerance of Pole and his friends for Catholic innovators. Furthermore, Contarini's failure at Regensburg and Morone's at Modena gave fresh support to the argument against moderation in dealing with the heretics. The Pope himself is said to have "opened up a new era"[24] in July 1542 when he appointed six Inquisitors-general and reestablished the Holy Office of the Inquisition. The significance of the bull

Licet ab initio as a radical shift in papal policy has often been overstated, although one need only name its first six executors to see that it marked another reverse of sorts for the party of reconciliation.[25] On the other hand, the bull may also be understood as a further effort by the Holy See to broaden the area of its authority and to make its impact on heterodoxy and false doctrine more direct. Once again the Vatican sought to replace local and temporary jurisdictions by that of the Roman Curia; and once again the personal endeavors of men like Sadoleto and Morone were supplanted by corporate action in the hands of the rigorists.

The Pope's most vital concern in the summer of 1542 went well beyond the parochial issues of Italian heresy, however, to the bull *Initio nostri hujus Pontificatus* and to its convocation of a Council at Trent. Far more pressing than the conduct of the Modenese Academicians was the matter of winning consent to peace from the Christian princes and their support for opening the Council on November 1.

Two weeks after the conciliar bull was published, the truce of Nice was suddenly shattered when Francis I declared war against the Emperor on July 12, 1542. The royal pretext was the murder of two French envoys to the Sultan on their return from the Porte a year earlier. Once again Cardinal Tournon had prevailed upon the King to resume the struggle against Charles V, and once again the Holy See was forced into the role of peacemaker from a position of honest neutrality, an attitude which so enraged the Emperor that he later forbade a single Spanish prelate to go to Trent. The French meanwhile opened a double offensive in the Netherlands and along the Pyrenees, against Luxembourg in the north and Roussillon in the south, while taking defensive measures for their interests in Italy.

Paul III immediately sought to end hostilities without waiting for the quieting effects of winter. In secret consistory on August 7 he created two *legati de latere* to negotiate peace, appointing Contarini to go to the Emperor and Sadoleto to Francis I.[26] The Venetian was expected to draw on his long association with Charles and Sadoleto on cordial relations with the French court; the Bishop of Carpentras held his see in France but not of it and was by now well established as a partisan of peace and the advocate of a holy war against the Turks, the King's allies of nearly seven years. Farnese now informed the nuncio to Spain that this mission was to "obtain peace or at least an observance of the truce"of 1538, and later reminded the nuncio to France that everything related to the Council depended on the status of relations between Charles and the Most Christian King.[27] So the legates were to work for a joint meeting between the princes, or for mutual assent to arbitration before the Pope or the Council.

Sadoleto received the legatine cross in Rome on August 11,[28] while Contarini received his in Bologna by courier. The Legate to France left on the seventeenth, carrying letters to the Dauphin, Tournon, the Duc d'Orléans, the Amiral d'Annebaut, Marguerite of Navarre, and other notables thought to have influence at court. Pole wrote Contarini on the fourteenth that he expected to see Sadoleto at Viterbo within the week,[29] but during the next forty-eight hours Contarini was stricken with an inflammation of the lungs while visiting a nephew in a Benedictine cloister at Padua, and was quickly taken by litter to his palace in Bologna. News of his illness "in extremis" reached Rome on August 20, and around midnight on the twenty-fourth the great Venetian breathed his last. The Pope, as Bembo put it, had lost "la prima colonna" of the Church.[30]

Sadoleto probably learned of his colleague's death while en route to Modena. Within a week he was joined by Contarini's replacement, the able Miguel da Silva, Bishop of Viseo in Portugal, and together they moved rapidly overland toward Provence, while snow and wind lashed the mountains.[31] Later, as Sadoleto made his way to Carpentras for a brief rest, he watched columns of French troops moving south to join the royal offensive at Perpignan. By September 22 Sadoleto was in Montpellier, where the King's secretary de Monluc tentatively scheduled a meeting with Francis I for the twenty-ninth.[32] On October 2, received cordially by the King at Beziers, the Legate was given the first of seven audiences spaced over a period of two months; his long and sententious dispatches to the Vice-Chancellor had already begun,[33] the first of them written from Montpellier on October 3. Having vaguely announced his mission as the promotion of "lo bene universale," Sadoleto heard the King defend his use of the Turkish fleet as a means of shortening the war and listened to royal doubts that the Emperor would submit to papal mediation.[34] The Legate found sympathy for peace in Cardinal Lorraine and du Bellay but deeply regretted the absence of Queen Marguerite, from whom he had hoped to find strong support for his mission.[35] Also absent from the court was François Tournon, still in Lyons, where he directed military operations against the imperialists while adroitly creating propaganda for the French cause in Rome and in the royal court for the benefit of the rather credulous Legate.

On October 5 de Viseo wrote Farnese from Barbastro in Aragon to say that his mission to the imperial court had already collapsed.[36] The discourtesy with which the Emperor received him was actually meant for the Pope, while Charles dismissed the Legation itself as an insulting absurdity. It was Francis I, ally of the Turk, who had broken the armistice of 1538; yet the Pope, Charles protested, still insists on remaining neutral. The Emperor looked upon himself as twice injured and therefore refused to listen to talk about peace, so that de Viseo saw no reason to stay longer.

Sadoleto, on the other hand, was pleased by his progress at the French court although certain that he would have to pursue his cause over a long period of time.[37] Francis' strategy with the Legate was apparently to play a waiting game, nourishing Sadoleto's hopes without committing himself either to peace or to papal arbitration.[38] Sadoleto accepted Francis' declarations literally and filled his reports with praise of the King, showing none of the watchful skepticism which his role required. Not content merely to seek royal observation of the truce, he ambitiously resolved to have the King submit his differences to the Pope.[39] It seemed sufficient to the Legate to promote the principle of arbitration in the most general terms without trying to define the issues or conditions under which it might be made acceptable; "such details," he felt, would only create obstacles to accord. He saw no contradiction between the King's outburst against Charles for making his own advances to the Porte, and Tournon's solemn profession of attachment to peace; he evidently discounted Tournon's veiled defiance of Rome[40] and saw no irony in reporting that the royal interest was to seek what the Legate referred to as "peace with honor." Nonetheless, Sadoleto was passionately devoted to the goal of his mission: "May God help me persuade the King of the urgency of peace," he wrote to Farnese, "for the alternative is a war more brutal than ever took place in Italy . . . ," and one which cannot result in anything but the ruin of Christendom.[41] In fact he believed that for the moment even the Council was less important than ending the war.

While Sadoleto pressed his program for negotiation, the Pope on October 16 commissioned Parisio, Morone, and Pole as his Legates at Trent. In the meantime de Viseo's letters from Barbastro reached the Curia. Knowing now that the war could not be ended soon and aware that tempers were too aroused for arbitration, the Pope on October 31 announced his decision to recall de Viseo and to have Sadoleto withdraw from the French court immediately.[42] Farnese explained this new turn of policy in a letter to Sadoleto on November 3; a colloquy might be proposed the following year, but for the present all efforts were to be applied to opening the Council, which was to be attempted, if need be, without support from the princes.[43] So Sadoleto in leaving the court was to drop his plea for peace and do his utmost to promote the Council. The effort to bypass the princes was further revealed in the Pope's direct appeal on November 3 to the French Cardinals, whom he now tried to order to Rome.

While Farnese's letters were in transit, however, Sadoleto unwittingly worked at cross purposes with the Holy See. Writing to the Vice-Chancellor from Angoulême on November 14, he explained that it seemed best, in the interest of securing the King's consent to arbitration, not even to mention the Council at this time: it was more desirable to commit the crown to peace and to the Legate's own plan for negotiation.[44] Because his majesty had already observed that a

Council was out of the question so long as hostilities continued, Sadoleto explained that he would not waste time trying to persuade the French Cardinals to obey the summons to Rome and advised the Pope to deal more tactfully with them in the future.[45]

On November 25, however, Farnese's instructions reached Sadoleto at Angoulême and he acknowledged them on the thirtieth, after conveying to the King the Pope's proposal for a colloquy the following year.[46] Francis replied that if he went to Italy for such a conference, he would take no fewer than 60,000 men with him; he considered the Council necessary but would send none of his prelates until peace was concluded. Nor would he now permit his Cardinals to go to Italy. For his own part, the Legate reiterated his conviction that a colloquy of peace offered "the last and only hope" of avoiding catastrophe. He left the court on December 4 and was in S. Felice, to which he continued because of the plague at Carpentras, on the twenty-ninth.[47]

Undertaken at great personal hardship to Sadoleto, the mission was still a total failure, not so much from his own obvious defects in its pursuit as from the basic futility of its purposes. If the Legation accomplished anything, it was to reveal the great indifference of the princes to intervention by the Holy See and their present disregard for the Council. It also disclosed the gravity of the Emperor's anger toward Rome and the King's persistent fear that the Council would work to his rival's political advantage.[48]

Otherwise the Legation throws some light on Sadoleto as a "man of action"; what we see is his great attachment to the cause of Christian peace and his equally great ineptitude in seeking it. Sadoleto's conduct at the royal court and his dispatches to Rome in particular suggest Pole's tendency to turn "from the hard, unpleasant, unchangeable realities of a problem to the ideal way in which it ought to be solved."[49] Sadoleto understood secular politics no better in this assignment than in his treatises on the crusade. Conscious though he was of princely power as a source of division and disorder, he seldom disciplined himself, whether as moralist or diplomat, to think in terms of the feasible. His concern was usually with what the princes should do rather than with what could actually be expected from them. And yet when directly confronted with individuals—whether Ercole d'Este or Ercole Gonzaga, Duke George of Saxony or William of Bavaria, or any of the three Popes he served—Sadoleto assumed the manner of a client before a patron, eager for signs of favor, willing to praise and idealize them, and invariably the subordinate.[50] Often a poor observer of the immediate and the particular, he preferred at the end of the Legation in 1542 again to see the world from a distance, which is to say, from Carpentras.

Before leaving Angoulême for the Comtat, Sadoleto informed Farnese of his intention to return to Carpentras for at least a month, certain that he would be permitted to wait out the rest of the winter there before receiving new orders.[51] But what then? Once back in Provence the fear of being called back to Rome became an obsession.

Still living in solitude at the priory, he wrote to Farnese on January 21, 1543, begging the Vice-Chancellor to define his status and thus settle the question once and for all. If the Pope intended to summon him to the Curia again, then His Holiness should know that it would be quite impossible for him to live in Rome without supplemental income. God himself, as St. Augustine put it, cannot command what cannot be done. This was no oblique allusion to penury but an open request for additional funds as the condition for returning to Rome. He advanced his case on the ground of merit no less than of need in the most arresting self-portrait of his later life:

I am certainly a familiar figure in many parts of Christendom and not entirely disdained. I am feared by the Lutherans as much as any one is and credited by them with the capacity to confound them with their own weapons. I am a person for whom able men in Italy and elsewhere have considerable respect, and when they resolve to turn their backs on the Pope and the Holy See, as is done in so many places, my reputation and authority among them retains their loyalty [e.g., in Modena?]. I was born and brought up honorably enough, I am versed in good letters and the liberal arts with a degree of recognition, and am neither ignoble nor base in spirit.[52]

For these reasons, he concluded, "I entreat Your Reverence to assist and preserve me lest I be called where I cannot go." Specifically, he put himself forward as one qualified for the Legation at Bologna, unfilled since the death of Contarini, or at least for access to some of its income. Only by such means would it be possible to settle in Rome and to live there in the manner which befits a Cardinal.

Then comes an even more impassioned petition. What Sadoleto wanted above all was the Pope's "perpetua licentia" to remain at Carpentras. Granted this, dear to him above all else, he would have nothing further to ask, for "of all the favors which I can expect from Your Reverence and His Holiness, this is and always will be the greatest, the highest of all."[53]

Farnese replied from Forli on March 13: because of the Emperor's intention to be in Italy in April and in view of his reported willingness now to reach an agreement with Francis I, the Pope would have to require Sadoleto to rejoin the Curia.[54] If Sadoleto came south for the Pope's meeting with Charles at Bologna, His Holiness in turn would give attention to the Cardinal's financial needs. And a month later he was ordered to Italy on the simple ground that he could not be spared.[55] Farnese went on to say that since the College had suffered so many deaths in recent years the living were under even greater obligation to take their places in Rome.[56] What Farnese failed to understand, however, was that the argument could be turned around. No one was more aware of these losses than Sadoleto, for they included some of his most sympathetic colleagues. In view of what the College had become without them he was more reluctant than ever to go back to Rome. The loss of Contarini was particularly painful, he explained to Negri, since it followed the death of other close friends. "By now there remain only a few . . . who have genuine esteem for me and respect for my convictions."[57] Farnese's reminder was therefore more frightening than compelling.

But Farnese had made it clear that the Pope insisted on Sadoleto's

7+

participation in new talks with the Emperor. The papal request became an "imperium," as Sadoleto put it, so toward the end of March he acquiesced, although the journey was not begun until May. From Modena he sent Fiordibello with a letter to Farnese at Bologna, "concealing nothing of my melancholy and making clear how difficult it has been for me to come to Italy and how inconvenient. . . ." He also asked for permission to return to Carpentras as soon as the colloquy ended, this being "the one and only favor I ask of the Supreme Pontiff." The rumor that the Pope had made him Legate to Bologna was unfounded, he wrote Paolo.[58] "If I am given what I want, I will return to you at home and remain with those dearest to me." He would reject a benefice at Bologna anyway if it required him to live, "as though in exile," away from the Contado.[59]

The Emperor reached Savona on May 24, and once the news got inland the Curia quickly came to life. However, Sadoleto's thoughts were not on the colloquy so much as on winning consent to leave for Carpentras when it ended. During a conversation with Paul III on June 6 he repeated the request for additional income, but even more emphatically renewed his petition to return to Provence. The Pope replied that for the present, at least, he could give no decision.[60]

This was hardly the time to importune the Pope with so personal a matter, for His Holiness was suddenly faced with the Emperor's firm opposition to the projected talks. Eager to continue to Germany and indifferent to further discussion of peace, Charles refused to go so far out of his way as Bologna and in fact seemed unwilling to meet the Pope anywhere. On June 8 the Cardinals had to reconsider their counsel that the Pope go no farther west than Bologna and that he treat with Charles only through nuncios if the Emperor declined to compromise on a site. When it came his turn to speak, Sadoleto impatiently challenged the pride of his colleagues with the argument that a face-to-face meeting between Pope and Emperor was indispensable to the cause of peace. So unique is the office of the Pope, he said, that there can be no alternative to direct talks with Charles V, particularly in view of rumors about bad relations between him and

Paul III; if the Emperor finds the Pope willing to proceed beyond Bologna toward Parma, he will be shamed into a conference. The age and infirmity of the Pontiff, or the risk of injuring his dignity, could not be taken as legitimate objections.[61]

Initially so unconcerned with the colloquy that he launched his efforts to leave Italy before it opened, Sadoleto now managed to change the mood of the consistory and thus to bring about the fourth and last encounter between Paul III and Charles V.[62] On June 11 the Pope set out for Parma, leaving behind the Cardinals of pro-French persuasion, and reached the city on the fifteenth. At a secret consistory in the episcopal palace three days later he designated Cervini and Parisio as his Legates to the Emperor at Cremona, apparently with instructions to determine a mutually acceptable meeting place. Even then, however, there was no certainty that Charles would consent to see the Pope. Sadoleto looked disconsolately at this episode, to him a dismal exhibit of self-seeking without any concern for the common needs of Christendom, and took comfort only in the thought that he had no personal responsibility for the chaos around him.[63]

After a week of negotiation, the Pope moved again, now to Busseto, a village between Parma and Piacenza, where he first met Charles on June 22. With him at this first meeting were Sadoleto, Cardinal Grimani, and the two Legates. The conference lasted through the twenty-fourth and ranged disjointedly over the Franco-Imperial war, the Emperor's alliance with Henry VIII, the disposition of Milan, the status of the Colonna, the advance of the Turks, and the opening of the Council. On the last day Paul III brought twelve Cardinals forward to exhort the Emperor to peace with France,[64] but his Majesty flatly refused and added that he would also oppose the convocation of the Council anywhere under present circumstances. He likewise defended his alliance with England and made it impossible to reach a settlement over Milan. The Pope, on the other hand, refused to abandon his neutrality, so that the issue of the conference was entirely barren. If anything, the tension between Empire and Papacy was more strained after Busseto than before.

Charles started north on the twenty-fifth, while the Pope returned to Bologna, his court regrouped except for Sadoleto, who took leave of the Curia at Parma to return to Provence.⁶⁵ While the Bishop hastened to Carpentras for two more—as it turned out, the last— years of "blessed tranquility," Paul III suspended the Council *ad beneplacitum*, opening thereby another interim of restless waiting.⁶⁶

On his way north Sadoleto stopped briefly at Milan,⁶⁷ where he met his friend Speciano, a cultivated statesman and soldier, who questioned the Cardinal rather closely about his willingness to leave the Pope. As Speciano put it, Sadoleto was about to cut himself off from matters of public concern in order to retreat to his books, in spite of his station and responsibility. Put in these terms, Sadoleto conceded, the decision was ignominious. But why not say that he left the court because he found himself accomplishing nothing in it, being consistently opposed in whatever he proposed for the good of the Church? In the solitude of his diocese he could at least pursue goals which would be of some value to it. Sadoleto answered, in other words, that he left the Pope not simply to enjoy private leisure, but because he found it vain to struggle against prevailing opinion in the Curia or against the conduct of the princes. So long as Christian princes are willing to destroy the Church rather than protect it, "What was I to do? Was I to make myself a spectator of the common miseries?" Sadoleto argued here, as he had so many times before, that he gave up the *vita negotiosa* because he found among its prac- titioners neither the will nor the capacity to save the Church from disaster; and while admitting his preference for Carpentras he claimed that only there was he in a position, through study and contemplation, to work constructively for the welfare of the faith. In returning "to port" once more he had not abandoned the Church at all.⁶⁸

But just how is the word "princes" to be read in these remarks to Speciano? Who was it that Sadoleto had in mind when he spoke of "those in authority and power"? Did he refer only to the secular rulers, or did he also mean to include the Pope and the Cardinals? The letter seems to extend his judgments to the Curia as well as to the Emperor and his circle, suggesting a sense of isolation from the College as a whole.[69] Sadoleto's chronic disillusionment with the Curia appears to have been that not only of a humanist whose tastes were incompatible with public life, but also of a sensitive and offended reformer, who seemed to find himself in a permanent minority. Carpentras continued to be in his eyes a unique place of refuge, but its calm was nonetheless incomplete.

X

Embattled Bishop

Disrupting what Speciano imagined to be the deep quiet of Carpentras and the serenity of Sadoleto's life there was a series of crises which turned the diocese like the county into anything but the place of peace which Jacopo once trusted the region would become. In his utopian expectations for the Comtat Venaissin Sadoleto wanted to think that the little world around him would be high ground which the flood tides of religious discord and civil strife would never reach, or at least a quiet harbor in which he and his people could enjoy lasting refuge. His hope seemed to be that by remaining in Carpentras he could isolate himself from conditions over which princes and priests had lost control everywhere else. He was to find, however, that Provence belonged to the world quite as much as Italy.

For one thing, relations between Carpentras and Avignon had already taken a turn for the worse even before Sadoleto went to Bologna and Busseto. New conflicts with the Legation developed in 1541 when Alessandro Farnese, already Vice-Chancellor of the Church and Archbishop of Avignon, was appointed successor to Cardinal Clermont.[1] Sadoleto still declared that he was the "first personage and head" of the Comtat, but Farnese's Vice-Legates—initially Filberto Ferrero, Bishop of Ivrea, and then the heavy-handed Alessandro Campeggio[2]—promptly extended their jurisdiction at his expense. Farnese attempted to pacify the *contadini* and reassure the Sadoleti by appointing Paolo as rector of the county, but once again an exchange of charges reached the Vatican from both parties, the Bishop accusing Campeggio of corruption and misgovernment while the Vice-Legate complained of unwarranted interference from the see of Carpentras.[3] At the center of the controversy were the fiscal powers of a regime far more assertive than Clermont's and administered by ill-paid officials who lived from fees and fines. Avignon, which Sadoleto once praised as "the second Rome," now threatened his autonomy as much as the first by the time the Farnese family directly controlled each.

Moreover, the Sadoletti were under heavy pressure to resist the encroachments of the two Romes from lay representatives of the Comtat. These delegates, known as "Electi" or "Elus," were originally spokesmen for the Estates during interims between assemblies, but by 1531 they formed a standing commission of fifteen, empowered to speak for the lay population in all matters of public concern.[4] Vigilant guardians of traditional rights and privileges, they carried their grievances directly to the Roman Curia as dependents of the Holy See and closely supported Sadoleto in his struggle with the Legation.[5] Of equal concern to the delegates was the favored position of the Jewish bankers, whose rights were still being bitterly attacked when Sadoleto returned from Nice in 1538. A year later, having recently been given full inquisitorial powers over Vaudois heretics in Avignon and the county, he wrote Farnese to demand how he could be required to persecute Lutherans in the name of Christian orthodoxy while protecting Jewish bankers in their privileged power over indigent Catholic peasants. No group in the county, he claimed, is more indulged in Rome, where the Jews are laden with privileges which they buy "to fatten on the common people like wolves among cattle."[6] Sadoleto tirelessly sought support in the College and relief for his people from the Curia[7]; but he gained little except the gratitude of the delegates for his futile attention to their "welfare and tranquility."

The predicament of agrarian debtors further deteriorated from the quartering of French troops in the Comtat at various times from 1539 until 1544.[8] When Francis I occupied the papal states in 1539, he treated the region like a conquered country, goaded by hatred of the Pope and the house of Farnese. The troops which Sadoleto watched on his way to the royal court in 1542 were inflicting fresh abuse on the

countryside with their heavy requisitions and pillaging. At one time
the people of Carpentras were forced to feed 8,000 Swiss mercenaries
for several weeks and then to supply the King's army with huge
quantities of grain in 1544, after a time of drought and thin harvests.
The Estates again made useless protests and were finally relieved of
the occupation only through Sadoleto's efforts and the coming of
peace in September. Once more the *Electi* and the diocese worked
together, appealing broadcast for help in letters to Farnese, Tournon,
Cardinal Lorraine, and the Pope.[9]

Although it provided occasional leisure for its studious Bishop,
papal Provence seems an unlikely *portus* for one seeking to escape the
stress of public life. Certainly the Comtat enjoyed no immunities
from the violence and conflict with which these decades were charged;
but in spite of clerical politics, war, heresy, plague, and the mistral,
Sadoleto still preferred it to any other place he knew.

Yet his strifeless ideal for the diocese was realized in no part of its life,
not even in the little college which the Bishop founded and nurtured.
The academy became merely one more part of diocesan life over
which its benign and protective Bishop was unable to gain full control.
Among other things he discovered that the consuls or syndics of
Carpentras were determined to participate in the selection of teachers
for the college. When Volusene retired from his post in 1537, apparently
in order to write, the communal fathers chose as his successor a man
whom we know only as Cassandro, evidently hired while Sadoleto
was in Rome as a member of the reform Commission.[10] The new
master was well liked in the town and in good standing with its
council, but he displeased both the episcopal vicar and the absent
Bishop. Convinced that Cassandro was a heretic, the vicar firmly
demanded his dismissal and was supported by Sadoleto in Rome, who
at that time was awaiting a reply from Melanchthon![11] On the other

hand, certain members of the town council were determined that the master at least be given a hearing on the issue of heresy. What had the making of a serious dispute between the manse and the council ended suddenly, however, when Cassandro died in the summer of 1537.

On their own initiative, the consuls thereupon appointed one Jacques Bording, a humanist physician from Antwerp, to replace Volusene and his successor. The consul Centenier notified the Sadoletti of Bording's acceptance in October of 1537 and received their approval before Christmas.[12] Bording himself was well educated, having studied literature at Louvain and medicine at Paris before teaching Hebrew and Greek in the Collège at Lisieux. His conduct at Carpentras seems to have been highly satisfactory, but he remained for only three years. In 1540 he decided to move on to Montpellier and Bologna to resume his medical studies, and went to Italy with generous letters of introduction from Cardinal Sadoleto.[13] We do not know the identity of Bording's replacement, but it is said that Bording himself returned to Carpentras with the expectation of settling there permanently, only to find that he was obliged to leave because of his reputed attachment to Calvinism.[14] The suspicion of heresy which hovered over Cassandro became a reality in the case of his successor.

By the spring of 1544 the consuls again were searching for a principal at the college. This time their choice fell on the celebrated Claude Baduel, until recently the rector of the new university at Nîmes and a candidate who went out of his way to seek the vacant but far more modest post at Carpentras.[15] The striking feature of this appointment, made while Sadoleto was at Carpentras and blessed with his full approval, was that Baduel's heterodoxy lay in the past and present as well as in the future. A Nîmois by birth, he had studied at Louvain, Liège, and Marburg before going to Wittenberg, where he knew Melanchthon and received through him a letter to Marguerite of Navarre, who also heard well of him from Martin Bucer.[16] Baduel's association with Sturm, Bucer, and Melanchthon matured in 1538-39 at the very time when Sadoleto, for different reasons, was vainly trying to win their confidence.[17]

While teaching in Paris, Baduel was recommended through Queen
7*

Marguerite in 1539 to the consuls at Nîmes for consideration as rector of the young university there. He received the appointment and took up his duties in 1540, a vigorous pedagogue and serious classicist who set the curriculum defiantly against the whole course of scholastic studies. But when after great effort he brought one of his former professors from Louvain to Nîmes, the university became a cockpit in which the old curriculum, represented by Guillaume Bigot, was ranged against Baduel's passionate advocacy of the new learning. Fought out in lecture rooms, with placards on the streets and in the city council, the struggle temporarily ended in a truce at the start of 1544, but by then Baduel was eager to leave Nîmes entirely. He was weary of conflict and perhaps no less concerned over the risk of falling victim to a campaign against heresy recently launched in the Conseil de Toulouse; it has even been suggested that his motive for going to Carpentras was to find security behind the prestige of its Bishop.[18]

Baduel had associations in Provence through certain of the Isnard or Isnardi, an influential Provençal family later represented in the court of the rector as well as in the Calvinist ministry.[19] Baduel, however, was also an earnest scholar and teacher, who was intent upon vindicating his principles of humanist education in a place where he could defend them freely. So he applied for the post through Sadoleto and was appointed by the consuls in May 1544.[20] He accepted it in a letter to the Bishop on August 26 and at great length in a formal treatise written in September, when he elaborated his doctrine of classical studies and reviewed the afflictions he suffered across the Rhône. Evidently pleased to have the appointment, Baduel flattered the Bishop by describing Carpentras as the Athens of Provence and heir to the lost glory of pre-Christian Marseilles.[21]

Once in Carpentras, however, the new master played a double game, the disciple not only of Cicero but also of Sturm and Calvin. Embarrassed by his extravagant praise of Sadoleto, he explained to Calvin in a letter written from Carpentras that he had "yielded to circumstance" but added that he was still mindful of his "Christian vocation [and] the duty to confess Christ."[22] He wrote of his progress both in teaching the classics and in spreading his own sort of evangelism among "good men eager for the glory of Christ," including a certain papal *quaestor* who seemed particularly receptive to it. In fact Baduel appeared as zealous for the new theology as he was for the new learning, and throughout his brief tenure in the college he remained in contact with both Calvin and Bucer. How ironic that Baduel at Carpentras was also reading works by two Protestant reformers who in one way or another had already broken swords with Cardinal Sadoleto, Baduel's sponsor and superior in a Catholic diocese and a papal state.

Although he fell under attack from classicists and Catholics alike, Baduel's dismissal at the end of his first year at Carpentras was based on a purely neutral argument. In a letter of September 20, 1545, the consuls simply asked him to accept cancellation of his contract.[23] Owing to loss of tax money through the ravages of the plague and the death of so many citizens, they explained that the town was unable to pay his salary or to keep the college open for the coming year. The letter was cordial and correct but seems unmistakably a request that Baduel resign, with the promise that he would eventually be paid. By the start of 1546 he was back at Nîmes and in two years was declared a heretic at the *Grands Jours* of Auvergne. Five years later he was at Geneva, where he was ordained a Calvinist preacher and made professor of philosophy.[24]

Little wonder then that Sadoleto admonished Volusene, about to return to Scotland in 1546, to stand fast in the faith.[25] Carpentras had curiously become something of a haven for the heterodox in the decade of the 'forties, providing temporary asylum for the Vaudois Jacques Reynaud of Arles, Gabriel des Isnard, and the physician Valeriole, all of whom were friends of Baduel. The local Franciscan Conventuals, once the hosts of Pole, were reported to be contaminated with heresy in 1545 and were later placed under investigation by the Vice-Legate.[26] In no respect whatever, though, did either Sadoleto or the consuls deliberately offer refuge to these doctrinal vagrants. Even in appointing Baduel the Bishop no less than the council was merely seeking a good Latinist, while Baduel, like Sadoleto, counted himself a good Christian dedicated to the promotion of sound learning. Nevertheless, it is remarkable that while Sadoleto boasted of preserving true doctrine among his people, three of the four masters invited to teach in the college were found to be more faithful to the classics than to the dogma of the Church.

His involvement in the problem of local heresy, moreover, by no means ended with the affairs of the college. The papal enclave in France, like the region which surrounded it, was widely infected by religious dissent, as the Vice-Legate, the Pope, Francis I, and the Sadoletti were finally obliged to admit. And one of the most complex and frequently puzzling aspects of Sadoleto's ecclesiastical career concerns his relations with the Vaudois of Provence between 1539–1545.

I n the midst of his first quarrel with the Legation and the visiting papal commissioners in 1531 Sadoleto informed Clement VII that there was not a trace of Lutheranism in the entire province of Avignon.[27] However, by the time he returned from Nice in 1538 such claims were no longer possible, and Sadoleto reluctantly admitted that heresy had made extensive gains in recent years.[28]

In June 1539 Paul III entrusted him with full inquisitorial authority over the heretics of Avignon and the Venaissin.[29] The Cardinal appreciated the *diploma* as a sign of the Pope's confidence but confessed that he did not expect to have to use the powers and methods which it made possible. "I propose," he explained to Farnese, "to employ more lenient means: not those of fear or punishment, but arms more valid for changing the minds of the wicked, that is, truth and Christian clemency, which press confession of error from the heart rather than from the mouth."[30] Thereupon he turned at considerably greater length to the privileged status of the Jews; if we are to judge from his letters to Rome at this time, the Bishop seemed far more intent upon interesting the Holy See in the suppression of Jewish merchants and bankers than in starting a crusade against the Waldensian peasants of the region, although they were then growing in numbers and daring in Piedmont as well as the interior of Provence itself.

The Vaudois of southeastern France at this time were heirs of a vestigal mountain heresy which originated in the Middle Ages.[31] Having been persecuted in more recent times by the Duke of Savoy, they migrated into the valleys of the Luberon, a mountain chain laced with ravines which extends for forty miles from the Maritime Alps into Provence, and settled on the estates of Piedmontese land-lords. Others appeared in rising numbers at Cabrières (in the diocese of Carpentras), at Gordes, Goult, Bonnieux, and in French Provence at Mérindol, called the "Geneva" of the region. It is said that by 1540 there were probably 10,000 Vaudois families in the papal county alone.

The first general persecution of these people in the sixteenth century was organized by the Dominican Giovanni da Roma in 1528 and was taken up again by Cardinal Clermont in 1535, when he tried un-successfully to banish them from the province. By the time Sadoleto was made Cardinal the Pope as well as the French King was searching for the means of effective suppression. The Vaudois meanwhile had negotiated a loose accord with Swiss and German Protestants, although they were brought to it more through Farel's eloquence and their own hatred of the Roman Church than by any real doctrinal affinity for Lutheranism.[32] The effect of this alliance was to embolden the Vaudois (who were now being called "Lutherans" by their enemies) and to encourage the use of violence among them in opposing and harassing the hierarchy and the crown.

The policy of Francis I oscillated between leniency and repression in the decade 1535–45 but swung, at midpoint, toward broad repres-sion in the Edict of Fontainebleau during the summer of 1540.[33] The most severe and specific decree of the whole era, however, was an *arrêt* in the Parlement of Aix on November 18, 1540, which ordered total destruction for the village of Mérindol and condemned nineteen of its inhabitants to be burned alive. Although the Archbishops of Aix and Arles demanded its immediate enforcement, the President of the Parlement, Barthélemy Chassanée, refused and held the decree in abeyance. For one thing, an inquest conducted in the region by Guillaume du Bellay was favorable to the Vaudois and described them as innocuous, industrious, and obedient.[34] Having no faith in the techniques of forceful repression, du Bellay himself persuaded the king to withdraw his consent of December 14, 1540, to the execution of the *arrêt* of Aix and to give those suspected of heresy three months in which to renounce their creed and return to the true faith.

The Vaudois of both Mérindol and Cabrières thereupon drafted statements of their doctrine to present first to local authorities, lay and ecclesiastical, and eventually to the king. The Confession of Cabrières[35] was given simultaneously to Pietro Ghinucci, the impatient and militant Bishop of Cavaillon,[36] and to Sadoleto at Carpentras. Our sole accounts of Sadoleto's reaction to the document come from the Protestant Crespin and the sympathetic pen of J. A. de Thou,[37] who stated that although the Cardinal proposed certain revisions of the text and objected to its language with respect to the Pope and the Roman clergy, Sadoleto found the confession otherwise acceptable and offered to discuss it with the authors at S. Felice.[38] His tone in writing to the Vaudois, according to de Thou and Crespin, was at once critical and conciliatory; their account gains credibility from Sadoleto's reported statement that he hoped all such disputes would eventually be referred to the Council, and even more from mention of his doubts and disappointment after returning to Provence from Busseto in 1543. Even though the source is not of prime reliability, we have found such views expressed in Sadoleto's own hand at this time. Crespin also relates that before departing for Rome in 1542 Sadoleto managed to dissuade Alessandro Campeggio from carrying out a campaign which was about to strike at Cabrières, inasmuch as the Vaudois had submitted a confession of faith and offered, as a sign of their good will, to modify it as he recommended. In any case, it is certain that Sadoleto alone among the prelates of the county and the Legation opposed the use of force against the Vaudois in principle while trusting—no doubt somewhat naïvely—in the efficacy of persuasion and discussion. On the other hand, his willingness to hear, counsel, and forgive the heretics arose from his belief that they could be led back in time to the Church, an attitude shared by Chassanée and sporadically honored as public policy by Francis I at the behest of du Bellay and Marguerite of Navarre. Impatiently hostile to this position were the two Ghinucci, the Vice-Legate Campeggio, Cardinal Tournon, the Parlement of Aix, and the clergy of French Provence.

At the end of 1542 the season of calm faded into a time of new persecution, beginning with local action on the part of Pietro Ghinucci and the Aixois. In April the Bishop of Cavaillon paid a menacing visit to Mérindol, even though the village was not in his diocese or the county, and in August to Cabrières while Sadoleto was in Rome. For their part the Vaudois resorted to terror, plundering the abbeys of Senauque and St. Hilaire under the leadership of Eustache Marron, the Vaudois firebrand and captain of Cabrières. In 1543 the Vice-Legate led 400 papal troops against the town with the help of the Nuncio Dandino, but failed to capture it. While the Parlement and clergy of Aix collaborated with the Legation and Tournon supported their plans at court, Francis I consented to the execution of the *arrêt* against Mérindol. But once again his sister persuaded him to withdraw his consent in *lettres de surséance*. However, the party of moderation lost partisans on each front in the course of the year through the deaths of Guillaume du Bellay and the President Chassanée, who was replaced by Jean de Meynier, Baron d'Oppède, the most fanatic enemy the Vaudois ever faced.

In December Sadoleto wrote to Niccolò Ardinghelli, Farnese's secretary, to warn—for the last time, he said—against what looked to him like a perilous drift to violence in local policy toward the heretics. He predicted that a crusade against Cabrières would only bring catastrophe to the whole region, but admitted that his fears were not shared in the Legation at Avignon.

I feel that I have given sound admonition on the matter of Cabrières; but, as I say, since it is ignored and a different policy followed, one fraught with injury and shame for us, I have now resolved to withdraw from public issues of this kind in order not to waste my strength or what little authority I still have. . . .[39]

Once more there was the sense of being unheeded, of pleading without support and even a trace of self-pity in one who said he preferred "this quiet and obscure life" to that of power and authority. But he also concluded with the hope that the inhabitants of the province could be governed by the Legation with greater justice and moderation, and that the Curia would put its confidence in better men than those who were currently advising the Vice-Legate.

It is difficult to separate Sadoleto's long conflict with Avignon from his attitude toward the Vaudois, but in any case he enjoyed no visible support for his attitude toward either the Legation or the heretics. In March 1544 Pietro Gelido, a cameral official in the county, reported to Farnese that the whole region was in a state of dangerous disorder and that the Vaudois intended to build up a "Swiss canton" around Cabrières and Mérindol. A renegade Calvinist himself, Gelido went on to deplore Sadoleto's clemency toward the Waldensians and urged that the Cardinal be ordered to abandon his policy of reconciliation for an energetic campaign against the heretics.[40] Therefore Cortese must certainly have been misinformed when in the same summer he congratulated Jacopo for exerting himself to "put down and extinguish the impiety of wicked men."[41] Sadoleto had no discernible part whatever in building up the engine of repression which was put together at this time.

But Paolo Sadoleto did. In his capacity as rector he supported the advocates of repression in the local hierarchy and urged that the Papal Legation now cooperate with the French crown in suppressing the Vaudois in the county at the earliest possible moment.[42] In his view they were simple outlaws to be crushed once and for all, although he conceded that the problem of heresy itself, following his cousin's habitual argument, was more difficult and a matter to be treated by a future Council.[43] In the meantime Paolo joined the Vice-Legate, Ghinucci, and the Baron d' Oppède in formulating the strategy of their offensive, while Jacopo, almost unheard of during these months, was completing his *Oratio de pace*. The Cardinal was thus pleading for a holy war against the Turk while the rector worked for a crusade against the Vaudois.

Early in 1545 Baduel wrote Calvin from Carpentras to suggest that the Vaudois be cautioned against excessive and imprudent action, being himself concerned, it appears, over the conduct of men like Marron.[44] But it was too late. Francis I had already and decisively ordered the *arrêt* against Mérindol to be enforced. Pressure from Tournon, Gelido, and the Parlement of Aix was too great to withstand any longer; he also feared that the Vaudois of Provence might soon open a schism in France which could grow into a major domestic problem, and was further alarmed by extravagant reports of Vaudois strength. Control of the roads and passes through Provence to Italy by a hostile minority was not to be tolerated, and such fears had been skilfully nourished by the rigorists around him.

Leadership of the crusade in the south now passed to d'Oppède. By forging an endorsement to a set of royal orders to Captain Paulin de la Garde and the *armée de la mer* on its way to Roussillon, the Baron managed to enlist the support of additional troops, recently in combat as allies of the Turks, against the Catholic forces of the Emperor! Ordered to the field on April 13, the expedition numbered about 5,000, most of them French regulars, supplemented by forces provided by Agostino Trivulzio, the new Vice-Legate. The operation lasted only a week, but quickly became an orgy of destruction which laid waste to more than twenty towns and villages, with climactic assaults on Mérindol and Cabrières; those who did not flee to the mountains were slaughtered or sent to the galleys. So from the standpoint of d'Oppède and his colleagues the campaign was a complete success.[45]

This melancholy saga, corrupted in the telling by the confessional bias of chroniclers and historians alike, bears closely on the interpretation of Sadoleto. Jacopo has been idealized in Protestant accounts as a prelate of singular and heroic tolerance, and of firm resistance to the methods of force.[46] To certain Catholic historians, on the other hand, he was the victim of his illusions and even a churchman of questionable intent.[47] It is generally conceded that among the local clergy in Provence, in any event, he played a unique part in the drama. The real test, however, is his attitude toward the massacre of Cabrières and Mérindol. Ludwig von Pastor, following the account of the Protestant Benrath,[48] was willing to say that "It is certain that in 1545 the bloody chastisement of the Waldensians met with his approval," and that

"Even Sadoleto, otherwise the advocate of clemency, thought their chastisement just."[49] But in each instance the basis of these statements is a letter to Farnese from Carpentras dated April 23, 1545,[50] the author of which was not Jacopo at all, as von Pastor and Benrath incorrectly assumed, but Paolo, who explained as he wrote that Jacopo was then on his way to Rome.[51]

Paolo, to be sure, did rejoice in the capture of Cabrières as the "just punishment of its heretics and rebels," a "memorable lesson" to those who went long unpunished before the town was returned to obedience. The rector also expressed admiration for the genius of the massacre, Baron d'Oppède. Paolo took pleasure in reporting this news to his cousin, and indeed a Protestant contemporary understood that "Sadoleto acted most brutally against the Lord in Provence."[52] But the simple fact is that Jacopo, so far as the evidence reveals, neither supported the policy of forceful repression before the assault of April 1545 nor rejoiced in its success after the massacres took place. As far as we know, he remained mute about the episode once back in Rome.

This is not to say that he was ever sentimental in his attitude toward the Vaudois or that he tried to explain away their excesses. The contempt which he felt for Luther, Calvin, and Farel must certainly have fallen on Vaudois leaders like Marron. We know, however, that at least until the time of the Vaudois raid on Cavaillon in November 1544, Sadoleto steadfastly opposed the use of force against them as a matter of public policy if not also of principle; that he associated oppression of the Vaudois with the Vice-Legate's crude and authoritarian government; and that he tenaciously believed that the arts of persuasion would succeed where coercion was bound to fail.[53] The whole man must be changed, he said, and not merely his civil conduct. We know, too, if only by way of negative evidence, that Sadoleto took no part in the councils of war at Avignon in December 1544 or at Marseilles in March of the next year over the organization of military action against the heretics; and we know further of his conviction that the first purpose of government is the preservation of peace.[54] Horrified by the spectacle of internecine war in Germany, he liked its prospect no better in Provence. It is difficult to understand, therefore, why it has been argued that Jacopo experienced a dramatic change of heart on the issue of reconciliation after 1539 or 1542.

On the other hand, he also revealed certain weaknesses of his own in the affair of the Vaudois. Once again, for example, he overestimated the power of persuasion and the likelihood of saving men from error. He seemed willing again to believe that if the Church followed the ways of charity and patience, it would eventually triumph over wrong doctrine and disobedience. While trying to restrain Campeggio, Farnese, and Ghinucci, he advised the Vaudois to modify the style of their written confession and to "change certain words" in it. In contrast to Paolo he was, both in the strict and in the larger sense, the constant humanist, the man of moderation and clemency, the solitary irenic in his view of the Lutherans and the Genevans no less than in his attitude toward the Vaudois peasants of Provence. In none of these cases, however, did he comprehend the function or importance of leadership among the heretics any more than he understood the political implications of schism for Church and State, or the raw cleavages which now divided common men.

The old Bishop, capable of combat and willing to fight against injustice whether at the hands of papal magistrats or the Jews, showed an equal capacity for resignation when he found himself disregarded by colleagues and superiors. Such evidently was the case in the court of Clement VII and on the reform Commission under Paul III; we have seen it again after Busseto and in his letter to Rome about legatine policy toward the Waldensians. Knowing that he was out of step and sympathy with the local hierarchy, the Legation and the Curia, he chose to quit the struggle altogether.

This repugnance of conflict was by no means unique with Sadoleto. Erasmus once conceded that "So much do I hate contention and love concord that I am afraid when strife develops, I would rather abandon a part of the truth than disturb the peace. . . ."[55] Melanchthon wrote to his persecutor Nausea in 1540 to say that "I have tried, as God is my witness, to salvage something constructive out of this tangle of controversies, and I believe many good men approve of my judgment and efforts. For instinctively I shrink away from strife."[56] Erasmus,

Melanchthon, and Sadoleto were all capable, each in his own way, of withering anger and of engaging an enemy closely, but each was temperamentally averse to violence and aspired in his own style to be a promoter of concord. Curiously, however, it was the Cardinal among them—potentially the most influential—who gave up most readily and who valued strifeless calm most highly, sometimes without calculating the risks to follow if his own convictions were defeated.

We cannot, in any case, dismiss his thoughts and feelings about the punishment of the Vaudois by invoking a brusque change of heart. Considered whole, the issue is still seen darkly at best, through fragments of hearsay and scattered opinions, while at many crucial junctures no record whatever survives. We can do no more than conclude that all remaining primary evidence, as well as the crust of legend which has grown over the history of the Vaudois in Provence,[57] supports the conclusion that as long as Sadoleto was in the Comtat he stood virtually alone in opposing the use of force. Neither on this occasion nor at any other time in his life was Sadoleto willing to believe that violence could be the servant of faith in the controversy over Christian doctrine.

Soon after writing to Rome to protest against legatine policy in the county, Jacopo made a series of appeals to the Curia for full release from his episcopal duties. Although he had asked Farnese to recognize Paolo as his successor in 1542,[58] his petitions show added insistence during the first half of 1544, when the struggle with Campeggio neared its climax. His health was failing and his spirits showed new signs of fatigue and irascibility, even though the will to fight back against what he counted as encroachments on the rights and privileges of the Comtat was never stronger. However, he confided to Pole that he had been exhausted by all this contention and spoke in February 1544 of leaving Provence entirely.[59] A clearer sign of despair would be hard to imagine.

Sadoleto was very much disturbed by Farnese's tolerance for Campeggio and by a general trend toward arbitrary government at all levels of the Vice-Legate's regime. He warned the Vice-Chancellor that the avarice and injustice of the magistrates under Campeggio were producing "untold seditions and discontent," although whether by *seditioni* he meant to include the lawless forays of the Vaudois as a reaction to misgovernment we do not know. But he did say that unless current practices were stopped, the Legation would lose its honor in the province and find it impossible to be at peace with the *contadini*.[60] He reminded Farnese that Avignon and the Venaissin were an international crossroads, in full view of other nations, and that papal government there could not afford to be conspicuous for its faults.

While in the diocese Sadoleto confessed that he could not neglect the defense of its interests, but he was eager to give over its administration and routine to Paolo so that he could find time for quiet and repose, for "studio et contemplatione delle cose divine."[61] It was more than a vague aspiration, for he wrote Gualteruzzi in March to ask that the transfer be formally recognized in the Vatican.[62] More and more, he told Farnese, he longed for solitude and complete retirement. Official approval of his request did not materialize, however, even though Paolo in fact had succeeded his uncle and freely spoke in his capacity as rector for the diocese as well.[63]

In the midst of these plans for relief from "mundane cares" Sadoleto began to revise his treatise *De peccato originis*, of which he had completed a first draft in 1543.[64] The introduction was changed and the dedication made over to Paul III[65] in gratitude for permitting him to return to Carpentras and his studies, whereupon in the spring of 1544 he sent it to Farnese with the stipulation that it be circulated among friends in the College and shown to Cortese in particular. This was only the start of its progress through the hands of critics, for Sadoleto's zeal in returning to sacred studies was matched by an even greater anxiety over what he wrote. Mined almost entirely out of St. Paul and the Greek Fathers, the work itself again discloses the untheological quality of Sadoleto's doctrinal thinking as well as his ignorance of scholastic thought. It was merely an elaboration of his position in the Commentaries on Romans, again interpreting original sin as "amorem carnis atque mundi," the pursuit of the vanities and indulgence of the flesh.[66]

At the same time he produced another work, the *De purgatorio*, which has not survived, although we know from the same letter to Cortese that he wrote it in the belief that no other element of Catholic dogma stood in greater need of defense and exposition in view of Protestant counterclaims.[67] But this treatise he also submitted with trepidation, reminding Cortese how readily a Catholic apologist could be ambushed by men of his own faith. So once again an elaborate circuit of readers was plotted, from the Inquisitor-general to Pietro Bembo. Inconsequential as they are, Sadoleto offered these works as the fruits of his recent labor in defending the "honor and authority" of the Church. The treatises were all there was to redeem his pledge to defend the faith by his pen if relieved from service to the Curia in 1542.

As the year drew on his absence from Rome fell under new threats. After the Peace of Crépy in September Paul III revoked the conciliar suspension made after the colloquy of Busseto and convoked the Council for March 25, 1545, at Trent. In consistory on November 19 he appointed ten Cardinals to a new commission on conciliar affairs and on December 3 sent briefs to all absent members of the College, summoning them to Rome to assist in its preparation.

Having heard rumors of these developments, Sadoleto wrote Farnese on December 19 to state unequivocally that he could not comply because he was so destitute that he could not even finance a journey of four days, much less the long trip to Rome.[68] He explained that previous travel between Italy and Provence had worn out his mules as well as his wardrobe; the single means of paying for another trip, he concluded, would be to borrow more money on his Quirinal vineyard, which was already heavily mortgaged.[69] In the same letter he referred to the exhaustive strain which nomination to the College had placed on his resources—no greater than the 1,600 ducats he received from the diocese, he said, with the result that he had never since been out of debt. If the Pope could not find additional funds for him, therefore, he would have no choice but to remain at Carpentras until the Council opened.[70]

Then he wrote directly to the Pope, setting forth another account of his indigence before making a request for financial assistance. Sadoleto described himself as one whose entire ecclesiastical career was dogged by poverty; he had eschewed opportunities to acquire wealth under the Medici Popes, just as he had declined offers of cameral *subsidia* from Paul III.[71] In this long and rather self-righteous review of his career in the Church he recognized the generosity of the Farnese Pope toward him in the past and attempted to explain his refusal of it on past occasions by a resolve to "live within the limits of my priestly resources and to accept nothing in the nature of extra-ordinary funds. . . ."[72] With adequate and regular income from the start of his career, he said somewhat unconvincingly, he never would have left the Curia in the first place. And now, if supplemental funds should materialize, he would go to Rome without hesitation.

Sadoleto got his answer in a letter from Farnese which arrived in February 1545: the Pope refused his petition and ordered him to proceed to Rome immediately.[73] Farnese took this occasion to remind Sadoleto that he had only himself to blame for his present embarrassment in view of the Pope's previous offers of help, and Jacopo conceded the point. But in doing so he tried to explain why he had declined the Pope's generosity on several occasions in the past. He emphasized a distinction, twice proposed to Paul III,[74] between cameral subsidies or special grants from the pontifical treasury on the one hand, and regular income from ecclesiastical benefices on the other.[75] He took the view that it is improper to accept money which does not form part of a regular priestly income. Special papal subsidies were "extra-ordinary funds" which he would not accept. Although some might think it strange, there is a difference, he insisted, between a gift and a benefice. But was it a question of principle or self-protection? Sadoleto apparently feared the papal subsidy as a *quid pro quo*, granted to support him by augmenting his regular income so long as he remained in the Curia, whereas the ordinary benefice provided unrestricted revenue and permanent provision.

To depend upon pontifical subsidies was to live at the Pope's side and thus to be torn away from Provence, while to live on beneficed income was to enjoy a higher degree of personal freedom in the certainty that his resources would not be cut short by a change of residence. Having reached the highest rank of the hierarchy, Sadoleto found his position at Carpentras made suddenly precarious and therefore did what he could to protect it by means of a somewhat contrived though plausible argument.

At the time he wrote Farnese two of the three conciliar Legates were already en route to Trent. Sadoleto concluded his letter by stating, in effect, that he would go to Rome, but requested quarters in the Vatican palace so as not to be an inelegant spectacle while passing through the streets on the way to consistories.[76] And so while Tournon and d'Oppède marshalled their forces for the assault on the Vaudois, Sadoleto left Carpentras late in March 1545, for the last time.[77] He reached Rome in May,[78] pleased and possibly even a bit surprised to find himself welcomed, after an absence of three years, "with a great display of affection from this entire court. . . ."[79]

By now it is obvious that in Sadoleto's career there is a marked and even monotonous recurrence—or is it coherence?—of situation and response, as though a familiar cycle were often repeated with only slight variations. Rome was the starting point of his adult life in 1498 or 1499, and he died there in 1547; but during the interim of nearly fifty years he left Italy for Carpentras on five different occasions, protesting against every summons to return to the Curia with the same stubborn insistence, the same elaborate reasons for remaining in Carpentras, and the same convictions on each occasion but the first. Soon after his final journey Sadoleto interpreted the cycle for Duke William of Bavaria:

Although time and time again I tried to liberate myself from these cares and concerns of the City in order to live in my church at Carpentras in the service of God, myself, and my people, and to pursue those studies the knowledge of which is the freest and the reward the most pleasant, I was nonetheless unable, by whatever fate or condition of fortune I do not know . . . to gratify my will or to lead the life in which learned and wise men have always considered happiness to reside. For no matter how often I went there, always having obtained the Pope's consent, just as often was I recalled to Rome at his order and command. If this moving back and forth had issued from mine and not another's will, such inconstancy would disgrace me. . . . But since if there is any fault it is certainly not mine but rather to be attributed to the times and the daily changes they bring forth, I ask you . . . to ascribe this frequent change of place to the desire of the Pope, and that in turn to the age we live in.[80]

Uprooted for the last time, the fourth in the name of a Council yet to materialize, Sadoleto cautioned that it would be a mistake to expect too much from it now. The Bishop of Carpentras, having left his diocese in new convulsions, was returning to Rome to die.

XI

The Old Cardinal

The word used to denote the Council in ciphered correspondence between Trent and the Vatican was "la fornace"—the furnace,[1] and in leaving Carpentras for Rome the old Cardinal was moving from one cauldron of controversy to another. Sadoleto was now a melancholy and in some ways a defeated man, a fugitive from conflict called back against his will to the city which he first saw as an exuberant young scholar fifty years earlier. The expatriot was returning to his fatherland almost as a stranger.

He went to Rome with little outward interest in the Council, as though he was smothered in thoughts of his diocese and in anxieties about his personal affairs. Once in the Curia again, what little comment he made about it was cryptic or skeptical,[2] the word itself a synonym for futility and misplaced hope. His first letter to Paolo from Rome, which was not written until the end of July, failed to speak of Trent or to mention the cloud of uncertainty which hung over it. Jacopo explained his silence by a general want of good news.[3] He could only report that His Holiness had dismissed the accusations directed against the Sadoletti from Avignon, although the Cardinal admitted that these charges were far more serious than he had imagined.

After ten weeks he was still troubled by debt and penury. During this time he had been obliged to spend over a thousand scudi, partly borrowed, for various purchases and the payment of old debts. What seemed like a large sum "went up in smoke" and left him, by a changed metaphor, "redutto al verde." Advances of 200 scudi from his cameral allowance, which the Pope arranged when Sadoleto suffered a new attack of malaria, were trifling, he said, because of high prices and the extent of his needs.[4] Yet His Holiness had been very generous, promising to provide Sadoleto with a minimum income of 2,000 scudi and to give him a new benefice when a proper vacancy was open. The Pope also invited him to live in the Vatican, presumably to reduce Jacopo's expenses and to have him nearby for consultation "in matters of importance." Sadoleto felt it was necessary to add, however, that the Supreme Pontiff appeared to be perfectly sincere in these discussions. Then quite abruptly, and no less casually, Jacopo announced that he in turn had agreed not to request further leave from the Curia: "I have promised," he wrote, "that I shall not try again to absent myself from His Holiness."[5] Nothing else was said about the terms of the engagement. Evidently pleased and even somewhat surprised by the Pope's interest in him, Sadoleto took further comfort in the hospitality of the court and then returned to the details of his own financial distress. But poverty is relative; there was still money enough to order imported wine and various provincial delicacies for his Roman table.

Grateful though he was for the Pope's sympathy and help, the Cardinal was hardly slavish in his conduct toward the Farnese during the following months. He scrupulously took notice of events in the personal and family affairs of Paul III, expressing grief and consolation over the death of Costanze Farnese, daughter of the Pope and wife of Bosio Sforza, and joy at the birth of twins to Ottavio Farnese and Margaret of Austria.[6] Yet his attention to the aggrandizing plans of the Farnese dynasty was anything but sympathetic when the Pope asked for consent from the College to invest Pierluigi with Parma and Piacenza, rich duchies of the Papal States which were to be alienated from the Church on the most contrived pretext and given as fiefs to the younger Farnese.[7] Paul III ran into general opposition when he first proposed his plan on August 12 and again in consistory on the nineteenth, for this was the crudest display of his nepotism to date. Juan Alvarez and De Cupis, Dean of the Sacred College, led an opposition which was reinforced by the protests of Sadoleto, Carpi, and Pisani,[8] while Caraffa showed his antipathy by visiting the pilgrimage churches during the consistory in which Pierluigi's investiture was finally confirmed.[9]

To the extent that the Council was a matter for supervision by the College and the special congregation, Sadoleto in these months did not emerge as a consistently active or influential figure. At no time during any of his sojourns in Rome did he ever show a capacity either for leadership or for adhering to well-defined factions. Even in the crush of the Curia he somehow managed to remain a solitary man—widely acquainted, but without strong or numerous friendships, and without forceful impact on his colleagues.

At the same time, however, the collective effect of the College on the conciliar Legates and the evolution of the Council in the latter months of 1545 was itself limited and generally inconclusive. It is often difficult to know precisely where major decisions about the Council were being made, or under whose auspices. Certainly there was no uniform or coordinated progress toward its convocation after it failed to open, as scheduled, in March, but rather a chaos of judgments and proposals from the Legates, the Pope, and the Emperor, and from King Ferdinand, the Protestants, and the French. Never in the pre-Tridentine era was communication more snarled than during the months between March and November, 1545. Opinions issuing from Rome, Trent, Worms, Vienna, Brussels, Paris, and Bruges were in constant collision, each place representing a distinctive point of view. The time and place of the Council, questions of attendance and participation, the real intentions of Pope and Emperor, the issue of war or peace with the Lutherans, the advisability of further doctrinal discussions, the suitability of Trent, the authority of the Legates, and the agenda of the Synod were questions which were debated all over Europe.

At times almost a third party to these controversies, the Pope was also disturbed by fresh rumors of his personal hostility to the Council, but he was determined not to proceed without the support of the College and to convoke it only with firm support from his Cardinals. As in the case of curial reform and the consistorial commissions of previous years, he was reluctant to move alone or to take major decisions without their approval. Paul III was entirely willing, when aroused, to lash out against a faction or minority in the Curia and was seldom timid or irresolute, but he habitually moved with the College, or at least with a majority of its members, and seldom very far ahead of it. At this juncture, however, he found the Cardinals overwhelmingly disposed at last to have the Council opened at Trent, and to the great relief of the Legates the consistory of November 6, 1545, fixed its convocation for December 13, *Gaudete* Sunday.[10]

Pole's earnest remarks to the fathers at the first formal session in January of the next year signified a momentous achievement which few could have foretold with assurance when he arrived at Trent in May, just as Sadoleto reached the Curia. This hour was the work of generations, brought on no less by Luther and the schism than by the internal disorders of the Church and the inability of the Roman Curia to reform itself. Trent came about not only through the detachment of great blocks of believers from the authority of Rome, but likewise through the failure of the Church to maintain uniform doctrine and discipline within itself. The reform projects of Oliviero Caraffa, the admonitions of Egidio da Viterbo, and the reforming intensity of Contarini were forms of response to the condition of the Church; so too were the partial alienation and sometimes bitter anti-curialism of Sadoleto, the searching consciences at Viterbo, and the fury of the illiterate Vaudois of Provence.

Sadoleto's reactions to the issues raised during the first twenty months of the Council can hardly be called those of a "typical" Catholic reformer, if indeed such a model exists at all. Although he voted with Caraffa and Morone on several important divisions, his performance was uniquely his own and at times so singular as almost to defy explanation.[11] His view of Christendom and the Council remained global rather than curial; he persisted in seeing the issues of religious crisis as a humanist with irenic concern but without the curialist's sensitivity to papal politics and dynastic interests. Massarelli could refer with certainty to the French faction in the College, most of whom uniformly obstructed the apparent wishes of the Emperor.[12] Caraffa and De Cupis, as members of the special congregation on the Council, voted steadily against Charles, whereas Morone and Sadoleto in particular showed no such consistency, even though Sadoleto and Caraffa were often on the same side of a vote.[13] Certainly no member of the commission on conciliar affairs was less partisan, less attached to national interest, or more independent of the Pope's dynastic wishes than the Bishop of Carpentras. In the opinion of an ambassador from the anti-curial Signory of Venice, he was the "very mirror of sound learning, high principles, and innocence in this court."[14]

In September 1545 the Pope ordered all the Cardinals to Rome without exception, but when the Council opened there were only thirty at his side,[15] ten of whom were deputized for the special commission. In a tactful and friendly letter to Diego Mendoza, the imperial envoy to Venice and soon the Emperor's ambassador to the Curia, Sadoleto wrote of being very much occupied with the "cares and concerns which the turbulence and rudeness of the times have inflicted upon the Church," and expressed his own hope that Charles V would assist rather than block the progress of the Council.[16] Shortly after the first session started, Juan de Vega, then imperial ambassador to the Curia, notified Charles of reports that either Sadoleto or Morone, or else Sadoleto and Cortese, might be sent to the Council as additional Legates.[17] Both the Pope and the deputies were dissatisfied with the slow start and the modest accomplishments of the fathers to date, and once again in April there was talk of attaching six more Cardinals —Sfondrato, Sadoleto, and Morone among them—to the three then already at Trent, men who "might strengthen the Council by their authority and erudition."[18] But by then, reported Madruzzo, the prospect of war in Germany would probably require their continued presence in Rome. Such a delegation was never formed, but the fact that Sadoleto's was the only name mentioned on each of three different occasions suggests that his standing in the Curia was still high.

Like Sadoleto at an earlier time, the Legates at Trent had acquired new perspectives on the Curia and the image of Rome in the rest of Christendom. "As to the Roman court," they wrote on March 7, "two things scandalize the world and deprive it of authority: one is avarice, the other its pomp and luxury. . . ."[19] Comment on its moral climate was joined to close criticism of the major agencies of curial government. Furthermore, they argued, the question of reform is enormously complex and something which provokes a great variety of opinions, of which even the most radical and extreme deserve to be heard or discussed. What was said and written during these weeks formed a catalogue of grievances against the Curia for its encroachment on episcopal authority and jurisdiction, and equally notable is the number of ideas and complaints which recur so often in Sadoleto's letters and treatises. The statements of the prelates against curial avarice, papal exemptions and dispensations, priestly ignorance and illiteracy, and their plea for practices which "conform to the discipline of the ancient Church"[20] run strikingly parallel to many of Sadoleto's own complaints and remedies.[21] So too does their emphasis on the urgency of removing popular hatred of the clergy and of winning respect and obedience for the Holy See through a sweeping reformation.

In other respects, however, Sadoleto disputed the decisions of the Council. Coinciding with the discussion of reform in the general congregation of the fathers was an attempt by the theologians to resolve the question of theological tradition and the biblical canon, a problem of definition provoked as much by Catholic humanists like Erasmus and Sadoleto as by the heretics themselves. At Trent this vexed question was solved simply and quickly by what was, in effect, a restatement of previous decrees on the canonicity of both the Old and New Testaments by earlier councils. Pole's proposal to examine each book of the Bible individually, together with his suggestion that the Greek and Hebrew texts be admitted with the Vulgate, was defeated.[22] The general congregation elected to accept all books on equal authority, choosing to receive them "simpliciter" before considering the necessity of correcting textual errors and abuses.

Sadoleto was conspicuous among those in the curial congregation in Rome who were astonished by these decrees, in a way which recalls the objections that Pole had vainly raised at Trent.[23] According to Giovanni Battista Cervini, Cardinal Santa Croce's procurator in Rome, most of the congregation was distressed by the inattention of the fathers to the defects of the Vulgate and the need for its revision. And while no one appeared to defend the reasoning of the conciliar fathers when the decrees were being criticized, Cervini concluded by adding that Sadoleto, in particular, was displeased by the willingness of the Council to accept St. Jerome's version so complacently.[24]

At Trent the fathers argued that nothing would be gained from a public concession of errors in the Vulgate text and that any revision should be undertaken discreetly and quietly. The Dominican and Franciscan theologians showed neither any patience for the subtleties of comparative exegesis, nor any serious doubts about the authorship of St. Jerome, while conciliar opinion generally held that long usage alone justified the position taken in their first decree on the Scripture. The consistorial deputies, however, were still not satisfied, implying that the theologians at Trent simply failed to grasp the magnitude of the problem and the hazards of revision.[25] Differences of opinion were exchanged for two months before the curial congregation yielded; the fathers in turn agreed to correct and publish a new edition of the Bible but held fast to the primacy of the Vulgate. Their success was another victory for the regulars and a triumph for the scholastics, represented by men like the Dominican De Soto, over the consistorial humanists and partisans of the new exegesis in the manner of Cardinal Sadoleto.

The Latinist in Sadoleto also showed in other ways. From time to time he returned to the familiar role of pontifical *scriptor*, drafting briefs for Paul III in the same periods and phrases that distinguished his style in the days of the Medici Popes.[26] He may likewise have assisted in the expansion and reorganization of the Vatican Library which took place under Paul III, during whose reign the collection grew in size and system, although Sadoleto probably did not work, as Pastor suggests he did, in cooperation with Marcello Cervini in developing new catalogues of its Greek and Latin manuscripts.[27]

Whether Sadoleto lived in the Vatican palace in the course of this last sojourn in Rome we do not know,[28] but by June of 1546 he occupied quarters in his third titular church, S. Pietro in Vincoli, with which he had been invested the previous October. He was not especially pleased by the apartments there and found them more attractive than convenient, although he liked the view from the Esquiline and its proximity to his vineyard.[29] More disquieting, however, was his nagging antipathy for Rome and the life he had to lead there. "I remain in the city against my will," he wrote Paolo, for "it is wholly foreign to my tastes. I am determined to endure it until I find an honorable opportunity to leave, but when such a chance arises I shall not pass it up." He knew that he was needed and valued in the Curia, "but nothing pleases me any longer except solitude and silence." Paolo had heard such complaints before. But he must have been less prepared to read that his cousin did not intend to return to the Venaissin when he left, but rather to seek a place of absolute isolation in which he could throw off all "the anguish and cares of these times." Carpentras, even S. Felice, now seemed too much of the world to qualify.

During these weeks, while he grew more restive and reiterated the same objections to Rome which he first expressed thirty years earlier, the special congregation discussed the possibility of suspending the Council.[30] On June 9, 1546, when De Vega reported this prospect to the Emperor, the Curia learned that Charles was committed to immediate war against the Schmalkaldic League and that he was now waiting to learn of the Pope's decision about entering or supporting the offensive. On June 22 Paul III laid the question before a general consistory at his summer palace in S. Marco. A reading of the treaty evoked immediate protest from the French and Venetian ambassadors, who in turn were supported by Sadoleto, Caraffa, and Morone.[31] The war and the Pope's participation in it were opposed in Venice as a threat to commerce and in France as a step toward imperial encirclement.[32] Caraffa's objections were consonant with his francophilia; but what of Sadoleto's and Morone's? Possibly they too were frightened by the prospect of an over-mighty Emperor, yet both were high in Charles' esteem less than a year later, and while Sadoleto had always shown great deference toward the French crown, he was never aligned with the French faction in the College. It is just as plausible that what he objected to was the use of papal arms and subsidies against the Lutherans now that the Council had opened. Nor is there any reason to assume that he might have felt differently about the use of force against the Lutherans than he did about an armed crusade against the Vaudois. Otherwise, however, the Pope enjoyed the full support of the College. Ottavio Farnese received command of the papal army, which numbered over 12,000 men, and Alessandro Farnese the legatine cross for a new mission to the Emperor.

During the Vice-Chancellor's absence Vasari went feverishly to work at the end of the summer on a series of frescoes in the Palace of the Cancelleria, to be disclosed in honor of the Legate when he returned from Germany. Vasari's speed was more remarkable than the painting itself, which was intended to glorify the achievements of the Farnese pontificate. One of the major scenes was conceived as a tribute to the Pope's nominations to the Sacred College, and singled out for recognition were Contarini, Sadoleto, Pole, and Bembo. Of these Contarini had been dead for four years; Pole was at Trent; and Bembo, Sadoleto's oldest friend, died not long after the frescoes were completed.[33] Once again Sadoleto counted the losses, which, by the following spring, also included the "saintly and illustrious Vittoria Colonna."[34]

In the meantime, now reduced to twenty-four resident Cardinals,[35] the Sacred College went through another process of fragmentation. There were always the imperialists, menacing the Pope with the threat of withdrawing to a national synod. Directly opposed to them were the so-called "ecclesiastici," who fully supported the procedural policies of the Cardinal-Legate Marcello Cervini at Trent.[36] There was also what Giovanni Battista Cervini referred to as "La fattione [*sic*]

Paul III Conferring Honors
Detail of Fresco by Giorgio Vasari

Fiametta," which included Francesco Sfondrato and Morone: men who now tempered their support of the conciliar Legates with the reservation that although the aims of the fathers were themselves worthy, their timing and tactics were imprudent because of their irritating effect on the Emperor. Nowhere in his report on division in the College and congregation did the younger Cervini refer to Sadoleto, whose position, while obscure, lay between Morone's and Sfondrato's with respect to the order of procedure at Trent. He had clearly the reputation of being a rigorist in matters of sacerdotal reform, but at the same time he shared the feeling that good intentions at Trent would have to be modified by some respect for the Emperor's convictions. However fanciful Sadoleto often tended to be in matters of practical politics, he seemed now to believe that the Church could not afford to alienate Charles or to lose his support of the Council.

Having published the decrees on reform of March 3, the fathers, many of whom disliked Trent from the start, voted a week later for the removal of the Council to Bologna.[37] Although all but the Spanish delegates left Trent before the decree on translation to another site was discussed in Rome, the decision to move was plainly within the constitutional powers of the Council and received the Pope's full approval. Massarelli recorded the substance of a private letter from Rome describing the consistory of March 23, in which the issue of translation was discussed and then endorsed by all present except for Juan Alvarez de Toledo, Francisco Mendoza, and Cardinal Sadoleto.[38] Juan Alvarez was probably more outspoken, but the other two insisted that the Emperor should at least have been consulted. The Pope angrily retorted that for two years the Lutherans had refused to go to Trent and that nothing further could be expected from its proximity to them.

We have two other concurring accounts of this episode. One comes from the imperial ambassador De Vega, who protested against the translation to the Pope on March 24, only to be rudely received and scolded with the argument that the Council depended on the Pope and on no one else.[39] In his report to Charles V the envoy added the names of Badia and Morone to those of Sadoleto and the two Spaniards, observing that although it was Burgos who drew the most choleric reply from the Pope, all five spoke against the translation in consistory "like good cardinals." The third version is that of Bonifazio Ruggieri, ambassador from Ferrara to the Roman Curia, naming Sadoleto as an opponent of translation who declared that "he would be far more pleased to see the Council dissolve itself through the departure of the prelates than to have it translated" from Trent to Bologna.[40] Why such a contradiction of the Pope's stated wishes?

Luther once described Sadoleto as an arrogant Italian and a lackey of the Farnese Pope, but the caricature is neither accurate nor just.[41] Sadoleto to be sure was sometimes guilty of patronizing judgments about non-Italians, savants and heretics alike, but more important was his profound belief in the corporate nature of European Christendom and the desperate need of Christian unity. Out of this conviction came his undiminished horror of conflict between European princes, persuaded as he was that neither reason of state nor private injury could justify what he always regarded as civil war.[42] In order to guarantee the political and religious peace of Europe he pleaded for the necessity of cooperation between Pope and Emperor in a "holy conspiracy," a joint hegemony vaguely suggestive of Dante's, in which there might be two distinct and complementary spheres of authority.[43] Because the Pope's jurisdiction is spiritual, his is the function of supreme arbiter among the princes; but Christendom likewise depends for its security upon the Emperor, who is the proper guardian of domestic peace. Similarly, he is responsible for war against the great foreign enemy—the only military enemy Sadoleto ever considered legitimate—the Turks.[44]

We must also recall Sadoleto's consistency in defending these arguments and convictions. As a partisan of the Council a decade earlier, after Mantua had to be abandoned as its projected site in 1537, he alone proposed its immediate convocation at Piacenza, choosing this location in order to accommodate the imperialists and to reassure the Germans.[45] It was likewise Sadoleto alone who dissuaded the College and the Pope in 1543 from refusing a direct colloquy with the Emperor when

Charles rejected a meeting with Paul III at Bologna: Busseto, albeit a failure, was nonetheless a result of Sadoleto's exertion to promote a "pia conspiratio" and to subordinate protocol and papal pride to the urgency of cooperation with the Emperor.[46] In the spring of 1547 he was willing again to take an independent position, ostensibly on the ground that the Emperor was entitled to participate in decisions affecting the site of the Council, which had originally been negotiated with his representatives in Germany.

By this time neither the Farnese Pope nor the Emperor was disposed to think of mutual concessions and collaboration. Paul III remained inflexible in his resolve to keep the Council at Bologna, or at least to resist imperial pressure for its restoration to Trent. Nevertheless, the question was still discussed by the Cardinal-deputies in Rome well into the summer. Most of them were opposed to a return to Trent, even at the risk of a rupture with the imperialists; but Sadoleto and Morone, joined now by a few others, continued to argue against the recent translation to Bologna, while Guidiccioni defended the Pope's claim that the Lutherans would never participate anyway.[47]

Early in September, in order to placate Charles, the Pope agreed to delay the reopening of the Council, which had been scheduled for the fifteenth of the month at Bologna. The fathers complied by postponing the meeting of the next session *sine die*. But all prospects of compromise abruptly ended on the tenth, when Pierluigi Farnese was murdered at Piacenza by Ferrante Gonzaga, the imperial viceroy, and a band of disgruntled nobles. The Farnese were certain that Charles was neither ignorant of the assault nor innocent of complicity in it, and Rome was now stricken with fears that Gonzaga might soon appear as a new Frundsberg or Charles of Bourbon. Bewildered, frightened, and furious, the Farnese Pope did what his predecessors usually did in such a crisis and immediately sought an alliance with France and Venice. It was as though the panic of 1527 had come back like the plague.

In the midst of these fears and alarms in the Curia, Charles was at Augsburg, serene and assured. Among other things he reflected on the matter of finding an acceptable candidate to succeed Paul III—a kind of solicitude which would doubtless have cheered the angry and suffering Pope had he known of it. (Reports of the Pontiff's poor health had grown common during the past eighteen months, and at the time of Pierluigi's assassination he was suffering from an acute attack of gout.) Charles had long considered himself the victim of inept and "unsuitable" Popes and showed no great enthusiasm for any particular candidate; it was simply a process, he reminded Mendoza, of observing the conduct of those few who seemed "more suitable and less objectionable" than the rest. In his ponderous and inconclusive way, however, he was satisfied with Mendoza's four candidates: Cortese, Sadoleto, Sfondrato, and Morone.[48] The author of the *Oratio de pace* and prime mover of the conference at Busseto was worthy at least of consideration. Several weeks later Lancellotti recalled that Sadoleto was assumed to be no less *papábile* in 1534 after the death of Clement VII.[49]

As it turned out, Sadoleto's health was more precarious than the Pope's at the end of a summer which took a heavy toll in the Sacred College. Ardinghelli died on August 22 and Badia on September 6, while in the meantime Ascanio Sforza, Sirleto, and Sadoleto agonized with what were probably malarial fevers.[50] Cervini found Sadoleto gravely ill on August 27 and noted the illness again on the thirtieth, but the Cardinal lingered on for seven more weeks.[51] At this time he was living at Sta. Maria in Trastevere, apparently having given up his apartment on the Esquiline in order to be closer to the Vatican. After the middle of August we hear of him only as some one seriously ill. He died on October 18, 1547, at the age of seventy.[52]

When news of the Cardinal's death reached Modena a week later and Lancellotti recorded it in his diary, he mentioned a rumor that Sadoleto had been murdered on papal orders:

They say that Pope Paul did not like him *caldemente* because when in consistory he tried to make his son Pierluigi Duke of Parma and Piacenza, Sadoleto refused to consent; and when His Holiness tried to make his nephew [*sic*] Cardina Farnese pontifical coadjutor, the Most Reverend Sadoleto also objected: and dealt likewise with another proposal. . . . [*sic*] It is said that he was made to die for such contradictions.[53]

Ciacconius recorded but dismissed the legend that Sadoleto, for unknown reasons, was poisoned.[54] To the popular imagination of this era a natural death was an unnatural end to the life of a public figure, but the rumor in this case is scarcely credible. More significant is the accurate account by a Modenese diarist of Sadoleto's opposition to Paul III and the Farnese family. Even in death Sadoleto was remembered as a Cardinal who was no man's man.

His code name in secret correspondence between Trent and the Curia had been either "mio padre" or "Don Bernardino."[55] The first has the ring of respect and affection for the venerable and somewhat irascible Bishop of Carpentras, but "Don Bernardino" seems better to convey his spirited independence, his willingness to be counted with a minority, or to stand quite alone.

Two funeral orations were delivered in Sadoleto's honor by friends in Rome. One was given the day after his death by Gianpietro Caraffa,[56] the critic of Contarini and later the persecutor of Morone and Pole. Caraffa was also an able scholar; but like his uncle, Oliviero Caraffa, he was first a priest for whom liberal learning was not an end but a means. If more learned than Sadoleto, Caraffa cannot be called a humanist; though primarily a prelate, he was also a theologian and canonist, the founder of the Theatines, a reforming Bishop and Cardinal, and one of the original members of the Roman Oratory of Divine Love as he was of the new Roman Inquisition.[57]

The second orator was Jacopo Gallo,[58] a relatively obscure man of letters, without place or influence in the Curia, who delivered his tribute at S. Lorenzo. Together, Caraffa and Gallo signify two traditions which Sadoleto tried to reconcile in his own life. One of the orators recalled Jacopo's youthful and exuberant classicism in the casual company of the Leonine humanists; the other represented the earnest mood of Oliviero Caraffa's household on the Piazza Navona and the sober dilemmas of the Farnese era. One calls to mind the *vita contemplativa* and the other its opposite, one the humanist gardens and the other the Curia; one the Quirinal and the other the Vatican.

And yet there is continuity in the fact that one Cardinal Caraffa received Sadoleto in Rome at twenty, and another memorialized his death in Rome at seventy. Oliviero's hospitality opened a new world to the young student from Modena and Ferrara. It provided new and rich associations which gave access to further patronage and preferment. But in Rome the direction of Sadoleto's maturing talents was uniformly toward a career in the Church by a kind of irreversible necessity at work even in Bembo's life. Bembo struggled and intrigued to go to Rome and then exerted himself just as desperately to leave it, returning to receive the Cardinal's hat which he had coveted from the start. But both he and Sadoleto were obliged to pay the price of preferment, and both discovered that patronage, under any auspices, was a system of obligations. In abandoning Ferrara and the Estense court, where Jacopo might easily have become a celebrity, he found himself no less a client of prelates and popes, whose favor was contingent on service and whose demands were ultimately proportional to their favors.

Sadoleto's career to a considerable degree may be seen as a quest for liberation and leisure, as an effort to break the chains of patronage while reaching for its rewards. One of the most common themes of his writing was a declared contempt for wealth and honors, both of which lay easily in his grasp during the earlier stages of his career—a point he made with tedious repetition in later years.[59] But more important to him by far was the achievement of independence and solitude. What Sadoleto failed to understand was that the sort of autonomy he sought was not the modest thing he imagined, but a rare and uncommon luxury. In some respects he also refused to acknowledge the hierarchical character of the Roman priesthood or to accept the elemental ties that bound him to obedience; he seemed unwilling to admit that he was not free to define his vocation in the Church with perfect liberty or to dispute the orders of the papal Curia. Yet because he was both an influential man of letters and a zealous prelate, Sadoleto increased his utility to the Pope and the claims which the Holy See placed on him by virtue of the things he accomplished *in otio*. Sadoleto's leisure was threatened and then all but destroyed by the profitable uses he made of it. His eloquent concern for the state of Christendom, which he felt best able to express at Carpentras, endowed him with the sort of authority which repeatedly forced him out of isolation. Yet even as a Cardinal he stubbornly tried to shut himself off from the world and from public service in the quiet of Provence, eschewing the kind of financial subsidy which might jeopardize it for that which promised to leave him his own master. Sadoleto was to find, however, that while he remained free to resist the demands of the Vatican, he was not free to ignore or defy them.

His autonomy was further restricted by financial need. Having assumed broad responsibilities for the younger Sadoletti—the victims of princely adversity, he became deeply involved in the loose net of services and rewards by which the Holy See contained, if not always effectively, its dependents. In order to provide a respectable dowry for the daughter "whom human frailty has given me," Pietro Bembo was willing to make himself a pauper and to surrender his personal freedom.[60] In Sadoleto's case the frailty of nepotism surrounded him with a drove of kinsmen, whose needs in turn only increased Jacopo's dependency on papal provision.[61]

Thus, for very practical reasons, Jacopo was limited in the extent to which he could insist upon seclusion in Provence. There, too, he was in full view of the papal Legation and found himself bound more closely than others of his rank to Rome. On the other hand, he also took seriously the "officium boni pastoris." If reluctant to merge its identity with the whole episcopate of Christendom, he nonetheless could never neglect the welfare of his flock, so that while in the Venaissin he spent his life more at Carpentras than in his rural retreat at S. Felice. Both the clergy and laity of his diocese deplored the Bishop's final departure for Rome and honored his absence with continuing signs of respect and affection.[62] Sadoleto never forgot Carpentras and was occupied to the end of his life with the see, whether inquiring about the leaking roof of the cathedral or watching for marks of the conscientious priest in a new vicar.[63]

8*

Nor in later life was he able to disregard the predicament of the universal Church. The religious schism and his own experience in the service of three Popes had the effect of tempering the tone of Sadoleto's classicism. Certainly the ring of the *De Cajo Curtio*, his youthful Vergilian poem, is dulled in *De purgatorio*. Sadoleto moved from a poetic glorification of "Laocoön" to the explication of St. Paul, claiming with naïve zeal that he would here "disclose the whole mystery of the death and cross of Christ."[64] The erstwhile poet had evolved by stages into a quasi-philosophic humanist and exegete, writing in the latter half of his life as theologian, moralist, and reformer. During his last two years in Rome he turned again to the treatise *De peccato originis*, which was sent now to Isidoro Chiari in January 1546,[65] not long before the conciliar theologians rendered obsolete and almost meaningless all such private efforts of dogmatic definition and apologetics. He also began another work on ecclesiastical government, of which only enough remains—or was ever started—to identify it as another appeal for the reform of Christian morality and as a further example of his rigid and absolute moral idealism.[66]

The *Hortensius*, completed in 1535, was the last complete work he wrote in the genre of secular classicism, and it properly belongs to the earlier half of his literary career. In the works which followed he was preoccupied with different aspects of the schism. Yet we cannot conclude that the humanist in him lived no more or that his youthful values were now altogether burnt out. Just a year before his death Sadoleto wrote at some length to Ranuccio Farnese on the subject of the young Cardinal's education.[67] It is a letter drawn directly from the *Hortensius* and from the whole fabric of Sadoleto's humanist conviction. If we must acknowledge the unity of circumstance in the role of the Cardinals Caraffa, so too must we recognize the coherence of his intellectual values in the counsel he gave Ranuccio in 1546.

Sadoleto knew that certain of the Farnese were advising the Pope's grandson to turn aside from the liberal arts in order to start the study of civil law,[68] just as the son of Giovanni Sadoleto was once expected to do at Ferrara. Sadoleto felt obliged to disagree with the Farnese once more in his letter to Ranuccio:

If you were born with scant resources and only modestly provided with the means of achieving distinction, then I too would suggest that you turn to the law. For it is a fitting and open road to those in humble circumstances for acquiring great honors; nor is the civil law studied for any other reason than to come through it to some knowledge of men and a better condition of fortune.[69]

But these things, he said, you already possess. The law is sordid, inevitably involving disputes over money, and never with the praise of man and the knowledge of God. Philosophy, on the other hand, is the most difficult and rewarding of all the *scientiae* of man, for

having abandoned those cares and tribulations which pertain to profit and acquisition, and having counted them nothing, it undertakes the formation and elevation of man, so that lifted from this common infirmity, it renders him similar to God, seeking nothing which is external and transitory, while counselling others that all good is to be sought in virtue.[70]

Pericles ruled Athens in wisdom for forty years because, as a student of Anaxagoras, he was educated in the knowledge of nature and had exercised his mind in the liberal arts, acquiring *prudentia* from these studies for use in the affairs and government of men. Here once more then is Sadoleto's defense of a secular wisdom which leads men to the image of divinity and sets them apart from the generality of mankind.[71] Here too is a defense of the liberal arts as a body of knowledge superior to the law, which inferentially is made to signify the *vita activa* as well. Sadoleto evidently hoped to turn Ranuccio Farnese toward those "sacred silences" which he himself had once hoped to find in Rome.

Thus the career which began with dazzling recognition from a Medici Pope had closed with a stern summons to duty from the Farnese Pope. The wheel of fortune, to which Sadoleto so often referred, had come full circle in taking him back to Rome and the Papal Curia. His body remained in the City for ninety-nine years, buried somewhere in the basilica of St. Peter in Chains, where Michelangelo's "Moses" sits flanked by the figures of Rachel and Leah, one representing the active life and the other the contemplative. An eighteenth-century chronicler of Sadoleto's life abbreviated the Cardinal's feelings for place in the paraphrase, "Mihi Roma carcer,

Carpentoracte paradisus."[72] Rome had turned out to be an elegant prison and a form of servitude, whereas at least until the final years of his life Provence had remained an earthly paradise.

The final liberation took place in 1646, when a canon of the cathedral which Sadoleto had helped to build received the Bishop's remains for reburial at Carpentras.[73] Not a trace of his tomb can be found at S. Pietro in Vincoli. The chains were broken at last, and Sadoleto was taken home to St. Siffrein and his beloved Provence. If in late life he found even the Venaissin to be an imperfect place of refuge, it was the best that could be done for a reforming humanist who was never willing to accept the world's disorder.

APPENDIXES

APPENDIX I

Sadoleto's Authorship of the *Consolationes Philosophicae*

The attribution of this work to Sadoleto has never, to my knowledge, been questioned. Tiraboschi includes it among Sadoleto's *Opere Stampate*, using the title of an edition published at Frankfurt in 1577: *Consolationes Philosophicae ac Meditationes in adversis ad Joannem Camerarium Dalburgium Pontificem Vormaciensem.*[1] It also appears in the Verona edition of Sadoleto's works as *Philosophicae Consolationes et Meditationes in Adversis: Jacobi Sadoleti Cardinalis Joanni Camerario Dalburgio Pontifici Vormaciensi, Jacobus Sadoletus cubicularius Apostolicus,* S., and dated "Romae, ex palatio Apostolico vii. kal. Novemb. Anno salutaris nostrae, MDII."[2] Modern biographers and other scholars have likewise attributed this work to the young Sadoleto.[3]

P. S. Allen did raise the question of Sadoleto's friendship with Dalberg and suggests that after completing his studies at Ferrara Sadoleto "perhaps accompanied a university friend to Germany." The author of the treatise certainly alludes to his close ties with the Bishop,[4] although to be sure the connection may have been no more than epistolary. But there is no evidence that Sadoleto ever travelled in Germany before going to Rome. It is not this aspect of the treatise, however, which brings Sadoleto's authorship into doubt.

The letter was written to console Dalberg on the death of his mother. The author speaks as one who some years earlier had suffered the death of his own mother and who now asks Dalberg likewise to seek comfort "in the books of the ancients."[5] The crucial word is in the clause "itidem ego dulcissimae genetricis meae crudelissima nece gravissimum vulnus accepi," where "genetricis" seems obviously to be the synonym of *matris*. But Sadoleto's mother long survived the death of Dalberg himself in 1503. In a letter to Giovanni Sadoleto in March

221

1511, for example, Jacopo sent affectionate greetings to his "cherished mother"[6]; and later, in the epitaph to Giovanni, he restricted the monument to the use of his father, recently dead, his mother, still living, and himself.[7] From the same inscription we know too that Giovanni Sadoleto was married only once. And finally, the death of Francesca Machiavelli was noted by Lancellotti in his journal on March 6, 1537.[8] It is difficult to believe that Sadoleto would have falsified his mother's death in order to console a man whom in all probability he never saw.

The content of the treatise, to be sure, clearly suggests the Stoicism of Sadoleto's later philosophical works, particularly as it is expressed in his *De liberis recte instituendis* (1533). Joly observes that the work is "a consolation which does not console,"[9] and in this sense it is a plausible view of death from the pen of a rigorous young Senecan. The manner of the treatise is correct for one writing to a man twice his age, the author confessing that he regards Dalberg "ut patrem." On the other hand, the letter was written "from the Apostolic Palace" by one who referred to himself as a papal chamberlain, but once again there is no corroboration of either clause in Fiordibelli or in Sadoleto's own reminiscences.

Sadoleto and Erasmus: 1534-1536

The last surviving exchange of letters between Sadoleto and Erasmus took place between October 1534 and December 1534, and bears largely on issues related to Sadoleto's Commentaries on Paul's Epistle to the Romans. It began when each wrote to inquire about the mystery of the other's silence—Erasmus on October 31 and Sadoleto on November 1.[1] Erasmus, however, confessed to an anxiety far more severe and self-accusing, fearful that he had chilled Sadoleto's good will in the course of evaluating his work on the first Epistle.[2] At the same time he arranged to send the Bishop one of the three copies he had recently bought of Melanchthon's Commentary on Romans, evidently the edition of 1532, a gesture which Giulio Vallese and Giuseppe Toffanin regard as a kind of cryptic warning, intended to say that "Melanchthon also was a theologian."[3] Toffanin further raises the possibility that Jacopo's treatise brought on an estrangement between himself and Erasmus, on the ground that Erasmus may now have suspected his friend of moving into the arena of controversial or polemical theology.

A more specific clue, however, is Erasmus' statement in a letter to Boniface Amerbach that Sadoleto had shown ingratitude for his criticism of the Commentaries.[4] We know also from a letter to Damian à Goes that Erasmus felt he had warned the Bishop in vain that this treatise was clearly headed toward trouble.[5] For his part, when he wrote to Erasmus again on December 9, 1534, Sadoleto warmly and casually assured his friend of continuing affection and expressed his appreciation of Erasmus' efforts as a critic of this work. "How I wish," he wrote, "that you might always be near me as my 'corrector et magister' . . .", reminding Erasmus that honest criticism is an obligation which strengthens ties between friends.[6] With this letter, said P. S. Allen, "Erasmus' apprehensions were finally laid to rest."[7] And although he never overcame his reservations about the Commentaries, Erasmus in the last year of his life was willing to describe Sadoleto as "illud eximium huius aetatis decus Iacobus Sadoletus, admirabili sermonis nitore, et copia plane Ciceroniana, nec deest affectus episcopo Christiano dignus."[8]

M. Renaudet has recently stated that "Sadoleto probably remained the most loyal friend Erasmus had," and Professor Schätti observes that among the Catholic reformers of the 1530's none was closer to Erasmus than Sadoleto.[9] But why then is there not a single trace of further correspondence from either side between December 1534 and July 1536, when Erasmus died? Why do Erasmus' previously recurrent references to Sadoleto vanish so abruptly from letters written during the last eighteen months of his life? The most likely basis for conjecture is the mutual misunderstanding which developed while Sadoleto was working on the Commentaries. Dr. Allen may have been perfectly correct in the opinion that Erasmus dismissed his fears of having alienated the Bishop when he received Sadoleto's letter of December 9, 1534; but the inference cannot be supported by anything from Erasmus' hand.

It is just as plausible to suggest that although each accepted the other's assurances of respect and esteem, Sadoleto may have chosen to avoid the risk of future misunderstanding altogether and thus decided not to ask Erasmus to read the *Hortensius*, for example, while it was being circulated for criticism. Erasmus in turn seems clearly to have found the Bishop rather deaf to admonition,[10] and may well have been content to be spared from future consultation. In any event the exchange of manuscripts ended with the last surviving exchange of letters at the end of 1534. We cannot infer a serious strain in their relations after this point. Nevertheless, the exchange of manuscripts in preparation was usually the ritual test and symbol of confidence between humanists of this generation. We may conclude therefore that by tacitly agreeing no longer to involve one another as "corrector et magister," Sadoleto and Erasmus removed a crucial link in their friendship through an honest effort to protect and preserve it.

BIBLIOGRAPHY

NOTES

INDEX

Abbreviations Used in Bibliography and Notes

Allen	Erasmus. *Opus Epistolarum Des. Erasmi Roterodami.* Edited by P. S. and H. M. Allen. 12 vols. Oxford, 1906–58.
Arch. Vat.	Archivio Segreto Vaticano.
ARG	*Archiv für Reformationsgeschichte.* Leipzig and Berlin, 1903–.
BHR	*Bibliothèque d'Humanisme et Renaissance.* Geneva, 1941–.
Bib. Vat.	Bibliotèca Apostolica Vaticana.
Comment.	Sadoleto. *Jacobi Sadoleti . . . in Pauli Epistolam ad Romanos Commentariorum libri tres.* The edition cited is in *Opera,* IV.
CR	*Corpus Reformatorum.* Edited by K. G. Bretschneider and H. E. Bindseil. Halle, 1834–.
CT	*Concilium Tridentinum: Diariorum, actorum, epistolarum, tractatuum nova collectio.* Edited by the Görres-Gesellschaft. Freiburg, 1901–.
Epistolae	Sadoleto. *Jacobi Sadoleti S.R.E. Cardinalis Epistolae quotquot extant proprio nomine scriptae nunc primum duplo auctiores in lucem editae.* 3 vols. Edited by V. A. Costanzi. Rome, 1760–64.
HJG	*Historisches Jahrbuch der Görres-Gesellschaft.* Bonn, 1880–.
Lettere	Sadoleto. *Lettere del Card. Iacopo Sadoleto e di Paolo suo Nipote, tratti degli originali che si conservano a Parma nell' Archivio governativo e pubblicate da Amadio Ronchini.* Modena, 1872.
LPR	*Lettere di Principi.* Edited by G. Ruscelli. 3 vols. Venice, 1581. (Not to be confused with the MS series "Lettere di Principi" in the Vatican Secret Archives, cited as Arch. Vat., Lett. di Prin.).
Mon. ref. Luth.	*Monumenta reformationis Lutheranae ex tabulariis S. Sedis secretis. 1521–25.* Edited by P. Balan. Ratisbon, 1884.
Mon. saec. XVI.	*Monumenta saeculi XVI. historiam illustrantia.* Vol. I *Clementis VII epistolae per Sadoletum scriptae.* Edited by P. Balan. Innsbruck, 1885.

Mon. Tri.	*Monumenta Tridentina. Beiträge zur Geschichte des Konzils von Trient.* Edited by A. von Druffel and Karl Brandi. Munich, 1884–89.
Mon. Vat.	*Monumenta Vaticana historiam ecclesiasticam saeculi XVI. illustrantia ex tabulariis Sanctae Sedis apostolicae secretis.* Edited by Hugo Laemmer. Freiburg im Breisgau, 1861.
NB	*Nuntiaturberichte aus Deutschland 1533–1559 nebst ergänzenden Aktenstüken.* Preussisches historisches Institut zu Rom. Edited by Walter Friedensburg. 12 vols. Gotha, 1892–1908.
Opera	Sadoleto. *Jacobi Sadoleti Cardinalis et Episcopi Carpentoractensis viri disertissimi, Opera quae extant omnia.* 4 vols. Verona, 1737.
QF	*Quellen und Forschungen aus italienischen Archiven und Bibliotheken.* Preussisches historisches Institut zu Rom. Rome, 1898–.
RB	*Regesten und Briefe des Kardinals Gasparo Contarini.* Edited by Franz Dittrich. Braunsberg, 1881.
RQ	*Römische Quartelschrift für christliche Alterthumskunde und für Kirchengeschichte.* Rome, 1887–.
RSR	*Archivio della R. Società Romana di Storia Patria.* Rome, 1878–.
SHPF	*Bulletin de la Société de l'histoire du Protestantisme français.* Paris, 1851–.
WA	*D. Martin Luthers Werke. Kritische Gesamtausgabe.* Weimar, 1883–.
ZKG	*Zeitschrift für Kirchengeschichte.* Gotha and Tübingen, 1876–.

Bibliography

I. MANUSCRIPT SOURCES

AVIGNON: Musée Calvet

MS. 1290. Epistolae familiares C. Baduelli a Joanne Fontano interprete collectae Nemausi.

MS. 4180. Dossier concernant les Recteurs du Comté Venaissin.

MS. 4188. Epistolae familiares nobilis et egregii domini Joannis Baptistae de Centenariis.

MS. 5128. C. F. H. Barjavel. Généalogies de divers familles vauclusiennes nobles et non nobles.

MS. 5512. Autographes et documents divers.

CARPENTRAS: Bibliothèque Inguimbertine

MS. 558 (L. 535). Inventarium jurium mensae episcopalis Carpentoractensis.

MS. 1559. Recognitiones prioratus N. D. de Grezo pro in Christo reverendo domino Jacobo Sadoleto epistopo Carpentoractensi, perpetuo commendatario ejusdem prioratus.

MS. 1680. Bonet de Saint-Bonet. Mémoires pour servir à la vie du Cardinal Sadolet (1759).

MS. 1797. Documents concerning Sadoleto's Legation to France in 1542.

THE VATICAN: Bibliotèca Apostolica Vaticana
Cod. Barberini Latini:

834. Jacobi Sadoleti epistola de iustificatione.

2157. Miscellaneous correspondence of Sadoleto; Latin and Italian, autograph letters and copies.

2517. Letters of Mario Maffei, principally to Sadoleto.

2799. Diarium Blasii de Cesena.

5695. Miscellaneous correspondence of Sadoleto, 1538–45.

Cod. Ottoboniani Latini:

489. Oratio Jacobi Sadoleti de emendanda vitiis curia Romana.

IIII. Miscellaneous briefs and letters.

3139. Letters of Jacopo and Paolo Sadoleto, Bembo and Accolti.

Cod. Vaticani Latini:

3436. Correspondence of Sadoleto and Sturm.

3294. Miscellaneous letters of Sadoleto.

THE VATICAN: Archivio Segreto Vaticano
Acta Camerarii. Tomes 2–8.
Acta Vicecancellarii. Tomes 4–6.
Armario XL. Tomes 12 and 50. Miscellaneous letters of Sadoleto.
Armario XLV. Tome 42. Miscellaneous letters of Sadoleto, 1522–40.
Carte Farnesiane. Tomes 19–21. Documents concerning Sadoleto's Legation to France in 1542.
Lettere di Principi. Tomes 4–14. Miscellaneous correspondence.
Nunziatura di Germania. Tome 59. Correspondence concerning Sadoleto's Legation to France in 1542.
Nunziature diverse. Tome 238. Miscellaneous briefs.

PARIS: Bibliothèque Nationale
Rés 4°Lb²⁹ 35a. Jacobi Sadoleti de bello suscipiendo contra Turcos ad Ludovicum Regem Galliarum oratio. (Rededicated and addressed to Francis I.)
MS. 2870. Sylva ad Octavium et Franciscum Fregusos.

II. PRINTED PRIMARY SOURCES

WORKS BY SADOLETO

Epistolarum libri sexdecim, nunc multo quam antehac umquam diligentius recogniti, atque in lucem aediti. Cologne, 1590.

Jacobi Sadoleti Cardinalis et Episcopi Carpentoractensis viri disertissimi, Opera quae extant omnia. 4 vols. Verona, 1737.

Jacobi Sadoleti S.R.E. Cardinalis Epistolae quotquot extant proprio nomine scriptae nunc primum duplo auctiores in lucem editae. 3 vols. Edited by V. A. Costanzi. Rome, 1760–64.

Jacobi Sadoleti Epistolarum Appendix. Accedunt Hieronymi Nigri et Pauli Sadoleti vitae ac rariora monumenta. . . . Edited by V. A. Costanzi. Rome, 1767.

Jacobi Sadoleti S.R.E. Cardinalis Epistolae Leonis X. Clementis VII. Pauli III. nomine scriptae. Accessit Antonii Florebelli de Vita ejusdem Sadoleti commentarius et epistolarum liber. Edited by V. A. Costanzi. Rome, 1759.

Lettere del Card. Iacopo Sadoleto e di Paolo suo Nipote, tratte degli originali che si conservano a Parma nell' Archivio governativo a pubblicate da Amadio Ronchini. Modena, 1872.

Miscellaneorum ex MSS. libris Bibliothecae Collegii Romani Societatis Jesu. Vol. I. *Clarorum vivorum Theodori Prodromi. Dantis Alighierj. Franc. Petrarchae. . . . et Jacobi Sadoleti epistolae ex codd. MSS. Bibliothecae Collegii Romani S. J. nunc. primum vulgatae.* Edited by Pietro Lazzari. Rome, 1754.

Iacobi Sadoleti Cardinalis De Christiana Ecclesia ad Iohannem Salviatum Cardinalem. Edited by Cardinal Angelo Mai, in *Spicilegium Romanum.* Vol. II, 101–78. Rome, 1839.

Elegantissimae orationes duae. Altera Iacobi Sadoleti, De emendandis viciis Curiae Romanae : Altera Samuelis Macieovii, qua exceptus Petrus Gamratus, cum veniret in episcopatum Cracoviensem. Cracow, 1561.

Sadoleto on Education. A Translation of the De Pueris recte Instituendis. Translated by E. T. Campagnac and K. Forbes. Oxford, 1916.

Sadoleto, Elogio della Sapienza (De laudibus philosophiae). Translated by Antonio Altamura and Giuseppe Toffanin. Naples, 1950.

WORKS BY OTHERS

Albertini, Marcello. "Il Diario di Marcello Albertini (1521–1536)," edited by Domenico Orano, RSR, Vol. 18 (1895), 319–417.

Argentré, Charles du Plessis d', ed. *Collectio judiciorum de novis erroribus.* 3 vols. Paris, 1728–36.

D'Attichy, Ludovico Donio. *Flores historiae sacri collegii S.R.E. Cardinalium.* Vol. III. Paris, 1660.

Aubery, Jacques. *Histoire de l'exécution de Cabrières et de Mérindol. . . .* Paris, 1645.

Beccadelli, Lodovico. *Monumenti di varia letteratura.* Edited by L. Morandi. 2 vols. Bologna, 1797–1804.

Bembo, Pietro. *P. Bembi card. epistolarum familiarium libri vi, eiusdem, Leonis X. Pont. Max., nomine scriptarum. libri xvi.* Venice, 1552.

—— *Opere del Cardinale Pietro Bembo.* Vols. I–IV. Venice, 1729; Vols. I–V. Milan, 1808–10.

Bonamicus, P. (Buonamici, Filippo). *De clariis pontificiarum epistolarum scriptoribus ad Benedictum XIV, Pont. Max., liber.* Rome, 1770.

Bullarium privilegiorum Comitatus Venaissini. Carpentras, 1780.

Calvin, John. *Calvini opera quae supersunt omnia.* Edited by G. Baum, E. Cunitz, and E. Reuss. 59 vols. Brunswick and Berlin, 1863–1900.

Calvin, John. *Trois traités comprenant en un volume l'épitre à Sadolet, le traité de la sainte cène, le traité des scandales.* Translated by Albert-Marie Schmidt. Paris, 1935.

——— *Recueil des opuscules, c'est à dire, petits traitez de M. Jean Calvin.* Geneva, 1566.

Camerarius, Joachimus. *De Philippi Melanchthonis ortu, totius vitae curriculo & morte narratio.* Leipzig, 1696.

Ciacconius, Alphonsus. *Vitae et res gestae Pontificum Romanorum et S.R.E. Cardinalium ab initio nascentis Ecclesiae usque ad Clementem IX.* . . . Vol. III Rome, 1677.

Concilium Tridentium: Diariorum, actorum, epistolarum, tractatuum nova collectio. Edited by the Görres-Gesellschaft. Freiburg, 1901–.

Contarini, Gasparo. *Gasparis Contarini Cardinalis opera.* Paris, 1571.

——— *Regesten und Briefe des Kardinals Gasparo Contarini.* Edited by Franz Dittrich. Braunsberg, 1881.

Corpus Catholicorum. Werke katholischer Schriftsteller im Zeitalter der Glaubenspaltung. Münster, 1919–.

Corpus Reformatorum. Edited by K. G. Bretschneider and H. E. Bindseil. Halle, 1834–.

Corvisieri, C. "Compendio dei processi del Santo Uffizio di Roma (da Paolo III a Paolo IV)," RSR, Vol. 3 (1880), 261–90, 449–72.

Crespin, Jean. *Histoire des martyrs persecutez et mis à mort pour la verité de l'Evangile, depuis le temps des apostres iusques à present.* Edited by Caniel Benoit. 3 vols. Toulouse, 1885–89.

Erasmus. *Opus Epistolarum Des. Erasmi Roterodami.* Edited by P. S. and H. M. Allen. 12 vols. Oxford, 1906–58.

Fontana, B., ed. "Documenti Vaticani contro l'eresia luterana in Italia," RSR, Vol. 15 (1892), 71–166, 365–474.

Fontana, Vincenzo Maria. *Syllabus magistrorum sacri palati apostolici.* Rome, 1663.

Gairdner, James, and R. H. Brodie, eds. *Letters and Papers, Foreign and Domestic, of the Reign of Henry VIII.* Vols. VII–XIV. London, 1883–98.

Giraldi, Lilio. *Lilius Gregorius Gyraldus de poetis nostrorum temporum.* Edited by Karl Wotke. Berlin, 1894.

Hergenroether, Joseph, ed. *Leonis X Pontificis Maxima Regesta.* 2 vols. Freiburg im Breisgau, 1884–91.

Herminjard, A. L., ed. *Correspondance des réformateurs dans les pays de langue française.* 9 vols. Geneva, 1866–97.

Lancellotti (Tommasino de' Bianchi). *Cronaca Modenese*, in *Monumenti di storia patria per le provincie Modenesi*. 12 vols. Parma, 1861–84.

Lazzari, Pietro, ed. *Miscellaneorum ex MSS. libris bibliothecae Collegii Romani Societatis Jesu*. Vol. I. Rome, 1754.

Lettere di Principi. Edited by G. Ruscelli. 3 vols. Venice, 1581.

Lettere di Principi. MS series. Vatican Secret Archives.

Le Plat, J. *Monumentorum ad historiam Concilii Tridentini potissimum illustrandam spectantium amplissima collectio*. 7 vols. Louvain, 1781–87.

Löscher, Valentin Ernst, ed. *Vollständige Reformations-Acta und Documenta oder umständliche Vorstellung des evangelischen Reformations-Werks*. . . . 3 vols. Leipzig, 1720–29.

Luther, Martin. *D. Martin Luthers Werke. Kritische Gesamtausgabe*. Weimar, 1883–.

Mai, Cardinal Angelo. *Spicilegium Romanum*. 10 vols. Rome, 1839–44.

Melanchthon, Philip. *Philippi Melanchthonis opera quae supersunt omnia*, in *Corpus Reformatorum*. Edited by K. G. Bretschneider. Vols. I-VIII. Halle, 1834–40.

———— *Epistolarum D. Erasmi libri xxxi et P. Melanchthonis libri vi. Quibus adiunciunt Th. Mori & Lud. Vivis Epistolae*. London, 1642.

Monumenta reformationis Lutheranae, ex tabulariis S. Sedis secretis. 1521–25. Edited by P. Balan. Ratisbon, 1884.

Monumenta saeculi XVI. historiam illustrantia. Vol. I. *Clementis VII epistolae per Sadoletum scriptae*. Edited by P. Balan. Innsbruck, 1885.

Monumenta Tridentina. Beiträge zur Geschichte des Konzils von Trient. Edited by A. von Druffel and Karl Brandi. Munich, 1884–89.

Monumenta Vaticana historiam ecclesiasticam saeculi XVI. illustrantia ex tabulariis Sanctae apostolicae secretis. Edited by Hugo Laemmer. Freiburg im Breisgau, 1861.

Nausea, Friedrich. *In magnum illum laudatae felicisque memoriae Erasmum Rotterodamum, nuper vita functum Monodia*. Cologne, 1536.

Nuntiaturberichte aus Deutschland 1533–1559 nebst ergänzenden Aktenstüken. Preussisches historisches Institut zu Rom. Edited by Walter Friedensburg. 12 vols. Gotha, 1892–1908.

Omont, H., ed. "Journal du cardinal Jérôme Aléandre," *Notices et Extraits des Manuscrits de la Bibliothèque Nationale*, XXXV (1895).

Paquier, Jules, ed. *Lettres familières de Jérôme Aléandre (1510–1540)*. Paris, 1909.

Paris de Grassis (Paride Grassi). *Il Diario di Leone X*. Edited by M. Armellini. Rome, 1884.

Pole, Reginald. *Epistolarum Reginaldi Poli S.R.E. Cardinalis et aliorum ad ipsum collectio*. Edited by A. M. Quirini. 5 vols. Brescia, 1744–57.

Raynaldus, Odoricus. *Annales ecclesiastici. Accedunt notae chronologicae, criticae, . . . auctore J. D. Mansi.* Vols. XII (31), XIII (32), XIV (33). Lucca, 1754–55.

Relazioni degli ambasciatori veneti al Senato. 3rd Series. *Relazioni di Roma.* Edited by E. Albèri. Florence, 1839–63.

Sanuto, Marino. *I Diarii,* 58 vols. Venice, 1879–1903.

Seckendorf, Viet Ludwig von. *Commentarius historicus et apologeticus . . . de Lutheranismo.* Leipzig, 1694.

De Thou, Jacques-Auguste, *Jac. Augusti Thuani historiarum sui temporis tomus primus—septimus.* London, 1733.

Zambotti, Bernardino. *Diaro Ferrarese dall' anno 1476 al 1504.* Edited by Giuseppe Pardi. Bologna, 1928–33.

III. SECONDARY WORKS

André, J. F. *Histoire du gouvernement des recteurs pontificaux dans le Comtat-Venaissin d'après les notes recueillés par Charles Cottier.* Carpentras, 1847.

Andreoli, E. and B. S. Lambert. *Monographie de l'église cathédrale Saint-Siffrein de Carpentras.* Paris, 1862.

Angeleri, Carlo. *Il Problema religioso del Rinascimento.* Florence, 1952.

Arnaud, Eugène. *Histoire des Protestants de Provence, du Comtat-Venaissin et de la principauté d'Orange.* 2 vols. Paris, 1884.

Aubenas, Roger and Robert Ricard. *L'Eglise et la Renaissance (1449–1517).* Vol. 15 of Histoire de l'église depuis les origines jusqu' à nos jours. Edited by A. Fliche and V. Martin. Paris, 1951.

Audin, J. M. V. *Histoire de Léon X.* 2 vols. Paris, 1844.

—— *Histoire de la vie, des écrits et doctrines de Calvin.* 5th ed. 2 vols. Paris, 1851.

Bainton, Roland. *Bibliography of the Continental Reformation.* Chicago, 1935.

Balan, Pietro. *Clemente VII e l'Italia de' suoi tempi, studio storico. . . .* Milan, 1887.

Barjavel, C. F. H. *Dictionnaire historique, biographique et bibliographique du département de Vaucluse.* 2 vols. Carpentras, 1841.

Barotti, Giovannandrea. *Memorie istoriche di letterati Ferraresi,* 2nd ed. 2 vols. Ferrara, 1792–93.

Bataillon, M. *Erasme en Espagne.* Paris, 1937.

Batiffol, Pierre. *La Vaticane du Paul III á Paul V, d'après des documents nouveaux.* Paris, 1890.

Benoit, Fernand. "Le Cardinal Jacques Sadolet évêque de Carpentras," *Annuaire de la Société des amis du palais des papes,* XIV (1925), 35–47.

—— *La Légation du cardinal Sadolet auprès de François Ier en 1542, d'après sa correspondance avec le cardinal Farnese.* Monaco and Paris, 1928.

Benoit, Fernand. "Lodovico Beccadelli à Carpentras et ses amours avec Elisa Gallas," *Mémoires de l'Institut historique de Provence,* I (1924), 7–11.

—— *La Provence et le Comtat-Venaissin.* Paris, 1940.

—— *La Tragédie du sac de Cabrières.* Vol. II of Bibliothèque de l'Institut historique de Provence. Marseilles, 1927.

Besson, Joseph Antoine. *Mémoires pour l'histoire ecclésiastique des diocèses de Genève, Tarantaise, Aoste et Maurienne, et du décanat de Savoye.* Nancy, 1759.

Bianconi, Alfredo. *L'Opera delle compagnie del "Divino Amore" nella riforma cattòlica.* Città di Castello, 1914.

Bieber, Margarete. *Laocoön. The Influence of the Group since its Discovery.* New York, 1942.

Bonnet, Jules. *Aonio Palerio, étude sur la réforme en Italie.* Paris, 1863.

—— "La Tolérance du cardinal Sadolet," SHPF, XXXV (1886), 481–95, 529–43; and XXXVI (1887), 57–72, 113–26.

Borsetti, Ferrante. *Historia almi Ferrariae gymnasii.* 2 vols. Ferrara, 1735.

Bourrilly, V. L. *Guillaume du Bellay, seigneur de Langey. 1491–1543.* Paris, 1904.

Brandi, Karl. *The Emperor Charles V. The Growth and Destiny of a Man and of a World-Empire.* Translated by C. V. Wedgwood. London, 1939.

Brezzi, Paolo. *Le Riforme cattòliche dei secoli XV e XVI.* Rome, 1945.

Brotto, Giovanni and Gasparo Zonta. *La Facoltà teologica dell' università di Padova,* Padua, 1922.

Brown, G. K. *Italy and the Reformation to 1550.* Oxford, 1933.

Buschbell, Gottfried. *Reformation und Inquisition in Italien um die Mitte des XVI. Jahrhunderts.* Paderborn, 1910.

Caillet, Robert. *Un Prélat bibliophile et philanthrope, Monseigneur d'Inguimbert Archevêque-évêque de Carpentras, 1683–1757.* Lyons, 1952.

Cantimori, Delio. *Eretici italiani del Cinquecento.* Florence, 1939.

—— "Recenti studi intorno alla riforma in Italia a ai riformatori italiani all'estero (1924–1934)," *Rivista storica italiana,* Series V, XIV (1936), 83–110.

Cantù, Cesare. *Gli Eretici d'Italia.* 3 vols. Turin, 1864–66.

Capasso, Carlo. *Paolo III (1534–1549).* 2 vols. Messina, 1924.

Cardauns, L. *Von Nizza bis Crépy. Europäische Politik in den Jahren 1534 bis 1544.* Rome, 1923.

—— *Zur Geschichte der kirchlichen Unions- und Reformbestrebungen von 1538 bis 1542.* Rome, 1910.

Cardella, Lorenzo. *Memorie storiche de' cardinali della santa Romana chiesa.* 9 vols. Rome, 1792–97.

Carrière, Victor. *Introduction aux études d'histoire ecclésiastique locale.* 3 vols. Paris, 1934-40.

Carrier de Belleuse, Albert. *Liste des abbayes, chapitres, prieurés, églises de l'ordr de Saint-Ruf (chanoines réguliers de Saint-Augustin) de Valence-en-Dauphiné.* Rome, 1933.

Catalogue général des manuscripts des bibliothèques publiques de France. Départements. Tome XXXVI, Carpentras. 3 vols. Paris, 1903.

Cavazzuti, Giuseppe. *Lodovido Castelvetro.* Modena, 1903.

Celier, Léonce. "Alexandre VI et la réforme de l'église," *Mélanges d'archéologie et d'histoire,* XXVII (1907), 65-124.

———— "L'Idée de réforme à la cour pontificale du concile de Bâle au concile de Latran," *Revue des questions historiques,* LXXXVI (1909), 418-35.

Chaillot, Pierre. *Précis de l'histoire d'Avignon au point de vue religieux et dans ses rapports avec les principaux événements de l'histoire générale.* Avignon, 1852.

Charpenne, Pierre. *Histoire de la réforme et des réformateurs de Genève.* Paris, 1861.

Cherubelli, Paolo. *Il Contributo degli ordini religiosi al Concilio di Trento.* Florence, 1946.

Chledowski, Casimir von. *Der Hof von Ferrara.* Berlin, 1914.

Christoffel, R. "Des Cardinals Gasparo Contarini Leben und Schriften. Eine kirchengeschichtliche Studie über einen altkatholischen Reformationsversuch der römischen Kirche im zweiten Viertel des sechzehnten Jahrhunderts," *Zeitschrift für historische Theologie,* V (1875), 2 Heft.

Church, Frederic C. *The Italian Reformers. 1534-1564.* New York, 1932.

Cian, Vittorio. *Un' illustre nunzio pontifico del Rinascimento : Baldassar Castiglione.* Vatican City, 1951.

———— *Un Decennio della vita di M. Pietro Bembo. 1521-1531.* Turin, 1885.

Cistellini, Antonio. *Figure della Riforma pretridentina.* Brescia, 1948.

Cornelius, C. A. *Historische Arbeiten, vornehmlich zur Reformationszeit.* Leipzig, 1899.

Cosenza, Mario E. *Biographical and Bibliographical Dictionary of the Italian Humanists and of the World of Classical Scholarship. 1300-1800.* (Microfilm.)

Cristiani, L. *L'Eglise à l'époque du concile de Trente.* Vol. 17 of Histoire de l'église depuis les origines jusqu' à nos jours. Edited by A. Fliche and V. Martin. Paris, 1948.

David, Marcel. *De l'organisation administrative, financière et judicaire du Comtat-Venaissin sous la dominion des papes (1229-1791).* Aix, 1912.

Dittrich, Franz. "Beiträge zur Geschichte der katholischen Reformation im ersten Drittel des 16. Jahrhunderts," HJG, V (1884), 3 Heft, 319–98; and VII (1886), 1 Heft, 1–50.

—— *Kardinal Gasparo Contarini (1483–1542). Eine Monographie.* Braunsberg, 1885.

Döllinger, J. J. *Beiträge zur politischen, kirchlichen und Kultur-Geschichte der sechs letzten Jahrhunderts.* 3 vols. Regensburg and Vienna, 1862–82.

Dorez, Léon. "Antonio Tebaldeo, les Sadolet et le cardinal Jean du Bellay," *Giornale storico della letteratura italiana*, XXVI (1895), 384–89.

—— *La Cour du Paul III d'après les registres de la trésorie secrète.* 2 vols. Paris, 1932.

Doumergue, E. *Jean Calvin, les hommes et les choses de son temps.* 7 vols. Lausanne, 1899–1927.

Drei, Giovanni. *I Farnese. Grandezza e decadenza di una dinastia italiana.* Rome, 1954.

Dupront, Alfonse. "Du Concile de Trente: Réflexions autour d'un IVe centenaire," *Revue historique*, CCVI (1951), 262–80.

Ehses, Stephen. "Ein Gutachten zur Reform des päpstlichen Gnadenwesens aus dem Jahre 1538," RQ, XIV (1900), 102–19.

—— "Kirchliche Reformarbeiten unter Papst Paul III vor dem Trienter Konzil," RQ, XV (1901), 153–74.

Ferrajoli, Alessandro. "Il Ruolo della corte di Leone X," RSR, Vols. 34–39 (1911–1916).

Fornery, Joseph. *Histoire ecclésiastique du Comté Venaissin et de la ville d'Avignon.* 3 vols. Avignon, 1909.

François, Michel. *Le Cardinal François de Tournon, homme d'état, diplomate, mécène et humaniste (1489–1562).* Paris, 1951.

Friedensburg, Walter. "Beiträge zum Briefwechsel der katholischen Gelehrten Deutschlands im Reformationszeitalter," ZKG, XVIII (1898), 2 Heft, 233–297; and XX (1900), 2 Heft, 242–59.

—— "Das Consilium de emendanda ecclesia, Kardinal Sadolet und Johannes Sturm von Strassburg," ARG, XXXIII (1936), 2 Heft, 1–69.

—— "Giovanni Morone und der Brief Sadolets an Melanchthon vom 17. Juni 1537," ARG, I (1904), 4 Heft, 372–80.

—— *Kaiser Karl V und Papst Paul III (1534–1549).* Leipzig, 1932.

—— "Zwei Aktenstücke zur Geschichte der kirchlichen Reformbestrebungen an der Römischen Kurie 1536–1538," QF, VII (1904), 251–67.

Gaffarel, Paul. "Les Massacres de Cabrières et Mérindol en 1545," *Revue historique*, Vol. 107 (1911), 241-71.

Garin, Eugenio. "Desideri di riforma nell' oratoria del Quattrocento," *Quaderni di Belfagor*, I (1948), 1–11.

Gasquet, Cardinal Francis. *Cardinal Pole and his Early Friends.* London, 1927.

Gaufrès, M. J. "Les Colleges protestants. Nîmes," SHPF, XXIII (1874), 289–304; 337–48; 385–95; and XXIV (1875), 4–20.

―――― *Claude Baduel et la réforme des études au XVIᵉ siecle.* Paris, 1880.

Gilmore, Myron P. *The World of Humanism.* New York, 1952.

Girard, Joseph. "Les Etats du Comtat Venaissin depuis leurs origines jusqu' à la fin du XVIᵉ siècle," *Mémoires de l'Academie de Vaucluse*, 2nd Series, VI (1906), 27–101, 179–218, 287–303; and VII (1907) 1–58, 141–78.

Gnoli, Domenico. "Descriptio urbis o censimento della popolazione di Roma avanti il sacco borbonico," RSR, XVII (1894), 376–520.

―――― *La Roma di Leone X.* Milan, 1938.

―――― "Secolo di Leone X?" *Rivista d'Italia*, II (1898), 625–50; and III (1899), 39–55.

Gollob, H. *Friedrich Nausea. Probleme der Gegenreformation.* Vienna, 1952.

Gothein, E. *Ignatius von Loyola und die Gegenreformation.* Halle, 1895.

Granget, E. A. *Histoire du diocèse d'Avignon et des anciens diocèses dont il est formé.* 2 vols. Avignon, 1862.

Grillo, Giacomo. *Poets at the Court of Ferrara: Ariosto, Tasso, and Guarini.* Boston, 1943.

Grimm, Harold J. *The Reformation Era. 1500–1650.* New York, 1954.

Haile, Martin. *Life of Reginald Pole.* New York, 1910.

Harbison, E. Harris. *The Christian Scholar in the Age of the Reformation.* New York, 1956.

Hefele, Karl J. and J. Hergenröther. *Conziliengeschichte.* Vols. IX–X. 2nd ed. Freiburg, 1887–90.

Hermelink, Heinrich and Wilhelm Maurer. *Reformation und Gegenreformation. Handbuch der Kirchengeschichte für Studierende.* Vol. III. Tübingen, 1931.

Herzog, J. J. and Albert Hauck. *Realencyklopädie für protestantische Theologie und Kirche.* 3rd ed. 24 vols. Leipzig, 1896–1913.

Hofmann, W. von. *Forschungen zur Geschichte der kurialen Behörden vom Schisma bis zur Reformation.* Bibliothek des kgl. preussischen historischen Instituts in Rom, Vols. XII–XIII. Rome, 1914.

Hughes, Philip. *Rome and the Counter-Reformation in England.* London, 1942.

Jedin, Hubert. *Geschichte des Konzils von Trient*. Vol. I. *Der Kampf um das Konzil*. Freiburg, 1951.

—— *Katholische Reformation oder Gegenreformation? Ein Versuch zur Klärung der Begriffe nebst einer Jubiläumsbetrachtung über das Trienter Konzil*. Lucerne, 1946.

—— *Das Konzil von Trient. Ein Ueberblick ueber die Erforschung seiner Geschichte*. Rome, 1948.

—— *Il Tipo ideale di vescovo secondo la riforma cattòlica*. Brescia, 1950.

Joachimsen, Paul. *Die Reformation als Epoche der deutschen Geschichte*. Munich, 1951.

Joly, Aristide. *Etude sur Sadolet. 1477–1547*. Caen, 1856.

Kalkoff, Paul. *Forschungen zu Luthers römischem Prozess*. Bibliothek des kgl. preussischen historischen Instituts in Rom. Vol. II. Rome, 1905.

—— "Zu Luthers römischem Prozess," ZKG, XXXI (1910), 1 Heft, 48–65; XXXII (1911), 1 Heft, 1–67; and XXXIII (1912), 1 Heft, 1–72.

Kampschulte, F. W. *Johann Calvin, seine Kirche und sein Staat in Genf*. Vol. I. Leipzig, 1869.

Kawerau, Gustav. *Die Versuche, Melanchthon zur katholischen Kirche zurückzuführen*. Schriften des Vereins für Reformationsgeschichte, No. 73. Halle, 1902.

Lauchert, Friedrich. *Die italienischen literarischen Gegner Luthers*. Freiburg im Breisgau, 1912.

Lehmann, Oscar. *Herzog Georg von Sachsen im Briefwechsel mit Erasmus von Rotterdam und dem Erzbischof Sadolet*. Neustadt, 1889.

Leva, Giuseppe de. "La Concordia religiosa di Ratisbona e il cardinale Gasparo Contarini," *Archivio Veneto*, Anno II, IV (1872), part 1.

—— *Storia documentata di Carlo V, in correlazione all' Italia*. 5 vols. Venice, 1863–94.

Levi, I. "Clément VII et les Juifs du Comtat Venaissin," *Revue des études juives*, XXXII (1896), 63–87.

Liabastres, J. *Histoire de Carpentras, ancienne capitale du Comté-Venaissin*. Carpentras, 1891.

Lortz, Josef. *Die Reformation in Deutschland*. 3rd ed. 2 vols. Freiburg, 1948.

Marangoni, Giuseppe. "Lazaro Bonamico e lo Studio Padovano," *Nuovo Archivio Veneto*, N.S. I, I (1901), 118–52, 301–19; II (1901), 131–97.

Martin, J. "Le Saint-siège et la question d'Orient au seizième siècle. Projets de croisade sous la regne de Léon X," *Revue d'histoire diplomatique*, XXX (1916), 35–56.

9+

Maulde, R. de. *Les Juifs dans les états français du Saint-Siège au moyen âge, documents pour servir à l'histoire des Israélites et de la Papauté.* Paris, 1886.

Mestwerdt, Paul. *Die Anfänge des Erasmus.* Leipzig, 1917.

Moncallero, G. L. *Il Cardinale Bernardo Dovizi da Bibbiena umanista e diplomatico (1470–1520).* Florence, 1953.

Moreau, E. and Pierra Jourda. *La Crise religieuse du XVIᵉ siècle.* Vol. 16 of *Histoire de l'église depuis les origines jusqu'à nos jours.* Edited by A. Fliche and V. Martin. Paris, 1950.

Mossé, Armand. *Histoire des Juifs d'Avignon et du Comtat Venaissin.* Paris, 1934.

Navenne, Ferdinand de. *Rome, le Palais Farnèse et les Farnèses.* Paris, 1923.

Nitti, Francesco S. "Documenti ed osservazioni reguardanti la politica di Leone X," RSR, XVI (1893), 181–289.

——— *Leone X e la sua politica, secondo documenti e carteggi inediti.* Florence, 1892.

Nolhac, Pierre de. *Erasme en Italie.* Paris, 1898.

Pallavicini, Pietro. *Vera concilii Tridentini historia.* 3 vols. Antwerp, 1670–77.

Pandolfi, T. "Giovan Matteo Giberti e l'ultima difésa della libertà d'Italia negli anni 1521–1525," RSR, XXXIV (1911), 131–237.

Paquier, Jules. *Jérôme Aléandre de sa naissance à la fin de son séjour à Brindes (1480–1529).* Paris, 1900.

——— *De Philippi Beroaldi junioris vita & scriptis (1472–1518).* Paris, 1900.

Pardi, Giuseppe. *Lo Studio di Ferrara nei secoli XV° e XVI°.* Ferrara, 1903.

——— *Titoli dottorali conferiti dallo Studio di Ferrara nei secoli XV° e XVI°.* Lucca, 1900.

Paschini, Pio. *Roma nel Rinascimento.* Bologna, 1940.

Pasolini, Guido. *Adriano VI.* Rome, 1913.

Pastor, Ludwig von. *History of the Popes from the Close of the Middle Ages.* Translated by R. F. Kerr. Vols. VII–XII. 3rd ed. St. Louis, 1950.

——— *Die kirchlichen Reunionsbestrebungen während der Regierung Karls V.* Freiburg, 1879.

——— *Die Stadt Rom zu Ende der Renaissance.* Freiburg, 1906.

Pecchiai, Pio. *Roma nel Cinquecento.* Bologna, 1948.

Pericaud, Antoine. *Fragments biographiques sur Jacques Sadolet, évêque de Carpentras.* Lyons, 1849.

Perrin, Charles. *Etats pontificaux de France au seizième siècle.* Paris, 1847.

——— *De Jacobo Sadoleto, cardinali, episcopo Carpentoractensi, disquisitio historica.* Paris, 1847.

Pieper, Anton. *Zur Entstehungsgeschichte der ständigen Nuniaturen.* Freiburg, 1894.

Piromalli, Antonio. *La Cultura a Ferrara al tempo di Ludovico Ariosto.* Florence, 1953.

Polman, Pontien. *L'Elément historique dans la controverse religieuse du XVIe siècle.* Gembloux, 1932.

Renaudet, Augustin. *Erasme et l'Italie.* Vol. XV of Travaux d'Humanisme et Renaissance. Geneva, 1954.

——— *Etudes érasmiennes (1521–1529).* Paris, 1939.

Reumont, Alfred von. *The Carafas of Maddaloni : Naples under Spanish Dominion.* Translated from the German. London, 1854.

——— *Geschichte der Stadt Rom.* 3 vols. Berlin, 1867–70.

——— *Vittoria Colonna, marchesa di Pescara, vita, fede a poesia nel secolo decimosesto.* Translated by Giuseppe Müller and Ermanno Ferrero. 2nd ed. Turin, 1892.

Reusch, Franz H. *Der Index der verbotenen Bücher.* 2 vols. Bonn, 1883–85.

R[icard], Abbé. *Histoire du cardinal Sadolet suivie des pièces justicatives.* Avignon, 1872.

Rice, Eugene F., Jr. "Varieties of Renaissance Wisdom, a Study in the Secularization of an Idea." Unpublished Ph.D. dissertation, Department of History, Harvard University, 1952.

Richard, P. "Les Origines et développement de la secrétairerie d'état apostolique (1417–1823)," *Revue d'histoire ecclésiastique,* XI (1910), 56–73, 505–29.

Ritter, S. *Un Umanista teologo Jacopo Sadoleto (1477–1547).* Rome, 1912.

Rodocanachi, Emmanuel. *Les Pontificats d'Adrien VI et Clément VII.* Paris, 1933.

——— *La première Renaissance. Rome au temps de Jules II et de Léon X.* Rome, 1912.

——— *Le Réforme en Italie.* 2 vols. Paris, 1921.

Rossi, P. A. *Marc' Antonio Flaminio.* Rome, 1931.

Rückert, Hans. *Die Rechfertigungslehre auf dem tridentinischen Konzil.* Bonn, 1925.

Sarpi, Paolo. *Istoria del Concilio Tridentino.* Edited by Giovanni Gambarin. 3 vols. Bari, 1935.

Schenk, W. *Reginald Pole, Cardinal of England.* London, 1950.

Schmidt, Charles G. A. *La Vie et les travaux de Jean Sturm.* Strasbourg, 1855.

Schottenloher, Karl. *Bibliographie zur deutschen Geschichte im Zeitalter der Glaubenspaltung.* 6 vols. Leipzig, 1933–40.

Schreiber, Georg, ed. *Das Weltkonzil von Trient. Sein Werden und Wirken.* 2 vols. Freiburg, 1951.

Schultess-Rechberg, Gustav von. *Der Kardinal Jacopo Sadoleto, ein Beitrag zur Geschichte des Humanismus.* Zurich, 1909.

Schweitzer, Vincenz. "Beiträge zur Geschichte Pauls III," RQ, XXII (1908), 132–42.

Scott, Izora. *Controversies over the Imitation of Cicero as a Model for Style and Some Phases of their Influence on the Schools of the Renaissance.* New York, 1910.

Simar, Théophile. *Christophe de Longueil, humaniste (1488–1522).* Louvain, 1911.

Tacchi-Venturi, Pietro. *La Vita religiosa in Italia durante la prima età della compagnia di Gesù.* Rome, 1910.

Terris, Jules de. *Les Evêques de Carpentras. Etude historique.* Avignon, 1886.

Tiraboschi, Girolamo. *Bibliotèca Modenese o notizie della vita e delle opere degli scrittori nati degli stati del serenissimo signor Duca di Modena. . . .* Vol. IV. Modena, 1783.

Toffanin, Giuseppe. *Il Cinquecento.* 3rd ed. Milan, 1929.

—— "Umanesimo e teologia," BHR, XI (1949), part 2, 204–14.

Vallentin, Roger. "Notes sur la chronologie des Vice-Légats d'Avignon," *Mémoires de l'Académie de Vaucluse,* IX (1890), 200–13.

Visconti, Alessandro. *La Storia dell' Università di Ferrara, 1391–1950.* Bologna, 1950.

Wolfe, Gustav. *Quellenkunde der deutschen Reformationsgeschichte.* 2 vols. Gotha, 1915–16.

Zanta, Léontine. *La Renaissance du Stoïcisme au XVI siècle.* Paris, 1914.

Notes

Chapter I: The Young Scholar

1. G. Conversino, *Dragmalogia de eligibili vitae genere*, cited in H. Baron, *The Crisis of the Early Italian Renaissance* (Princeton, 1955), I, 113, and II, 490, n. 37.

2. A. Piromalli, *La cultura a Ferrara al tempo di Ludovico Ariosto* (Florence, 1953), pp. 17–22.

3. See G. Barotti, *Memorie istoriche di letterati ferraresi* (Ferrara, 1792), I; C. von Chledowski, *Der Hof von Ferrara* (Berlin, 1914); G. Grillo, *Poets at the Court of Ferrara* (Boston, 1943); and especially Piromalli, *La cultura a Ferrara*.

4. *Epistolae*, III, 155.

5. Cf. Jacopo's statement: "Io sono nato et allevato assai honoratamente. . . .", *Lettere*, No. XXXII, p. 79. The complete genealogy of Giovanni's family and its collateral branches is extremely difficult to establish. The best single source is Lancellotti (Tommasino de' Bianchi), *Cronaca Modenese* (Parma, 1862–84), I–XI. It may be supplemented by G. Tiraboschi, *Bibliotèca Modenese* (Modena, 1783), IV, 413–67. Two variants of the genealogy appear in C. F. H. Barjavel, "Généologies de divers familles vauclusiennes nobles et non nobles," Avignon, Musée Calvet MS. 5128, fols. 93–96; these, however, are often erroneous and admittedly speculative.

6. Giovanni's wife has been mistakenly identified as Madeleine Bembo, Pietro's aunt: Abbé Ricard, *Histoire du cardinal Sadolet* (Avignon, 1872), p. 17, and Jules de Terris, *Les évèques de Carpentras* (Avignon, 1886), p. 221. Her proper maiden name is found in the epitaph composed by Sadoleto for Giovanni's tomb, Tiraboschi, *Bibliotèca Modenese*, IV, 418, and in Lancellotti's identification of her in his *Cronaca*, VI, 263. One branch of the Ferrarese Machiavelli operated the most important banking dynasty in the Duchy, Piromalli, *La cultura a Ferrara*, pp. 36–37.

7. See F. Borsetti, *Historia almi Ferrariae Gymnasii* (Ferrara, 1735), II, 56, for the dispute which surrounded his appointment.

8. Lancellotti, *Cronaca*, VIII, lxiii.

9. Tiraboschi, *Bibliotèca Modenese*, IV, 420 ff. Guilio was one of the interlocutors in Lilio Giraldi's *De poetis nostrorum temporum* (c. 1515). Jacobo praised his erudition at the start of his *In Pauli Epistolam ad Romanos*, *Opera*, VI, 7B, and dedicated this treatise to Giulio.

10. Alfonso alone, moreover, appears to have taken the full course of legal studies at Ferrara, receiving his degree in civil law in 1514. See Giuseppe Pardi, *Titoli dottorali conferiti dallo Studio di Ferrara nei secoli XV° e XVI°* (Lucca, 1900),

pp. 114–15. References to "Io. Sadoletus" (e.g., p. 107) mean Giovanni, of course, and not Jacopo Sadoleto.

11. For Sadoleto's early years it is necessary to rely almost entirely on Fiordibello's quasi-official *Vita* in Sadoleto's *Opera*, I, 1–20. Fiordibello himself was a Modenese banker's son who studied law and the arts before joining Sadoleto's household in Provence in 1533. Lauchert, *Die italienischen literarischen Gegner Luthers* (Freiburg im Breisgau, 1912) pp. 474–75; Lancellotti, *Cronaca*, VI, 263 and VII, 347.

12. On the University, see Borsetti, *Historia*; A. Visconti, *La Storia dell' università di Ferrara, 1391–1950* (Bologna, 1950); and G. Bertoni, La bibliotèca Estense e la coltura ferrarese ai tempi del duca Ercole I, 1471–1505 (Turin, 1903).

13. Bembo to Sadoleto, 1503, *P. Bembi card. epistolarum familiarium* (Venice, 1552), p. 85; Sadoleto to Bembo, 1531, *Epistolae*, I, 401–2. The standard work on Bembo is still G. Mazzuchelli, in *Scrittori d' Italia* (Brescia, 1760), II, Part 2, 733–69, for details of his life and works. See also V. Cian, *Un Decennio della vita di M. Pietro Bembo* (Turin, 1885), and M. Santoro, *Pietro Bembo* (Naples, 1937).

14. The exact date is unknown. Early biographers put it in 1502 or 1503, e.g. Tiraboschi, *Bibliotèca Modenese*, IV, 425–26. A more modern study, A. Ferrajoli, "Il Ruolo della corte di Leone X," RSR, XXXVIII (1915), 256, calls attention to a line in Sadoleto's funeral oration on the death of Cardinal Caraffa in which he stated he had lived in Caraffa's household for twelve years. Because his patron died in January 1511, Jacopo must then have joined the Cardinal in 1499 at the latest, and most likely in 1498. However, Sadoleto was incurably careless in his memory of time and dates.

15. E. H. Wilkins, *A History of Italian Literature* (Cambridge, 1954), p. 185.

16. Fiordibello, *Vita*, in *Opera*, I, 2. In a treatise written twenty years after Giovanni died Jacopo causes a hostile interlocutor to remark that Giovanni sent him to Rome to prepare himself for public life and to win influence at the Curia in the belief that Jacopo would later return to Ferrara. *De laudibus philosophiae*, *Opera*, III, 178; see above, pp. 78–79.

17. A de Reumont, *The Carafas of Maddaloni*, Eng. trans. (London, 1854), p. 139. See also R. and F. Silenzi, *Pasquino* (Milan, 1933), ch. 1, and D. Gnoli, "Descriptio urbis o censimento della populazione di Rome avanti il sacco borbonico," RSR, XVII (1894), 391.

18. L. Celier, "Alexandre VI et la réforme de l'église," *Mélanges d'archéologie et d'histoire*, XVII (1907), 65–124.

19. J. E. Darras and J. Bareille, *Histoire de l'église* (Paris, 1875–89), XXXII, 482.

20. Sadoleto to Colocci, 1529, *Epistolae*, I, 309–18.

21. Sadoleto to Bembo, 1528, *ibid.*, I, 227.

22. Sadoleto's associations were exclusively with the Academy founded by Pomponio Leto and revived under Colocci, rather than with the Gymnasium Romanum. See Pio Pecchiai, *Roma nel Cinquecento* (Bologna, 1948), pp. 387–93.

23. Composed at Ferrara though not published until he was in Rome; see A. Joly, *Etude sur J. Sadolet. 1477–1547* (Caen, 1856), p. 31.

24. Lilio Giraldi, *De poetis nostrorum temporum*, ed. K. Wotke (Berlin, 1894), pp. 15–16.

25. *De Laocoöntis statua*, *Opera*, III, 245–46. The best recent monograph is Margarete Bieber, *Laocoön, the Influence of the Group since its Discovery* (New York, 1942). It is possible that the Sperlonga Laocoön, discovered in 1957, may be the original and the Vatican group a copy.

26. *Opera*, III, 245–46. For Bembo's praise, see his letter to Sadoleto of May 5, 1506, *Epistolarum familiarium*, pp. 92–93.

27. The list of benefices held over his lifetime is in Ferrajoli, "Il Ruolo . . . Leone X," RSR, XXXVIII, 219; this canonry is cited in Arch. Vat. Reg., Vol. 1001, fol. 186. It was held by various members of Sadoleto's family for over fifty years after Jacopo renounced it first in favor of Giulio Sadoleto in 1518.

28. The texts of Beroaldo which implicate Sadoleto are in J. Paquier, *De Philipi Beroaldi junioris vita et scriptis* (Paris, 1900), p. 72. See also Ferrajoli, "Il Ruolo . . . Leone X," RSR, XXXVIII, 259–60, and XXXIX, 559 ff. S. Ritter, *Un Umanista teologo Jacopo Sadoleto* (Rome, 1912), dismisses Beroaldo's allusions as baseless. Others, however, have accepted the alliance as a certainty, e.g. D. Gnoli, "La Lozana e le cortigiane nella Roma di Leone X," in *La Roma di Leone X* (Milan, 1938), pp. 205–7. See also Gianfrancesco Lancellotti, *Poesie italiane e lettere di Monsignor Angelo Colocci* (Jesi, 1772), p. 117n.

29. A treatise of 1502 entitled *Philosophicae consolationes et meditationes in adversis* and dedicated to Johann Dalberg has traditionally been accepted as Sadoleto's; however, I have raised some questions about this attribution in the Appendix.

30. *De bello suscipiendo contra Turcos ad Ludovicum Christianissimum Regem oratio*, *Opera*, II, 287–331. The same work was later rededicated to Francis I, "Francisco Francorum regi Christianissimo Jacobus Sadoletus," Paris, Bibliothèque Nationale, Rés. 4° Lb^{29}35a (MS).

31. The date of the treatise is uncertain, though it seems closer to 1510 than 1500, which Ritter lists as the year of publication, *Un Umanista*, p. 85.

32. The funeral was held up until December, when Sadoleto delivered his oration on Caraffa at Santa Maria sopra Minerva, Bib. Vat., Vat. lat. 9539, fols. 399–409.

33. Jacopo to Giovanni, Rome, March 19 [1511], Arch. Vat., Arm. XLV, tome 42, fol. 19. Ferrajoli notes that Sadoleto must have meant to say "minor orders," for he was still a subdeacon in 1513, "Il Ruolo . . . Leone X," RSR, XXXVIII, 426.

34. Bembo may also have been in Caraffa's household for a short time; see Fiordibello, *Vita*, in *Opera*, I, 3; and Santoro, *Pietro Bembo*, p. 33. We know that he joined Fregoso's in 1512, Mazzuchelli, *Scrittori*, p. 378.

Chapter II: Papal Secretary: The Court of Leo X

1. Raynaldus, *Annales ecclesiastici* (Lucca, 1754–55), XII, 7; E. Rodocanachi, *La première Renaissance: Rome au temps de Jules II et de Léon X* (Paris, 1912), p. 116. Sadoleto and Bembo are listed, with their servants, in the important "Rotulus" of the Leonine court in A. Ferrajoli, "Il Ruolo . . . Leone X," RSR, XXXIV (1911), 363–91. Mazzuchelli reports Bembo's annual stipend as 3,000 scudi, *Scrittori*, p. 739.

2. The basic work on the Apostolic Secretariat is Giovanni Carga, "Informatione del secretario et secretaria di nostro signore et di tutti gli offitii che da quello dependono" (1574), in H. Laemmer, *Mon. Vat.*, Appendix II, pp. 457–68; see also P. Bonamicus, *De clariis pontificiarum epistolarum scriptoribus* (Rome, 1770). The best modern account is P. Richard, "Leo origines et développement de la secrétairerie d'état apostolique (1417–1823)," *Revue d' histoire ecclésiastique*, XI (1910), 56–73, 505–29. It may be supplemented by W. von Hofmann, *Forschungen zur Geschichte der kurialen Behörden vom Schisma bis zur Reformation*, Bib. des kgl. preuss. hist. Instituts in Rom, Vols. XII–XIII (Rome, 1914), *passim*.

3. Other members of the Secretariat at this time included Sadoleto's friends, Colocci and Beroaldo the younger, Giovanni Poggio and Emilio Ferreri; Bonamicus, *De clariis . . . scriptoribus*, p. 84; Bembo put the total number at thirty, *Epistolarum familiarium*, p. 5.

4. G. L. Moncallero, *Il Cardinale Bernardo Dovizi da Bibbiena* (Florence, 1953), pp. 374–85.

5. F. Nitti, "Documenti ed osservazioni riguardanti la politica di Leone X," RSR, XVI (1893), 181–289, and Moncallero, pp. 364 ff.

6. Sadoleto to Bembo, *Epistolae*, I, 18–20; Egidio's oration is in J. Harduin, *Acta conciliorum* (1700–16), IX, 1576 ff. Sadoleto's interest fell on the address of Egidio rather than of his friend G. Francesco Pico or the strong *Libellus ad Leonem X* by the Camuldensian reformer Vincenzo Quirini. It is significant that the *Libellus* advanced precisely the line of argument which Sadoleto later used in his own address to Paul III in December 1536 as well as that contained in the *Consilium de emendanda ecclesia* (1537–38), urging that reform begin with the Pope and the Curia. Cf. H. Jedin, "Vincenzo Quirini und Pietro Bembo," *Miscellanea Giovanni Mercati*, IV (1946), 423, and *Geschichte des Konzils von Trient* (Freiburg, 1951), I, 102 f.

7. Hergenroether, *Leonis X . . . regesta*, Fasc. IV, Nos. 8494–95; Arch. Vat., Acta cancell. 1, fols. 2, 3ᵛ.

8. Jedin, *Geschichte*, I, 110; F. Dittrich, "Beiträge zur Geschichte der katholischen Reformation im ersten Drittel des 16. Jahrhunderts," HJG, V (1884), 343.

9. The most important were the distinguished Cajetan and Egidio da Viterbo; Dittrich plausibly includes Giberti, but to add Sadoleto as well is hardly justifiable, *Beiträge*, HJG, VII (1886), 21.

10. Hofmann, *Forschungen*, XIII, 153; P. Richard, "Les origines et développement de la secrétairerie d'état apostolique," pp. 507–8. These examples represent only a fragment of the tasks entrusted to Sadoleto. The principal depository of manuscript material connected with the Leonine Secretariat is Arch. Vat., Reg. Vat., Vols. 889–1214. The *libri secretorum* most relevant to his functions are Vols. 1194, 1197 and 1198; and for Bembo's, Vols. 1203–4; see Aloys Schulte, *Die Fugger in Rom. 1495–1523* (Leipzig, 1904), I, 254–56. The most accessible printed collection is *Jacobi Sadoleti S.R.E. Cardinalis Epistolae Leonis X. Clementis VII. Pauli III nomine scriptae*, ed. V. A. Costanzi (Rome, 1759), pp. 1–128. Many of Bembo's are in his *Epistolarum Leonis decimi pontificis*; and for a brief discussion of Bembo's role in editing and publishing the 581 letters in this collection, see F. Sydow, *Die leonischen Briefe des Petrus Bembus* (Rostock, 1893), pp. 28–43.

11. Largely because Sadoleto insisted toward the end of his life that he had openly disputed the indulgence policies of Leo X; see Schulte, *Die Fugger im Rom.*, I, 40, and p. 137 above.

12. Signed jointly by Sadoleto and "Balandrinus," Schulte, *Die Fugger im Rom.*, II, No. 84, pp. 135–43 and I, p. 63; Hergenroether, *Leonis X . . . regesta*, Fasc. VII, No. 14,825; Pastor, *History*, VII, 328 ff.; H. S. Lea, *History of Auricular Confession and Indulgences of the Latin Church* (Philadelphia, 1896), III, 385 ff.

13. Schulte, *Die Fugger im Rom.*, II, No. 99, pp. 157–61; No. 101, p. 163; No. 102, pp. 163–65.

14. The commissioner was Johannes Heitmars, who claimed to have found Livy's *De bello Macedonico*. Sadoleto instructed the Archbishop to pay Heitmars, on delivery of the MS., the sum of 147 ducats "ex pecuniis indulgentiarum," Schulte, *Die Fugger im Rom.*, II, No. 111, pp. 188–89.

15. Marino Sanuto, *I Diarii* (Venice, 1879–1903), XXIV, 679.

16. For a tendentious but very provocative discussion of Leonine patronage, see D. Gnoli, "Secolo di Leone X?", *Rivista d' Italia*, II, 625–50; and III, 38–55.

17. Sadoleto elaborated this theme for Leo X in a letter to Francesco de Rossi, Rome, 1517, *Epistolae Leonis X*, pp. 68–69.

18. He may also have considered the land an investment; see Ferrajoli, "Il Ruolo . . . Leone X," RSR, XXXVIII, 437 ff. On the general subject of the humanist gardens, D. Gnoli, *La Roma di Leone X* (Milan, 1938), pp. 136–63.

19. Sadoleto to Colocci, Carpentras, 1529, *Epistolae*, I, No. CVI, 309.

20. *Ibid.*, pp. 311–12. To use the phrase "castigatum & prudentem Beroaldum" is generous in view of the poet's allusion to the want of such virtues in Sadoleto as a suitor of Imperia. Maffei, writing to Sadoleto in 1517, cites most of these men as mutual friends, Bib. Vat., Barb. lat. 2517, fol. 45ᵛ.

21. Pastor, *History*, VI, 557–58. Müntz states that Sadoleto once accompanied Erasmus to the artist's studio, *Raphaël* (Paris, 1881), p. 282; and Audin identifies Raphael as the builder of Sadoleto's villa, *Léon X* (Paris, 1884), I, 480.

22. Castiglione's letter is in C. Martinati, *Notizie storico-biografiche intorno al Conte Baldassare Castiglione* (Florence, 1890), p. 83.

23. Erasmus, who condemned Ciceronians in a body, made exceptions of

9*

Sadoleto and Bembo. See Izora Scott, *Controversies over the Imitation of Cicero* (New York, 1910), pp. 22–23, and her translation of the *Ciceronianus*, pp. 116 ff.; Giorgio Santangelo, *Il Bembo critico e il principio d' imitazione* (Florence, 1950). Erasmus found Sadoleto a far less slavish Ciceronian, willing, for example, to express religious themes in religious language, *Ciceronianus*, p. 117. Comparisons of their Latin style were made by Giraldi, *De poetis nostrorum temporum*, pp. 15–16.

24. S. Ritter, *Un Umanista*, p. 86, follows Tiraboschi, *Bibliotèca Modenese*, IV, 437 f., in accepting Sadoleto's authorship of a work entitled *Illustrium imagines*, 1517. The original attribution was suggested by Jacopo Strada in a dedicatory letter to Jacob Fugger in Strada's *Epitome Therauri Antiquitatum* (Zurich, 1557). Fiordibello does not mention it and Paolo Sadoleto did not include it in his collection of Jacopo's works; Tiraboschi admits that the text itself leaves the matter of authorship in doubt.

25. Also named with Sadoleto as one of Imperia's admirers, Menagiana, II, 129. V. Cian, *Un buffone del secolo XVI. Fra Mariano Fetti* (Milan, 1891); for Leo X's fascination with Mariano and his kind, see Gnoli, "Secolo di Leone X?", III, 51, 55.

26. His collaborator was often Mario Maffei, Bishop of Aquino, a dissolute and indifferent prelate who was Sadoleto's friend for forty years; Rodocanachi, *Le première Renaissance*, p. 183, and Ferrajoli, "Il Ruolo . . . Leone X," RSR, XXXVIII, 261 ff.

27. A full account is in Th. Simar, *Christophe de Longueil* (Louvain, 1911); also D. Gnoli, *Un Giudizio di lesa Romanità sotto Leone X* (Rome, 1910). Cf. Erasmus' comment in *Ciceronianus*, in Scott, *Controversies*, pp. 112–15.

28. *Epistolae*, I, 464–65.

29. *Ibid.*, pp. 45–48, 53–55, 86 ff.

30. Pastor, *History*, VIII, 229–30, agrees to this effect with Gnoli, *Un Giudizio*, p. 40, and Reumont, *Geschichte der Stadt Rom* (Berlin, 1867–70), III, part 2, 351.

31. *Responsio pareanetica* (1527); Raynaldus, *Annales*, XXXI, 263–64; Renaudet, *Etudes érasmiennes* (Paris, 1939), pp. 296 ff.

32. M. Bataillon, *Erasme en Espagne* (Paris, 1937), pp. 114 f.

33. Aleander to the Vice-Chancellor, Worms, January 1521, in *Mon. ref. luth.*, No. 14, p. 40.

34. Paquier, *Lettres*, p. 224, n. 1; Santoro, *Pietro Bembo*, pp. 41 ff. We cannot be sure that Sadoleto and Erasmus ever met, P. de Nolhac, *Erasme en Italie* (Paris, 1898), p. 70, n. 1.

35. *Epistolae Leonis X*, p. 94. Erasmus had written to the Pope from Louvain, September 13, 1520, Allen, IV, No. 1143. On his own initiative Sadoleto stoutly opposed publication of a later attack on Erasmus by Diego Lopez de Zuniga in April 1521; Bataillon, *Erasme*, pp. 24, 98–99; Renaudet, *Etudes*, p. 283, n. 3.

36. Ferrajoli, "Il Ruolo . . . Leone X," RSR, XXXVII, pp. 352–53.

37. Arch. Vat., Reg. Vat., Vol. 1001, fol. 166; Ferrajoli lists his benefices, pp. 219–20. However, in citing Jacobo's dispensation from fiscal immunity over his benefices (p. 221), Ferrajoli neglects to add that such exemptions were commonly

enjoyed by most curialists and members of a Cardinal's *famiglia*, Jedin, *Geschichte*, I, 352–53.

38. J. Fornery, *Histoire ecclésiastique du Comté Venaissin* (Avignon, 1909) III, 220. Sixtus IV conferred the diocese on Giulio della Rovere.

39. Abbé Ricard, *Sadolet*, pp. 34 ff. See also C. de Cottier and J. d'Inguimbert, *Recueil de divers titres sur lesquels sont fondés plusiers droits et privileges dont jouit la ville de Carpentras* (Carpentras, 1782), pp. 10–14.

40. F. Cistellini, *Figure della riforma pretridentina* (Brescia, 1948), pp. 269–83; the names of Giberti and Contarini are also missing from the *elenco* of 1524. Authority for Sadoleto's membership in the Oratory previously rested on the list in A. Caracciolo, "Vita et gesti di Giovanni Pietro Carafa" (1619), cited in A. Bianconi, *L'Opera delle compagnie del Divino Amore nella riforma cattolica* (Citta di Castello, 1914), pp. 46–47.

41. The question of Bembo's religion is discussed by Cian, *Un Decennio*, pp. 20–21. A defense of his piety made by Bernardo Morsolin, "La Ortodossia di P. Bembo," *Atti del R. Ist. Veneto*, III, Ser. II (1885), 1–43, is closely questioned by Cian in *Gior. della. lett. ital.*, V (1885), 432–40.

42. Rome, May 28, 1517, Arch. Vat., Arm. XLV, Vol. 42, fol. 42ᵛ.

43. Described by Paris de Grassis, *Diarium*, in Pastor, *History*, VII, Appendix No. 40, pp. 492–93.

44. "Iacobi Sadoleti episcopi Carpent. Leonis X. Pontificis Maximi a secretis in promulgatione generalium indulgentiarum Oratio in Beata semper Virginis ad Minervam habita xix kal. Aprilis MDXVIII." *Opera*, II, 257–64.

45. Sanuto, *I Diarii*, XXV, 322. The version in *Opera*, II, contains no reference to Venice; the ambassador evidently won his point.

46. Allen, III, No. 858, p. 365; see also Renaudet, *Etudes*, pp. 103–4.

47. The original draft is in Arch. Vat., Arm. LIV, Vol. 5, fols. 125–28.

48. P. Kalkoff, *Forschungen zu Luthers römischem Prozess* (Rome, 1905), 94–96.

49. Luther, WA, Vol. II, 23–25; V. E. Löscher, *Vollständige Reformations— Acta und Documenta* (Leipzig, 1720–29), II, 437–40; P. Kalkoff, "Zu Luthers römischem Prozess," ZKG, XXXIII (1912), 22, 47.

50. Kalkoff, ZKG, XXXIII, 47.

51. *Opera*, II, 168–71.

52. *Epistolae*, I, 31 f.

53. *Ibid.*, 34.

54. Bembo to Longueil, August 20, 1520, *Epistolarum familiarium*, p. 205.

55. Sadoleto to Longueil, *Epistolae*, I, 81. (Costanzi dates the letter "3 Kal. Jan."; Simar holds that it should be "3 Kal. Feb.," i.e. January 30, 1521, *Christophe de Longueil*, p. 170, n. 3.) It is difficult to know what Sadoleto meant in saying that he had withdrawn himself "in portum", although there are indications of partial isolation from the Curia, e.g., the statement of Micheli that Sadoleto was now "somewhat sequestered, so that one is not able to talk to him as one would like to." Micheli to Tiepolo, 1519, Sanuto, *I Diarii*, XXVII, 224.

56. Later, feeling that his cousin might be tempted to stay indefinitely in Rome rather than return to Carpentras, Sadoleto warned him of the perils

involved by likening the Curia to a fish net, from which escape, once in it, is almost impossible. Jacopo to Paolo Sadoleto, Carpentras, 1535, *Epistolae*, II, 325–26.

57. Cian, *Un Decennio*, pp. 9–10. Sadoleto later told Erasmus that Bembo had to quit the Curia for the sake of his health, *Epistolae*, I, 87, and 250.

58. The alliance with Morosina, whose husband did not die until 1523 or 1525, began in 1513. While they were in Rome, where she had an apartment in the Borgo, they kept the relationship discreet, but in Venice and Padua she lived openly as his mistress and bore him three children; marriage, of course, would have cost him his benefices.

59. Gnoli makes a good deal of Bembo's exasperation with the Leonine court, "Secolo di Leone X?", III, 39–40.

60. January 18, 1521, in *Mon. ref. luth.*, No. 13, p. 38; and *Epistolae Leonis X*, pp. 95 ff.

61. *Ibid.*, Nos. LXXII–LXXX.

62. *Calendar of Letters, Dispatches, and State Papers relating to the Negotiations between England and Spain*, II, *Henry VII, 1509–25*, ed. G. A. Bergenroth (London, 1866), No. 338.

63. Arch. Vat., Lett. di Prin. 11, fols. 192–97. The treaty itself is in A. Theiner, *Codex diplomaticus* (Rome, 1862), III, 524–29; for a summary of its contents, Nitti, *Leone X*, pp. 431–33.

64. Blasius Baronius de Martinellis, "Diarium," Bib. Vat., Barb. lat. 2799, fols. 48ᵛ–49.

Chapter III: Papal Secretary: The Court of Clement VII

1. "Il diario di Marcello Albertini (1521–1536)," ed. Domenico Orano RSR, XVIII (1895), 325; cf. Sanuto, *I Diarii*, XXXII, 383.

2. Tiraboschi, *Bibliotèca Modenese*, IV, 429. Fiordibello erroneously states that he went to Carpentras immediately after the death of Leo X, *Vita*, in *Opera*, I, 5.

3. *Cronaca*, I, 383. This translation and all that follow, unless otherwise indicated, are mine.

4. Rome, April 14, 1522, LPR, I, 88. To my knowledge the only biography of Negri is by V. Costanzi in *J. Sadoleti Epistolarum Appendix*, pp. lxxiii–cviii. Notes on his career are in Tiraboschi, *Storia della letteratura italiana* (Milan, 1824), VII, Part IV, 2322; and M. Foscarini, *Della letteratura veneziani libri otto* (Padua, 1752), I, 211. A Venetian, Negri studied under Pomponazzi at Padua before turning to law; and from Padua, where he held a minor benefice, he went to Rome in the reign of Julius II. He probably met Sadoleto through the Academy. Negri was secretary to Francesco Cornaro from 1529–33 and later was Contarini's vicar from 1538–41. Negri's letters to Micheli contain important material on Sadoleto's life in Rome.

5. Sadoleto to Longueil, July 2, [1521], *Epistolae*, I, 91.

6. *Relazioni degli ambasciatori veneti al Senato. Relazione di Roma*, ed., E. Albèri, Ser. II, Vol. III, 75.

7. G. Pasolino, *Adriano VI* (Rome, 1913), pp. 21 ff.; E. Rodocanachi, *Les Pontificats d'Adrien VI et de Clément VII* (Paris, 1933), pp. 62–63.

8. Rome, August 14, 1522, LPR, I, 98.

9. Allen, V, Nos. 1324 and 1338. Cf. Renaudet, *Etudes*, pp. 6 ff., and Bataillon, *Erasme en Espagne*, p. 157.

10. Letter of A. Germanello, January 5, 1523 (Gonzaga Archives, Mantua), cited in Pastor, *History*, IX, 115, n. 4.

11. March 17, 1523, LPR, I, 113.

12. Rodocanachi, *Adrien VI et Clément VII*, pp. 64–65.

13. C. Cantù, *Italiani illustrati* (3rd ed.; Milan, 1875), III, 136, which probably follows Tiraboschi, *Bibliotèca Modenese*, IV, 429.

14. March 17, 1523, LPR, I, 113.

15. April 7, 1523, *ibid.*, p. 114.

16. *Ibid.*, p. 113.

17. *Ibid.*, p. 114.

18. *Epistolae*, I, 97.

19. As a youth Petrarch and his mother lived at Carpentras from 1313–17 while his father stayed at Avignon, then congested by the sudden influx of the papal court. The poet remembered Carpentras fondly in later life: ". . . urbs parva quidem sed provincie parve caput. Tenes ne memoria tempus illud quadriennii? Quanta ibi iucunditas, quanta securitas, que domi quies, que ve in publico libertas, que per agros otia, quod ve silentium!" Petrarch, *Prose*, eds. G. Martellotti et al. (Milan and Naples, 1955), p. 1094.

20. Situated in a corner formed by the confluence of the Rhône and the Durance, the Venaissin is flanked by mountains: Ventoux, de la Lance, and the long plateau of the Luberon on the South. In Sadoleto's time the diocese embraced twenty-three parishes and included around seventy-five clergy in the chapter and the parishes; see Ricard, *Sadolet*, pp. 159–62. The diocese was suppressed in 1802 and joined to that of Avignon in 1818.

21. L. Dorez, "Antonio Tebaldeo, les Sadolet et le cardinal Jean du Bellay," *Giornale storico della letteratura italiana*, XXVI (1895), 384. Sadoleto referred to Avignon as "the other Rome," *Epistolae*, I, 139.

22. LPR, I, 118ᵛ.

23. *Ibid.*

24. Negri to Micheli, quoting Sadoleto, December 8, 1523, *ibid.*, p. 119ᵛ. Favonio, implicated with Sadoleto and imprisoned, was later mentioned as an alternative to Blosio Palladio for the second secretarial post under Clement VII, *ibid.*, p. 118ᵛ.

25. *Mon. saec. XVI*, I, No. I, 1. Cortese later recalled Sadoleto's visit to Lérins when requesting papal dispensation to study certain works of the Lutherans; Sadoleto evidently had no trouble in getting a consent, *Epistolae*, I, Nos. XXXIII and XXXV. Such dispensations, however, were more difficult under Paul III; cf. F. Dittrich, RB, No. 288, p. 87.

26. Bembo to Sadoleto, Padua, February 15, 1524, in Bembo, *Opere* (Venice, 1729), III, 54. Mazzuchelli, *Scrittori*, II, part 2, 743.

27. Fiordibello, *Vita*, in *Opera*, I, 5; and, among others, Joly, *Etude*, p. 127. Ferrajoli's view of the three year commitment is far more plausible, "Il Ruolo . . . Leone X," RSR, XXXVIII, 233.

28. Letter to Clement VII, Bib. Vat., Barb. lat. 2157, fol. 54.

29. Campeggio to Sadoleto, Vienna, 1524, *Mon. Vat.*, No. XII, 12.

30. Carpentras, 1537, *Epistolae*, II, 502; the same theme appears in his commentary on Ps. 93, *Opera*, III, 297A–298B.

31. P. Polman, *L'Elément historique dans la controverse réligieuse du XVIe siècle* (Gembloux, 1932), p. 366.

32. T. Pandolfi, "Giovan Matteo Gilberti e l'ultima difésa della libertà d'Italia negli anni 1521-1525," RSR, XXXIV (1911), 145–49, 170 ff.

33. Arch. Vat., Nunz. diverse 238, fol. 88^v.

34. *Mon. Vat.*, No. 179, p. 398.

35. Hofmann, *Forschungen*, XIII, 124; Pastor, *History*, X, 335; Ferrajoli, "Il Roluo . . . Leone X," RSR, XXXVIII, 269. Accolti was arrested in 1535 for malfeasance as Legate in Ancona, having been made Cardinal in 1527, Dorez, *La Cour de Paul III* (Paris, 1932), I, 97. Blosio Palladio, Pietro Carnesecchi, and Sadoleto's private secretary J. F. Bini later served as Domestic Secretaries.

36. A. Pieper, *Zur Entstehungsgeschichte der ständigen Nuntiaturen* (Freiburg im Breisgau, 1894), p. 5.

37. Most of these letters are in *Mon. saec. XVI*; others appear in *Mon. ref. Luth.*; *Mon. Vat.*,; and *Epistolae Leonis X*.

38. *Mon. saec. XVI.*, No. 35, p. 50.

39. *Ibid.*, Nos. 36, 38. On two previous occasions Sadoleto had saluted Henry VIII in the name of a Medici Pope as "defender of the faith," congratulating him for his apologetical attack on Luther, *Letters and Papers, Foreign and Domestic relating to the Reign of Henry VIII*, III, part 2, No. 1740; and *Mon. saec. XVI*, No. 5, p. 5.

40. January 21, 1525, *ibid.*, No. 47. Among the recipients was the Landgrave Philip of Hesse, Sadoleto sharing the ignorance of the commission on Lutheran affairs in not knowing that Philip had supported Luther since the end of 1523; cf. Pastor, *History*, IX, 119.

41. *Mon. saec. XVI*, Nos. 239–240.

42. *Ibid.*, No. 102, pp. 138–39.

43. *Ibid.*, No. 112.

44. *Ibid.*, No. 110.

45. Machiavelli went to Rome after the battle of Pavia in March 1525, to obtain papal support for his *Istoria* but was no less interested in the defense of Florence against the imperial armies. Guicciardini did not share the Pope's momentary enthusiasm for Machiavelli's plan to arm the people of the Romagna and set forth his doubts to Machiavelli in a letter of June 19, 1525, Pandolfi, RSR, XXXIV, 209–12 and M. Brion, *Machiavel* (Paris, 1948), pp. 387–93. Sadoleto wrote on July 8 that he had been given no instructions on the subject,

Opere di Niccolò Machiavelli (Florence, 1813), III, 165–66. See especially R. Ridolfi, *Vita di Niccolò Machiavelli* (Rome, 1954), pp. 318–25.

46. Rome, June 20, 1525, *Mon. saec. XVI*, No. 115, p. 159.

47. These dispatches are found largely in *Mon. ref. Luth.*, Nos. 167, 173, 177, 179, 182, 184–87, 192, 194, 199, 204, 214–15, 220, 223, 228, 241, 244, 250 (Campeggio); 191, 195, 207, 213, 227, 229, 233, 240, 252, 257, 265 (Rorario); 203 (Burgo). Others, with some duplication, are in *Mon. Vat.*, Nos. XI–XVI, XIX (Campeggio); XVII–XVIII (Rorario). Instructions from Sadoleto to these missions are in *Mon. saec. XVI*, Nos. 12–14, 26–27, 273.

48. *Mon. ref. Luth.*, No. XV, p. 15.

49. *Mon saec. XVI*, Nos. 154–55.

50. Fiordibello, *Vita*, in *Opera*, I, 7; Raynaldus, *Annales*, XXXI, No. 10, p. 556; Gregorovius, *History*, VIII, part 2, 501; Abbé Ricard, *Sadolet*, p. 42.

51. June 16, 1526, *Mon. saec. XVI*, p. 233; July 2, 1526, Arch. Vat., Arm. XL, Vol. 12, fol. 6.

52. The text in *Mon. saec. XVI*, No. 275, is inaccurate; for an account of the several versions of this letter see Pastor, *History*, IX, 313, n. 4; a summary of its contents follows, pp. 313–16.

53. *Mon. saec. XVI*, No. 178.

54. *Mon. saec. XVI*, No. 276.

55. Negri to Micheli, Rome, October 24, 1526, LPR, I, 234–35.

56. October 18, 1526, *Mon. saec. XVI*, No. 185, p. 244. Sadoleto also described the raid to Burgo in a letter of October 23, Arch. Vat., Arm. XL, Vol. 12, fol. 160.

57. Letter to Micheli, Rome, July 17, 1525, LPR, I. 164.

58. September 17, 1524, *Epistolarum Reginaldi Poli*, ed. A. M. Quirini (Brescia, 1744–57), I, No. XVI.

59. Erasmus said he first heard of Sadoleto from Niccolò Leonico, Allen, IX, No. 2443, p. 166. Niccolò Leonico Tomeo, a humanist and Aristotelian scholar who taught at Padua, was Pole's teacher and should be distinguished from Niccolò Leoniceno, Sadoleto's master at Ferrara.

60. Froben published the work in August 1524. Sadoleto and Giberti received two of the first copies, Renaudet, *Etudes*, p. 230 and Allen, V, p. 573, n. 1; for Sadoleto's reply, see Allen, V, No. 1511.

61. Allen, V, intr. to No. 1519.

62. Erasmus to Sadoleto, Basle, February 25, 1525, *ibid.*, No. 1555.

63. Basle, August 31, 1525, *ibid.*, VI, No. 1604, p. 158.

64. Cf. Luther's unflattering comment; "Aber da ist kein Verstand in der heiligen Schrift nicht, wie man klärlich sieht in seinem Comment über den 51 Psalm. . . ." WA, Vol. IV, No. 4341, p. 235.

65. *Jacobi Sadoleti Episc. Carpentoracti, Interpretatio in Psalmum Miserere mei, Deus*, S. M. M. T. Romae, F. M. Calvus, 1525. It was reprinted in Rome in 1531 and 1532, and by Gryphius at Lyons in 1533 and 1537; see Ritter, *Un Umanista*, p. 48. My references are to the version in *Opera*, III, 262–93.

66. Sadoleto to Giberti, *ibid.*, pp. 262–63.

67. Lancellotti, *Cronaca*, II, 360. For recognition of Jacopo's services to Modena see Lancellotti's statement at the time of Sadoleto's death, *ibid.*, X, 190.

68. For the history of the Jews in the region see R. de Maulde, *Les Juifs dans les états français du Saint-Siège au moyen âge* (Paris, 1866); Israel Lévi, "Clément VII et les Juifs du Comtat Venaissin," *Revue des Etudes juives*, XXXII (1896), 63–87; I. Loeb, "Les Juifs de Carpentras sous le gouvernement pontifical," *ibid.*, XII (1886), 34–161; A. Mossé, *Histoire des juifs d'Avignon et du Comtat Venaissin* (Paris, 1934). In Carpentras itself there were only fifty-four Jewish families in 1522, but nowhere else in the region had anti-Jewish sentiment been stronger, Mossé, pp. 88, 97.

69. *Mon saec. XVI*, No. 234.

70. Letter to Micheli, LPR, II, 68. Sadoleto was reluctant to divulge the treatise but agreed to send the first part to Clement VII when the Pope asked to see it, *Epistolae*, I, pp. 405–6, 449.

71. *Ibid.*, Nos. XLII, XLVI–LV, LVIII, LXXIV. None of these letters bearing on the case gives a complete account of the issues, but the best available summary is No. LII, pp. 149–50.

72. In May 1526 he obtained a brief from the Pope recognizing the authenticity of an important relic at Carpentras, a nail said to have pierced the right hand of Christ in the crucifixion: de Terris, *Les Evêques de Carpentras*, p. 227; Granget, *Histoire du diocese d'Avignon* (Avignon, 1862), II, 61. Later, in a letter to Erasmus, he defended the use of images and the veneration of the saints as legitimate concessions to popular piety against what Sadoleto regarded as misplaced criticism on the part of Erasmus. Sadoleto to Erasmus, Carpentras, 1530, *Epistolae*, I, 373–74; for Erasmus' reply, Allen, IX, No. 2443, pp. 162–63.

73. Cian, p. 178; E. H. Wilkins, *Studies in the Life and Work of Petrarch* (Cambridge, 1955), p. 284.

74. *Mon. saec. XVI* contains 184 briefs written by Sadoleto in the name of Clement VII between January 31, 1524, and October 18, 1526; but only seven for the following months, i.e. after the Colonna raid, and none after April 16, 1527.

75. Rome, March 18, 1527, *Mon. saec. XVI*, No. 291.

76. Rome, April 15, 1527, LPR, II, 72ᵛ.

77. Negri to Sadoleto, Venice, July 2, 1527, *Epistolae*, I, 190; Jacopo recalled his own prevision to Negri again in September, *ibid.*, No. LXXI, 193.

78. For the dating of Sadoleto's departure, see *Epistolae*, I, 217–18, 238, 250.

79. May 17, 1527, *ibid.*, No. LXV, 171, 173.

80. June 18, 1527, *ibid.*, No. LXVII, 179.

81. *Ibid.*, p. 171.

82. *Ibid.*, p. 196, and letter to Erasmus, November 20, 1527, *ibid.*, No. LXXXVII, 250. Sadoleto of course was only one among hundreds who lost valuable libraries at this time; Piero Valeriano summarized the afflictions of lettered society in his *De literatorum infelicitate* (Venice, 1620).

83. *I Diarii*, XLV, 20.

84. Giberti was made a hostage at the end of the siege. In February 1528

he escaped to Verona but later rejoined the Pope at Viterbo. Eager though he was to leave Rome to devote himself to his diocese, Giberti never fully deserted Clement VII before the Pope died. See F. Dittrich, "Beiträge zur Geschichte der katholischen Reformation im ersten Drittel des 16. Jahrhunderts," HJG, VII (1886), part 1, 11 ff. Aleander, as eager as Sadoleto to get away, left Rome in March 1527 for his diocese at Brindisi.

Chapter IV: Fugitive

1. Allen, IX, No. 2443, pp. 164–65; *Epistolae*, I, 437.

2. "Il diario di Marcello Alberini," RSR, XVIII, 325.

3. Bembo felt that Sadoleto was to be congratulated for extricating himself from the court, rather than censured for leaving it, *Epistolarum familiarium* (1552) p. 251.

4. *Epistolae*, III, 376.

5. Sadoleto to Bini, Carpentras, June 18, 1527, *Epistolae*, I, 178; and to Negri, September 9, 1528, *ibid.*, 193. He used the same argument to Clement VII, Carpentras, September 9, 1528, Arch. Vat., Arm. XLV, Vol. 42, fol. 41.

6. Negri to Sadoleto, July 4, 1527, *Epistolae*, I, 191.

7. Sadoleto to Bini, Carpentras, June 18, 1527, *ibid.*, p. 178.

8. ". . . la fortuna m' è pure stata sempre troppo crudele." *Ibid.*, p. 181. Elsewhere, however, it was not *fortuna* which had taken him from Rome, but his own deliberate resolve (*voluntas*), *ibid.*, p. 250; and to Coloccio, p. 316.

9. *Ibid.*, p. 250.

10. Sadoleto to Negri, *ibid.*, p. 193; and to Clement VII, September 1, 1527, Arch. Vat., Arm. XLV, Vol. 42, fol. 41.

11. Sadoleto to Negri, Carpentras, September 9, 1527, Bib. Vat., Cod. Barb. lat. 2157, fol. 1; the version in *Epistolae*, I, 193 f., is slightly different.

12. Sadoleto to Clement VII, April 17, 1528, Arch. Vat., Lett. di Prin. 5, fols. 169–70.

13. Sadoleto to Bini, Carpentras, June 18, 1527, *Epistolae*, I, 179.

14. *Epistolae*, I, 172, 283, 352, and Arch. Vat., Lett. di Prin. 6, fol. 274.

15. E.g., *Epistolae*, I, 172, 176, 196; and Arch. Vat., Arm. XLV, Vol. 42, fol. 42.

16. *Epistolae*, I, 325.

17. Letters to Salviati, *ibid.*, pp. 224–25, 393; also Bib. Vat., Cod. Ottob. lat. 3139, fols. 345ᵛ–46.

18. *Epistolarum familiarium* (1552), p. 95. Bembo told Erasmus that Sadoleto should never have returned to Rome in 1524, *ibid.*, p. 251.

19. *Epistolae*, I, 352.

20. *Ibid.*, II, 247–48.

21. March 13, 1536, *Epistolae*, II, 304.

22. Sadoleto to Salviati, May 1528, *ibid.*, p. 224; and to Coloccio, 1529, *ibid.*, pp. 316–17.

23. Sadoleto to Cardinal Juan Alvarez de Toledo, Carpentras, January 19, 1545, *ibid.*, III, 382; and to Paul III, January 21, 1545, *ibid.*, 387. Applied to his departure in 1527, these claims seem nothing but a clumsy invention. If such an agreement had been made, why did Sadoleto never mention it immediately after the event? And why then did he tell Bini, on June 18, 1527, that the Pope had consented to an absence of three or four months? *Ibid.*, I, 179.

24. *Ibid.*, pp. 323, 332.

25. Sadoleto became deeply attached to the château and gardens at St. Félix-de-Malemort, seven miles west of Carpentras, where since the thirteenth century his predecessors had developed a summer retreat. See Robert Caillet, *Un Prélat bibliophile en philanthrope, Monseigneur d'Inguimbert, Archevêque-évêque de Carpentras* (Lyons, 1952), pp. 73 ff. No longer a temporal fief of the diocese in the sixteenth century, it remained under episcopal jurisdiction as a priory of St. Ruf; Bibliothèque Inguimbertine (Carpentras) MS. 1740, fol. 24, and MS. 540, fol. 14. Sadoleto found S. Felice "in no way inferior to our Quirinal gardens," being blessed with water and fruit trees as his Roman villa was not, *Epistolae*, I, 241, 275–76.

26. Cf. P. Mestwerdt, *Die Anfänge des Erasmus* (Leipzig, 1917), pp. 69–70, for a discussion of the "Kirchlichkeit oder Unkirchlichkeit" of the humanists.

27. Sadoleto to Erasmus, Carpentras, 1528, *Epistolae*, I, 251–52.

28. *Ibid.*, pp. 337–38.

29. Letters to Cajetan, 1530, *ibid.*, p. 320; and to Fregoso, *ibid.*, p. 323.

30. Sadoleto hoped to have Bini promoted to fill the position he had vacated in the Secretariat and wrote to Cardinal Gonzaga and Bembo in his behalf, *ibid.*, Nos. LXVIII, LXXV. Later, as Domestic Secretary, Bini wrote a treatise *Del perfetto segretario* (ca. 1535).

31. Letters to Accolti, 1531, Bib. Vat., Cod. Ottob. lat. 3139, fol. 329; Fregoso, *Opera*, III, 294A; and G. F. Pio, *Epistolae*, I, 362.

32. Letters to Negri, 1531, *Epistolae*, I, 399; and to Blosio, 1531, Arch. Vat., Lett. di Prin. 6, fol. 244.

33. *Epistolae*, I, 274.

34. *Opera*, III, 294A–95B.

35. In *Gasparis Contarini Cardinalis Opera* (Paris, 1571); see also H. Jedin, *Il tipo ideale di vescovo secondo la riforma cattolica* (Brescia, 1950).

36. *Opera*, III, 296A–98B.

37. Sadoleto, *ibid.*; cf. Contarini, *Opera*, pp. 403, 410–11.

38. Sadoleto, *Opera*, III, 296B; Contarini, *Opera*, p. 431. Contarini especially condemned the spread of absenteeism and the high living of those who had abandoned their sees for Rome, *ibid.*, p. 412.

39. Jean Montaigu, professor of law in Avignon, wrote Boniface Amerbach in 1527 to ask what the latter knew of reports about the evil condition of the Curia and "almost all the Roman clergy." With respect to the Avignonese clergy he wrote: "Presbiteri nostri adhuc non cessant, non emendantur, nihil timent, non fiunt aliorum periculo cautiores. Nescio an remittet illos Deus in aliud seculum."

In A. L. Herminjard, ed., *Correspondance des réformateurs dans les pays de langue française* (2nd ed.; Geneva, 1866–97), II, No. 201, pp. 32–33.

40. Sadoleto, Commentary on Ps. 93, *Opera*, III, 298A, from Hosea 4:15.

41. Carpentras, Bib. Inguimbertine, MS. 558 (L535), fols. 8–19. The survey is dated May 3, 1527, and evidently took place on the day of his arrival, or was at least ordered at that time.

42. Founded in the eleventh century and named for the first Bishop of Avignon, the order was then widespread in Provence and Dauphiné; its members, known as the canons regular of St. Ruf, followed the Augustinian rule. See A. Carrier de Belleuse, *Etudes et documents sur l'ordre de Saint-Ruf* (Avignon, 1933). Their monastery at Carpentras was located just outside the walls, opposite the present Hôtel Dieu, Cottier et d'Inguimbert, *Receuil de divers titres*, p. 44.

43. Bib. Inguimbertine, MS. 1559.

44. Carpentras, MS. 1740, fols. 17–24; MS. 558 (L535), fol. 473. It was through his rights over the order that Sadoleto enjoyed the use of his summer residence at S. Felice.

45. Excluded from the present study, however, is the material contained in the important *Secretariatus*, a chronicle of the diocese under Sadoleto's jurisdiction. This record of over 2,000 folio pages is in the Bib. Inguimbertine, MSS. 1358–59, and covers the years 1520–46.

46. Carpentras, MS. 1740, fol. 13.

47. Among the more useful studies of papal government in Avignon and the county are those of M. David, *De l'organisation administrative, financière et judicaire du Comtat-Venaissin sous la dominion des papes 1229–1791* (Aix, 1912); J. F. André, *Histoire du gouvernement des Recteurs pontificaux dans le Comtat-Venaissin* (Carpentras, 1847); C. Cottier, *Notes historiques concernant les Recteurs du ci-devant Comté-Venaissin* (Carpentras, 1806); A. Mossé, *Histoire des Juifs d'Avignon et du Comtat Venaissin* (Paris, 1934), pp. 63 ff.; E. A. Granget, *Histoire du diocèse d'Avignon et des anciens diocèses dont il est formé* (Avignon, 1862), Vol. II; V. Faudon, *Essai sur les institutions judiciaux, politiques et municipales d'Avignon et du Comtat-Venaissin sous les papes* (Nîmes, 1867); and R. Vallentin, "Notes sur la chronologie des Vice-Légats d'Avignon au XVIᵉ siècle," *Mémoires de l'Académie de Vaucluse*, IX (1890), 200–13.

48. M. David, *De l'organisation . . . Comtat-Venaissin. . . .*, pp. 67–70.

49. Sadoleto to Alessandro Farnese, Carpentras, 1544, *Lettere*, p. 93.

50. Arch. Vat., Arm. XLV, Vol. 42, fols. 51–53; Cottier, *Notes historiques* pp. 186–87.

51. Sadoleto to Blosio, Carpentras, July 29, 1531, Arch. Vat., Lett. di Prin. 6, fol. 244. Paolo was more blunt: Lett. di Prin. 7, fols. 432, 490.

52. For Jacopo's replies, Lett. di Prin. 6, fol. 268; and letter to Accolti, August 16, 1531, Bib. Vat., Cod. Ottob. lat. 3139, fols. 328–30.

53. The Legate apparently used his own funds, *Epistolae*, I, 420.

54. R. de Maulde, *Les Juifs*, pp. 315–24.

55. *Ibid.*, Articles IV and XXIII of the protest.

56. De Maulde, p. 81; Mossé, p. 77.

57. E.g., letters to Paolo, Carpentras, November 7, 1535, *Epistolae*, II, 318; and Avignon, November 26, 1535, *ibid.*, p. 321.

58. E.g., Erasmus' praise: "Agamemnon hoped for ten Nestors; we, even more ardently, wish that the Church of Christ might have ten Sadoletos." Allen, VIII, No. 2315, p. 431.

59. Cf. Negri's image of Jacopo's life as one spent in "total quiet, free of all tribulation, virtually a heaven on earth. . . ." Letter to Sadoleto, Rome 1532, *Opera*, I, 195.

60. Particularly, it seems, for Bembo's circle at Padua: Sadoleto to Bonamico, Carpentras, 1534, *Epistolae*, II, 213.

61. Sadoleto to Clement VII, Carpentras, July 29, 1531, *ibid.*, p. 420, where he stated that there was not a trace of Lutheran heresy in the entire province. How then are we to interpret the report which Jean Montaigu made to Amerbach in a letter of May, 1533? "The Vaudois, who are partisans of Luther's sect, are badly treated here [Avignon]. Several have been burned and others are seized every day; it is said that there are over six thousand adherents to his sect." Herminjard, *Correspondance*, III, p. 42, n. 21.

62. Sadoleto to G. Niccolai, Carpentras, 1531, *Epistolae*, I, 408–10.

63. May 5, 1528, *ibid.*, p. 224.

64. Bib. Vat., Barb. lat. 2517, fols. 87ᵛ–89. Appointed vicar at Cavaillon by Cardinal Clermont, Jacopo found that the regime of Maffei's procurator had become a reign of terror and expropriation, and in the following spring he urged Maffei to return immediately, *ibid.*, fol. 31.

65. The constant pedagogue, Sadoleto felt that the whole province had suffered from educational famine until the advent of Clermont: Sadoleto to Clement VII, Carpentras, July 29, 1531, *Epistolae*, I, 421. Except in civil law the same illiteracy prevailed in Carpentras, where after great pleading he persuaded certain parents to give their sons a liberal education. Traditionally, however, law alone was studied seriously. But Sadoleto was sure that proper instruction would redeem his people from avarice and from "every sordid and wicked desire." Letter to Negri, *ibid.*, pp. 168–69.

66. *Epistolae*, II, 197–98. Bonamico had already expressed his doubts. See G. Marangoni, "Lazaro Bonamico e lo studio Padovano," *Nuovo Archivio Veneto*, n.s. I, Vol. II (1901), 134.

67. Jacopo to Paolo, Carpentras, November 7, 1535, *Epistolae*, II, 315–16.

68. Sandys, *History*, II, 247; R. C. Christie, "Florence Volusene," *Dictionary of National Biography*, XX, 389–90.

69. Volusene originally wanted to find a post in an Italian university but fell ill at Avignon on his way south. He knew of Sadoleto from Thomas Starkey and was again reminded of Carpentras by Antonio Bovisi, a friend of Starkey's, whom Volusene saw at Lyons en route to Italy in the fall of 1535: Christie, "Florence Volusene," p. 389, who based his account on Sadoleto's letter to Cardinal Lorraine, 1536, *Epistolae*, II, 383–85.

70. Sadoleto to Bembo, Carpentras, September 3, 1532, *ibid.*, p. 57. Pole had hoped to settle quietly at Avignon and resume his studies there, but he disliked

the climate and especially the ferocious Alpine winds, M. Haile, *Reginald Pole* (New York, 1910), pp. 92–93; and W. Schenk, *Reginald Pole, Cardinal of England* (London, 1950), p. 25.

71. Lancellotti, *Cronaca*, V, 179.

72. Exceptions were his journeys to Lyons and Marseilles in 1533. In the course of his trip to Marseilles he was in Avignon when the tomb of Petrarch's Laura was reportedly located in the Minorite church, and was present when Francis I, en route to his meeting with the Pope, ordered the tomb opened. Sadoleto supported the claim that the sonnet found in the casket was written by Petrarch, but Bembo and Beccadelli later disagreed. The incident is described in a letter from Maurice de Sève to Jean de Tournes, Lyons, August 25, 1565, in Abbé de Sade, *Mémoires pour la vie de François Pétrarque* (Amsterdam, 1764), III, Pièces justificatives, Nos. 4, 10; see also A. Bartoli, *Storia della letteratura italiana* (Florence, 1884), VII, 198–207.

73. Maffei to Clement VII, Bib. Vat., Barb. lat. 2157, fol. 58.

74. *I vini d' Italia giudicati da Paolo III* (Rome, 1890), cited in Dorez, *La Cour de Paul III*, I, 75.

75. Paolo has been incorrectly identified as the son of Bishop Sadoleto's brother Giulio in Schultess-Rechberg, *Der Kardinal Jacopo Sadoleto* (Zurich, 1909), pp. 51, 60; as the son of the Bishop's brother Alfonso, in Ricard, "Vie de Mgr. Paul Sadolet, évêque de Carpentras," Carpentras Bib. Inguimbertine, MS. 1719, fol. 1, and in Barjavel, "Généologies," Avignon, Musée Calvet, MS. 5128, fol. 93; and simply as "fratris filius," in *Gallia Christiana*, I, col. 911. Paolo and Jacopo were second cousins, but because they habitually referred to one another as "zio" and "nipote," i.e. as "uncle" and "nephew," I sometimes perpetuate the error by adopting their own terms. For Paolo's biography see Costanzi's *Vita* in *J. Sadoleti Epistolarum Appendix*, pp. 195–208.

76. Sadoleto to Accolti, Carpentras, 1532, Bib. Vat., Ottob. lat. 3139, fol. 355; to Jean du Bellay, *Opera*, I, 123A. Bembo once used the phrase "cum Paolo fratris tui filio," letter to Jacopo, Padua, 1532, *Epistolarum familiarium* (1552), p. 108.

77. Sadoleto to Bembo, *Opera*, I, 25A. Paolo's identity is confirmed by Lancellotti, who describes Paolo as "Fiolo fu de M. Jacomo Sadoleto cusino del predetto M. Alfonso," *Cronaca*, IX, 12, and again as "Fiolo fu alevo del R.mo Cardinale M. Jacomo Sadoleto cusino del preditto M. Jacomo. . . .", *ibid.*, p. 199.

78. *Ibid.*, I, 259, 389, 426; III, 80; XI, 12; XIII, 43.

79. Allen, X, introduction to No. 2864.

80. Fregoso later took the treatise to Italy to have it printed, Sadoleto to Negri, May 17, 1529, *Epistolae*, I, 275. Although Lyons was now emerging as the literary capital of France, Sadoleto's only connection and interest in the city was with Gryphius; see A. F. Johnson, "Books Printed at Lyons in the Sixteenth Century," *The Library*, Ser. IV, Vol. III, No. 3 (1922), 145–74.

81. Sadoleto to Fregoso, May 1528, *Epistolae*, I, 233.

82. Sadoleto to Bembo, Carpentras, June 26 [1529], *ibid.*, p. 294; the date may be established from a letter to Fregoso of August 13, p. 301.

83. *Ibid.*, II, 1–10.

84. Sadoleto considered himself "juri potestatique subjectus" in referring to Francis I, *Opera*, I, 124B; he felt free, however, to decline the King's invitation but went out of his way to praise Francis as a just, righteous, and faithful sovereign, e.g., in *In Epistolam Pauli ad Romanos*, *ibid.*, IV, 5, 309B. Sadoleto dedicated this treatise to Francis I (*Epistolae*, II, No. CCIX) as well as the brief *De duobus gladiis interpretatio* (1534–35).

85. L. Celier, "Alexandre VI et la réforme de l'église," p. 99. Accolti to Sadoleto, Rome, January 20, 1532, Bib. Vat., Ottob. lat. 3139, fol. 343; and July 8, 1532, *ibid.*, fol. 357.

86. Accolti to Sadoleto, Rome, May 15, 1532, Bib. Vat., Ottob. lat. 3139, fol. 350.

87. Sadoleto to Accolti, June 19, 1532, *ibid.*, cols. 355–56ᵛ.

88. The delegation thus represented each order of the College, a device proposed to Accolti by his kinsman Cardinal Ancona. Accolti's description of his procedure is singularly vivid; the letter was dated July 15, 1532, *ibid.*, fols. 356ᵛ–58.

89. Sadoleto to Clement VII, October 4, 1532, Arch. Vat., Lett. di Prin. 7, fol. 489.

90. He mentioned the fact in thanking Accolti for his services in a letter of August 30, Bib. Vat., Ottob. lat. 3139, fol. 360. But he was not yet alarmed, having heard that Clement was ill in late summer and evidently unable to attend to the matter.

91. Sadoleto left Carpentras on September 29; Clement, accompanied by a splendid retinue, reached Marseilles on October 11: Raynaldus, *Annales*, XXXII, 317–20. For the negotiations between Clement and Francis I, see Michel François, *Le Cardinal François de Tournon* (Paris, 1951), pp. 112 ff., and Jedin, *Geschichte*, I, 228.

92. Ferrajoli, "Il Ruolo . . . Leone X," RSR, XXXVIII, 229; Sadoleto to Fregoso, May 27 [1534], *Epistolae*, II, 295. Paolo was later confirmed in the title by a brief dated February 14, 1535, Arch. Vat., Arm. XL, Vol. 50, fol. 311. This was the start of a career in which he became rector of the county (1541–46), papal secretary (1552–55) under Julius III, assistant to Ippolito d'Este, and rector again (1567–72). He died in 1572. See *Lettere*, pp. xv–xviii. Paolo in turn was a nepotist in his own right; see his letters to Cardinal Farnese, *ibid.*, Nos. LXIV–LXVII.

93. *Epistolae*, II, 124 (incorrectly dated 1533 in both Costanzi and the Verona edition). On his return to Carpentras Sadoleto wrote a rather trivial treatise, *In duo Iohannis loca de Nicodemo et de Magdelena*, which he dedicated to Clement VII. It concludes with an expression of gratitude for the "tranquil and blessed life" which was now his, and with the plea that retirement at Carpentras be "perpetual and inviolate." The treatise is in Cardinal Mai's collection, *Spicilegium Romanum* (Rome, 1839), II, 180–230.

94. Tiraboschi, *Storia della letteratura italiana*, VII, part 1, 461. Another son of Marguerite Sadoleto and J. B. Sacrati, Jacopo became Bishop of Carpentras

(1572–93) and Rector of the County (1572–76); his procurator, coadjutor, and successor were all Sadoletti, Fornery, *Histoire ecclésiastique*, III, 229 ff.

95. Sadoleto to Accolti, January 21, 1532, Bib. Vat., Ottob. lat. 3139, fol. 346; Ercole at this time appears to have been in serious financial trouble.

96. *Epistolae*, II, 309, 314–15. Jacopo advised Paolo to assume the late Jacopo's debts and felt sure that the Pope would provide help in the form of a new ecclesiastical pension. At the same time Paolo was to attend to the leasing of the Bishop's Quirinal vineyard.

97. Jacopo argued that for Paolo to seek a pension from the Pope through Cardinal Farnese was thoroughly honorable and legitimate, while forbidding him to seek help from Francis I instead, *ibid.*, pp. 334–35.

98. E.g., *Epistolae*, II, 281. To Paolo he wrote of Carpentras as a place were everything is abundant but money, December 28, 1535, *ibid.*, p. 337. Of Sadoleto's various biographers only Ferrajoli has examined his financial position with any care. He estimated Jacopo's gross annual income at 2,688 ducats, Bembo's at 1,665, and thereupon challenged the legend of Sadoleto's poverty, "Il Ruolo . . . Leone X," RSR, XXXVIII, 222. Earlier biographers assumed that he received only the episcopal income attached to Carpentras, e.g., Ribier, *Lettres et mémoires d'état* (Paris, 1666), I, 116; du Tems, *Clergé de France*, II, 30; Granget, *Histoire du diocèse d'Avignon*, II, 49. Although Ferrajoli emphasizes Sadoleto's nepotism and the size of his household, he fails to concede the extent and effect of Jacopo's largesse to his dependents. Sadoleto's complaint of poverty, however, did not become insistent until after he entered the Sacred College; see below, chapter VIII.

99. Sadoleto saw himself as one who had eschewed "wealth and honors" while in papal service (e.g., letter to Burgos, *Epistolae*, III, 382) and at Carpentras (letter to Salviati, *ibid.*, I, 393). His attacks on avarice in the hierarchy were equally numerous, e.g., Sadoleto to G. Niccolai, 1531, *ibid.*, p. 410.

100. Despite the fact, as V. Schweitzer suggests, that few prelates were more conspicuously nepotistic, CT, XII, 119, n. 1.

101. Accolti, for example, used this argument in pressing Jacopo's claims for Paolo on Clement VII, Accolti to Sadoleto, 1532, Bib. Vat., Ottob. lat. 3139, fol. 357. Sadoleto did so in a letter to Salviati, 1528, *Epistolae*, I, 224.

Chapter V:
Exegete, Pedagogue, and Theologian

1. "Otium porre est, ubi Roma non est." *Epistolae*, I, 283. Cf. Cicero, *De officiis*. 3. 1.

2. *In Psalmum nonagesimum tertium interpretatio*, *Opera*, III, 296–376. Sadoleto reported his progress on the work to Fregoso on October 15, 1528, Bib. Vat., Barb. lat. 2157. See Cardinal Mercati, "Un Salterio Greco e una catena greca del salterio posseduti dal Sadoleto," in *Miscellanea Pio Paschini* (Rome, 1949), II, 205–11, for Sadoleto's use of Greek texts and commentaries.

3. Allen, VII, No. 2315, p. 443.

4. The commentary also argues the merits of what Sadoleto called the "historical method" of exegesis, based on the analysis of language and a literal interpretation of the text, *Opera*, III, 299A. He goes on to defend the authority of the Septuagint against the Vulgate, insisting that Greek is the proper tool of biblical studies: *ibid.*, pp. 336A; 342B–43B; 355A–56B. Latin is ancillary to it, while Hebrew like Cabbalistic studies serves only as a minor aid in Christian scholarship. Sadoleto to Fregoso, *Epistolae*, I, 232–33; II, Bo. CLXXXVI.

5. *Ibid.*, I, 351.

6. Allen, VIII, No. 2315, p. 435. Sadoleto commented on Erasmus' melancholy in a letter to Fregoso, 1530, *Epistolae*, I, 369.

7. Allen, VIII, No. 2864, p. 297. Erasmus looked upon Sadoleto, says Renaudet, as the best example of those liberal Catholics through whom reform of the Church would materialize, *Etudes*, p. 263.

8. E.g., Sadoleto to Fregoso, 1530, *Epistolae*, I, 369 f. Yet he claimed to have done his best to obtain preferment for Erasmus from Clement VII, Sadoleto to Erasmus, 1530, *ibid.*, p. 375.

9. *Ibid.*, I, 337; see also Nos. CXXII and CXLIX.

10. Allen, IX, No. 2443, p. 159.

11. Sadoleto to Erasmus, 1528, *Epistolae*, I, 251–52.

12. Allen, VIII, No. 2315, p. 431.

13. *De pronuntiatione* (1528), *De pueris statim ac liberaliter instituendis* (1529). Allen, VII, intro. to No. 1949, p. 327; Renaudet, *Etudes*, p. 292; Allen, VIII, intro. to No. 2189, p. 217.

14. He completed it in the summer of 1530, *Epistolae*, I, 385 f. The following citations are to the version in *Opera*, III, 66–126. There is an English translation by E. T. Campagnac and K. Forbes, *Sadoleto on Education. A Translation of the De Pueris recte Instituendis* (Oxford, 1916). See also B. C. Weber, "The Views of Cardinal Sadoleto on Education," *Modern Language Journal*, XXVI, 452–54. The question of whether Montaigne was influenced by the treatise is answered negatively by Pierre Villey, "Montaigne a-t-il lu le traité de l'éducation de Jacques Sadolet?", *Bulletin du Bibliophile*, VI (1909), 265–78. The first edition was published by Sabio in Venice in 1533 and again in 1534. Gryphius issued it in 1533 and 1535; other sixteenth-century editions followed at Paris (1534), Strasbourg (1535), and Basle (1538, 1556).

15. *Opera*, I, 73A.

16. *Opera*, III, pp. 86A, 105A.

17. *Ibid.*, p. 125B; Sadoleto to Pole, 1534, *Epistolae*, II, 240.

18. *Opera*, III, 119B.

19. *Ibid.*, p. 121B.

20. *Ibid.*, pp. 70B–71A; 126B.

21. *Epistolarum Reginaldi Poli*, I, No. XII, 399.

22. Sadoleto to Bembo, 1532, Bib. Vat., Barb. lat. 2157, fols. lxxvi ff. Bembo to Sadoleto, Padua, 1533, *Opere del Cardinale Pietro Bembo* (Milan, 1808–10), I, 237–39.

23. Pole to Sadoleto, *Epistolarum Reginaldi Poli*, I, XII, 399–400.

24. Sadoleto to Pole, 1532, *Epistolae*, II, 110-11.

25. Sadoleto to Pole, July 1533, *Epistolae*, II, 183 f.

26. Sadoleto to Pole, 1534, *ibid.*, p. 238.

27. Pole tried to get help from Sadoleto in coaxing Lazaro Bonamico away from the Paduan Aristotelians and back to Platonic and thence to "celestial philosophy." However, Sadoleto was much more eager to have Bonamico retain his teaching post than to support Pole. *Ibid.*, Nos. CCI and CCIII. For Bonamico's career see G. Marangoni, "Lazaro Bonamico e lo Studio Padovano," *Nuovo Archivio Veneto*, N.S. I, Vol. I (1901), 118–52, 301–19; and Vol. II (1901), 131–97. I largely concur with S. A. Nulli, *Erasmo e il Rinascimento* (Turin, 1955), pp. 354–59 in his comment on Sadoleto's defense of a secularized concept of wisdom. But I seriously question the statement that the Paduan humanists by 1530 were more preoccupied with "religious than with literary issues," (*ibid.*, p. 355).

28. *Epistolarum Reginaldi Poli*, I, No. XVI, 417.

29. Bembo to Sadoleto, Padua, 1532, *Epistolae*, II, 64.

30. Bonamico later urged Sadoleto not to delay completion of the *Hortensius* and recalled Jacopo's pledge in the *De liberis* (*Opera*, III, 104) to elaborate his defense of the liberal arts in the *De laudibus philosophiae*. Bonamico to Sadoleto, Pavia, 1534, *Opera*, I, 111A.

31. Sadoleto to Giberti, 1532, *ibid.*, p. 68B.

32. *Epistolae*, I, pp. 385–86; 399; 403; 447.

33. On May 1532 Sadoleto told Bembo about plans to return to the *Hortensius* at the end of the summer in the hope of completing it, *ibid.*, p. 50. Bembo assumed that Sadoleto wrote rapidly, but Jacopo represents himself as plodding and anxious, letter to Paolo, 1535, *ibid.*, II, 323.

34. P. de Nolhac, *Erasme en Italie* (Paris, 1898), p. 68.

35. Each of his major works was a dialogue, with Sadoleto in the role of protagonist. Toffanin suggests that his literary model in the *De laudibus philosophiae* was either the platonic dialogue, or the form used by Valla in *De voluptate*, "Umanesimo e teologia," BHR, XI (1949), part 2, 210.

36. *Opera*, III, 134B–35B. While Sadoleto was preparing the rejoinder to Fedra's "accusation," Thomas Starkey wrote a treatise ranging over many of the same issues, *A Dialogue between Reginald Pole and Thomas Lupset*, ed. Kathleen M. Burton (London, 1948), in which Pole argues that there are times when public service is futile. Starkey thought highly of Sadoleto, whom a colloquist describes as "one of the wisest men of our time," but Starkey's praise was inspired by the *De liberis* and not by Jacopo's defense of the contemplative life in the *De laudibus* (which was unfinished when Starkey wrote his *Dialogue*).

37. *Opera*, III, 136B, 178A.

38. *Ibid.*, p. 178. Giovanni Sadoleto, Caraffa, and Fedra were dead by the time Sadoleto wrote the *Phaedrus*.

39. *Ibid.*, p. 129. For a close analysis of the work, see A. Altamura and Giuseppe Toffanin, *Sadoleto, Elogio della Sapienza* (Naples, 1950). On Sadoleto as philosopher, see Joly, *Etude*, pp. 95–99; Schultess-Rechberg, *Der Kardinal*

Jacopo Sadoleto, pp. 46 ff.; L. Zanta, *La Renaissance du Stoïcisme au XVIᵉ siècle* (Paris, 1914), pp. 8–13; G. Toffanin, "Umanesimo e teologia," pp. 205–14; and Eugene F. Rice, Jr., "Varieties of Renaissance Wisdom, a Study in the Secularization of an Idea" (Unpublished Ph.D. dissertation, Dept. of History, Harvard University, 1953), chap. III.

40. Toffanin, "Umanesimo e teologia," p. 214.

41. *Opera*, III, 202B–203A.

42. *Epistolae*, II, 160.

43. *Opera*, III, 242B.

44. *Jacopi Sadoleti Episcopi Carpentoractis in Pauli Epistolam ad Romanos Commentariorum libri tres.* The version cited below with the abbreviation *Comment.* is the one in *Opera*, IV, which follows the first edition published by Gryphius at Lyons in 1535; it therefore lacks the passages which Sadoleto added in the Gryphius edition of 1537.

45. *Epistolae*, II, 300.

46. For Sadoleto's patristic orientation, see Ritter, *Un Umanista*, pp. 34–35, and P. Polman, *L'Elément historique*, pp. 358–59. For Sadoleto's own accounts of his theological formation, see his letters to Giberti, 1532, *Epistolae*, II, 79; to G. Brice, 1534, *ibid.*, p. 245; to Erasmus, 1532, *ibid.*, p. 22; and to Fregoso, *ibid.*, p. 150.

47. Sadoleto to Erasmus, June 1533, *ibid.*, II, 172–73. See also his letter to Brice, June 1534, *ibid.*, p. 245.

48. *Comment.*, p. 206A.

49. *Ibid.*, pp. 208B–209B; letter to Fregoso, April 1533, *Epistolae*, II, 150–54.

50. Sadoleto to Brice, *ibid.*, p. 245.

51. *Ibid.*, II, 148–49. For comment on his assurance of divine inspiration, see D. Cantimori, "Atteggiamenti della vita culturale italiana nel secolo XVI di fronte alla Riforma," *Rivista storica italiana*, Ser. V, I (1936), 50–51.

52. Sadoleto to Giberti, 1532, *Epistolae*, II, 80. For a recent estimate of Augustine's exegetical and linguistic faculties, see M. Pontet, *L' Exégèse de S. Augustin* (Paris [1946]), pp. 195 ff.

53. E. Gothein, *Ignatius von Loyola*, p. 124; cf. Lauchert, p. 398.

54. Letter to Fregoso, *Epistolae*, II, 153.

55. *Comment.*, p. 66B.

56. *Ibid.*, p. 213A.

57. *Ibid.*, pp. 215B–216A.

58. *Ibid.*, p. 215B.

59. *Ibid.*, p. 234A.

60. "Sed licet nihil ex nobis sit dignum, nihil vim aut rationem ullam meriti continens, tamen aliquid a nobis proficiscatur necesse est, in quo confidat [sic] Dei gratia, & justitia, id porro non est operis, sed bonae dumtaxat erga Deum voluntatis, quae solum per fidem Christi contingere nobis potest." *Ibid.*, pp. 100B–100A. The *confidat* in this passage is more plausibly *considat*, as in the Venetian edition of 1536, fol. 57ᵛ: Ritter, *Un Umanista*, p. 112, n. 5.

61. *Comment.*, p. 66A.

62. *Ibid.*, p. 210A. Cf. also pp. 206B, 209A, 213A, 216A, 234B.

63. *Ibid.*, pp. 214B–215A.

64. *Ibid.*, p. 216A.

65. *Ibid.*, p. 206A.

66. Cf. his summary of this position in the dedicatory letter to Francis I, *Epistolae*, II, 256–57.

67. *De trinitate.* IV. 1. 3.; XI. 8. 14.

68. Denzinger, *Enchiridion symbolorum* (28th ed.; Freiburg im Breisgau, 1952), No. 178, can. 5 (Council of Orange); Aquinas, *Summa Theologica*, Iª 2ᵃᵉ, q. 113, a. 8; and 2ª 2ᵃᵉ, q. 6, a. 1. See Ritter *Un Umanista*, pp. 119–20.

69. *Hebrews*, WA, Vol. LVII, 116. 1.

70. *Opera omnia* (Leyden, 1706), col. 1238.

71. See E. Gilson, *L'Esprit de la philosophiae médiévale* (Paris, 1932), chap. VI; also A. Renaudet, "Autour d'une définition de l'humanisme," BHR, VI (1945), 7–49.

72. *Opera*, III, 320B–321A.

73. See RB, *inedita*, No. 20, p. 70, for Contarini's warning (1537) to apologists whose zeal for orthodoxy outruns their knowledge of patristic and medieval theology.

74. For Sadoleto's replies, see his letters of April 3, 1533, and November 13, *Epistolae*, II, Nos. CLXXXVI and CLXXXVII.

75. Sadoleto to Erasmus, *ibid.*, No. CLXXXIX. However, he still felt under obligation to Gryphius and had the first and second editions printed at Lyons.

76. Erasmus twice expressed such fears to Amerbach in the spring of 1534, Allen, X, Nos. 2927, 2928; for Amerbach's views, *ibid.*, No. 2931. Writing to Sadoleto in October 1534, Erasmus finally asked if he had offended the Bishop, *ibid.*, XI, No. 2971, pp. 44–45. See Appendix II above for a commentary on Erasmus' concern.

77. Sadoleto to Erasmus, November 1, 1534, *Epistolae*, II, 251–52 (also in Allen, XI, No. 2973). This letter crossed Erasmus' of October 31, which Sadoleto answered on December 9, when he tried to put his friend at ease about his criticism of the Commentaries, Allen, XI, No. 2982. This is Sadoleto's last surviving letter to Erasmus, whose last to Sadoleto is that of October 31.

78. Allen, XI, No. 3043, p. 208.

79. Basle, December 15, 1535, *ibid.*, No. 3076, p. 259.

80. The Commentaries were not ready for publication until the end of 1534: *Epistolae*, II, 251, and Allen, XI, No. 2982, p. 53.

81. *Epistolae*, II, 244.

82. In Brice, however, Sadoleto may have hoped to find a willing procurator in Paris and a sympathetic critic of the Commentaries. The Bishop knew Brice's recent Latin translations of Chrysostom's sermons (*Sexdecim homiliae Chrysostomi*, 1533) and addressed him as "one who is running the same race", *ibid.*, p. 245. But from this letter it seems that Brice was not altogether pleased by Jacopo's interpretation of Chrysostom.

83. *Ibid.*, pp. 245–46.

84. C. du Plessis d'Argentré, *Collectio judiciorum de novis erroribus* (Paris, 1728), I, viii.

85. See Elizabeth Armstrong, *Robert Estienne, Royal Printer. An historical Study of the Elder Stephanus* (Cambridge, 1954), pp. 201 ff.

86. I concur with Lauchert, p. 398, n. 1, that the disapproval of the Sorbonne took place in 1535, that is, after the printing of the first edition and after the censure in Rome. Ritter, however, places the Sorbonne's censure in 1534, *Un Umanista*, p. 60. But the evidence is inconclusive in each case, for neither the text of the curial censure nor that of the Sorbonne has survived, so far as I have been able to discover.

87. In an undated letter, incontestably written in the spring of 1535, Sadoleto thanked Brice for continuing attention to the matter and urged him to treat further with the faculty, from which, it appears, no final word had yet come. *Epistolae*, II, 283–84; cf. Ritter, *Un Umanista*, p. 59, n. 2 and 4.

88. Badia (1484–1547) was once professor of theology at Ferrara, Venice and Rome before succeeding Sylvester Prierias in the office of Magister. See V. M. Fontana, *Syllabus magistrorum sacri palati apostolici* (Rome, 1663), p. 127.

89. The bull *Inter Solicitudines* required approval of books published in Rome by the Magister sacri palatii and of diocesan ordinaries for those published elsewhere; see Mansi, *Sacrorum conciliorum*, XXXII, p. 913. The Magister's authority was broadened in 1525: Negri to Micheli, LPR, I, 160ᵛ, and B. Fontana, "Documenti Vaticani contro l'eresia luterana in Italia," RSR, XV (1892), 71–166, 365–474.

90. Negri to Micheli, December 6, 1635, LPR, III, 37–38; Benoit, "Le Cardinal Jacques Sadolet," pp. 44–45; K. J. von Hefele and J. Hergenroether, *Conziliensgeschichte*, IX, 901.

91. This much, at least, may be gathered from Sadoleto's letter to Bini, August 20, 1535, *Epistolae*, II, 300. See also Dittrich, RB, No. 268, p. 79, and Contarini to Sadoleto, *ibid.*, p. 262; Dittrich, *Contarini*, p. 485; Lauchert, p. 398; and Joly, *Etude*, p. 170.

92. Sadoleto to Bini, *Epistolae*, II, 298–99.

93. Sadoleto further criticized Badia's conduct in a letter to Blosio, Carpentras, August 30, 1535, in Ferrajoli, "Il Ruolo . . . Leone X," RSR, XXXVIII, 448.

94. Sadoleto to Bini, *Epistolae*, II, 299–300; by mid-August, therefore, Sadoleto learned that Badia found unacceptable the clarifications he had received from Carpentras.

95. *Ibid.*, p. 300.

96. Paolo was to stop first at Modena to see the new Duke, Ercole II, *Epistolae*, II, 308–9. Further instructions followed concerning the debts of Paolo's mother and late brother (*ibid.*, pp. 314–15), although by that time Paolo was already in Rome. There he was to express the Bishop's gratitude to the Pope for a confirmation of privileges (Sadoleto had made the request in a letter to Paul III in December 1534, *ibid.*, No. CCXI, and informed His Holiness of Paolo's mission on September 8, 1535, *ibid.*, pp. 302–3); Paolo was also to report from

the Curia on the effect of the censure on Jacopo's reputation (*ibid.*, pp. 321–22). Other charges included a decision about finding a new tenant for the Quirinal property and a pension for Alfonso Sadoleto from the Pope. Meanwhile, Paolo was to have the *De laudibus philosophiae* copied in Rome and delivered to friends there and in Padua, Paolo to Bembo, November 22, 1535, *Opera*, II, 201–2.

97. Negri to Micheli, December 6, 1535, LPR, III, 37ᵛ.

98. *Epistolae*, II, 319–20. Sadoleto did not congratulate Contarini on his nomination until November 6, 1535, *Epistolae*, II, 339; the first correspondence between them dates from this time, Dittrich, *Contarini*, p. 215.

99. Jacopo to Paolo, November 26, 1535, *Epistolae*, II, 321. His attitude toward Badia had now begun to soften.

100. Sadoleto to Contarini, November 26, 1535, *ibid.*, pp. 342–49.

101. E.g., *De spiritu et littera*, ch. 60; *De natura et gratia*, ch. 35.

102. Sadoleto to Contarini, *ibid.*, p. 347.

103. He went on to agree, however, to make whatever revisions Contarini proposed and stated that he had recently sent to Lyons his own correction of a "grave error" which he found himself. *Ibid.*, pp. 348–49.

104. Contarini to Sadoleto [s.d.], in Dittrich, RB, pp. 261–62. Contarini explained that he had not yet finished reading the Commentaries, being interrupted by the events surrounding his elevation.

105. RB, p. 262.

106. Sadoleto had requested this intervention in his letter of November 26, *Epistolae*, II, 347. Gryphius by then was willing to reprint the treatise to include Sadoleto's emendations.

107. Sadoleto to Paolo, November 26, *Epistolae*, II, 322; here too he showed genuine appreciation of Contarini's part in the controversy. When writing to Micheli on December 6 Negri reported that Sadoleto had made his peace with Badia and that the Commentaries had been "approved and released." LPR, III, 38.

108. Lauchert, p. 395; Ritter, *Un Umanista*, p. 66, n. 6. In the Verona edition, which does not contain these revisions, the insertion would appear on p. 215B of Vol. IV, following the line ". . . sed quo tamen libertas animi nostri non constringatur."

109. This would appear in the Verona edition on p. 247B; see Lauchert, p. 392, n. 3.

110. *Epistolae*, II, 393.

111. RB, *inedita*, No. 12, p. 264.

112. Jedin cites Badia's acquiescence to illustrate the predicament of the pre-Tridentine Church on questions of doctrinal definition, *Geschichte*, I, 297. The second (corrected) edition was published at Lyons in the early spring of 1536, the third by Sabio in Venice in May 1536, and a fourth at Lyons in 1537.

113. Sadoleto mentioned Tournon's interest in writing to du Prat, October 14, 1532, *Epistolae*, II, 94; he was also careful to cultivate and maintain Tournon's friendship, e.g., *Epistolae*, No. CLXXVI, presumably in view of the Cardinal's political influence.

114. John 3:1–23, and 20:17. Sadoleto received the commission from the

Pope while at Marseilles in October 1533, *Epistolae*, II, 165–66. The treatise, discovered by Cardinal Mai, is in his *Specilegium Romanum*, II, 180–230. At the same time Sadoleto completed another exegetical work, dedicated to Francis I, in which he sought to relate Isaiah 53 to Mark 15–28 and Luke 22:35–39, showing the fulfillment of prophecy with respect to the suffering Messiah in two texts of the Gospel; this work, *In locum Evangelicum de duobus gladiis interpretatio*, is in *Opera*, III, 377–90. Both works belong to the period in which the Commentaries were written.

115. This is not to say that the method or manner of these men was uniform. Erasmus, for example, made no continuing effort in the *De libero arbitrio* to resolve and define his conclusions dogmatically, recognizing his own limitations as a theologian; for an analysis of his own *via media*, see Renaudet, *Etudes*, pp. 233 ff.

116. Cf. A. Dupront, "Du concile de Trente: Réflexions autour d'un IVe centenaire," *Revue historique*, CCVI (1951), 262–80.

117. The issue was most evident during the debate on the sacred canons and the interpretation of Scripture. See A. Walz, "Die Dominikaner und Trient," in G. Schreiber, ed., *Das Weltkonzil von Trient* (Freiburg, 1951), II, 491–93.

118. The general congregation of theologians at Trent in June 1546 numbered thirty-eight, and of these all were regulars but eight: Walz, *ibid.*, p. 495; CT, V, 262. Of the five theologians in the commission on justification four were Dominicans. For the role of the regulars generally, see P. Cherubelli, *Il Contribuo degli ordini religiosi al Concilio di Trento* (Florence, 1946).

119. CT, I, 105. Pighius' treatise *De libero hominis arbitrio et divina gratia libri X* (Cologne, 1542), an attack on Calvin's doctrine of grace, was dedicated to Sadoleto. For its content, see the close analysis in the *Dictionnaire de théologie catholique*, XII, 2098–2100.

120. See Dupront in his review of Cherubelli, BHR, XI (1949), 287.

Chapter VI: Curial Reformer and Cardinal

1. Report of A. Soriano, November 15, 1535, in *Relazioni degli ambasciatori veneti al Senato. Relazione di Roma*, Ser. II, Vol. III, 313–14.

2. CT, IV, 2; Raynaldus, *Annales*, XXXII, 411; Jedin, *Geschichte*, I, 252.

3. There are some interesting contrasts between the congratulatory letters sent to Paul III at the time of his election. Sadoleto's, deferential and cautious, ends with a request for the confirmation of his episcopal rights and privileges including that of remaining in his diocese; *Epistolae*, I, 262–66. Erasmus' letter, on the other hand, is a vigorous plea for Christian unity, curial neutrality, peace, the Council, and moderation in dealing with doctrinal differences; Allen, XI, No. 2988, pp. 61–63. And while Sadoleto shared these hopes and expectations, Erasmus had nothing to ask of the Pope for himself.

4. *Epistolae*, II, 326.

5. *Ibid.*, p. 304.

6. *Ibid.*, p. 323.

7. Grassi to Sadoleto, Rome, December 12, 1535, *ibid.*, pp. 356–57. Sadoleto's answer was evasive, January 20, 1536, *ibid.*, pp. 359–60. Evidently he had already been approached as a possible tutor to the young Cardinal when Grassi's inquiry arrived, although I cannot find the invitation to which Grassi seems to allude. Alessandro Farnese (1520–89), a son of Pierluigi, was made Vice-Chancellor in August 1535 following the death of Cardinal Ippoliti de' Medici; later he became Archbishop of Avignon and Legate in 1541. Relations between him and the Sadoletti were to be necessarily constant, if not always congenial. See Dorez, *La Cour du Paul III*, II, 275 ff.

8. RB, *inedita*, No. 10, p. 262.

9. Sadoleto to Contarini, March 13, 1536, *Epistolae*, II, 394–97.

10. *Ibid.*, p. 396.

11. *Epistolae*, II, 388.

12. RB, p. 264.

13. Paul III to Sadoleto, May 8, 1536, Avignon, Musée Calvet, MS. 5512, fol. 15.

14. The earliest summons in the name of the second reform Commission was sent to Caraffa on June 23, 1536 (Raynaldus, *Annales*, XXXII, 428–29). The others were written in mid-July.

15. Sadoleto to Fregoso, May 27 [1536], *Epistolae*, II, 294. (Costanzi erroneously dates this letter 1535, which from its content is impossible; in *Opera*, I, 66A, it is dated 1536.) Writing from S. Felice to Bembo on the same day, Sadoleto also mentioned his decision to attend the Council at Mantua, "Maximo omnino meo cum incommodo." Bib. Vat., Barb. lat. 2157, fol. cxx.

16. Sadoleto to Contarini, March 13, 1536, *Epistolae*, II, 396; see also his letters to Fregoso of May 27, *ibid.*, p. 294, and to Negri on June 2, *ibid.*, p. 408.

17. Arch. Vat., Acta Vicecancellaria 6 (Farnese), fol. 37ᵛ.

18. *Ibid.*, fol. 39; *Epistolarum Reginaldi Poli*, I, 463.

19. Such at least is the view which Friedensburg defends very emphatically, ARG, XXXIII, 2 Heft, 8, against those who claim that Contarini was "the soul of the whole movement" (Pastor, *History*, XI, 155). Capasso supports Pastor and quotes the Mantuan orator's view that the Commission materialized "per opera et instigazione del card. Contarino," *Paolo III* (Messina, 1924), I, 654, n. 4.

20. RB, No. 292, p. 89; and *Epistolarum Reginaldi Poli*, I, 461.

21. The letters to Caraffa and Pole are in Raynaldus, *Annales*, XXXII, 428–29 (1536); the others may be found in CT, IV, No. 11, pp. 26 ff.

22. *History*, XI, 155.

23. Contarini's references to "various learned men, Italian, Spanish and French," suggests that the original group may have been changed; see his letter to Pole of July 12, *Epistolarum Reginaldi Poli*, I, 463. For the so-called "Italianization" of the Curia and College, see Hofmann, *Forschungen*, XII, 238–42.

24. Back in Rome, Giberti squarely refused the Pope's invitation to the Dataria, whereupon it was offered to that formidable enemy of reform, Bartolomeo Guidiccioni. Pastor, *History*, XI, 173–74; Ehses, RQ, XV (1901), 166, and CT, IV, 156.

25. *Epistolae*, II, 430.

26. Bib. Vat., Barb. lat. 2517, fol. 95ᵛ.

27. *Epistolae*, II, 420–21.

28. *Ibid.*, Nos. CCLII, CCLV, CCLXXXVIII; K. Schätti, *Erasmus von Rotterdam und die Römische Kurie* (Basel, 1954), p. 150.

29. Friedensburg, "Zwei Aktenstücke zur Geschichte der kirchlichen Reformbestrebungen an der Römischen Kurie 1536–1538," QF, VII (1904), 254; S. Ehses, "Kirchliche Reformarbeiten unter Paul III. vor dem Trienter Konzil," RQ, XV (1901), 153 ff., 397 ff.; Pastor, *History*, XI, 165, n. 1; and Cristiani, 35 f. Cf. Schweitzer, "Beiträge zur Geschichte Pauls III," RQ, XXII (1908), 133 ff., and Rodocanachi, *Réforme en Italie*, II, 27.

30. *Jacobi Sadoleti Card. de Romanae curiae et cleri moribus reformandis oratio* (Cracoviae, 1561). I have consulted this version in the British Museum as well as a sixteenth-century MS. copy in the Vatican Library, Cod. Ottob. 489, fols. 50–54. Citations below follow the text in CT, IV, No. 15, pp. 108–19, which is based on the Vatican MS.

31. CT, IV, 109–10.

32. *Ibid.*, pp. 110–11.

33. *Ibid.*, pp. 113–14. Like other sixteenth-century reformers, Sadoleto followed the aphorism of Ecclesiastes 10:2: "Qualis sacerdos, talis populus," to account for the fallen morality of his generation. Cf. his observations in the Commentary on Ps. 93, *Opera*, III, 296A, and Contarini in his *De officio episcopi*, *Opera*, pp. 403, 410–11, as well as Nausea in CT, XII, 389–413.

34. CT, IV, 114–15.

35. It also carries an implied justification of his decision to quit the Curia in 1527. Nevertheless, Sadoleto retained a personal affection for Clement VII and would not tolerate Sturm's criticism of the Pope, as though Sadoleto in his own mind distinguished between the man and his failures in office.

36. It is noteworthy, however, that Maffei expected his friend merely to be amused by the argument from astrological signs, Bib. Vat., Barb. lat. 2517, fol. 98.

37. Bib. Vat., Barb. lat. 2799, fol. 439.

38. Bataillon, *Erasme en Espagne*, p. 534, citing the statement of S. Hosius to Pole that this promotion would have included Erasmus "if a cruel death had not begrudged them [i.e., Pole, Contarini, Sadoleto] this honor." Cracow, April 7, 1537, RB, No. 322, pp. 96–97.

39. The ceremony of ordination, held in the Sistine Chapel on the 23rd, is described at some length by Blasius, "Diarium," fols. 440–42. Later in the day a dispute over protocol developed when certain of the "novi creati" decided to forego the traditional rite of thanksgiving in order to return to their quarters in the city, while Sadoleto, Pole, and Jaccobazzi repaired to the *Sala Regia* as prescribed. The new Cardinals received their titular churches on January 15, 1537, Sadoleto's first being S. Calisto; he later exchanged it in turn for S. Balbina and S. Pietro in Vincoli.

40. *Epistolarum Reginaldi Poli*, II, 14–16. It is also said that Paul III at one time accepted Pole's request that the nomination be deferred but "suddenly changed

his mind" just before the nomination of December 22, Schenk, *Reginald Pole*, pp. 74–75.

41. Bib. Vat., Barb. lat. 2517, fol. 105. His answers to letters of congratulation are in *Epistolae*, II, Nos. CCLXII–CCLXXXV.

42. Sadoleto to Ercole II, Rome, December 23, 1536, *ibid.*, pp. 434–35.

43. *Cronaca*, V, 222; the celebration is described on pp. 222 ff. Lancellotti later noted that the excitement attending it seemed to have aggravated the illness of Sadoleto's mother, who died on March 6, 1537, *ibid.*, p. 263.

44. *Ibid.*, p. 227.

45. Fiordibello, *Vita*, in *Opera*, I, 13.

46. *Epistolae*, II, 468, 481.

47. RB, No. 309, p. 94. He protested to the Pope, however, against his failure to bring Aleander into the College, being himself aware perhaps of Aleander's resentment at the reservation *in petto*: Sadoleto to Paul III [s.d.], *ibid.*, pp. 459–60.

48. *Ibid.*, p. 471; Dittrich, *Contarini*, p. 376. Sadoleto apparently had to ask for lodging *in palazzo* after reaching Rome; he explained that the request sent to Cardinal Farnese was a financial necessity, having previously discussed his need with Contarini, Arch. Vat., Lett. di Prin. 13, fol. 217. Although this letter is undated, we know from Negri that Sadoleto had "rooms in the palace" while on the Reform Commission: January 28, 1537, LPR, III, 51.

49. February 23, 1537, *Epistolae*, II, 488–89.

50. In any case, as he saw it in February, he would leave Rome in March; cf. his letter to Maffei, November 2, 1536, *ibid.*, p. 420.

51. Letter to Nausea, *ibid.*, p. 489.

52. Friedensburg, QF, VII (1904), 254 ff., and "Das Consilium de emendanda ecclesia, Kardinal Sadolet und Johannes Sturm von Strassburg," ARG, XXXIII (1936), 2 Heft, 9 ff.; Dittrich, *Contarini*, pp. 345–48.

53. Aleander's manifest desire to play up his own importance in the consistory necessarily damages the value of this record. We may question both the completeness of the account and his willingness to dismiss Sadoleto's memorial so categorically. Cf. Friedensburg, QF, VII, 255.

54. *Ibid.*, p. 261.

55. Although he identified himself with the majority of the deputies, Aleander was himself dissatisfied with their views. It was finally decided that the twelve Cardinals present were to draw up separate opinions from which a final draft would be written, with the understanding that this final version be published before the opening of the Council in May. Friedensburg, ARG, XXXIII, 9–10. However, by distributing copies of the memorial, the secrecy on which the Pope had insisted was jeopardized and soon lost: Rodocanachi, *Réforme en Italie*, II, 31–33, esp. 31, n. 1. For Aleander's own recommendations, see his *De convocando concilio sententia*, CT, XII, No. 16, 119–27, which emphasizes the urgency of reforming the clergy and of convening the Council. This treatise tends to spare the Holy See and attributes the loss of its authority to wicked and godless priests.

56. Friedensburg, QF, VII, 262–63.

57. *Ibid.*, pp. 254–55; cf. ARG, XXXIII, 9.

58. L. Celier, "Alexandre VI et la réforme de l'église," p. 92; Hofmann, *Forschungen*, XII, 307 ff.

59. "Consilium delectorum cardinalium et aliorum praelatorum de emendanda ecclesia, S. D. N. Paulo III jubente conscriptum & exhibitum anno MDXXXVIII," in Le Plat, *Monumentorum ad historiam Concilii Tridentini* (Louvain, 1781–87), II, 596–605. Summaries and extracts may be found in Pastor, *History*, XI, 165–69; Friedensburg, ARG, XXXIII (1936), 2 Heft, 11–13; Rodocanachi, *Réforme en Italie*, II, 28–31; Dittrich, *Contarini*, pp. 364 ff.; Jedin, *Geschichte*, I, 339–41.

60. At this point in his German translation of the *Consilium*, Luther wrote in the margin: "Ja der mus gethan haben. Wolt Gott, er solt leben und euch schendliche Buben bezahlen und anzeigen, wie Gottselig ihr mit worten und wercken jung und alt gebessert haben." WA, Vol. L., 304. Melanchthon marvelled that such "heroes" as Sadoleto and Aleander supported the prohibition, *Epistolarum D. Erasmi libri XXXI et P. Melanchthonis libri IV* (London, 1642), p. 735ᵛ.

61. Le Plat, *Monumentorum*, II, 596.

62. *Ibid.*, p. 597. This was the basic prescription of the deputies, which assumes the sufficiency of existing law for the governance of the Church.

63. As a Cardinal, Bembo reminded Contarini, then under attack from Roman colleagues for his negotiations with the Lutherans at Regensburg, how difficult it is to find agreement in the College: "You are well familiar with the character of the College, or rather with human nature. There are as many opinions as there are men." RB, No. 731, p. 188.

64. Sarpi, *Istoria del Concilio Tridentino*, ed. Giovanni Gambarin (Bari, 1935), I, 134–35.

65. R. Christoffel, "Des Cardinals Gasparo Contarini Leben und Schriften," *Zeitschrift für die historische Theologie*, V (1875), 2 Heft, 222. But after Caraffa became Pope, the *Consilium* was placed on the Index of 1559.

66. Schönberg evidently sent a copy of the *Consilium* to a friend in Germany, possibly Cochlaeus, for reasons which remain obscure and controversial. Sleidanus cites the argument that Schönberg thereby hoped to obstruct the progress of reform (*Commentary*, Bk. XII), but this is still a moot question. For discussion of it see Ehses, HJG, XXXIX, 600 ff.; Friedensburg, ARG, XXXIII (1936), 2 Heft, 13; Pastor, *History*, XI, 171, n. 3; and Dittrich, *Contarini*, p. 369.

67. "S. D. N. P. Paulo III Bartholomaus Guidiccioni de ecclesia et emendatione ministrorum eorumque abusum per generale concilium facienda," CT, XII, No. 27, 227–56; see also Jedin, *Geschichte*, I, 342, and Tacchi-Venturi, *La Vita religiosa durante la prima età della Compagnia di Gesù* (Rome, 1910), p. 24.

68. CT., XII, 229. For later Catholic objections to the *Consilium*, see Le Plat's "Monitum ad lectorem," *Monumentorum*, II, 594–95.

69. *De potestate pontificis in usu clavium epistolae*, and *De potestate pontificis in compositionibus epistolae*, *ibid.*, pp. 605–15.

70. *Ad principes populosque Germaniae exhortatio* (1538), in *Opera*, II, 331–68; the quotation, p. 362A.

71. Contarini reiterated the argument in his *Consilium quatuor delectorum*. CT, XII, 208–15; see also Jedin, *Geschichte*, I, 344–45, and Dittrich, *Contarini*, pp. 370, 402.

72. The problem of terminology is perplexing. I am uneasy about using such a term as the "center" and readily agree that even among its constituents there was by no means an authentic homogeneity. Dittrich refers to Contarini's position as the "Midpoint" of the Italian reformers, RB, p. iii, and Pastor to the Catholic moderates in Germany as the "Partei der Mitte," *Die kirchlichen Reunionsbestrebungen während der Regierung Karls V* (Freiburg, 1879), pp. 126 ff. For Bataillon they were "les héritiers de l'idéal irénique d'Erasme" and may be collectively known as the "Erasmians" (*Erasme en Espagne*, pp. 534–36), a group which is meant also to include Isidoro Chiari, Marguerite de Navarre, Gropper, Pighius, Valdés, and Vives. Renaudet calls Sadoleto an "Italian Erasmian" (*Etudes érasmiennes*, p. 99. Cf. his *Erasme et l'Italie*, p. 217) and Ritter identified him "sopratutto con Erasmo," *Un Umanista*, p. 5. Jedin, however, distinguishes the terms "Erasmian" from "irenic," qualifying Sadoleto by the latter, *Geschichte*, I, 294, 321. For G. K. Brown, Contarini and his associates in the Commission were the Catholic "mediatizers," *Italy and the Reformation to 1550* (Oxford, 1933), *passim*; and more recently they have been related to a movement of Catholic "Evangelism" which flourished between 1532–42, Eva Maria Jung, "On the Nature of Evangelism in Sixteenth-century Italy," JHI, XIV (1953), 511–27. In view of their misplaced confidence in reconciliation with the Lutherans, Joachimsen refers to at least part of the group as the "Illusionists," *Die Reformation als Epoche der Deutschen Geschichte* (Munich, 1951), p. 232. The risk in every case, however, is that of imparting to the reformers a unanimity which at best was tenuous and occasional; they formed a transient faction in the College, which broke down under later and different pressures. Professor Schätti reminds us of the fact that "Pure Erasmians are rarely found." *Erasmus von Rotterdam und die Römische Kurie*, p. 164.

73. The Duke's letter, dated March 24, was read on April 9, 1537; his purpose was to make the offer of hospitality contingent on a security force in the Pope's pay, Arch. Vat., Arch. consist., Acta vicecan. 5, fols. 51–52.

74. *Ibid.*, fol. 56; the bull announcing and explaining the delay was published on May 15, Raynaldus, *Annales*, XXXII, 447. See also Ehses, RQ, XV (1901), 164.

75. *Epistolae*, II, 494 f.

76. Sadoleto suggested Piacenza because of its proximity to the Emperor and his troops; Schönberg argued for Bologna, *ibid.*, p. 495.

77. *Ibid.*, p. 496. Contarini showed similar fears in a letter to Pole, May 12, 1537, *Epistolarum Reginaldi Poli*, I, 32.

78. Upon presenting Caraffa and Sadoleto with additional revenue from the funds of the Dataria, the Datary had this to say to them: "Signori, see what you are doing. You have 700 scudi a month from this source and you want to ruin it. Such destruction will be your responsibility." Quoted in Jedin, *Geschichte*, I, 345, n. 66. Moreover, if the recommendations in the *Consilium* had been applied to

Sadoleto, he would have been deprived of his see (Le Plat, II, 600), certain of his benefices and dispensations (*ibid.*, p. 599), papal recognition of Paolo as coadjutor *cum successione* (*ibid.*), and permission to resume residence as a Cardinal in the Comtat (*ibid.*, p. 601), even if he retained title to the diocese.

79. Cf. L. Cardauns, *Zur Geschichte der kirchlichen Unions- und Reformbestrebungen 1538 bis 1542* (Rome, 1910), p. 58.

80. Conclusio LXXXIX, "Resolutiones," WA, Vol. I, 627.

Chapter VII: Conciliator

1. Erasmus to Sadoleto, Freiburg, 1530, Allen, VIII, No. 2315, p. 434; and 1531, *ibid.*, IX, No. 2443, pp. 164–67.

2. *Epistolae Leonis X*, pp. 95–96; see also Nos. LXXXII–LXXXIII.

3. Allen, V, No. 1313, p. 127.

4. *Epistolae*, II, 501–2.

5. Sadoleto to Farnese, 1543, *Lettere*, pp. 78–79, in which Jacopo boasts that he is "feared by the Lutherans as scarcely anyone else. . . ."

6. *Epistolae*, III, 34; see also his *Ad principes populosque Germaniae exhortatio* in *Opera*, II, 342B and *passim*; and Gothein, *Loyola*, p. 126.

7. *Epistolae*, II, 84.

8. I cannot share the contrary view of O. Lehmann, *Herzog Georg von Sachsen im Briefwechsel mit Erasmus von Rotterdam und dem Erzbischofe Sadolet* (Neustadt im Saxony, 1889), p. 58.

9. *Epistolae*, II, 504–5; Lehmann, pp. 61–62.

10. *Epistolae*, II, 513.

11. The text of the original letter is in G. Kawerau, *Die Versuche, Melanchthon zur katholischen Kirche zurückzuführen* (Halle, 1902), 174–77. See also W. Friedensburg, "Giovanni Morone und der Brief Sadolets an Melanchthon vom 17. Juni 1537," ARG, I (1904), 4 Heft, 372–80. Costanzi deleted the addressee's name and removed all references to Melanchthon from the version which appears in *Epistolae*, II, 477–99; the letter is also in CR, III, No. 158, pp. 379 ff. Citations below are from Kawerau, who first brought the letter to light. For Erasmus' letters to Melanchthon, see Renaudet, *Etudes*, p. 325 and Allen, V, Nos. 1452, 1466, 1496.

12. The phrase is Friedensburg's, ARG, XXXIII (1936), 20.

13. WA, *Tischreden*, Vol. IV, No. 4341, 235.

14. Kawerau, *Die Versuche*, pp. 175–76.

15. CR, III, No. 1595, p. 393; and to Veit Dietrich, *ibid.*, No. 1599, p. 399.

16. October 11, 1537, *ibid.*, No. 1615, p. 421.

17. ZGK, V (1881), 162–63.

18. CR, III, No. 1651, pp. 488–89; and No. 1663, p. 506.

19. *Ibid.*, p. 507. See also Kawerau, *Die Versuche*, p. 38, and G. Ellinger, *P. Melanchthon* (Berlin, 1902), p. 363.

20. Braccetto was a Catholic friend of Melanchthon who forged a reply to

Sadoleto, having previously revealed his intentions to the Nuncio Girolamo Rorario, Kawerau, *Die Versuche*, pp. 39, 58. See also Aleander to Paul III, in NB, III, *Legation Aleanders 1538–1539* (Gotha, 1893), No. 16, pp. 127–29.

21. *Epistolae Leonis X*, p. 105.

22. See J. Lortz, *Die Reformation in Deutschland* (3rd ed.; Freiburg im Breisgau, 1948), II, 155–59; P. Polman, *L'Elément historique*, pp. 362–65; Jedin, *Geschichte*, I, 318 ff.

23. In Friedensburg, "Beiträge zum Briefwechsel der katholischen Gelehrten Deutschlands im Reformationszeitalter," ZKG, XVIII (1898), 275 f.

24. ZKG, XX (1900), 244–47; German translation in ZKG, XIX (1899), 42–44.

25. ZKG, XVIII (1898), 288. See also M. Spahn, *Johann Cochläus* (Berlin, 1898), p. 263.

26. *Epistolae*, II, 510. The reference here is unquestionably to Melanchthon (as Kawerau suggests, *Die Versuche*, p. 81), and not to Sturm (as in Gothein, *Loyola*, p. 127).

27. ZKG, XX (1900), 247–49.

28. *Epistolae*, III, 7.

29. Sadoleto referred gratefully to Morone's letter of October 19, 1537, when he wrote to the Nuncio from Rome on November 22, in ARG, I (1904), 4 Heft, 375–76. Soon to be the "ablest Italian expert on German affairs" (Jedin, *Geschichte*, I, 270), Morone from the start identified his views with those of Contarini, for whom he had great respect; cf. Morone's letters to Cardinal Farnese in F. Dittrich, *Nuntiatur G. Morones vom deutschen Königshofe. 1539. 1540.* (Paderborn, 1892), pp. 142, 166.

30. Morone's letter of October 19 has disappeared, but we can deduce its contents from Sadoleto's of November 22; the Nuncio's reply to the latter was lost in transit. Sadoleto sent a duplicate on February 22, 1538, with a covering note from Paolo. These are in ARG, I (1904), 4 Heft, 375–77.

31. *Ibid.*, p. 379. Morone later suggested that since Aleander was again in Germany as Nuncio, it would be well to offset the hatred which he inspired among the Lutherans by sending another Italian in whom they had some confidence, and suggested either Sadoleto or Contarini. NB, II, No. 105, p. 320.

32. NB, II, pp. 230–31; see also Friedensburg, ARG, I (1904), 4 Heft, 377, n. 2.

33. NB, II, No. 66, pp. 229–30.

34. This letter, like the one to Morone, was lost and a duplicate sent from Rome on February 22, 1538, ARG, I (1904), 4 Heft, 377. Morone replied from Prague on March 25 to say that he had forwarded the letter to Mosheim, *ibid.*, p. 380.

35. NB, IV, 588–89. In September 1539 Mosheim was stripped of his benefices by the Bishop of Passau and subsequently fled to Mainz and Cologne. See M. Heuwieser, *Rupert von Mosham* (Gotha, 1913), pp. 115–92 (cited by Jedin, *Geschichte*, I, 566).

36. Allen, VIII, No. 2315, pp. 433–34; and 1531, *ibid.*, IX, No. 2443,

pp. 161–62, in which Erasmus defended himself against the implication that he had been too lenient with the Protestants.

37. *In magnum illum . . . Erasmum Rotterodamum . . . Monodia* (Cologne, 1536); see also Andreas Flitner, *Erasmus im Urteil seiner Nachwelt* (Tübingen, 1952), pp. 22 ff.

38. Allen, XI, No. 3076, p. 208.

39. R. G. Villoslada, "La Muerte de Erasmo," *Miscellanea Giovanni Mercati*, IV (1946), 406.

40. Dolet's *Cato christianus* (1538), the first book to be published at his press in Lyons; see O. Douen, "Etienne Dolet. Ses opinions religieuses," SHPF, XXX (1881), 341–42.

41. Bib. Vat., Cod. lat. 5695, fol. 100.

42. Arch. Vat., Arch. consist., Acta Vicecancellarii 5, fol. 75^v; CT, IV, No. 98, p. 142.

43. *J. Sadoleti Epistolarum Appendix*, pp. 231–32.

44. *Ibid.*, pp. 25 ff.; Raynaldus, *Annales*, XXXII, 475.

45. P. Jourda, *Marguerite d'Angoulême* (Paris, 1930), I, 231 f.; Dorez, *La Cour du Paul III*, I, 299.

46. *Epistolae*, III, 33.

47. *Ibid.*, Nos. CCCV and CCCXII.

48. Bib. Vat., Barb. lat. 2157, fol. cxxiii.

49. Dittrich, *Contarini*, pp. 417–18; Pastor, *History*, XI, 508. Contarini chose Negri as his vicar and left to him the work of completing various projects of diocesan reform at Belluno. Negri had resigned from the service of Cardinal Francesco Cornaro in 1533 to remain at Venice: LPR, III, 21. He remained Contarini's vicar at Belluno from 1538 to 1541; see Costanzi, *De vita H. Negri*, in *J. Sadoleti Epistolarum Appendix*, pp. lxxxix ff.

50. Bib. Vat., Barb. lat. 5695, fol. 96.

51. Arch. Vat., Arm. XLV, Vol. 42, fol. 62^v; and *Epistolae*, III, Nos. CCCIII. CCCVII, CCCVIII.

52. *Epistolae*, III, 42.

53. E.g., his letters to Cajetan, 1530, *Epistolae*, I, 320; to Paolo, 1535, *ibid.*, II, 337; to Catarino (Polito), 1538, *ibid.*, III, 57; to Bembo, 1539, *ibid.*, p. 128; to Farnese, 1544, *ibid.*, p. 378; and to Paolo, 1545, Bib. Vat., Barb. lat. 5695, fols. 100 ff.

54. E.g., *Epistolae*, II, 451.

55. E.g., a letter to Gualteruzzi requesting that his monthly stipend of 210 ducats be paid to one Bastiano Montaguti in order to discharge part of a debt which Sadoleto owed to Ramondo Vidal of Avignon, Carpentras, July 16, 1538, Bib. Vat., Barb. lat. 5695, fol. 96. See also Ferrajoli, "Il Ruolo . . . Leone X," RSR, XXXVIII, 224–25.

56. Ferrajoli, *ibid.*, pp. 219, 221.

57. According to Ferrajoli the total revenue from all the benefices Sadoleto ever held is 2,688 ducats (*ibid.*, p. 222). Such computation fails to deduct the income he lost by assigning certain of these benefices to kinsmen, and fails to include

the special provision he received as Cardinal. In his letter to Gualteruzzi of July 16, 1538, he referred to 210 ducats "della paga di S. Giovanni," (Bib. Vat., Barb. lat. 5695, fol. 96) indicating that he like Contarini and others received a monthly stipend of this amount from the Camera. (See also Dittrich, *Contarini*, p. 324; and Pastor, *History*, VII, 20.) He later referred to a monthly *subsidio* of 200 scudi, which was nevertheless "piccolo a li mei bisogni," (1545), Bib. Vat., Barb. lat. 5695, fol. 100.

58. *Epistolae*, III, 42, 138.

59. P. Pecchiai, *Roma nel Cinquecento*, pp. 21 f.; L. von Matt and H. Rahner, *Ignatius of Loyola*, tr. John Murray (Chicago, 1956), p. 57. Complete maintenance for an "ordinary person" in Italy during the 1530's probably required between 25 to 30 ducats a year.

60. *Epistolae*, III, 183.

61. Arch. Vat., Arm. XLV, Vol. 42, fol. 64.

62. *Lettere*, No. XXVIII, p. 69.

63. Fiordibello, *Vita*, in *Opera*, I, 18.

64. He once stated that while his poverty was conspicuous and humiliating in Rome, it would be an asset in going to a Council "come Vescovo mediocre," arguing that what was embarrassing to him in the Curia would enhance his prestige among the conciliar deputies. *Epistolae*, III, 379, 385, 390.

65. Tacchi-Venturi, *La Vita religiosa durante la prima età della Compagnia di Gesù*, p. 162.

66. *Opera*, I, 278A.

67. *Epistolae*, III, 63.

68. Sadoleto described this commission in a long letter to Caraffa, Arch. Vat., Arm. XLV, Vol. 42, fols. 62–63.

69. The basic work is Sanjanello, *Historica monumenta ordinis S. Hieronymi congr. B. Petri di Pisa* (Venice, 1758–62); see also Fr. Hélyot, *Dictionnaire des ordres religieux* (Paris, 1848), II, 588–97, and M. Heimbucher, *Die Orden und Kongregationen der katholischen Kirche* (Paderborn, 1933), I, 592–96.

70. Sadoleto to Caraffa, Arch. Vat., Arm. XLV, Vol. 42, fol. 62; and again, *Epistolae*, III, 126.

71. Beccadelli, *Monumenti di varia letteratura*, ed. L. Morandi (Bologna, 1797–1804), Vol. I, part II, 64.

72. *Ibid.*, pp. 66–67. He wrote to Campeggio in August 1541, *J. Sadoleti Epistolarum Appendix*, No. 5, p. xxviii.

73. *Ibid.*, No. 6, p. xxx.

74. Pole to Campeggio, Viterbo, March 6, 1542, *ibid.*, No. 7, p. xxxi.

75. *Epistolae*, III, No. CCCVI.

76. The definitive monograph is by W. Friedensburg, "Das Consilium de emendanda ecclesia, Kardinal Sadolet und Johannes Sturm von Strasburg," ARG, No. 130, XXXIII (1936), 1–69, which also contains the Latin text of the three letters in question.

77. Luther's German translation and his glosses on it are in WA, Vol. L, 284–308. Melanchthon also saw the *Consilium* early in 1538.

78. "Johannes Sturmius cardinalibus ceterisque praelatis delectis s.p.d." Strasbourg, April 3, 1538, in Friedensburg, "Das Consilium," ARG, No. 130, XXXIII, 28–51.

79. *Ibid.*, pp. 44–45.

80. *Ibid.*, pp. 32, 34, 35. The "dialogues" to which Sturm refers are unquestionably Sadoleto's Commentaries on Romans even though Sadoleto spoke of having written "those commentaries" eleven years ago in a letter to Sturm of 1538, Friedensburg, p. 52.

81. RB, *inedita*, No. 30, p. 296; NB, IV, 576.

82. *Aequitatis discussio super consilio delectorum* (Leipzig, 1538). See Dittrich, *Contarini*, p. 372; and for Sadoleto's opinion of the work, see his letter to Cochlaeus, *Epistolae*, III, 53.

83. "Jacobus Sadoletus Joanni Sturmio s.d." in Friedensburg, "Das Consilium," ARG, No. 130, XXXIII, 51–53, and in *Epistolae*, III, 104–8.

84. Sturm vainly sought to find a copy of Sadoleto's letter from du Bellay and others in Paris but was unable to until the summer of 1539. Schmidt, *Sturm*, p. 45, and Friedensburg, "Das Consilium", ARG, No. 130, XXXIII, 22. For Sturm's account of his difficulties, see his reply to Sadoleto, Strasbourg, July 18, 1539, in Friedensburg, p. 54.

85. *Ibid.*, p. 52.

86. *Epistolae*, II, 510. He made the same concession to Morone, ARG, I (1904), 376.

87. WA, *Tischreden*, Vol. IV, No. 4463, pp. 324–25.

88. Early in 1539 it was rumored that a papal agent was in Germany to offer Melanchthon a yearly pension of 500 or even 1,000 ducats if he went to Italy, Dittrich, *Contarini*, p. 512. Cochlaeus sent Contarini a copy of Sadoleto's letter to Sturm which the Bishop had forwarded to Germany for Cochlaeus' approval. Cochlaeus to Contarini, February 20, 1539, RB, *inedita*, No. 5, pp. 374–75. NB, IV, 589; ZKG, XIX (1898), 243.

89. F. H. Reusch, *Der Index der verbotenen Bücher* (Bonn, 1883–85), I, 399, n. 1; so, too, ironically, was Cochlaeus' *Aequitatis discussio super consilio delectorum Card.* (1538) because of its concessions to Sturm of a free council in Germany, *ibid.*, p. 398.

90. It was completed in rough draft before Sadoleto left Rome in April 1538, and later revised at Carpentras, *Epistolae*, III, 29. Citations here are to the version in *Opera*, II, 331B–367B. See Ritter, *Un Umanista*, pp. 75–76.

91. *Opera*, II, 342A.

92. *Ibid.*, pp. 343B–344A.

93. *Ibid.*, pp. 345, 362B; Sadoleto had in mind the forthcoming Council at Vicenza, decreed originally for May 1538 and then prorogued for April 1539.

94. "Sacrosanctis Salvationis et Redemptoris nostri," Hergenroether, *Leonis X . . . regesta*, Fasc. VII, No. 14,825, p. 62; J. Fornery, *Histoire ecclésiastique*, III, 222, for the indulgence on St. Siffrein.

95. *Opera*, II, 350.

96. *Ibid.*, pp. 343B–354A; 362A–65A.

97. *Ibid.*, pp. 354B–55A.
98. *Ibid.*, pp. 256B–61A.
99. *Ibid.*, p. 358B: Rom. 3:28; Eph. 2:8–9; Rom. 3:23–24.
100. John 15:14; Rom. 2:6; Rev. 22:12; Rom. 2:10; Gal. 5:5.
101. *Ibid.*, p. 360B.
102. *Ibid.*
103. *Epistolae*, III, 29–30.
104. *Ibid.*, pp. 33–34; 53.

Chapter VIII: Controversialist

1. *Epistolae*, III, 285.
2. Santoro, *Pietro Bembo*, pp. 55–59. Sadoleto was among those who recommended his nomination to the Pope, *Epistolae*, III, 58–60; but it was Alessandro Farnese who was most effectual in securing it. See Ferrajoli, "Il Ruolo . . . Leone X," RSR, XXXVII, 456–58.
3. In RB, No. 400, p. 113.
4. Letters to Contarini, *Epistolarum Reginaldi Poli*, II, Nos. LXV, LXXII.
5. *Ibid.*, No. LXXX.
6. Beccadelli completed his *Vita del Petrarca* in 1540; for his remarks on the sojourn at Carpentras and his visits to Vaucluse, see *Le Rime di M. Francesco Petrarca* (Padua, 1732), pp. xix–xx. Cf. the interesting account of F. Benoit, "Lodovico Beccadelli à Carpentras et ses amours avec Elisa Gallas," *Mémoires de l'Institute historique de Provence*, I (1924), 7–11.
7. *Epistolarum Reginaldi Poli*, II, 193 ff.
8. *Epistolae*, III, 70; Arch. Vat., Arm. XLV, Vol. 42, fol 62ᵛ.
9. *Epistolae*, III, 73, 128, 148.
10. *Ibid.*, pp. 177–79.
11. *Ibid.*, pp. 114–19.
12. (1) 1523–24: completion of the *Phaedrus* and the Commentary on Psalm 51. (2) 1527–36: Commentary on Psalm 93; "Oratio in Judeos" (1531); *De liberis recte instituendis* (1532); *In duo Johannis loca de Nicodemo et de Magdalena* (1533); *De duobus gladiis interpretatio* (1533–34); *In Pauli Epistolam ad Romanos Commentariorum libri tres* (1535); *De laudibus philosophiae* (1535–36). (3) 1538–42: completion and revision of *Ad principes populosque Germaniae exhortatio* (1538); *Ad senatum populemque Genevensem* (1539); *De christiana ecclesia* (1538 ff.); *De obitu optimi ac praestantissimi cardinalis Federici Fregoso Homilia* (1541); *De regno Ungariae ab hostibus Turcis oppresso et capto Homilia* (1541); resumption of work on the "De gloria" (c. 1539). (4) 1543–45: *De peccato originis* (1543); *De purgatorio* (1544); *De pace, ad Imperatorem Carolum Caesarem Augustum oratio* (1545). (It is possible that the fragment *De republica christiana* was written in Rome during the last three years of his life, but the history of this treatise cannot be satisfactorily established. For the complete list of Sadoleto's works, see Lauchert, pp. 387–89, and Ritter, *Un Umanista*, pp. 85–87.)

11+

13. Citations below are to the text in *Opera*, II, 171–86; it may also be found in *Calvini opera*, V, 385–416, and in *Epistolae*, III, 74–98. The original MS. is in the Geneva Archives, Portefeuilles historiques, No. 1208. The edition published by Michel du Bois (Geneva, 1540), is said to be closer to the original than that of Gryphius (Lyons, 1539), which Sadoleto revised for publication.

14. RB, No. 506, p. 133.

15. *Calvini opera*, X, No. 165, p. 332.

16. Cf. P. Charpenne, *Histoire de la Réforme et des réformateurs de Genève* (Paris, 1861), p. 333; F. W. Kampschulte, *Johann Calvin* (Leipzig, 1869), I, 352; C. Cantù, *Italiani illustrati* (3rd ed.; Milan, 1875), III, 158; E. Moutarde, *Etude historique sur la réforme à Lyon* (Genève, 1881), p. 46; M. François, *Tournon*, p. 460. The assumption that Sadoleto attended the conference has been rejected by C. V. Cornelius, *Historische Arbeiten vornehmlich zur Reformationszeit* (Leipzig, 1899), p. 248, and by E. Doumergue, *Jean Calvin* (Paris, 1899–1927), II, 678, as well as by Herminjard, *Correspondance*, V, 261.

17. Sadoleto's letter of transmittal is in Herminjard, V, 261–62. On March 27 the Small Council agreed that a "response aymable" be written to the "Cardinal of Carpentras," Cornelius, p. 248.

18. *Opera*, II, 172B, 180B, 182B–83A.

19. *Ibid.*, pp. 176 ff.

20. See Dittrich, *Contarini*, pp. 489–92.

21. *Epistolae*, III, 101–2.

22. RB, *inedita*, No. 39, p. 303.

23. *Epistolae*, III, 68–69.

24. Sadoleto to Farnese, July 29, 1530, *ibid.*, 115–19.

25. In ARG, XXXIII (1936), 2 Heft, 54–68.

26. Herminjard, *Correspondance*, V, p. 322, n. 3; see also *Calvini opera*, X, No. 174, for previous discussion of the reply.

27. *Calvini opera*, X, No. 178, p. 361. The reply was dated September 1. Calvin's own French translation was ready by the end of October: Calvin to Farel, October 27, 1539, *ibid.*, No. 194, p. 426.

28. *Calvini opera*, V, 385–416. The *Responsio* contains some arresting passages on Calvin's conversion, especially pp. 411–12; see also John T. McNeill, *History and Character of Calvinism* (Oxford, 1954), pp. 116–18.

29. *Calvini opera*, V, 385–87. It is interesting to notice how careful Sadoleto, Sturm, and Calvin all were to vaunt themselves on their restraint and moderation in dealing with the issues in controversy: e.g. Sadoleto to Sturm, ARG, XXXIII (1936), 2 Heft, 53; and Calvin to Sadoleto, *Calvini opera*, V, 387.

30. *Ibid.*, pp. 396–99.

31. *Ibid.*, p. 399.

32. *Ibid.*, p. 407, referring to the passage in Sadoleto, *Opera*, II, 571–72.

33. WA, *Briefwechsel*, Vol. VIII, No. 3394.

34. E.g., Eck to Contarini, ZKG, XIX (1898), 243.

35. RB, *inedita*, No. 30, p. 297.

36. E.g., letters to Clement VII, September 1527, Arch. Vat., Arm. XLV,

Vol. 42, fols. 41–42; to Contarini, *Epistolae*, II, 390 ff.; to Duke George of Saxony, *ibid.*, III, 1–8.

37. Its published title in the edition of Cardinal Mai, in *Spicilegium Romanum* (Rome, 1839), II, 101–78. Cardinal Mai published only the first part of the treatise and took the liberty of deleting certain passages "so that nothing would be done against the author's intent," on the ground that Sadoleto was unable to complete his revision of the text.

38. Writing to Pighius in February 1539, Sadoleto said he had already finished "a good part" of his study (*Epistolae*, III, 71). See also Ritter (*Un Umanista*, pp. 76–80), who, like Mai (*Spicilegium Romanum*, II, xi), places the start of the work three years earlier; but Sadoleto himself clearly placed it after his return to Carpentras from Nice in 1538 (*Epistolae*, III, 255).

39. *Epistolae*, III, 292 ff.; he praised the *Enchiridion* extravagantly (e.g., pp. 293, 297), though he also protested against the omission of purgatory from its treatment of the sacraments, pp. 298–300.

40. *Ibid.*, No. CCCXIX, 70–71; see also Pighius to Farnese, in ZGK, I (1902), 1 Heft, 118.

41. Mai, *Spicilegium Romanum*, II, 158, 176–77.

42. *Ibid.*, pp. 119–20.

43. *Ibid.*, pp. 136, 139. Cf. *De Officio episcopi* (1516), in Contarini's *Opera*, fol. 403. See also Dittrich, *Contarini*, pp. 283–97.

44. Cf. Nausea's analysis of sacerdotal corruption and his belief that the crisis in the Church had come about as an uprising of the laity against the clergy, in J. J. Döllinger, *Beiträge zur politischen, kirchlichen und Kultur-Geschichte der sechs letzten Jahrhunderte* (Vienna, 1882), III, 152–66.

45. *Epistolarum Reginaldi Poli*, II, No. LXV, 148.

46. *Epistolae*, III, 252; Gothein, *Loyola*, p. 129; T. Phillips, *Life of Reginald Pole*, pp. 262–63.

47. Schultess-Rechberg, *Der Kardinal Jacopo Sadoleto*, p. 69.

48. *Epistolae*, III, 295. He had once proposed a general plan for reform to Clement VII through a special body of pious and erudite prelates, Arch. Vat., Lett. di Prin. 5, fol. 169.

49. *Opera*, III, 1–14.

50. *Epistolae*, I, 275.

51. *Ibid.*, III, 231.

52. Once again in poor health Sadoleto continued to rely on Pole to protect his residence at Carpentras and to see to it that "I may be permitted to live on here *in honesto otio*," Sadoleto to Pole, 1540, *Epistolae*, III, 183.

53. Arch. Vat., Acta Vicecan. 5, fol. 131^v-32; Ehses, RQ, VI (1901), 166 ff.

54. RB, No. 523, p. 138.

55. Sadoleto to Cervini, March 16, 1541, *Epistolae*, III, 260.

56. RB., No. 519, p. 137.

57. *Ibid.*, pp. 137–38.

58. *Epistolarum Reginaldi Poli*, III, cclxxxv ff.

59. *Ibid.*, p. cclxxix.

60. See G. de Leva, "La Concordia religiosa di Ratisbona," *Archivio Veneto*, IV (1872), part 1, 1–36; Jedin, *Geschichte*, I, 308 ff.; Dittrich, *Contarini*, pp. 550–651; Pastor, *History*, XI, chap. X.

61. The text is in Dittrich, *Contarini*, pp. 651–63.

62. 1541, RB, No. 701, p. 177. Dittrich, *Contarini*, pp. 619–20. The correspondence from his Legation is in RB, Nos. 528–860.

63. The text is in Beccadelli, *Monumenti*, I, part II, 149 ff.; see also Jedin, *Geschichte*, I, 309, and Dittrich, *Contarini*, pp. 669–70.

64. *Lettere*, p. xxi.

65. Cited in Dittrich, *Contarini*, p. 682.

66. *Epistolarum Reginaldi Poli*, III, xlvi–xlviii; and No. XI, p. 24.

67. RB, No. 733, p. 188. Dittrich, *Contarini*, p. 717.

68. *Epistolarum Reginaldi Poli*, III, xlv; RB, No. 731, pp. 187–88.

69. Pole to Contarini, July 16, 1541, *Epistolarum Reginaldi Poli*, III, No. XIII, 26–30.

70. *Lettere*, p. xxii; *J. Sadoleti Epistolarum Appendix*, No. 5, pp. xxvi–vii; RB, No. 777, 202–3.

71. Sadoleto referred to them as the "due cedule," "schedae," or "schedulae," the smaller ("minore") being Contarini's letter on justification from Regensburg on May 25. See his letter to Polito, *Epistolae*, III, 267, and Beccadelli, *Monumenti*, I, part II, 162.

72. *Epistolae*, III, 265–66.

73. *Ibid.*, pp. 267–68.

74. *Ibid.*, pp. 268–69. Catarino had become Sadoleto's principal adviser in matters of doctrine; for comment on Catarino as polemicist, see Lauchert, pp. 30–133.

75. "Sadoleti de Justificatione," Bib. Vat., Barb. lat. 834, fols. 53–56; Beccadelli, *Monumenti*, I, part II, pp. 162–67 (on which following citations are based); CT, XII, No. 40, 322–25; Dittrich, *Contarini*, pp. 692–97; Ritter, *Un Umanista*, pp. 108 ff.

76. Beccadelli, *Monumenti*, part II, I, 185.

77. Sadoleto to T. Campeggio, August 1, 1541, *J. Sadoleti Epistolarum Appendix*, No. 5, p. xxvii.

78. *Lettere*, p. xxii; also in RB, No. 852, p. 224.

79. Dittrich, *Contarini*, pp. 684–85. In the Diet, however, Contarini aroused neither respect nor affection in Protestant hearts. Calvin mocked his concern for creature comfort, marking him as one who took pleasure "seulement à cuysine, au buffet, à la gardrobe et à l'establ e des évesques. Voilà comme la court romaine se veult acquiter de la reformation des églises." *Calvini opera*, V, 659. The Legate was hardly flaunting his wealth, however, and had to ask for cameral advances soon after arriving at Regensburg. Melanchthon's observations were far more astute and divined the nature of the Legate's instructions: "Many here wonder why Contarini, for all his reputed command of Christian doctrine and his celebrated integrity, is so unwilling to say what he feels." *Epistolarum . . . Melanchthonis* (London, 1642), pp. 18c, 38e.

80. Cardauns, *Kirchlichen Unions- und Reformbestrebungen*, p. 207; Reusch, *Index*, I, 565–66.

81. J. *Sadoleti Epistolarum Appendix*, p. xciii, note (a).

82. *Epistolarum . . . Melanchthonis*, fol. 780d; cf. Luther, WA, Vol. I, 627.

83. *Geschichte*, I, 311.

84. Paolo Brezzi, *Le Riforme catholiche dei secolo XV e XVI* (Rome, 1945), pp. 62–63. Even more serious, however, was the rising emnity of Pole and Caraffa.

Chapter IX: Arbiter and Legate

1. Sadoleto to Farnese, January 3, 1543, *Lettere*, No. XIV, pp. 34–36. See also Sadoleto to G. Poyet, February 17, *ibid.*, p. 302, and CT, IV, No. 166, pp. 212–13.

2. Sadoleto to Campeggio, J. *Sadoleti Epistolarum Appendix*, No. 6, p. xxx.

3. Pastor, *History*, XII, 145, n. 1; the bull itself is in CT, IV, No. 184, pp. 226–31.

4. Brown, *Italy and the Reformation*, pp. 93 ff.; G. Cavazzuti, *Lodovico Castelvetro* (Modena, 1903), pp. 18 ff.; Dittrich, *Contarini*, pp. 803 ff.

5. Pastor, *History*, XII, 502.

6. Sadoleto to Castelvetro, Rome, June 12, 1542, *Epistolae*, III, 317–18.

7. Dittrich, *Contarini*, pp. 816–17.

8. These letters are in RB, *Anhang*, Nos. 14a–18, pp. 390–97.

9. *Ibid.*, No. 14a, pp. 390–91. The fact remains that Castelvetro's library included works by Luther, Zwingli, Calvin, Bucer, Oecolampadius, Melanchthon, and Bullinger: Brown, *Italy*, p. 97.

10. July 15, 1542, *Epistolae*, III, 319–20.

11. July 13, 1542, RB, *inedita*, No. 89, p. 353.

12. Alfonso's hospitality raises the question of his own relations to the Academy, but his name is not to be found elsewhere in documents bearing on the issue.

13. An English translation of the *Confessio fidei* is in Brown, *Italy*, pp. 295–97; the original is in the Estense Library.

14. Brown, p. 296, following Lancellotti, *Cronaca*, VII, 251–53.

15. *Lettere*, No. XIX, p. 46.

16. G. T. Mennrich, *Biographie d'Aonio Paleario* (Strasbourg, 1861), pp. 25 ff.; Rodocanachi, *Réforme en Italie*, I, 300–11; Brown, *Italy*, pp. 207–8; J. Bonnet, "La tolérance du cardinal Sadolet," SHPF, XXXV (1886), 489; M. Young, *Life and Times of Aonio Paleario* (London, 1860), I, 306.

17. Sadoleto to Bonamico, 1536, *Epistolae*, III, 371–73.

18. *Ibid.*, pp. 377–79; Gryphius published at least two editions, in 1532 and 1552.

19. *Epistolae*, II, 189; Rodocanachi, *Réforme*, I, 274 ff. Accused of heresy and cited to appear in Rome in 1546, he was charged again *in absentia* under Paul IV and put to death in the reign of Paul V.

20. *Epistolae*, I, 353. See P. A. Rossi, *Marc' Antonio Flaminio* (Rome, 1931);

Rodocanachi, *Réforme*, I, 292–300; Brown, *Italy*, pp. 240–41; Reusch, *Index*, I, 384–85.

21. C. Corvisieri, "Compendio dei processi del Santo Uffizio di Roma," RSR, III (1880), 297, 288; see also A. de Reumont, *Vittoria Colonna*, tr. G. Müller and E. Ferrero (2nd ed.; Turin, 1892), pp. 176–77.

22. See R. H. Bainton, *Bernardino Ochino* (Florence, 1940), chap. 3.

23. D. Cantimori, *Eretici italiani del cinquecento* (Florence, 1939), chap. 4.

24. Pastor, *History*, XII, 500.

25. Caraffa, Juan Alvarez de Toledo, P. P. Parisio, B. Guidiccioni, Laurerio, and Badia.

26. Arch. Vat., Arch. consis., Acta cam. 3, fol. 207; Acta cam. 4, fol. 96ᵛ; Masserelli, *Diarium*, CT, I, 417; Cardauns, *Nizza bis Crépy*, pp. 266–67. The basic monograph on Sadoleto's Legation is Benoit, *La Légation du cardinal Sadolet auprès de François Iᵉʳ* (Monaco and Paris, 1928).

27. Farnese to Poggio, August 19, 1542, in Pastor, XII, Appendix, No. 17; Sadoleto to Farnese, Asti, September 7, 1542, Arch. Vat., Nunz. di Ger. 59, fol. 279.

28. Arch. Vat., Acta cam. 4, fol. 96ᵛ.

29. *Epistolarum Reginaldi Poli*, III, No. XXXVIII, 61.

30. RB, No. 927, p. 24; cf. Sadoleto to Negri, *Epistolae*, III, 326.

31. Arch. Vat., Acta cam. 5, fol. 64. Sadoleto reported on his talks with de Viseo in a letter to Farnese from Asti on September 7, loc. cit.; also in *Lettere*, No. XX, p. 48.

32. Sadoleto to Farnese, Montpellier, October 3, 1542, Arch. Vat., Nunz. di Ger. 59, fols. 280–84 (copy).

33. There is an abundance of manuscript material on the Legation, much of which has been published. I have followed the documents in the Vatican Archives: (1) Nunz. di Ger. 59, fols. 279–310; (2) Carte Farnesiane 19, fols. 63–69; (3) Lett. di Prin. 12, fols. 47–57, supplemented by the published texts in Benoit, *Légation*; Ferrajoli, "Il Ruolo . . . Leone X," RSR, XXXVIII, 272–80; and Sadoleto, *Lettere*, pp. 47 ff. For a full account of the sources, see Benoit, pp. 21–22; his own edition of many of these letters is uniquely valuable for the fact that he deciphered the more important of them, using the code in Nunz. di Ger. 59.

34. Nunz. di Ger. 59, fols. 280 ff.; Benoit, *Légation*, No. IV.

35. *Ibid.*, No. V, pp. 41–42; on his eagerness for Queen Marguerite's help, see also his letter to Farnese, Toulouse, October 22, 1542, Nunz. di Ger. 59, fol. 296.

36. Arch. Vat., Lett. di Prin. 12, fols. 47 ff.

37. He expected to follow the King to Bordeaux and thence to Paris: letter to Farnese, Montpellier, October 17, 1542, Nunz. di Ger. 59, fol. 292ᵛ; cf. Tournon's outline of the royal itinerary in Sadoleto, *Lettere*, p. 65.

38. Francis did not officially recognize Sadoleto's legatine commission or ratify his powers until November 12, and since the King's recognition had also to be registered by the Parlement of Paris, the Legate was technically not accredited until December 4, 1542, three days after he left the court at Angoulême. *Collection*

des ordonnances des rois de France. Catalogue des actes de François Ier (Paris, 1870–90), No. 12801, p. 383. A copy of the royal letter patent is in the Bibliothèque Inguimbertine at Carpentras, MS. 1797, fol. 121; and the Parlement's confirmation of Sadoleto's powers in fols. 119–20, where his status is recognized on condition that the Bull of appointment in no way derogates "the authority, privileges, franchises, and liberties of the Gallican Church."

39. He first set forth his proposal to Francis I at Montpellier on October 9, Nunz. di Ger. 59, fols. 292 ff.; Benoit, *Légation*, pp. 17–18.

40. Tournon advised Sadoleto that the princes would no longer tolerate coercion from Rome and told the Legate to expect no more than a brief armistice at best, Cardauns, *Nizza bis Crépy*, pp. 268–69.

41. Nunz. di Ger. 59, fol. 294^v; fol. 295^v.

42. Acta cam. 4, fol. 100; CT, II, 403–4; Benoit, *Légation*, p. 52, n. 1.

43. Farnese explained the Pope's decision as the result of de Viseo's failure in Spain: Farnese to Sadoleto, November 3, 1542, Lett. di Prin. 14, fols. 228–29; *Lettere*, 66–68. Farnese sent a duplicate of this letter on November 12, which is in Benoit, *Légation*, No. X, pp. 52–54.

44. Nunz. di Ger. 59, fols. 296–302.

45. Sadoleto to Farnese, Angoulême, November 16, 1542, *ibid.*, fols. 302–5; Benoit, *Légation*, No. XII, pp. 67–69. In a later dispatch Sadoleto advised the Pope to address Francis "alquanto più dolce" with respect to summoning the French Cardinals, Benoit, pp. 70–71; and in his letter of the thirtieth he confessed that the Briefs to them seemed "un poco rigorosi," *ibid.*, No. XIV, p. 74. Sadoleto felt obliged to remind the Pope that these Cardinals were virtual dependents of the French crown, for which see M. François, *Tournon*, p. 446.

46. Nunz. di Ger. 59, fols. 305^v–10; also in Carte Farnesiane 19, fols. 63–69; Benoit, *Légation*, No. XIV, pp. 71 ff.

47. *Lettere*, No. XXXII, p. 77.

48. Nunz. di Ger. 59, fol. 307^v.

49. Hughes, *Rome and the Counter-Reformation in England*, pp. 37–38.

50. E.g., *Epistolae*, II, No. CCLVIII; and Vol. III, Nos. CCCLXIII, CCXCV, CCCXCIV and CCCXCX.

51. Angoulême, November 30, 1542, Nunz. di Ger. 59, fol. 309.

52. *Lettere*, No. XXXII, pp. 78–79.

53. *Ibid.*, pp. 80–81.

54. Benoit, No. XVI, 78–79.

55. April 17, 1543, Arch. Vat., Lett. di Prin. 14, fols. 229^v–230^v.

56. In 1543 the Sacred College numbered fifty-six; of these, twenty-seven were then in Rome, twenty-nine "variis in locis absentes." The absentees included the three Cardinal-Legates at Trent, the Legates to Parma and Perugia, ten "French" Cardinals, etc.; Sadoleto was still listed as Legate to Francis I. Arch. Vat., Arch. consis., Acta cam. 4, fols. 105^v–106.

57. *Epistolae*, III, 326.

58. *Ibid.*, pp. 328–29. Benoit states that Sadoleto received the Legation in Bologna soon after reaching Italy (*Légation*, p. 79, n. 1). The fact is, however, that

it lay vacant although nominally under its Vice-Legate Conversini until Morone was invested with it in April 1544. See P. Vizano, *Dieci libri della Histoira della sua patria* (Bologna, 1602–8), part 2, p. 31; S. Muzzi, *Annali della città di Bologna della sua origine al 1796* (Bologna, 1840–49), VI, 504; Eubel, *Hierarchia*, III, 24.

59. *Epistolae*, III, 329. It is difficult to understand why Sadoleto is said to have tried to emancipate himself from Carpentras so that he could indulge his ambition to live more sumptuously in Italy (as in Benoit, *Légation*, pp. 5, 15–16). His restlessness in the peninsula was never so obvious as it was during this brief sojourn in 1543.

60. *Epistolae*, III, 332.

61. *Ibid.*, p. 333.

62. Pallavicini, *Vera concilii tridentini historia*, I, Bk. 5, chap. 3; Pastor, *History*, XII, 173; Friedensburg, *Kaiser Karl V und Papst Paul III* (Leipzig, 1932), pp. 59–60.

63. Jacopo to Paolo, Parma, July 17, 1543, *Epistolae*, III, 335.

64. Acta cam. 4, fol. 118.

65. Acta cam. 3, fol. 226.

66. Peace was then fourteen months away, coming in September 1544; Crépy inspired Sadoleto to write his *Oratio de pace* (c. 1545), which he dedicated to Charles V, *Opera*, II, 264–87. It is another treatise in the manner of his earlier exhortations to the crusade. The Emperor, however, seems to have been little impressed by it. See Joly, *Etude*, p. 211.

67. *Epistolae*, III, 341 ff.

68. *Ibid.*, p. 346. Cf. his letter to Bembo of November 3, 1527, *Epistolae*, I, 207–8.

69. Letter to Speciano, p. 343.

Chapter X: Embattled Bishop

1. Farnese was appointed in March 1541; see Fornery, *Histoire ecclésiastique*, II, 530–31; R. Vallentin, "Notes sur la chronologie des Vice-Légats d'Avignon au XVIe siècle," *Mémoires*, IX, p. 202.

2. Ronchini, *Lettere*, pp. vii–ix; Alessandro Campeggio (1504–54), Archbishop of Bologna, was the son of Sadoleto's friend Lorenzo Campeggio.

3. Paolo to Farnese, *J. Sadoleti Epistolarum Appendix*, pp. 245–46; Jacopo to Farnese, *Lettere*, No. XXXV, pp. 89 f.; Jacopo to Pole, *Epistolae*, III, 348 ff.; Paolo to Farnese, March 23, 1545, Bib. Vat., Barb. lat. 5695, fols. 105–6.

4. The "Electi comitatus Venayssini," as they were called in a text of 1399, the first in which the title was mentioned: Girard, "Les états du Comtat Venaissin depuis les origines jusqu'à la fin du XVI siècle," *Mémoires de l'Académie de Vaucluse*, 2nd Ser., VI (1906), 182. See also Mossé, *Histoire*, pp. 67–68.

5. E.g., the *Electi* to Farnese, August 10, 1544, Avignon, Musée Calvet MS. 4188, fols. 14v–15; and August 20, 1544, *ibid.*, fol. 5.

6. 1539, *Epistolae*, III, 117.

7. Letters to Simonetta, *ibid.*, 136 ff.; to Contarini, No. 138 ff.; to Farnese, 149; and to Paul III, Bib. Vat., Barb. lat. 2157, fol. cxxix.

8. The *Electi* to Paul III, August 10, 1544, Avignon, Musée Calvet MS. 4188, fol. 14ᵛ f.

9. The *Electi* to Farnese, September 21, 1541, Avignon, Musée Calvet MS. 4188, fol. 5; to Tournon, same date, fol. 17ᵛ f.; to Paul III, May 28, 1542, fol. 12 f.; and Paolo to Farnese, July 1542, *Lettere*, No. XVIII, p. 43.

10. The consul Centenier reviewed the circumstances of the appointment in a letter to Sadoleto, February 12, 1538, Avignon, Musée Calvet MS. 4188, fols. 44ᵛ–46.

11. Paolo to Centenier, Rome, December 12, 1537, *ibid.*, fol. 52.

12. Centenier to Paolo Sadoleto, October 20, 1537, *ibid.*, fol. 51; Paolo to Centenier, Rome, December 12, 1537.

13. *Epistolae* III, 236–38; and 238–40.

14. Barjavel, *Dictionnaire*, p. 60. After fugitive interludes in Antwerp, Hamburg, and Rostock, Bording was appointed court physician to Christian III of Denmark.

15. M. J. Gaufrès, *Claude Baduel et la réforme des études au XVIᵉ siècle* (Paris, 1880), and "Les Collèges protestants . . . Nîmes," SHPF, XXIII (1874), 289–304, 337–48, 385–95; continued in Vol. XXIV (1875), 4–20. See also E. Droz, "Claude Baduel, Traducteur de Bucer," BHR, XVII (1955), 347–50. I have used the collection of letters in Avignon known as "Epistolae familiares C. Baduelli a Joanne Fontano interprete collectae Nemausi," Musée Calvet MS. 1290.

16. CR, II, p. 732; *Calvini opera*, X, No. 125, p. 217.

17. Cf. Baduel to Melanchthon, recalling association with him and Bucer in years past, Avignon, Musée Calvet MS. 1290, fols. 100ᵛ–103.

18. Gaufrès, *Baduel*, p. 127.

19. Avignon, Musée Calvet MS. 1290, fols. 42, 44–45ᵛ.

20. *J. Sadoleti Epistolarum Appendix*, pp. lxxi–lxxii. The consuls, in their letter of appointment, also refer to Baduel's initiative in writing to Sadoleto and to Sébastien de Blégier, a consul at Carpentras: consuls to Baduel, April 27, 1544, Musée Calvet MS. 1290, fol. 89.

21. *J. Sadoleti Epistolarum Appendix*, pp. xxxii–lxxix; Gryphius published the treatise as *De officio & munere eorum qui juventutem exercent* (1544).

22. *Calvini opera*, XX, No. 4141, col. 374.

23. Musée Calvet MS. 1290, fols. 102ᵛ f.

24. The debt to Baduel was still unpaid in 1547, but by then Sadoleto had decided not to honor it; Jacopo to Paolo, Rome, July 31, 1547, Bib. Vat., Barb. lat. 5695, fol. 100ᵛ.

25. Volusene appears to have written Sadoleto for advice on how he should conduct himself amid the doctrinal warfare then raging in Scotland; Jacopo replied from Rome sometime in 1546, *Epistolae*, III, 433 ff.

26. CT, V, No. 15.

27. *Epistolae*, I, 424.

28. September 28, 1538, *ibid.*, III, 36–37.

11*

29. *Ibid.*, pp. 102–3; Raynaldus, *Annales*, XXXIII, 514.

30. *Epistolae*, III, 116.

31. The definitive monograph and bibliography is P. Gaffarel, "Les Massacres de Cabrières et Mérindol," *Revue historique*, Vol. 107 (1911), 241–71. The leading contemporary accounts are those of Jacques Aubery, *Histoire mémorable de la persécution et saccagement du peuple de Mérindol et Cabrières et d'autres circonvoisins appelés Vaudois* (1556), more accessible in the later edition entitled *Histoire de l'exécution de Cabrières et de Mérindol* (Paris, 1645); J. Crespin, *Histoire des Martyrs persecutez et mis à mort pour la verité*, ed. D. Benoit (Toulouse, 1885–89), the original edition published in French in 1554 and translated into Latin by Baduel in the same year; De Thou, *Historiarum sui temporis tomus primus* (London, 1733), covering the years 1543–51. For secondary accounts, see F. Benoit, *La Tragédie du sac de Cabrières* (Marseilles, 1927); Vicomte de Meaux, *Les Luttes religieuses en France au XVIᵉ siècle* (Paris, 1879); J. Liabastres, *Histoire de Carpentras* (Carpentras, 1891); Granget, *Histoire du diocèse d'Avignon*, II, 39–86; P. Chaillot, *Précis de l'histoire d'Avignon au point de vue religieux* (Avignon, 1852); C. H. Gaillard, *Histoire de François premier* (3rd ed.; Paris, 1819), Vols. V–VI, *passim*.

32. By 1535 the Provençal Vaudois had made contact with Farel, Viret, Bucer, and Capito, and immediately won enthusiastic support in Germany. See Arnaud, *Histoire*, I, 13 f.; Gaillard, *Histoire*, IV, 325–26; Granget, *Histoire*, II, 72–73.

33. E. Lavisse and A. Rambaud, *Renaissance et réforme* (Paris, 1894), p. 501. The Dominican Mathieu Ory, who reviewed and probably censured Sadoleto's Commentaries on Romans, was also appointed Inquisitor of the Faith for the whole realm in June 1540.

34. V. L. Bourrilly, *Guillaume du Bellay* (Paris, 1904), pp. 315–17; Gaffarel, "Les Massacres," pp. 246–47. Du Bellay's original report has not survived, the above being de Thou's account of it (*Historiarum*, I, 224), which Bourrilly considers wholly reliable.

35. The text, written in French, is in SHPF, VIII (1859), 507–10. See also de Thou, *Historiacum*, I, 224–25.

36. In 1541 the diocese of Cavaillon passed to Girolamo Ghinucci, a papal diplomat and curialist who was Auditor of the Camera at the start of Leo X's proceedings against Luther; see L. Cardella, *Memorie storiche*, IV, 147–48. Ghinucci succeeded Mario Maffei but soon died, to be followed by his brother Pietro, who quickly won notoriety for his persecution of the Vaudois.

37. De Thou, *Historiarum*, I, 225; Crespin, *Histoire*, I, 401–2; and SHPF, VII (1859), 510. Cf. the account of J. Bonnet, "La Tolérance," SHPF, XXXV, 536–37, following Crespin.

38. De Thou gives an account of Sadoleto's response to the confession (*Historiarum*, I, 225), which is probably a paraphrase of Crespin's version of Sadoleto's letter to the Vaudois of Cabrières, *Histoire*, I, 401–2.

39. *Lettere*, No. XXXV, 89–90.

40. Cited in Benoit, *La Tragédie*, pp. 11–12.

41. Herminjard, *Correspondance*, V, 362, n. 4.

42. Paolo to Farnese, Cavaillon, November 23, 1544, *Lettere*, No. XLIV, 109–10.

43. *Ibid.*, No. XLVI, 115–16.

44. *Calvini opera*, XX, No. 4141, cols. 374–75. For Calvin's paternal interest in the Vaudois, see his letter to Bullinger, Geneva, *ibid.*, XI, No. 586, col. 773. It is plausibly said, however, that Calvin's support hurt the Vaudois more than it helped, for such assurance emboldened their leaders to turn violently on the Church in Provence, Gaillard, *Histoire*, IV, 326–27. Melanchthon and the German princes had previously interceded before Francis I in their behalf, *Calvini opera*, XI, No. 31, col. 220.

45. For the later trial of Baron d'Oppède and the snarled political and constitutional issues it involved, see Aubery's account in the *Histoire de l'exécution*, and Gaffarel, *Histoire*, pp. 262–70.

46. E.g. Crespin and de Thou; Bonnet, "Un Magistrat bernois du XVIe siècle," SHPF, XXIII (1874), 14.

47. Dom Charles Poulet, *Histoire de l'Eglise en France* (Paris, 1946–49), III, 27.

48. J. J. Herzog and Albert Hauck, *Realencyklopädie für protestantische Theologie und Kirche* (3rd ed.; Leipzig, 1896–1913), XVII, 331.

49. *History*, XI, 500, n. 2; XII, 486.

50. Paolo Sadoleto to Farnese, April 23, 1545, *Lettere*, No. LXIX, pp. 122–23; a duplicate, dated April 25, was sent by another courier. Benrath gives a German translation of this passage, in the mistaken belief that Jacopo wrote it, in order to demonstrate a decisive change in Sadoleto's attitude toward the Vaudois. As further proof, Benrath cites Jacopo's letter to Farnese of May 31 (No. L in the *Lettere*), but even though the Cardinal wrote this letter, it contains no reference whatever to Cabrières or the Vaudois.

51. In his letter of April 23, Paolo advised Farnese that Jacopo should by then be approaching Rome, having mentioned the Bishop's departure in a previous communication of March 23, Bib. Vat., Barb. lat. 5695, fol. 105ᵛ.

52. Myconius to Calvin, 1546, *Calvini opera*, CII, No. 812, col. 363.

53. Cf. his letter to Farnese, July 29, 1539, *Epistolae*, III, 116.

54. *Lettere*, No. XXXV, 89–90; and *Epistolae*, III, 351. He also felt that in view of general hostility to Campeggio's regime in the County, a crusade against the Vaudois would only serve to increase popular resentment against Rome and the Legation.

55. Allen, V, No. 1331, p. 159.

56. *Epistolarum . . . Melanchthonis*, p. 530 f.

57. For the interpretation of Sadoleto's attitudes towards the Vaudois which Benrath wanted to qualify, see François, *Tournon*, p. 217; de Meaux, *Les Luttes religieuses*, p. 31; Perrin, *De Jacopo Sadoleto* (Paris, 1847), p. 46; Bourrilly, *Guillaume du Bellay*, p. 115; J. Bonnet, "La Tolérance," SHPF, XXXV (1886), 481, 531; Arnaud, *Histoire*, I, 40; K. J. von Hefele and J. Hergenroether, *Histoire de l'église* (Paris, 1891), V, 463; Gaillard, *Histoire*, IV, 326, and V, 238.

58. *Epistolae*, III, 307–8. Ronchini places his effective retirement even earlier, *Lettere*, p. 14. The start of Paolo's episcopate has been dated both in 1541, E.

Andreoli, *Monographie de l'église cathédrale Saint-Siffrein de Carpentras* (Paris, 1862), p. 238; and in 1547, i.e. after Sadoleto's death, Fornery, *Histoire*, III, 227.

59. *Epistolae*, III, 354–55.

60. *Lettere*, No. XXXVI, 93.

61. *Ibid.*, p. 95.

62. March 20, 1544, Bib. Vat., Barb. lat. 5695, fol. 98.

63. In February 1544, Paolo asked Farnese to relieve him of his duties as Rector because Jacopo had decided to withdraw from diocesan administration altogether, *Lettere*, No. XXXVII, pp. 96–97. But because Farnese was unable to find a successor, Paolo was required to remain in office (*ibid.*, No. LV, p. 131).

64. Lauchert, p. 411; Ritter, *Un Umanista*, pp. 81–83.

65. It was rededicated to Niccolo Gaddi with a letter which is in Ritter, *Un Umanista*, pp. 141–42; cf. *Lettere*, No. LXXIV, pp. 173–74.

66. Ritter, *Un Umanista*, pp. 162, 167, 177.

67. *Epistolae*, III, 359–60.

68. *Ibid.*, pp. 378–79.

69. *Ibid.*, pp. 383–84.

70. But once again he stated his intention, as he had before, to attend the Council: *ibid.*, pp. 379–80, 385, 390.

71. *Ibid.*, pp. 387 f.

72. *Ibid.*, pp. 388–89. He refused a papal subsidy in the fall of 1538; see his letter to Paul III of October 15, 1538, *ibid.*, pp. 41–43.

73. As Sadoleto acknowledged in his letter to Farnese of February 22, 1545, *Lettere*, No. XLVIII, pp. 119–20.

74. *Epistolae*, III, 43, 389.

75. *Lettere*, No. XLVIII, p. 120.

76. *Ibid.*, p. 121.

77. Paolo to Farnese, March 23, 1545, Bib. Vat., Barb. lat. 5695, fol. 105.

78. In the consistory of May 11 Sadoleto chose to succeed the late Pier Paolo Parisio as Cardinal of S. Balbina, Arch. Vat., Arch. consis., Acta cam. 5, fol. 245ᵛ. According to Acta cam. 3, fol. 264, he had arrived several days earlier.

79. Jacopo to Paolo, Rome, July 31, 1545, Bib. Vat., Barb. lat. 5695, fol. 100.

80. Sadoleto to Duke William, Rome, July 16, 1545, *Epistolae*, III, 400–1.

Chapter XI: The Old Cardinal

1. CT, X, Appendix, No. 30, pp. 888–89; *Mon. Tri.*, I, 2 Heft, No. 289, p. 263. The special congregation on conciliar affairs now consisted of De Cupis, Caraffa, Sadoleto, Guidiccioni, Crescenzi, Morone, Cortese, Badia, Sfondrato, and Ardinghelli: De Vega to Charles V, June 9, 1546, CT, XI, No. 36, p. 55.

2. E.g., *Epistolae*, III, Nos. CCCCXVIII and CCCCXX.

3. Rome, July 31, 1545, Bib. Vat., Barb. lat. 5695, fols. 100–101ᵛ. This

letter is often nearly illegible; I am grateful to Prof. A. L. Pellegrini of Vassar College for generous help in working through these four difficult pages.

4. *Ibid.*, fol. 100.

5. *Ibid.*, fol. 100^{r-v}.

6. Sadoleto to Paul III, Rome, May 26, 1545, *Epistolae*, III, No. CCCCXVII; and August 29, 1545, *ibid.*, No. CCCCXXIII.

7. Cristiani, *L'Eglise à l'époque du Concile de Trente*, pp. 92–95; Drei, *I Farnese*, pp. 36–39.

8. Pastor, *History*, XII, 231. Further opposition came from Cardinal Tournou: François, *Tournon*, pp. 215–16, where Sadoleto is rather inappropriately included among the "French Cardinals."

9. August 26: Bib. Vat., Vat. lat. 6978, fol. 151.

10. Farnese to the Legates, November 7, 1545, CT, X, No. 184, p. 232. The Legates attributed the decision to the "holy and prudent resolution of the Pope," letter to Farnese, November 8, 1545, *ibid.*, No. 186, p. 253. At this time they were still trying to find a permanent secretary for the Council as a result of Beccadelli's resignation to return to the service of Ranuccio Farnese. The Vice-Chancellor first proposed Paolo Sadoleto, September 16, 1545, CT, X, p. 193; *Mon. Tri.*, I, No. 193, p. 188; Massarelli, *Diarium*, I, in CT, I, pp. 178, n. 3, and 318, n. 4. Evidently, however, there was not sufficient enthusiasm for him at Trent. After both Flaminio and Priuli declined the post (*Mon. Tri.*, I, 3 Heft, Nos. 292, p. 315; 306, p. 337; and 332, p. 379), Massarelli became *de facto* secretary in February 1546, Pastor, *History*, XII, 247.

11. The number of his surviving letters falls off sharply after Sadoleto reached Rome in 1545; such was also the case in 1536. The large volume of his correspondence after 1527 derives in large measure from Jacopo's separation from his friends in Italy, but once back among them, the need for letters was much reduced. We therefore know least of Sadoleto from his own hand at the beginning and the end of his career. Fatigue and illness also had their effect during his last two years in Rome; there is a postscript to his letter to Paolo of July 31, 1545, explaining that the Cardinal had been forced to take to his bed before he could finish it, Bib. Vat., Barb. lat. 5695, fol. 101^v.

12. His list included Trivulzio, De Cupis, Caraffa, and Georges d'Armagnac, CT, I, p. 261.

13. The declared hostility of Mendoza and the imperialists to Caraffa was plain to the conclave of May 1555, Cristiani, *L'Eglise*, pp. 148–49; for Morone's relation to the Spanish party and the French in the conclave of 1550, *ibid.*, pp. 106–7.

14. Giovanni Antonio Venier to the Council of Ten, Rome, February 16, 1546, ZKG, V (1881), 1 Heft, 610.

15. Arch. Vat., Acta cam. 8, fol. 3.

16. Rome, 1546, *Epistolae*, III, No. CCCCXXXVI.

17. De Vega's letters to Charles V: Rome, January 31, 1546, CT, XI, No. 18, p. 28; and February 7, 1546, *ibid.*, No. 20, p. 34.

18. Bernardino Maffei to Card. Cervini, Rome, April 17, 1546, CT, X,

No. 374, p. 463. They would be nominally under Farnese, CT, XI, No. 29, p. 47.

19. The Legates to Farnese, Trent, March 7, 1546, CT, IV, No. 360, p. 502.

20. *Mon. Tri*, I, 469 ff.; p. 480.

21. Commentary on Ps. 93, *Opera*, III, 297; Letter to the Germans, *ibid.*, II, 347A; *Epistolae*, I, 410; *ibid.*, III, 255.

22. P. Hughes, *Rome and the Counter-Reformation in England* (London, 1944), pp. 41–42. For support of his view and the argument for a return "ad fontes," both Hebrew and Greek, see the comment of Father Johannes, CT, XII, No. 75, pp. 537–38.

23. CT, X, No. 373, p. 462.

24. G. B. Cervini to Cardinal Cervini, *ibid.*, Appendix II, p. 891. Sadoleto's reservations were a matter of record in his writing, where he repeatedly stated his preference for the Septuagint (*Opera*, III, 270A, 286A, 299A, 336A, 355A), and used the Greek text in order to correct the Vulgate (*Opera*, IV, 8A, 10B; *ibid.*, II, 24, 360B–61A).

25. CT, X, Nos. 398 and 414.

26. E.g., Paul III (Sadoleto) to the Legates, Rome, 1546, *Epistolae Leonis X*, No. CIV, 190 ff.

27. E. Müntz, *La Bibliothèque du Vatican au XVIe siècle* (Paris, 1886), pp. 79–80; Pastor, *History*, XII, 545. Cervini did not become librarian until after Sadoleto's death, P. Battifol, *La Vaticane de Paul III à Paul V* (Paris, 1890), p. 18.

28. He had asked Farnese for "cantone in Palazzo," Carpentras, February 22, 1545, *Lettere*, No. XLVIII, p. 122, and later had the Pope's assurance that he could have an apartment here, Jacopo to Paolo, Rome, July 31, 1545, Bib. Vat., Barb. lat. 5695, fol. 100.

29. See his very important letter to Paolo, Rome, June 8, 1546, *Epistolae*, III, 431.

30. De Vega to Charles V, Rome, June 9, 1546, CT, X, No. 36.

31. G. B. Cervini to Cardinal Cervini, Rome, June 22, 1546, *ibid.*, Appendix II, No. XIV, p. 899; NB, IX, 90, n. 1; B. Maffeo to Cervini, Rome, June 23, 1546, CT, X, No. 447, pp. 535–36.

32. NB, IX, 90, n. 1. Pastor very much oversimplifies the motives of the opposition by citing only the complaint against a provision in the treaty which condones the sale of ecclesiastical properties in Spain to raise money for the war, *History*, XII, 291.

33. January 18, 1547; see Santoro, *Pietro Bembo*, p. 76.

34. *Epistolae*, III, 458–59.

35. Arch. Vat., Acta cam. 8, fol. 35. The total in 1545 was sixty-three; for the complete list, see O. Clemen, RQ, XXV (1911), 185–88.

36. CT, X, Appendix II, No. XLV.

37. The conventional view is that the vote of March 11 was produced by the outbreak of spotted fever at Trent and the death of one of the delegates; cf. Pastor, *History*, XII, 351 ff. But both the Pope and a majority of the fathers had long since decided to remove the Council to Rome or Bologna; see the letter of Cardinal Sforza to the Legates, Rome, October 20, 1546, CT, No. 562B, p. 693.

The Pope himself issued an order for the translation to Bologna on February 17, 1547, Brandi, *Charles V*, pp. 574–75.

38. Massarelli, *Diarium*, IV, CT, I, p. 633.

39. 1547, CT, XI, No. 13, p. 150.

40. NB, IX, 528.

41. WA, *Tischreden*, Vol. IV, No. 4341; and *Briefwechsel*, Vol. VIII, No. 3394. Sadoleto was not a cultural chauvinist, as we know in part from his defense of Longueil. But he was still an Italian who was pleased, for example, to notice that there was also progress in the arts in France and Germany, reasoning that "Those endowed with such talent are certainly not barbarians." *Phaedrus, Opera*, III, 130.

42. E.g., his *Oratio* of 1536, CT, XII, No. 15, pp. 109–10; *Opera*, III, 2B, 3B–4A, 5A, 12; and his letter to Duke William of Bavaria, *Epistolae*, III, 403–5.

43. See his letters to Duke George of Saxony, 1538, *ibid.*, 4–5; and to Mendoza, 1546, *ibid.*, 448.

44. *Oratio de pace, Opera*, II, 281, 283B–84A, 285A. Sadoleto considered Francis another guardian of the peace but not the equal of the Emperor.

45. Sadoleto to Salviati, 1537, *Epistolae*, II, 495–96.

46. Jacopo to Paolo, Parma, June 17, 1543, *ibid.*, III, 333. Cf. Massarelli's emphasis on the desperate need of "la confidentia tra S. Stà et S. Mᵗᵃ Ces.," CT, I, p. 281; and Mignanelli's admonitions of danger from "la inconfidentia manifesta, che si vede tra N. S.ʳᵉ et l'Imperatore. . . .", CT, X, No. 26, p. 41.

47. NB, X, 55–56; Pastor, *History*, XII, 368; Schweitzer, "Beiträge," RQ, XII (1908), 140–41.

48. Charles V to Mendoza, Augsberg, September 19, 1547, CT, XI, No. 12, p. 925.

49. "Tutta Roma teneva per certo che manchando el papa lui [Sadoleto] seria stato papa." Entry for October 25, 1547, *Cronaca*, X, 190.

50. CT, XX, p. 902.

51. CT, XI, p. 904. Cf. NB, X, 420.

52. Eubel, *Hierarchia*, III, p. 27, n. 9, says October 19; Lancellotti, the eighteenth, *Cronaca*, X, 189.

53. *Ibid.*

54. *Vitae et res gestae Pontificium Romanorum*, III, 618B.

55. CT, X, Appendix, No. 30, pp. 888–89.

56. Fiordibello, *Vita* in *Opera*, I, 19.

57. Rodocanachi, *Réforme*, II, 90; Schenk, *Reginald Pole*, pp. 58–59. Although Sadoleto and Caraffa were never conspicuously close friends, their relationship remained cordial and unmarred by the sort of conflict which developed between Caraffa and Pole.

58. Not to be confused with an older Jacopo Gallo (d. 1505), the Florentine banker and patron of Michelangelo; for the elder Gallo's friendship with Sadoleto, see Bembo to Sadoleto, 1503, *Epistolae*, I, 7.

59. E.g., *Epistolae*, I, 393, 410 (1531); II, 394 (1536), 502 (1537); III, 382 (1544), 380 ff. (1545), 386 ff. (1545) *Lettere*, pp. 19–20 (1545).

60. Bembo to Ascanio Sforza, 1543, *Opere*, V, 151–52. Bembo's last years brought him great financial distress. Unable to support himself in Rome, he returned to his diocese at Gubbio, aided somewhat in 1544 when the Pope conferred the Bishopric of Bergamo on him, Santoro, *Pietro Bembo*, pp. 64–65.

61. For the disposition of the Quirinal vineyard, still mortgaged, see Ferrajoli, "Il Ruolo . . . Leone X," RSR, XXXVIII, 440.

62. E.g., their letter to Sadoleto, Carpentras, February 15, 1546, Avignon, Musée Calvet MS. 4188, fol. 28.

63. Jacopo to Paolo, Rome, June 8, 1546, *Epistolae*, III, 430. Sadoleto to Niccolò Pietello, Rome, 1546, *ibid.*, No. CCCCXXXI. The *Electi* continued to turn to him; their last appeal, written a month before he died, was a request for help in recovering a common pasture which Bishop Ghinucci had appropriated, Carpentras, September 20, 1547, Musée Calvert MS. 4148, fol. 33.

64. Sadoleto to Contarini, Carpentras, November 26, 1535, *Epistolae*, II, 345.

65. Rome, January 20, 1546, *ibid.*, III, No. CCCCXXVIII.

66. "De republica christiana," in *Epistolae Leonis X*, pp. cxii–cxix; also in P. Lazzari, *Miscellaneorum ex MSS. libris bibliothecae Colegii Romani Societatis Jesu* (Rome, 1754), I, 608 ff.; see also Ritter, *Un Umanista*, p. 85; and Joly, *Etude*, p. 40.

67. Sadoleto to Ranuccio, Rome, September 20, 1546, *Epistolae*, III, No. CCCCXXXIV.

68. Ranuccio's humanist tutors had included Ludovico Beccadelli and Lazzaro Bonamico, Drei, *I Farnese*, p. 34.

69. *Epistolae*, III, 440.

70. *Ibid.*, p. 442.

71. *Ibid.*, p. 443.

72. *Opera omnia*, I, 80.

73. Abbé Ricard, *Sadolet*, pp. 152–53, 169–70.

Appendix I: Sadoleto's Authorship of the *Philosophicae Consolationes*

1. *Biblioteca Modenese*, IV, 454.

2. *Opera*, III, 30A.

3. Ritter, *Un Umanista*, p. 85; Schultess-Rechberg, *Der Kardinal Jacopo Sadoleto*, pp. 46 ff.; K. Morneweg, *Johann von Dalberg* (Berlin, 1887), pp. 297–300; Joly, *Etude*, p. 41; Allen, V, 527 f.

4. In using such phrases as "qua invicem juncti conglutinatique sumus benevolentia," and "pro amicitia nostra," *Opera*, III, 30, 65.

5. "Itaque sic accipias velim epistolam hanc, tamquam ad levandam animi tui molestiam atque tristitiam quam maxime accommodatam, ac tibi missam ab eo, qui te justissimis de causis non mediocriter amat, & huiusmodi perturbationis calamitatisque non est inexpertus. Paucis enim (ut scire te puto) ante annis, itidem ego dulcissimae genetricis meae crudelissima nece gravissimum vulnus accepi.

Quam ob rem, quae mihi ipsi tunc & dixi et consului: si quid etiam amplius ex antiquorum librorum lectione postea comparavi: tecum pro nostra benevolentia communicase decrevi." *Ibid.*, p. 31.

6. "abbracciate la mia veneranda matre in mia parte. . . ." Arch. Vat., Arm. XLV, Vol. 42, f. 19; and Ferrajoli, "Il Ruolo . . . Leone X," RSR, XXXVIII, *op cit.*, 426.

7. "optimo patri vita functo B. M. & Fran. Malchiavellae ejus unicae uxori, Matri suae charissimae viventi, & sibi fecit. . . . Huic monumento praeter treis hosce inseratur nemo." Tiraboschi, *Bibliotèca Modenese*, IV, 418.

8. "Mori e fu sepelita M.ª Francesca consorte fu de M.ʳᵒ M. Zohanne Sadoleto e madre del R.ᵐᵒ cardinale M. Jacopo Sadoleto; questa dona era mal sana, per la alegreza del figliolo fatto cardinale [ten weeks earlier] è sempre stato pegio. . . ." *Cronaca*, VI, 263.

9. *Etude*, p. 41.

Appendix II: Sadoleto and Erasmus: 1534–1536

1. Allen, XI, Nos. 2971 and 2973.

2. *Ibid.*, X, intro. to No. 2816 for the origins of Erasmus' concern.

3. Toffanin, "Umanesimo e Teologia," BHR, XI, part 2, 213–14, which includes the footnote citing Vallese's remarks in the introduction to his edition of the *Colloquia* (Naples, 1949), Vol. IV in the "Collezione Umanistica."

4. "Tametsi plane suspicor Sadoletum a nobis alienatum officio quo debeat nobis reddi amicior." Allen, XI, No. 2980, p. 52.

5. Erasmus to Damian à Goes, Basle, December 15, 1535, *ibid.*, No. 3076, p. 259.

6. Sadoleto to Erasmus, December 9, 1534, *ibid.*, No. 2982, p. 53.

7. *Ibid.*, X, intro. to No. 2816, p. 234.

8. *Ibid.*, XI, No. 3043, p. 208.

9. A. Renaudet, *Erasme et l'Italie* (Geneva, 1954), p. 239; K. Schätti, *Erasmus von Rotterdam und die Römische Kurie*, pp. 150, 154, 164. It is to Sadoleto's discredit, however, that he was not always a forceful public partisan of Erasmus when dealing with colleagues in the hierarchy. Thus while the Bishop was willing to write, "Erasmum meum amo incredibiliter," to Amerbach (1530; Allen, VIII, intro. to No. 2315, p. 429), he was cautious when asked to interpret Erasmus to Fregoso—willing to praise him for eloquence and erudition, but adding, "I know a little, but less than you imagine, about his integrity, honor and ingenuousness." (1530; *Epistolae*, I, 369–70).

10. Allen, XI, No. 3076, p. 259.

Index

Jewish bankers, *see* Venaissin
Justification: humanists *vs.* theologians on, 93; Sadoleto attacks *sola fide* doctrine, 137–39; his view in letter to Genevans, 145–46; his position disputed by Calvin, 148; Regensburg formula (Article V), 156–57; supported by Pole, 158; attacked by Sadoleto, 158–60

Lancellotti (Thommasino de' Bianchi), considers Sadoleto *papàbile*, 105, 212
Landsknechte, 51, 53, 56
Laocoön, 9–10
League of Cognac, 44
Leo X (Giovanni de' Medici), 4, 12, 13, 68, 137; nominates Sadoleto and Bembo to Secretariat, 14; reorganizes Secretariat, 14–15, 16; Sadoleto's duties under, 16–18, 23–25, 26–27; seeks Erasmus' support, 21; confers benefices on Sadoleto, 22–23; proposes crusade, 23–24; policy toward Luther, 24–25, 115–16; death of, 28, 250 n.64. *See also* Patronage
Leoniceno, Niccolò, 5, 253 n.59
Leonico Tomeo, Niccolò, 253 n.59
Leto, Pomponio, 18
Longueil (Longolius), Christophe, 23; his "trial" in Rome, 20–21
Lorraine, Cardinal of (Jean de Guise), 65, 67, 171
Louis XII, 11, 245 n.30
Loyola, Ignatius, 124, 128
Luther, Martin, 8, 252 n.40, 86, 108, 203, 210; early attitudes of Curia toward, 20; in Sadoleto's instructions to Cajetan, 25; ban against requested by Sadoleto, 27; deplores Sadoleto's exegesis, 47, 253 n.64; on difficulty of reform, 114; atti-

tudes of Erasmus and Sadoleto compared, 116–17; describes Sadoleto, 118; Sadoleto's knowledge of his works disputed, 134; praises Calvin's reply to Sadoleto, 149
Lutherans, 251 n.25, 258 n.61, 96, 111–12, 202, 208; Sadoleto boasts they fear him, 174–75
Lyons, 259 n.80, 280 n.16

Machiavelli, Francesca, *see* Sadoleto, Francesca (Machiavelli)
Machiavelli, Niccolò, 42, 252 n.45
Maffei, Mario, 9, 19, 65, 66, 101, 103, 248 n.26, 258 n.64, 290 n.36
Mai, Angelo, Cardinal, 281 ns. 37–38
Malaria, Sadoleto afflicted by, 124–25, 201
Mantua, Council of, 95, 269 n.15, 106; Sadoleto opposes delay of, 113–14
Marguerite d'Angoulême, Queen of Navarre, 170, 171, 189, 192, 273 n.72; at Congress of Nice, 126; supports Baduel, 183, 184
Marron, Eustache, 189, 192
Marseilles, Sadoleto meets Clement VII at, 63, 69
Massarelli, Angelo, 204, 209, 291 n.10
Maximilian I, 25
Medici, Caterina de', 69
Medici, Giovanni, Cardinal, *see* Leo X
Medici, Giulio de', Cardinal, *see* Clement VII
Medici Popes, judged by Sadoleto, 103, 116. *See also* Patronage; Reform sentiment
Melanchthon, Philip, 7, 108, 117, 123, 124, 134, 136, 140, 148, 149, 183, 193, 289 n.44
    Sadoleto's letter to (1537), 117–20, 121–22, 274 n.11; interpreted by Luther, 135; described by Cochlaeus, 120–21; defended by Sadoleto,

The roman type used in this book is known as Bembo (Aldine) Series 270.   It is a modern recutting of a fount designed by Francesco da Bologna (Griffi) for the Venetian printer-publisher, Aldus Manutius, and is named for Cardinal Pietro Bembo, author of the treatise, *De Aetna* (1495), in which the original type was first used.   The italic is modeled on a design by Giovanni Antonio Tagliente, contemporary of Sadoleto and Bembo, mathematician, calligrapher, and papal scriptor.

Composed, printed, and bound by William Clowes and Sons, Limited, London and Beccles.

Typography and jacket design by Marcia Lambrecht of the Harvard University Press.